The MAVERICK Guide to

AUSTRALIA

Robert W. Bone

1986–87 EDITION

PELICAN PUBLISHING COMPANY
GRETNA 1985

ISBN: 0-88289-492-7
ISSN: 0730-0018

Excerpts from the poem "Dunciad Minor" courtesy of
A. D. Hope, % Curtis Brown (Aust.) Pty. Ltd.,
Sydney, Australia.

Manufactured in the United States of America
Published by Pelican Publishing Company, Inc.
1101 Monroe Street, Gretna, Louisiana 70053

For Christina and David,
Who had to sit this one out

ACKNOWLEDGMENTS

Sara and I want to thank the scores of friends Down Under and Up Top who gave us dinkum oil and an equal measure of sympathy in this project, especially the following:

Ian Anderson, John Anderson, John W. Baker, Kathy Bascombe, Bernadette Benjamin, Tanya Bova, Ken Boys, Barbara Brooks, Christine Bray, Robert Bulfield, Keith Castle, Cathy Clutterbuck, Ian Cotton, Ed Davis, Anne De Wolfe, Bob Doyle, Sally Edwards, Mike Fisher, Marlene Freedman, Sue Gallie, George Gibson, Gael Golla, George Golla, Jack Gregory, Anne Harpham, Barry Haynes, Ralph Hoger, Sandra Holmes, Alison Hudson, John Hudson, J. B. G. Hulton, Ian Johnson, Maggi Jones, Paul Kendall, Ed Kaptein, Sally Kaptein, Leonard Lueras, Sheree Lipton, Ruth Mackay, Alison Fan MacLaurin, Duncan MacLaurin, Stan Marks, Jim Matheson, Neil McDonell, Maureen Millar, Bob Miller, Steve Moir, Dan Myers, Gale Myers, John Myers, Geoff Odgers, Bill O'Reilly, Ros Orrock, Sylvia Pager, Alexandra Piechowiak, Robin Prestage, Brian Price, Jennifer Price, Eduard Rodgers, Anne Ross, Tony Salisbury, Jim Sanderson, Joan Sanderson, Hugh Schmitt, Jim Shrimpton, Cile Sinnex, Barry Stinson, Wayne Storey, David Tong, Henk van Helden, Dorothy Van Kuyl, David Ward, Ellen Ward, Maria Williams, Gary Woodman, Marion Woodman, Peter Wright, Ann Wu, Tong Wu, Sanford Zalburg, and especially Frumie Selchen.

Contents

CONTENTS

List of Maps

THE MAVERICK GUIDE TO AUSTRALIA

Map courtesy Australian Tourist Commission

1

Why Go Down Under?
An Introduction

Have you been to another planet yet? Or are you even likely to visit one in your lifetime? Most of us probably doubt that we'll live long enough. Or even if we do, surely it will be too expensive for just an average bloke, anyway.

But imagine for a moment what we might find if we did indeed take off from home to land in some obscure, though physically hospitable, corner of the universe: There are surely many strange animals there, some of which we've never seen or heard of before—not even in a zoo. Probably some of these creatures won't divide neatly into the great zoological classifications in the textbooks—a mammal (like us) who lays eggs, for example.

The dark of night, spangled of course with an unfamiliar pattern of constellations, obscures the origins of a cacophony of weird cries. Perhaps we'll catch sight of one bizarre bird with twin tall tails. He seems not to possess a voice of his own, but to burst forth instead with the vocal tricks of hundreds of other creatures—even with the realistic noises of nonliving and mechanical objects like lawn mowers and car horns.

Naturally, on this strange planet, there are flowers, plants, and trees that look, act, and smell like nothing else in your previous experience. Grass that cringes when you walk on it, for instance. Trees with elephantine, bottle-shaped trunks that actually do hold water. How about some lovely blossoms that thrive on a protein diet—by trapping and consuming insects?

And the insects themselves. Some of them seem to behave differently. Would you believe flies that catch and devour other flies—or even bees— on the wing? What about termites who don't tear down houses but instead construct some complex condominiums of their own—skyscrapers, relative to their own size, with some models of these buildings designed in thin wedges, always pointing north and south, and using the effects of the sun for central heating and cooling?

Some of the land itself on this other world should be very different. Let's color the ground red and occasionally sculpt it into strange, massive, and beautiful shapes that seem . . . well . . . unearthly.

Say there are thousands of square miles in some areas composed of nothing more or less than flat, glaringly white salt. Or put in a mountain that has been on fire constantly, always burning out of control, for thousands of years. And there are other vast acreages where fiery-colored precious stones are scattered willynilly just under the surface of the ground—where amateur gem hunters can strike it rich with little more equipment than that provided by patience and determination.

And all this—could it be where you can have snow in July and where Christmas means summertime?

If these conditions *were* on another planet, would you go see them if you could? Understandably, you might be worried about the inhabitants, if any. Would they be dangerous, aggressive, living in heaven knows what way and speaking some unintelligible gibberish?

The strange "planet" we have been describing—as you knew all along— is Australia, the world's largest island and smallest continent. Separated by thousands of miles of ocean from the more familiar paths around the globe, Australia has all the things we've been talking about and a thousand times more. There are strange things, indeed, alien to all other parts of our Mother Earth. And 200 years ago, the place might just as well have been another planet. It was almost that inaccessible to the rest of the world.

The people, of course, are not to be feared. Far from inhospitable, living in caves, and munching only on strange, yucky objects, they are by and large just like you and me. Fifteen and a half million strong, they're friendly, have many lovely homes, and run excellent hotels and superb restaurants. They are interested in art, fashion, movies, cars, music, sport, and talking to foreigners.

And most of all, the folks who are surrounded by all this weird and wonderful nature speak English! Er . . . well, it's English *most* of the time, although many a Yank, Pommie, and Kiwi (American, Englishman, and

New Zealander) has had to cock his ear carefully to catch the exact meaning of the common language that is sometimes mutilated before his very ears.

But once he does catch it, it's a fascinating game—one where the sound "A" comes out like "I," and words like "our" became "air." It's best learned over a "schooner." That's 15 ounces of beer if you're in Sydney or 7 ounces for elbow benders in Adelaide.

They call the language "Strine." That, you'll notice, is the word "Australian," itself spoken in Strine.

You may never completely master this condensed communication, but you'll have a wonderful time trying, once you learn the basics—like the fact that Strines like to eat something called "semmiches" (sometimes an "M-semmich," sometimes an "Xsemmich").

Note that "shower" comes out "share" in Strine ("Wine chevva cole share?"). In fact, Strine, spiced with a group of colorful slang terms (e.g., "dinkie-die"—the whole truth; "tucker"—something to eat), plus a whole new set of antipodean jokes, could turn out to be your cheapest and best souvenir of Australia.

Australia has the charm of Great Britain, the excitement of America, and the intelligence to have a character all its own.

There's a refreshing feeling of space in underpopulated Australia. It's still pioneer country, in many ways—one of the very few left. There's a wild Outback "Beyond the Black Stump" that most Australians themselves haven't ventured into. A century ago, explorers died of hunger in this wilderness, often while food lay all around them, free for the taking. These nutrients were strange and different, and hidden from view, although the Aborigines, of course, lived quite well on such "bush tucker."

Today you can get to many of the wild areas—but not all of them—by modern means of transportation. And if you have a penchant for rough living, you can explore even more rugged areas with a kangaroo-proofed Land Rover and other survival equipment.

Whether on safari or on the standard tours, you can pick up some tall tales and take some pictures the neighbors couldn't get in Greece or Japan last year. There's no other place in the world where you can readily hold a koala bear in your arms, go on a mile-long hike accompanied by a high-stepping emu, or climb a thousand feet on one single red rock.

The Confessional

You can, of course, visit Australia without using a guidebook. There are plenty of people to point you toward the things they consider interesting and significant or whose brother-in-law owns the concession stand there. You'll find lots of "free" literature where the freight is actually paid by advertising. They generally don't write about the places that don't pay up.

Unlike many guidebooks, this one contains no advertising, either overt or covert. The opinions expressed, and there are many, pro and con, are those of myself or my wife and coresearcher, Sara. Readers familiar with the other books in the series, *The Maverick Guide to Hawaii* and *The Maverick Guide to New Zealand,* know that we allow no one to use friendship or favors to influence our coverage of their commercial interests.

In the full spirit of confession, however, we have to say that unlike the Hawaii book, for which we accepted no economic assistance, we could not afford to remain quite so Simon-pure this time. If we were going to hit just a few high spots, as most visitors to Australia do, we might have been able to swing it all with no help. But the expense of visiting and revisiting the major parts of Australia to prepare the manuscript for this book was just too horrendous.

We did not make the traditional travel guide turn to members of the tourist industry to subsidize our research. We managed to forswear allegiance to any commercial interest, accepting instead an offer by the government-owned Australian Tourist Commission to cover a portion of our expenses.

We accepted the offer only on the firm understanding that no one from the ATC or anywhere else would have the right to see our words before they were published or to approve or disapprove anything we wrote. The ATC, for its part, was more than understanding. All it asked in return was that I write a book about Australia. I could be as critical as I liked, the Aussies said.

This I have done, and I wouldn't have had it any other way.

This book is the sixth edition of the Australia guide, and it has again been revised to reflect changes that have taken place in the country over the past 24 months. It is the second volume in the Maverick series, which began in 1977 with the publication of our guide to Hawaii. The Hawaii book has been widely accepted and has been published in a new, updated edition every year since. We have also written, and also regularly revise, *The Maverick Guide to New Zealand.* If you are stopping in Hawaii or New Zealand on the way to or from Australia, we firmly suggest reading those, too, and then tucking them in your suitcase. Both will pay for themselves if you spend a day—or maybe an hour—in these countries en route.

Our family has now traveled to virtually every part of the globe. We have been in travel journalism since 1968, when we joined the well-honed team assembled by the late Temple Fielding, author of *Fielding's Travel Guide to Europe.* Today we have no connection with the Fielding operation, though if the Maverick guidebooks show an influence by the Fielding techniques, it is a heritage of which we are very proud.

But while the Fielding books cover Europe and the Atlantic, ours are now tied to Pacific climes, where we have lived since 1971. As a U.S. citizen, my outlook is naturally American. Sara, however, is a New Zealander, and her antipodean attitudes are reflected throughout the text. Her common cultural background with the Australians has helped at least one poor Yank and the Aussies to understand each other.

Getting the Most Out of This Book

We have arranged this guide in a specific pattern that we believe will make for supersmooth reading. After a chapter on timely basics and two others on nature and people, we devote the next eight "area chapters" to the capitals and surrounding areas of the six states and two territories in Australia. The order—Sydney, Canberra, Melbourne, Hobart, Adelaide, Perth, Darwin (with Alice Springs), and Brisbane—represents a hypothetical clockwise swing around the continent.

But the chapters need not be read in that sequence, of course. In fact, those areas that you will not be visiting need not be read at all. Nevertheless, we advise you to peruse it all in advance of your trip so that you can determine which areas you will (and will not) be able to visit in the country.

Each of those area chapters is divided into exactly 12 numbered sections, and after you become familiar with them in one chapter you should know where to look for these same subjects in each of the others. The categories are as follows:

1. **The General Picture**	7. **Guided Tours and Cruises**
2. **Airports and Long-distance Travel**	8. **Water Sports**
	9. **Other Sports**
3. **Local Travel**	10. **Shopping**
4. **Hotels and Lodging**	11. **Night Life and Entertainment**
5. **Restaurants and Dining**	
6. **Sightseeing**	12. **The Address List**

We have set up this book to be used two ways. First, you should look it over before you leave home, to help plan for your trip. There are several ways to travel to Australia, for instance. These and their different price scales are thoroughly described in the following chapter. Also, the individual hotels and other facilities for which advance reservations are required or advisable are discussed throughout the area chapters.

Next, the book is also designed to be used on the scene—to help solve those day-to-day concerns that get in the way of smooth, fun traveling: how to get a bus to King's Cross, where to find a hamburger, when to look for kangaroos, and, most of all, how to budget money and time everywhere as you travel throughout Australia.

A Few Bits of Miscellaneous Advice

If you're serious about planning a great vacation in Australia, be sure to take advantage of the colorful and free literature available. Write to the Australian Tourist Commission and ask for the latest information. (The independent national consumer newsletter *The Travel Advisor* has rated the ATC as one of the most helpful foreign government tourist offices in America.) In the U.S.A. you'll find the ATC at 636 Fifth Ave., New York, NY 10111, and at 3550 Wilshire Blvd., Los Angeles, CA 90010. (Please do mention our name when you contact them.) They also have offices in London, Auckland, Tokyo, Frankfurt, and Singapore.

Write to other addresses you'll find throughout this book, both those in the U.S. and in Australia, and tell them of your interest. Many will respond with a considerable amount of up-to-date illustrated literature. (And again, tell 'em we sent you!)

If you have a well-stocked public library in town, you'll find many large picture books on Australia. The beauty of the land and the strong characteristics of its inhabitants have been attracting professional artists and photographers for years. These will help you decide what areas you want to explore yourself on the great southern continent.

And most of all, after you've made your trip, would you please write us (in care of the publisher) and tell us about it? The traveling experiences of persons such as you will help us tremendously in preparing the next edition of this guidebook.

Use either the enclosed letter/envelope form or, if that's not enough space, copy the address onto your own envelope and include as many pages as you like. Your reactions to both the book and the country are earnestly solicited and will be warmly appreciated.

"Good-on ya!"
Bob and Sara Bone

2

Smooth Sailings
and Happy Landings

The major cities of Australia, virtually all perched on the rim of the continent, are served by dozens of the world's airlines, plus about 14 large shipping companies.

One important exception is Canberra, the federal capital, which has neither seaport nor international airport. (It does have frequent flights to and from other Australian cities, however.) Visitors to Australia generally land first in Sydney, Brisbane, Melbourne, Cairns, Perth, and sometimes Darwin. And most often they come by air.

For diehard surface travelers, there are still a few ocean liners on the high seas bound for Australia (along with other countries) as part of their cruise schedules. In the following paragraphs we have considered mostly those who also list convenient ports in North America and presumably may be boarded there.

Sailing to Australia. Most international travelers today agree that ships are either (a) too expensive, (b) too time-consuming, or (c) both. But old salts who want to plow full speed ahead may still consider a few alternatives. Some of these cruises may be combined by travel agencies into sea/air excursions, in which you return home by plane (or vice versa, although most agree it's more fun to sail out and fly back home).

Two of the most elegant tours are the winter cruises sometimes launched in January or February by the Norwegian-owned **Royal Viking Line,** both leaving from—and returning to—San Francisco and Los Angeles. The 28,000-ton *Royal Viking Star* or *Royal Viking Sea* may make a leisurely cruise through the Pacific, stopping at several ports, including Sydney, where it arrives after three weeks. Unfortunately it appears that in 1986 there will be no crossing from the U.S. to Australia. However Royal Viking will embark on some interesting cruises through South Pacific islands, originating or terminating in Sydney or in Auckland, and air/sea arrangements are available. Plans for 1987 have not been announced at this writing. In any case, the lowest fares will break down to more than $200 a day, and maximums are well over three times that figure.

Details on the Viking operation are available from the Royal Viking Line, One Embarcadero Center, San Francisco, CA 94111 (Tel. 415–398–8000 or toll free 800–422–8000).

California's popular **Princess Cruises,** owned by P & O Lines, usually sends its British-registered, 600-passenger *Island Princess* or *Pacific Princess* from California to Australia and New Zealand once a year. Plans for 1987 are incomplete, but for 1986, anyway, the *Pacific Princess* has scheduled a 28-day cruise Down Under leaving from San Diego January 25 and calling at several ports including Lahaina, Honolulu, Bora Bora, Papeete, Pago Pago, Vava'u, Lautoka, Auckland, and Sydney. (The return trip will include some of the same ports.) Per-person fares will run a minimum of about $6,500 each way in 1986 and perhaps $7,500 in 1987.

For full information, write P & O/Princess Cruises, 2029 Century Park East, Los Angeles, CA 90067 (Tel. 213–533–1770 or toll free 800–421–0522), or contact their offices in New York, Chicago, Dallas, San Francisco, or Seattle.

Princess's adoptive parent, the century-old **P & O Lines,** generally assigns its 42,000-ton, 25-year-old *Oriana* to the Southampton-Sydney run, which calls at Port Everglades (Florida), then slices through Panama and briefly nuzzles other American ports, including Los Angeles and San Francisco, at the end of November. It hits Honolulu around early December before it heads for Auckland and Sydney, docking at the latter a few days before Christmas. One-way, per-person fares will run from around $3,000 for an inside bathless bunk up to $9,000 or so for posh staterooms near the pool for the 1986 voyage from Los Angeles to Sydney.

The 45,000-ton, 1,800-passenger *Canberra*, flagship of the P & O fleet, usually stops at Sydney from about February 19 through 21 on her 90-day around-the-world cruise, which generally leaves Southampton about January 7. You can board her in San Francisco three weeks later or in Honolulu in early February. Fares will run between about $2,000 and $8,000. (We came within a bosun's breath of climbing the gangplank for this cruise, but finally had to fly instead.) For details on the *Oriana* or the *Canberra* cruises, write Princess Cruises at the address above.

Two more possibilities are sometimes represented by cruises on Britain's venerable **Cunard Line,** both sailing from the U.S. in January.

Some years the massive, 67,000-ton *Queen Elizabeth 2* includes both U.S. ports (New York, Port Everglades, and Los Angeles) and Australian ports (Sydney, Hobart, Adelaide, and Fremantle) on her winter world cruise, but Australian ports are not a QE-2 option for 1986, and 1987 plans are unavailable at this writing. However Cunard's 24,000-ton *Sagafjord,* which often runs a Pacific cruise departing from Florida in the winter, has expanded its 1986 tour to a 102-day world cruise that includes four Australian ports. The *Sagafjord* will leave Fort Lauderdale January 9, travel the Panama Canal, then pick up passengers at Los Angeles January 20 and at Honolulu January 26. After calling at some Pacific island ports en route she will visit Sydney February 8, Hobart February 11, Adelaide February 13, and Fremantle (Perth) February 16. The *Sagafjord* will then continue around the world before returning to Fort Lauderdale April 18 and Los Angeles May 2.

Figure a minimum of about $250 a day on either vessel. More details on these Cunarders can be obtained from the Cunard Lines, 555 Fifth Ave., New York, NY 10017 (Tel. 212–661–7500 or toll free at 800–221–4700).

We have had no personal experience with any of these ship trips, and can offer no firm opinion on their quality. But in general we feel strongly that any cruise that does not permit you to break your trip for a significant period in Australia will not allow you the time to enjoy the things Australia is famous for.

Sorry, but two popular questions about ships must be answered in the negative. (1) There are no longer any regular passenger-carrying freighters available from North America to Australia. (From Europe, you could take the Polish Ocean Lines, but that's about it.) And (2) there is absolutely no passengership service across the Tasman Sea between New Zealand and Australia.

Well, for most of us, all of this has been merely drifting and dreaming. Let's now step ashore and return to the solid realities of the jet age.

The Air Ways to Australia. Want to fly First Class to Australia? You can, of course. You can get the champagne, red carpet, Captain Kangaroo treatment for tickets costing from $5,000 to $5,500 round trip from Los Angeles, San Francisco, or Vancouver to and from Sydney, Brisbane, or Melbourne.

But is it really worth it? With the advent of jumbo jets (wide-body DC-10s, 747s, 767s, etc.), the much cheaper Economy Class (sometimes called "Tourist" or "Coach") is nearly as comfortable for most of us. So what if you have to cough up a little extra for the liquor or the movies? Is it worth about $2,500 *additional* for a few shots of scotch, the rubber earphones, a pair of cheap slipper sox, a wider seat, and a fancier meal? No way!

Whopping amounts like that are what you'll save if you choose to go Economy instead of First Class. We've tried both categories on flights to and from Down Under, and we've decided we'd rather sit in the back of the plane, taking considerable comfort in the knowledge that we can use the savings to spend perhaps another month in Australia!

The Economy Class round-trip tickets from the West Coast gateways mentioned above normally run around $2,500. For that, you can probably stop off when and where you want on the way, travel any day of the week, and return any day of the week. You can tool around Australia for up to a year, or until the money runs out, whichever comes first.

As an Economy flyer, you can watch the movie, too. It'll be $2.50 extra (sometimes) for the earphones the First Class passengers are getting "free" in exchange for their weight in gold.

But is that the best you can do? Not at all. With any luck you can cut these costs down significantly, as most vacation passengers between the American West Coast and Australia do today by taking advantage of "excursion" or "promotional" fares. The picture for these bargain fares is becoming more cloudy as the airlines are becoming less officially regulated and more competitive by price. But one principle still applies: *You can fly much more cheaply if you're willing to accept some restrictions on your travel plans.*

The most common types of discount tickets available at this writing are variations on APEX—Advance Purchase Excursion—fares. These vary, depending on the season you travel in—sometimes worked out in three seasonal levels for "Low" (usually April through August), "Shoulder" (usually March and September through November), and "Peak" (December through February) periods.

The seasons are slightly different for different airlines, and sometimes changed for northbound and southbound flights. If you fly out in one season and back in another, your fare usually—but not always—is prorated. (Some airlines may charge the full higher rate on a round trip, but a good travel agent should help you avoid this kind of cruel surprise.)

To qualify for the APEX fare, you will have to pay for your ticket a specified number of weeks in advance; if you change your mind about going a percentage of the fare will not be refunded after a certain cutoff date. Also, there is sometimes no stopover privilege under the APEX fare, and you may be required to remain in Australia for a minimum of

10 days to two weeks. As a guess—and don't hold us to it, please—the low-season APEX fares from the West Coast (Los Angeles, San Francisco, or Vancouver) to Cairns, Brisbane, or Sydney on some airlines could be around $1,300 round trip in '86–87. High season might be around $1,700. (Add about $100 for Melbourne or $200 for Perth.)

Luckily the airlines offering the APEX fares to Down Under are highly competitive, and the number of routes and flights is increasing—factors that normally tend to hold back some of the phenomenally high fare increases seen on other routes. These airlines may try very hard to be able to advertise a round-trip fare of around $1,000 for as long as they possibly can before mortgaging their souls to the devil of increasing fuel prices—the bane of continued bargain travel overseas.

A point to remember about the APEX or any bargain fare is that your using them also allows your travel agent to set up some lower *internal* air fares in Australia. More on that later.

More miscellaneous fare points: In addition to the usual First and Economy Class fares, most airlines flying from North America to Australia or New Zealand also have a middlerange fare called Business Class or some equivalent term. These tickets have been running around $250 more than Economy Class each way, but there are certainly differences between airlines in what you get for the price.

On some airlines, it is a sort of second-class First Class. Business fliers may check in at a special counter without long lines. They may use the airline's V.I.P. lounge, and that could mean free drinks and peanuts. On the plane drinks will be free, ditto the stereo headphones. Seats are usually placed between First Class and Economy sections, and they are wider than those in Economy.

You'll be seated with other business folks, of course, and you may have a larger reading library (*Forbes, Barrons,* the *Wall Street Journal*) than the guys in the back seats. For better or worse, there will probably be fewer children, priests, hippies, servicemen, and old ladies around you. If Business Class is your thing—and your company will spring for the extra bills—then go for it!

But there's another interesting trend that may portend the future on the Pacific routes. That is to give some Business Class services and facilities free to the regular, full-fare Economy Class traveler and perhaps even to the discount-fare traveler. With the free drinks and free movies, this cuts back the need for flight attendants to fiddle around with filthy lucre, make change at 30,000 feet, etc.—really a much more dignified way to fly.

As we noted in the latest edition of our New Zealand guidebook, you should check out different fares very carefully. The airline that is cheaper this week may not be next week. If you're shooting for an aerial bargain, you'll have to aim better than ever before.

Airlines may quote you a fare for your ticket, but by the time you get around to actually buying it the price may have gone up. Generally speaking, once you pay for your ticket and take it home you'll be able to make your trip without paying any increase—as long as you use it inside of a year from the day you peeled out the dough.

Therefore, as soon as your plans are complete—even if they are for a trip that begins eleven months hence—it would be a good idea to buy that ticket and then store it in a bank safe-deposit box.

A way to keep up with the latest on cheap flights is to join clubs composed mainly of antipodean expatriates. Examples are the Australia New Zealand America Club, P.O. Box 178204, San Diego, CA 92117; the Australian Kangaroo Club, P.O. Box 4230, Irvine, CA 92716; the Australian-New Zealand Society, 41 E. 42nd St., New York, NY 10017; the Southern Cross Club, P.O. Box 19243, Washington, DC 20036; the Down Under Club, P.O. Box 3143, St. Paul, MN 55165; and the Friends of the Koala and Kiwi Association, 68 Scollard St., Toronto, Ont. M5R 1G2, or Suite 618, 470 Granville St., Vancouver, B.C. V6C 1V5. Many of these are composed of Australians and New Zealanders who want to head home for the Christmas (summer) holidays.

And from elsewhere around the country? There are several domestic air fares in the U.S. that can be used in conjunction with the rates across the South Pacific.

As an example, if a New Yorker buys a midweek special round trip to Los Angeles to connect with a West Coast–to–Australia APEX tour, his trip to and from Sydney might set him back about $1,600. At rates like these, it would cost only a little more for an easterner to vacation in Australia than a westerner—an almost negligible amount compared to the awesome differences of a few years ago.

Tours. Many travel agents and travel wholesalers (tour operators) make up their own tailored tours, either escorted or for FITs ("free and independent travelers"). Tour companies have several fly/drive deals, but we would only be interested in the ones that allow you to roam over several cities. An example of a good deal might be a 14-day tour that offers a car with unlimited mileage and vouchers for several hotels all over the country, currently running at about $800 per person, two sharing. (Be sure to add your air fare to these prices.)

Tour Operators. Here are a few North American travel wholesalers who offer Australian itineraries. Your travel agent will probably know of more. The 800 numbers are toll free. If they have no 800 number, or if it doesn't work from your area, try phoning collect. Many will accept charges from persons genuinely interested in tours to Australia. In any case, tell 'em we sent you.

U.S.A.

Australian Explorers
Rt. 9, Professional Bldg.
Parlin, NJ 08859
Tel. (800) 631–5650
Tel. (201) 721–2929

Australian Travel Service
116 South Louise St.
Glendale, CA 91205
Tel. (800) 423–2880
Tel. (800) 232–2121 (CA)
Tel. (818) 247–4564

Australian Travel Services Intl.
5655 South Yosemite,
Suite 200
Englewood, CO 80111
Tel. (303) 793–1930

Brendan Tours
510 W. Sixth St.
Los Angeles, CA 90014
Tel. (213) 488–9191
Tel. (800) 421–8446

Intercontinental Tours
16700 Roscoe Blvd.
Van Nuys, CA 91406
Tel. (800) 421–7233
Tel. (213) 820–8561

Koala Tours
2930 Honolulu Ave., Suite 200
La Crescenta, CA 91214
Tel. (213) 957–1656
Tel. (800) 535–0316
Tel. (800) 523–1853 (CA)

Maupintour, Inc.
1515 St. Andrews
P.O. Box 807
Lawrence, KS 66044
Tel. (800) 255–4266
Tel. (913) 843–1211

Pacific Dateline Tours
201 Shipyard Way
P.O. Box 1755
Newport Beach, CA 92663
Tel. (800) 854–0543
Tel. (800) 432–7294 (CA)
Tel. (714) 675–7620

Pacific International Tours
760 Market St., Suite 445
San Francisco, CA 94102
Tel. (415) 397–0611

Travel Directions Worldwide
11621 W. Bluemound Road
Milwaukee, WI 53226
Tel. (800) 558–0872
Tel. (414) 259–0162

World of Oz, Ltd.
3 E. 54th St.
New York, NY 10022
Tel. (800) 223–6626
Tel. (212) 751–3250

World Travelers, Inc.
19032 66th Ave. South, Suite C-107
Kent, Seattle, WA 98032
Tel. (800) 426–3610
Tel. (206) 251–0656

Canada

Destinations Pacific Tours
1530 W. Eighth Ave., Suite 203
Vancouver, B.C. V6J 4R8
Tel. (800) 663–3431
Tel. (604) 736–9881

Overland Tours
P.O. Box 100
Agincourt, Ont. M1S 3C6
Tel. (800) 268–6370
Tel. (416) 291–7334

Goway Travel, Ltd.
40 Wellington St. East
Toronto, Ont. M5E 1C7
Tel. (416) 863–0799
402 W. Pender St., Suite 716
Vancouver, B.C. V6B 1T9
Tel. (604) 687–4004

UTL Holiday Tours
22 College St.
Toronto, Ont. M5G 1Y6
Tel. (416) 967–3355
Tel. (800) 268–7295 (Ont.)
Tel. (800) 268–3782 (P.Q.)

M-H Tours
1118 St. Catherine West,
Suite 503
Montreal, P.Q. H3B 1H5
Tel. (514) 875–5300

Westcan Treks/Adventure Travel
17 Hayden St.
Toronto, Ont. M4Y 2P2
Tel. (800) 661–7265 (W. Can.)
Tel. (800) 268–3768 (E. Can.)
Tel. (416) 922–7584

Which airline to fly? Choosing an airline is like choosing a spouse: It's a very personal thing, but it has important practical elements, too. Briefly, you pick an airline based on how well the things it offers seem to suit your needs for the price to be paid. (Please see our discussion a few pages previous on air fares.) But you should also seek the advice of friends and objective fellow travelers whose opinions you respect.

There are seven carriers—two American and five foreign—who fly from Canada and the U.S.A. to Australia. In our own general order of preference for this trip they are Qantas, Continental, United, Air New Zealand, CP Air, UTA, and Air Niugini. Here's why:

Qantas Airways Limited. For some years, now, Flight QF-4 has left San Francisco every evening at 9 o'clock. It arrives in Honolulu around midnight, picks up more passengers, and then continues on to Sydney and sometimes Melbourne. It lands in Sydney at 6:30 or 7:30 or 8:30 A.M., depending on who's on daylight saving time. The total elapsed time is 16½ hours, counting the hour's breather in Hawaii.

These Qantas flights have now been augmented by others. On Saturday, QF-26 leaves Vancouver, B.C., and flies to Honolulu, then continues on to the northern Australian state of Queensland, arriving in Cairns, a popular coastal city and a jumping-off place for Great Barrier Reef excursions, or in the state capital of Brisbane. (San Francisco passengers for Cairns—and Vancouver passengers for Sydney or Melbourne—change places with each other in Honolulu.) On Thursdays QF-26 originates in Honolulu instead of Vancouver.

From Los Angeles, passengers have some more interesting choices. There are three QF-18 services that jet to Melbourne via Honolulu and Fiji, or Flight QF-12, which at this writing flies three days a week to Sydney and Melbourne via Tahiti. Another three days a week it makes a dramatic nonstop hop to Sydney in just 14 hours. That cuts about 3½ hours off the total elapsed time from LAX.

All Qantas flights from North America are in various versions of our favorite plane, the Boeing 747. Seats in the Economy section are 10 across with two aisles in a three-four-three configuration. There's a Business Class section, with wide lounge chairs two abreast, either just behind First Class or upstairs in the "bubble." And First Class features full-length sleeper chairs that practically recline into long, contoured beds.

You'll get a movie—sometimes two movies—plus dinner, supper, and breakfast. There are no charges in any class for drinks or headsets. Return flights over the same routes are similar, but a real mind-boggler is that because of the International Date Line the return nonstop, Flight QF-11, leaves SYD in the early afternoon and arrives LAX in the morning *of the same day!*

Many prefer to fly the airline of the country to which they are travel ing, and this, too, may be a good reason for choosing Qantas. On the Sydney runs, the flight and cabin crew members are stationed in Sydney, so you have a group of experts on the city to advise you on where to go and what to see after you get there.

The flights also feature Aussie beer and wines (both are justly famous). Often there are other Down Under specialties like lamb dishes and beef pies, Sydney rock oysters, and perhaps even a Pavlova for dessert. And if you can shut your eyes during the early-morning flights between Honolulu and Sydney—10 hours of flying time—or between Honolulu and Cairns—9 hours in the air—you might pick up a full night's sleep before breakfast.

Qantas's best bargains are its special APEX "Circle Eight" fares, which invite passengers to visit several cities in Australia and New Zealand (plus Fiji, Tahiti, and Honolulu) on the same trip. These offer 58 percent discounts off the normal Economy fares.

All APEX fares are sold in Peak and Low seasons. The lowest low-season, round-trip fares between the U.S. and Australia may still be around $1,000 as 1986 begins. (You can add round trips to Perth or Adelaide for $200 additional round trip.) The bargain period will probably continue from April through November, and for our money April through June and September through November are ideal months to travel in both Australia and New Zealand. (See our New Zealand book for more details.)

Continental Airlines. Flying into its eighth year over the South Pacific, Continental wins a solid second place in our book for these subequatorial runs. At this writing, the airline's Pacific Division offers one flight daily from Los Angeles and twice-weekly flights from San Francisco on nine weekly round trips to Australia and five weekly trips to New Zealand. Some flights are now targeted especially for Sydney and Melbourne without making stops in Auckland.

All Continental's McDonnell Douglas DC-10-30 jumbos destined for Down Under leave from Los Angeles as Flight 1 and from San Francisco as Flight 3 late in the evening, timed so that they arrive in Honolulu around 11 P.M., five hours' flying time later. Flights to the south leave Honolulu just after midnight. Flight 1 continues to Auckland nonstop from Honolulu in about 9 hours (15 hours total from California), and Flight 3 goes by way of Fiji, which adds 2 hours on to the elapsed time. Some Continental flights go on to Sydney and then Melbourne. The minimum total elapsed time between Los Angeles and Sydney will be 16½ hours—18½ hours to Melbourne. Flights back up from Down Under are all numbered "2" (to LAX) and "4" (to SFO).

Several of Continental's flights continue across the Tasman Sea between Auckland and Sydney and one weekly flight goes from Auckland to Melbourne. Travelers interested in making a maximum number of hops and stops may now fly the airline in a circular pattern after Hawaii—e.g., Los Angeles–Honolulu–Fiji–Sydney–Auckland–Honolulu–Los Angeles. The airline's policy of offering free stopovers in any class means that you can visit all these destinations for the price of one round-trip Los Angeles–Sydney fare.

Since Hawaii is a stop in both directions, passengers who begin and end their Continental flights in the fiftieth state also benefit from the circular route, visiting Australia and New Zealand (plus Fiji, if they want) for the price of a Honolulu-Sydney round trip. Of course you can hit the same destinations, and even more, by switching airlines with abandon. But this could drive your total ticket price into the stratosphere. Under today's fare structures, such "interlining" will add hundreds onto your excursion, not to mention the potential expense and confusion with different baggage weight and size rules for different countries and airlines.

Like other carriers in the Pacific, Continental now has three classes of service, which it calls Executive Gold (28 sleeper seats forward in a two-by-two configuration), Executive Silver (31 large seats amidships set up two-three-two), and Economy (narrower seats aft arranged two-five-two).

The airline uses a tape-TV full-screen projection system for in-flight movies. And Continental doesn't charge anybody in any class extra for headsets—or for drinks—on South Pacific flights.

Continental has simplified its ticket prices immensely by eliminating APEX fares and replacing them with something perhaps a little better— the only airline on these routes to do so at this writing. (So there are no advance purchase requirements, cancellation penalties, minimum lengths of stay, and other potentially confusing gobbledygook from the APEX rule book.) Instead fares are set up on a high-low, two-season plan for round-trip travel. Cheapest travel (from the U.S.) is April through November.

Continental Airlines began its Down Under flights at around the same time as the first edition of this book in 1979, and we have continued to receive letters from satisfied passengers since then.

United Airlines. Last year United, America's largest domestic airline, announced it had bought nearly all the Pacific services and routes of Pan American World Airways. Although the picture is not perfectly clear at this writing, indications are that if all government approvals are obtained as expected, beginning sometime in 1986 it will run former Pan Am schedules pretty much as they were.

If so, one of its most significant Australian flights will be the Boeing 747-SP used two days a week for a single leap over the 7,500 miles between Los Angeles and Sydney, covering that distance in one humongous 14-hour hop. For years Pan Am took this giant step alone until Qantas began flying its own SP over the same route in 1985. Whoever flies it, it is still the longest single commercial flight in the world, and it is expected that United will continue the high-altitude SP (special performance) service.

Other United South Pacific service will be a little different than those Pan Am routes that simply went Down Under via Honolulu. Pan Am is continuing its own California-Hawaii service basically unchanged. But since United is taking over Pan Am's runs from Honolulu to foreign ports, including Auckland and Sydney, it will be offering its own fare structures from the U.S. based on that routing.

APEX fares will no doubt continue to be comparable to those on other airlines. Although United traditionally has not offered a "business" class, it will continue Pan Am's former Clipper Class service (although we bet it will be renamed). Under the old system, anyway, these passengers were given low-density seating amidships with upgraded menus, lots of free drinks, headsets, and a kit full of doodads. More important, the seats were wider and generally more comfortable. But when no-nonsense Pan

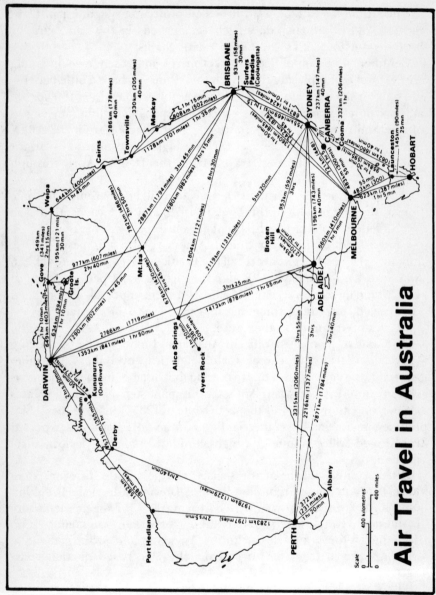

Air Travel in Australia

Map courtesy Australian Tourist Commission

Am was running things, at least, you couldn't see a movie from the business-class seats.

First Class passengers could watch movies in the nose seats but not upstairs in the "bubble." And Economy Class passengers, seated behind business class with two aisles in a three-four-three configuration, could go to the movies for an extra charge for headphones, a service that is provided free in all classes on some other airlines on these routes.

Pan Am has been pinching pennies in the Pacific for a long time, so we will look for changes from United to make these flights more competitive. But beyond that, we can only refer you to the 1987–88 edition of the *Maverick Guide to New Zealand.* By the time that is printed (in late 1986), United's Down Under plans will certainly have become much clearer.

Air New Zealand. Ten ANZ flights a week leave Los Angeles in the evening after dinner and make at least two stops before landing at Australian destinations 21 or 22 hours later—late morning, Australian time. The stops are at Honolulu and Auckland, or Papeete and Auckland. Two flights a week stop at Honolulu, Nadi, and Auckland.

ANZ now flies all Boeing 747-200s on these routes. In the Economy Class section, the rows of seats are currently separated by two aisles into a three-four-three configuration. Business class, called Pacific Class on this airline, is up the spiral staircase on the top deck, offering 16 sheepskin-covered seats separated two-by-two. In First Class, 16 wide, fully reclining sheepskin-covered sleeper seats are also two-by-two. Music and movies are offered free to everyone in all classes. The meals are usually excellent, and all drinks are now complimentary in any part of the aircraft.

We've enjoyed several trips ourselves on Air New Zealand, and it would probably be our first choice for flying to Auckland for a visit to New Zealand—certainly it would if we wanted to see something of Tahiti or Fiji along the way to either Auckland or Sydney.

CP Air, the Canadian international airline, has been traveling from Vancouver via Honolulu to Sydney for 3½ decades, building a reputation for good service over the 8,000-mile route. CP Air was the last to convert to double-aisle jets on these routes. It has now put aside its trusty DC-8s and has been flying Boeing 747 jets over the run, which includes a stop at Fiji on the way to Sydney. Flight 301 arrives in the Australian city after about 19 hours elapsed time.

The 400-passenger jumbo takes off from Vancouver every Wednesday and Friday and pauses in Honolulu in the late evening—at around the same time the opposite flight coming up from Sydney stops off in Honolulu. On the same two days Flight 311, a nonstop CP Air DC-10 from Toronto to Honolulu, connects with both flights so passengers to and from eastern Canada may interchange conveniently with the southern service. (On Friday, the DC-10 from Toronto now flies on from Honolulu nonstop to Auckland, New Zealand, and we suspect that could eventually expand to include the Wednesday flight, too.) The total travel time from Toronto to Sydney is about 22½ hours. (Or 19½ hours to Auckland.)

From Toronto, CP Air has no significant competition. From Vancouver, the choice is a little closer between CP Air and Qantas (although CP Air officials point out that theirs is the only same-plane service from Vancouver to Sydney). South of Honolulu, more competition is added by United, Continental, and Air New Zealand.

CP Air offers three classes of service. First Class features sleeper seats and all the other froufrous that First Class is supposed to have. Then there's business class, called Royal Canadian, with two-abreast seating. After that is Economy Class, composed of both full-fare and APEX-fare passengers. (There are now no extra charges for drinks, movies, etc. in any class.) Dinner and a movie are featured on the way to Honolulu on both flights.

We've flown CP Air on the Honolulu-to-Vancouver leg, and can report that service and amenities in First Class, anyway, were first rate. Our reader reports on the airline have continued to be favorable from all parts of the plane—especially since CP Air joined the jumbo-jet club in the South Pacific.

UTA French Airlines, as it's known in this country, or Union de Transports Aeriens, to use the official French name, has been expanding its service in the Pacific. It is now well suited to dedicated island-hoppers, if the fares remain competitive. Flying from Los Angeles to Sydney on UTA you normally make one exotic stop—in Tahiti—en route. At this writing, UTA flies *four times a week* to Papeete in eight hours nonstop, but recheck to see if you must remain in Tahiti at least overnight. Another UTA flight goes on direct to Sydney *once a week* in another 8½ hours. With a new weekly 5½-hour flight from Honolulu to Papeete, residents of Hawaii, too, can now take in Tahiti on the way to Australia. Or those who start in L.A. can set up UTA flights to hop to both Hawaii and Tahiti en route, although that dogleg configuration will surely cost them more.

UTA flies DC-10-30 aircraft on its major South Pacific runs, offering complimentary wine, beer, meals, and headsets. Movies are free and the actors *parlent anglais,* too. (So "I adore you!" won't come out like "Shut the door!") The Honolulu-Papeete round trips offer similar amenities but in 204-seat DC8s.

UTA now offers round-trip APEX fares between Los Angeles and Sydney, at this writing running between $1,100 and $1,500. Of course this could climb a bit by the time our ink is dry. *Parlez* with UTA or your travel agent.

Air Niugini, the national airline of Papua New Guinea, is technically speaking the new kid on the block since it has begun flying from an

American port (Honolulu) to Australia. Leaving Hawaii sometime after midnight Saturday, you'll have to jet first on a Boeing 707 (remember those?) to the capital city of Port Moresby, then change flights. More 707s fly on from there nonstop to Brisbane or Sydney. Or Fokker F-28 Fellowships, twinjet aircraft, hop nonstop from Port Moresby to Cairns, Australia.

The airline is partly owned by Ansett Airlines of Australia, by the way, and the flight crews are all Ansett or Trans-Australia Airlines veterans. As long as you can stomach the single-aisle, narrow-fuselage jets for long distances, you should have no hesitation about flying with them.

Transportation Within Australia

Getting around the country is a lot of fun, but it could be strenuous and expensive, too. We'll talk about it some more in the Transportation sections in the following area chapters, but some of your plans on how to go from one place to another should be considered before you leave home. For instance, any kind of transportation can be difficult on national holidays or at the beginning or end of school vacations ("school holidays"). These vary somewhat from state to state.

Domestic Air Travel. Australia boasts a long and honored aviation history. That befits a country that early embraced the airplane in its attempts to bridge vast, lonely distances in a sparsely settled land. The past is alive with Aussie air heroes, and passenger flights have developed to the point where Australia's airlines have been ranked safest in the world by *Flight International,* the respected British aviation magazine.

The half-century-old **Ansett Airlines of Australia** was an enterprise of that dynamic mogul of the transport business, Sir Reginald Ansett, whose name you may hear frequently. Its stock today is mostly owned by—and its policies dictated by—Rupert Murdoch, the newspaper and magazine king in Australia, Britain, and the U.S.

Ansett Airlines competes with the government-owned **Trans-Australia Airlines,** more often called TAA (and sometimes sounding like "T-I-I" to American ears). Both of these fly several models of modern jet aircraft, usually Boeing 727s or 737s, or McDonnell Douglas DC-9s. For long hauls, TAA depends on the jumbo-size European-built A300 Airbus and Ansett counters with one of the modern, wide-body Boeing 767s. First Class and Economy seats are available, and even Business Class is sold on a few routes by these two leaders. (Economy Class seats are divided into a two-four-two configuration on the domestic jumbos, so you may want to request a window or aisle seat.)

All seats are assigned ("allocated") in advance, usually in the departure lounges out by the gates, and you can request such options as smoking or nonsmoking, aisle or window, and even (photographers take note) forward or rearward of the wing and right or left side. You will have more choice of seat position if you arrive early and check in at the airport more than a half hour before the flight. Checking in at the city air terminals is convenient, but since seat allocations are made at the airport, you could find that your choice is already taken by the time your bus from town lets you out at the aerodrome.

Incidentally, to have greater choice in seats, try to avoid the early-morning weekday flights, especially between major centers. We once happened to arrive at Sydney Airport in time to hop on the 8 A.M. flight to Melbourne instead of the one we had reserved at 9. There we found ourselves bunched three abreast with battalions of bored businessmen. On a beautiful, clear winter day, we were trying to see the Sydney Opera House, etc., from an aisle seat on the wrong side of hundreds of fluttering financial pages.

If it's a toss-up between taking Ansett and TAA, we'd probably choose Ansett, although we have always gotten along fine on TAA, too. One reader who recently returned from two extensive business trips in Oz made no Bones about it: "I preferred Ansett Airlines by far over TAA. I thought that Ansett's aircraft were cleaner, their meals were better, and the service was much better," said Captain Charles Sweeney.

Another important company is **Ansett Airlines of Western Australia,** formerly MacRobertson Miller Airline Services, and now affiliated with Ansett Airlines. Headquartered in Perth, this airline flies several routes in the state of Western Australia, connecting towns and villages between Perth and Darwin, up in the "Top End" of the Northern Territory.

The workhorse of the fleet is the Fokker F-28, a fine twin-jet aircraft especially designed for quick takeoffs and landings on the short runways often existing in these far west outposts. But avoid the Fokker's Row 12. This back bank of seats is noisy, it has no windows, and the seats don't recline. Unfortunately for those in Row 12, the seats in Row 11 do! We felt like a pair of marsupials trapped in the same pouch for 1,116 miles and 2 hours and 40 minutes between Perth and Derby, all because we were last to show up for seat allocations on a busy holiday.

Some other domestic air companies include **East-West Airlines,** which historically flew principally in New South Wales and southern Queensland between Sydney and Brisbane, but which has recently expanded to include a few routes to Tasmania, the Northern Territory, and even Western Australia; **Air New South Wales,** covering some smaller airports mainly within that state; **Airlines of Northern Australia,** which buzzes hither and thither over the deserts almost entirely within the Northern Territory; **Airlines of Tasmania,** serving the island state; **Airlines of South Australia,** headquartered in Adelaide; and **Air Queensland,** formerly Bush Pilots Airways, which flies light planes on fascinating routes between communities along the Queensland coast as well as to islands in the Great Barrier Reef area.

Air Bargains in Australia. Get the latest dope directly from a travel agent or an airline representative, but North American visitors who hold APEX or other round-trip discount tickets to Australia generally qualify for two different bargains within the country on Ansett or TAA.

The first plan, the old reliable "See Australia" fare, offers approximately 30 percent discounts on air trips totaling more than 1,000 kilometers—621 miles—within the country. The tickets are only available to passengers from the U.S.A. and Canada traveling to Australia on low promotional fares. They do not have to be purchased outside Australia, but most travelers find it a lot easier to arrange them in advance of their trip.

If you're going to see anything of Australia at all, you'll have little trouble using up that 621-mile minimum. Round trip Sydney to Melbourne, for example, is nearly 900 miles, a trip that will cost about $A210 (at this writing) instead of the normal economy fare of around $A300. (These figures are in Australian dollars, so you can estimate at the prevailing exchange rates.)

The second—and newer—bargain is the "Go Australia Airpass," allowing savings of up to 40 percent on extensive domestic flights. It provides for 6,000 kilometers (3,726 miles) of travel, with up to five stopovers, for, say, $A500. Or you can fly for 10,000 kilometers, with up to eight stopovers, for perhaps $A800. This would allow an extensive trip around the country, for example one beginning at Cairns with stopovers at Brisbane, Sydney, Canberra, Melbourne, Perth, Alice Springs, and Mt. Isa before returning to Cairns. Both are available on Ansett or TAA. (Please don't hold us to these specific fares, however.)

Smaller airlines also offer some discounts off their regular Economy fares. East-West has a "Super Saver" fare, which must be purchased in North America. Air Queensland has a complicated five-route system providing bargain excursions to dozens of airports large and small in that interesting state.

Detailed information on all these is available in the U.S.A. from Trans-Australia Airlines in Los Angeles, Chicago, and New York; Ansett Airlines in Los Angeles and Toronto; East-West Airlines in Irvine, California; and Air Queensland, c/o GWF Travel Marketing in New York City.

All of Australia's domestic airlines seem to have some sort of special deal, many of them with complicated ifs, ands, and buts. Check them out at the offices mentioned, all of which will happily launch you into dozens of airports out in the wopwops.

Taking the train. For more than 100 years, railroad travel in Australia has been plagued by the shortsightedness and stubbornness of the original six different colonies, all of which—incredibly—adopted different track gauges. In the past decade this has been partly—but not totally—overcome. Today there are no sleepy 2 A.M. changes of carriage at Albury; rail travel has become sometimes convenient, occasionally comfortable, and often fun.

Australia's most prestigious train, the transcontinental *Indian Pacific,* travels 2,500 miles between Sydney (the Pacific Ocean) and Perth (the Indian Ocean), and may be only one of three in the world that carries a functioning piano on board in the lounge car. After traversing the rolling country of the east, it shoots across the great Nullarbor Plain in the west, at one point barreling along for 300 miles straight as an arrow, with not a single curve, over the longest stretch of straight track in the world.

Other passenger trains link Brisbane, Sydney, Canberra, Melbourne, Adelaide, etc. Famous for more than a century, *The Ghan* runs between Adelaide and Alice Springs, and *The Alice,* a brand-new train, also goes to Alice Springs, but leaves from Sydney. (This pair carry the other two pianos!) All three of these musical trains are discussed again in the chapters that follow.

If you're going to travel around Australia by train, you'll save a tank car full of dollars if you buy the "Austrailpass." Now stop, look, and listen, because this bargain *must be purchased outside of Australia.* There are six types, varying between a 14-day pass for about $A300 Budget Class and $A400 First Class and a three-month version for about $A750 Budget Class and $A1,000 First Class. Either allows you unlimited travel on all the rail systems of Australia, including city and suburban lines.

You'll have to pay extra for berths and meals on longrun trains, however. If the only train you're taking is the *Indian Pacific,* for example, ask your travel agent to make a careful comparison. The cost for the IP, usually quoted with berth and meals, just might come very close to the cost of a 14-day rail pass plus the approximately $A80 or $A90 charged extra each way for the berth and meals between Sydney and Perth.

With the Austrailpass you can generally hop off and on other trains whenever you want, making reservations where and when necessary. You can buy the pass through your travel agent or through the Australian Travel Service, 116 S. Louise St., Glendale, CA 91205. (See phone numbers under Tour Operators.) In Canada, they are also sold through Thomas Cook Canada in Toronto (Tel. 416–968–9409). We like this plan a lot.

Bargains by Bus. Besides booking on the scene, there are at least six types of passes you can use for bus ("coach") travel in Australia, but be careful to make the exact arrangements you want. There are two companies to deal with: One is **Ansett Pioneer,** which is represented in the U.S. by Ansett Airlines, 9841 Airport Blvd., Suite 1020, Los Angeles, CA

90045 (Tel. toll free 800–6–ANSETT in California, 800–4–ANSETT in the rest of the country, or 642–7487 within the 213 area code). The other is **Greyhound Australia,** which is now represented in the U.S. by Greyhound International in San Francisco at 50 First St., San Francisco, CA 94106 (Tel. 415–495–1210 or toll free at 800–828–1985).

(Until recently, Ansett was represented by the American Greyhound and the Australian Greyhound was represented in the U.S. by a New York tour agent. We don't want to confuse you, but someone may tell you that it's still true. Most mercifully, it is not—at least up to the moment the ink begins drying on this page!)

Ansett Pioneer, the large operation controlled by the same people as Ansett Airways, etc., offers some special bus plans which, like the Austrailpass, *must be purchased outside Australia.*

First and most famous is the "Aussiepass," which allows unlimited travel in Pioneer coaches throughout the country over the time period specified. The 1986 rates are not set at this writing, but as a general guide we'll guess they will be sold in three versions—15 days for about $A250 (extensions available at around $A10 per extra day), 30 days for about $A475, and 60 days for about $A700. (Remember, again, these are Down Under dollars, so the price you pay will depend on the current exchange rate.) There are also some "Super Aussiepasses" that include rooms and sightseeing, sold in two-, three-, and fiveweek blocks. (And although they don't publicize them in the U.S., there are also usually a couple of Aussiepass plans that may be purchased in Australia at somewhat higher rates.)

Ansett also sells an "Unlimited Sightseeing Pass" that allows you to take any number of the company's sightseeing tours (half-day or all-day narrated trips) at differing prices in capital cities and major tourist areas. We think you could live without this one. We have found that Pioneer sightseeing tours vary widely in quality, and we would rather make up our minds on tours only after arriving at each individual destination. If you already have the Aussiepass, you can get 50 percent discounts on most sightseeing tours anyway.

One American traveler writing in the *International Travel News* not long ago was critical of his own 60-day Aussiepass experience. Although the drivers were informative and pleasant and the buses comfortable, he said there was no provision made for passengers when an unexpected strike cut 12 days out of their excursion. Some routes only have one or two buses a week, making it impossible to stop over someplace for just a day or two. He also said the city sightseeing portions left a lot to be desired since some of the half-day and full-day tours advertised in the booklet he received were not available on arrival.

Ansett also offers its tried and true 21-day "Gold Pass to Australia." It

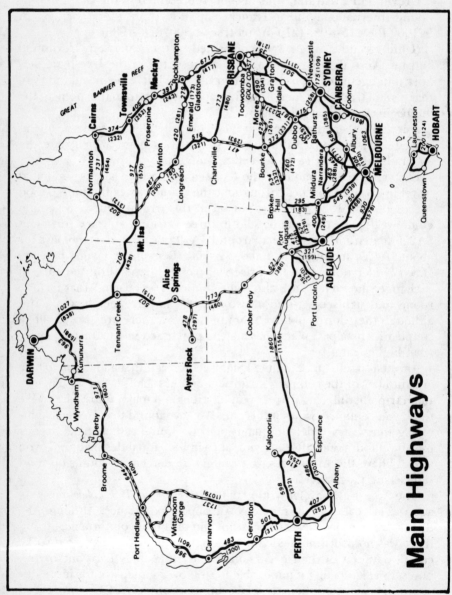

Map courtesy Australian Tourist Commission

allows 20 nights at certain hotels and 21 days of unlimited travel for about $A1,000 (at this writing, and on a share-twin basis), plus a couple of extras such as working out a personal itinerary for you, meeting you on arrival in Australia, etc. (It does not include meals or other expenses.) And in a change from previous years, there are no longer versions that include return domestic air trips.

Last on this busman's holiday, the other company, Greyhound Australia, offers a 14-day, 21-day, 30-day, and 60-day "Eaglepass" plan that is competitive with Pioneer's Aussiepass. At the moment the prices are similar, running from around $A250 to $A700—again, purchased before your arrival in the country. Besides this, Greyhound has inaugurated an interesting new "Aussie Explorer" route system that provides a single price for a circular journey, e.g., about $A400 for Sydney–Melbourne–Adelaide–Ayers Rock–Townsville–Sydney. The tickets are good for up to a year as long as you continue to use them in the same direction (no backtracking allowed). You can go virtually all around the country on this system for about $A700. That one sounds like an excellent deal, and we would very much like to hear from anyone who has done it.

Nearly all bus lines allow you to take two suitcases along. Children generally travel for half fare on all buses. Long-distance buses have lavatories and air conditioning on board, and usually don't stop at night. But neither the Aussiepass nor Eaglepass can guarantee that these modern devices won't "go crook" somewhere in the wild country Beyond the Black Stump.

Prior to the advent of mobile dunnies, the traditional Outback answer by the driver to the passenger who felt a call of nature hundreds of miles from any plumbing was to stop the coach and hand over a shovel with the instructions that the user could go dig in the desert as far away as was necessary to become inconspicuous.

According to the veteran bus driver who explained it to us, the passenger, who he said was most often a woman, soon learned that it was more practical to walk 100 yards or so *in front* of the bus—not to the rear. Under that procedure, she needed only to walk one way and then wave the shovel in the air as a signal to the driver that the job had been done, and that it was time to be picked up. (Trudging off *behind* the coach may seem more modest, but it was exactly twice as far to walk.)

Nevertheless, traveling by bus is quite respectable in Australia, and the meal stops are usually at fairly nice cafes. Many Americans say these long-distance trips are an ideal way to make good friends among the Aussies.

Rental Cars. There are three big outfits throughout Australia. Avis Rent-a-Car System, the good ole Number Two in America, is generally Number One Down Under. And Hertz Rent-A-Car, sometimes known as Kay/Hertz in Australia, is coming along right behind. The third biggie is Budget Rent-A-Car System. Rates on all three are similar, running from a minimum of about $A35 or $A40 per day for standard-shift minis up to about $A100 for large cars (for unlimited mileage—er, kilometrage?). You may find some also running 20 cents a kilometer, and sometimes "unlimited mileage" is only up to a specified number of miles.

Avis, incidentally, increases its rates during the "peak seasons"—winter on the Gold Coast and summer in Tasmania. Some others may, too. There are at least three other nationwide firms—Thrifty Rent-A-Car, L.R.C. Rent-A-Car (formerly Letz), and Natcar—and several regional operators. You'll find more about all of these in section 2 of each of the eight area chapters in this book.

The way to get the best deal, of course, is to shop for car rentals on the scene. All the above publish rate sheets. It may not make much difference renting a car for a day, but if you take an hour's research time to compare the different deals available, it could save you a hundred Aussie dollars or more over a long vacation.

By the way, don't go to the trouble of getting an international driver's license. If you're a genuine tourist, your regular U.S. license is good for a year in Australia. British, Canadian, and New Zealand licenses are also accepted.

Gasoline (called "petrol" Down Under) is extra and costs about 50 Australian cents per litre—perhaps $1.50 American per U.S. gallon. (If you rent a Leyland Mini, with manual transmission, you'll get about 30 miles per gallon.) Popular petrols include Shell, BP, Caltex, Mobil, Amoco, Golden Fleece, and AMPOL, and most of these stations will accept credit cards.

A few driving tips. Traffic signs are similar to the international signs we have at home today, and are generally clear and easily understood. As in Britain and New Zealand, you drive on the left, of course. You pass ("overtake") on the right. Until you get used to it, use caution making right-hand turns across the traffic lane (think "left turns narrow—right turns wide"), and don't forget to go *clockwise* around traffic circles ("round-abouts"). And the guy on the inside lane has the right of way, too! Also, watch carefully while pulling out from a parking lot into traffic. General-ly speaking, we prefer to rent an automatic-drive car, which gives us just one less thing to think about for the first 100 miles while we are grimly chanting, "Keep left! Keep left! Keep left!" and learning not to look for the rear-view mirror somewhere in outer space.

New South Wales has perhaps the toughest drunk driving law in the world, and other states are starting to follow suit. Three glasses of beer will take you to the legal limit. (See our discussions on beer in sections 11 of the area chapters.) And the alcohol hangs around in your body a long time, too. Recently, the host of a New Year's Eve party who allowed six guests to spend the night at his home so they would not be picked up for drunk driving was snagged himself by a police breath test while he was out buying his guests bacon and eggs for breakfast. His last drink had been taken nine hours earlier!

Don't forget that the vehicle on the right at intersections has the right of way unless otherwise indicated. And look out on main highways for the *ocker* (oaf) who comes off a little dirt country road insisting on his rights. Above all, remember that wearing a safety belt is the law in Australia. If you don't buckle up, you could be fined $A50!

If you're going to be traveling extensively in the Outback, there are many, many precautions to be taken. It's exciting country, but genuinely wild. Motorists are still found dead when they ignore the lessons of the past—forgetting to take extra water, getting bogged in "bulldust," etc. After you arrive in the country, look for some of the several publications with good advice and hints for effective motoring through specific rough areas.

Also, the Automobile Association in Australia offers a lot—road service, general driving assistance, travel information, maps, etc., *but only if you are already a member of an affiliated organization* like the American Automobile Association (AAA) or the Canadian Automobile Association. (And you'll be asked to prove it, too.)

Campers and caravans. You can rent campers (called campervans) and caravans (motor homes) from several places in Australia. Get a lot of good, up-to-date information on the subject from the Australian Tourist Commission (see chapter 1). Some family rates have been running about $A400 a week, including linens, dishes, and a free 625 miles (per week)—a good deal for combining sleeping and wheeling expenses. (But don't hold us to that. That rate is a sample one only.)

Camping grounds ("caravan parks") are located near cities and towns all over the country. With electric outlet you'll pay around $12 a day, $6 for "unpowered sites." And, of course, you can also rent or buy caravans in most parts of Australia.

We've never had the opportunity to evaluate caravan parks, but if you're serious about this kind of travel try to get hold of the annual *Caravan Camping Directory*, published by the NRMA (National Road & Motorists Association), 151 Clarence St., Sydney 2000, N.S.W. (If worse comes to worse, join the outfit for about 10 bucks.)

Hitchhiking. If you hitchhike elsewhere, you'll probably get away with it in Australia, too. Aussie drivers are gregarious, and hitching men and hitching couples usually seem to get along okay. As at home, it is considered dangerous for women to hitchhike, either alone or in pairs.

Members of the Society of the Upturned Thumb report good luck carrying (1) an American or Canadian flag, and (2) a signboard that can be marked with the immediate destination. Cops, like cops nearly everywhere, might interfere. Savants of the Australian open road say that when you see the "white hats," you should step back off the right of way. Then you're not standing on an illegal portion of the road.

Choosing a Travel Agent

Don't pick a travel agent blindly from the Yellow Pages. If you don't already have a trusted travel expert, your best bet is to ask your friends and associates who they've used—especially if they recently took a trip to Australia or the South Pacific.

After you have a few names of agencies in your area, call them up. Some just won't talk to you over the phone at all about your proposed trip. Throw those rascals out immediately. A good agency may understandably not feel like going into great detail over the phone, but you can get a pretty good feel for their operation if they seem pleasant and willing to jaw with you for a few minutes.

Ask them some questions about Australia. If they seem vague or confused, they just might not be able to do the job for you. If they seem to have facts and figures at their fingertips, then make a date to drop in and speak to someone about your ideas for a vacation.

We heartily recommend that you choose an aggressive, enthusiastic travel agency. Avoid "assembly-line" operations (and these can be the tiny, one-man offices or the giant, international outfits)—those who seem anxious only to ship you out in one of their own prewrapped packages or just to jet you off into space on any old flight. Australia is not a single, simple destination; there are many kinds of tours and other options, and a travel agency should be ready to spell them all out for you and then follow through and make your reservations.

Your travel agent should be a member of ASTA (the American Society of Travel Agents) or ARTA (the Association of Retail Travel Agents). The most respected agents today also have the initials "CTC" (Certified Travel Counselor) after their names. And of course the agency should be licensed by the ATC (the Air Traffic Conference), so that it can legally issue your tickets.

If your agent has been to Australia, that may be a help, but it's not an absolute requirement. Agents who have received only one or two "familiarization" trips hosted by commercial outfits in the travel industry may be inclined to book their clients with those few firms to whom they feel grateful for the freebies. (Incidentally, in case you missed it before, we have made no arrangements of any kind with any companies in connection with this book.)

It's quite possible for a good agent who has never been to Australia to be thoroughly familiar with many of its facilities and book you into a terrific vacation, and it's also possible for a dumb or gullible agent who has been to Australia a dozen times to completely foul up your trip.

A good travel agent will try to give you what you want, so we suggest that you rely on this book for the important basics and then let your travel agent try to put your requests into a final practical itinerary.

Remember, your travel agent's service should be free. They generally make their money from commissions (7 to 11 percent from airlines, 10 percent from hotels, tours, etc.). It costs them money in postage, cables, phone calls, and the like to set things up, of course, and if their client suddenly decides to cancel everything at the last minute, it's not unreasonable that the agency would then send the would-be customer a bill. We've heard that some travel agents charge their clients outright, anyway. Maybe they've got a good reason, but personally we'd stay away from those people.

If you prefer to make all your arrangements yourself, that can be a very satisfying experience. Just be sure to write letters that are specific about your requirements. (See our remarks on hotels, rental cars, bus tours, etc., before you do this.) And be sure to save all your confirmation letters and deposit receipts. You'll need those for proof at every turn.

Travel Facts and Figures

Here's a set of considerations that may be boring after you've learned them all, but they are essential for first-time visitors to Australia.

Weather and Climate. Antipodeans think it gets cold in their country. Don't believe it. Without the opportunity to experience the "temperate" zone in North America, bless their hearts, they don't know what cold really is. Even the island state of Tasmania—which Aussies sometimes describe in terms reserved in most places for deepest Siberia—grows an occasional palm tree. And how cold can any city be where practically the only snow is the white stuff that sometimes appears in the hills and mountains?

It does, however, get hot—damned hot—in Australia; more on that in a moment.

The most important thing to remember about weather and climate Down Under is that the seasons are exactly opposite to ours. When we're hot, the Australians are cold (or think they are). When we're cold, the Aussies are hot—or warm, depending on the part of the country.

Because of the upside-down weather pattern, remember that the hottest parts of the country are those in the north, while the temperature gets generally lower the further south you progress. This puts cities like

Brisbane and Darwin *up* in the tropics (closer to the equator), while Sydney, Canberra, and Melbourne are *down* in the cooler southland. (Perth, like Los Angeles, is in a separate category. It's west and warm nearly the year around.)

The seasons are considered to run like this:

Spring...September to November.
Summer...December to February.
Autumn...March to May.
Winter...June to August.

In practical terms, this means that the ideal time to visit Australia would seem to be during our northern winter—the southern warm months, September to April—when most Aussies are enjoying swimming, sailing, and other outdoor sports in temperatures in the 70s and 80s. (We've felt comfortable in a suit or sport jacket in sunny Sydney even in late May.)

Important exceptions are Darwin and the "Top End" districts of the Northern Territory, which will be suffering through the hot and humid summer monsoon season December to March, and also the desert Outback, where temperatures reach over 100 degrees F. around Christmastime.

Darwin is nicest during its dry season—about April to November. The skies are clear and the weather is usually ideal in Alice Springs and at Ayers Rock then, too. You'll find warm weather in Perth and in Brisbane also at that time of year. In Sydney, Canberra, and Melbourne, they think it's cold in the winter seasons because their daytime temperatures run between the mid-40s and the mid-60s on the Fahrenheit scale from June to August. Hobart does get down as low as 40 degrees F. in deepest July.

And snow? You'll find it in abundance, appropriately enough in the Snowy Mountains. Within easy traveling distance from Sydney and Canberra, they host a flourishing ski season at winter resorts there from June through September.

To sum it up optimistically, a country as large as Australia can always point to some area blessed with ideal vacation weather at any time of the year. By the same token, there is always some place in Australia that is not dependably comfortable at any particular time of the year.

However one of our own two-month trips took place under near-perfect conditions. We found ourselves generally in the southern part of the country in April (early autumn) and in the warmer northern areas in May (late autumn), and we enjoyed perfect traveling conditions nearly all the time.

Be aware, though, that spanning the temperate and tropical zones means a wider selection of wearing apparel. We usually take sweaters as well as shorts, for instance.

Packing and Wearing. The most important thing to remember is that the international baggage allowance for persons (including children) traveling between the U.S.A. and a foreign destination is two checked pieces of luggage and a small amount of hand luggage.

Technically, neither of the two checked bags may exceed 62 inches; that's adding up its length, width, and breadth. And unless you're traveling First Class, the two together may not exceed 106 inches, all told. Virtually no commercial suitcase made in America comes close to exceeding 62 inches, so the chances are you'll be okay if you take your two largest bags. (But if in doubt, measure it out.)

You're allowed one or more pieces of carry-on luggage small enough to fit under the seat (camera bag, airline bag, etc.), and the maximum outside dimensions of all those pieces combined may not exceed 45 inches per person.

If you have a third suitcase, it'll cost you an extra $100 or so to bring it to Australia. And another good reason for keeping your luggage down is that while traveling around Australia by plane, the official requirements are much more strict: You're allowed only one checked bag plus a piece of carry-on luggage. If you have extra checked bags, the airline may decide to charge you for them on a sliding scale of $2 to $10 per bag, depending on how far you're traveling.

This may occur if you buy additional domestic air tickets while you are in Australia. The Australian Tourist Commission has told us that as an international traveler you should get the second bag free as far as your next destination in Australia after the one you arrive at initially, and also from your next-to-last destination before leaving Australia. (Authorities have always been hard to pin down on this subject, however, and for whatever it's worth, we carried an extra bag on a dozen flights all around Australia again in '85, and no one said a word. We would like very much to hear from anyone who has any problems along these lines while traveling within the country.)

Now, what to take? If you're an experienced traveler, you'll believe us when we plead that you should travel as light as you possibly can. You may also know that it never seems to be possible to travel as light as you plan to. One principle to remember: If you're moving fast, you'll probably need more clothes, because there may not be time for laundering them en route.

The male traveler. Even if he's only in Australia on vacation, the American man will feel out of place on occasion if he doesn't have something to wear a tie with. Take at least a sport jacket or a blazer. A dark-colored suit, either summer or winter weight, would also be a good idea.

Australians don't like to think of themselves as class-conscious, to be sure. But in my experience, I nearly always receive a little better attention when wearing a coat and tie than wandering around bare-necked. Also, many of Australia's nicer restaurants have dress codes; like it or not, you just won't be allowed in without that noose around your neck. A couple of pairs of easy-care slacks will do for most day-to-day needs. A pair of jeans is a must if you're going to do any exploring in the bush.

Take maybe one or two long-sleeve shirts, two or three knit pullover shirts, and perhaps two two-way shirts with short sleeves, which can be worn with a tie or open-necked. (If you're going to be traveling entirely in winter, substitute another long-sleeve shirt or two for these.)

I'd have a sweater along any time of the year, either a pullover or cardigan. Some men might like a zipper jacket for cold weather.

There's considerable debate about top coats among antipodean traveling men. My personal choice is a knee-length all-weather coat (with or without lining), unless I plan to spend all the time in dependably warm weather. In that case, you could consider a folding raincoat. I also like to have a collapsible umbrella in the suitcase.

For your feet, try to find something that's comfortable but also looks good with your suit or jacket. Hush Puppies or similar suedes might do it. I felt equally at ease in good dining salons, tramping around animal reserves, and exploring old gold mines in shoes like that last year. Of course businessmen on the job may prefer to have a pair of black leather shoes along, as well.

Take an old, well-broken-in pair of sneakers or running shoes, too, if you'll be trudging over sand and gibbers in the Red Centre—certainly for clambering up Ayers Rock or for picking your way carefully over the coral at the Great Barrier Reef.

We saw no great need for a hat, except possibly for days of excessive rain or sun. A roll-up or crushable model to keep in a coat pocket most of the time is not a bad idea. And if you want to buy an Aussie bush hat, well, there are many to choose from.

Throw in underwear, pajamas, lightweight robe, ties, etc., to suit your fancy, and several pairs of socks. As a general guide, automatic laundries do exist in Australia, but they are hard to find as compared with the U.S.A. (You'll find automatic washing machines available for guest use more often in the less expensive "family" hotels and motels.)

In the good ole summertime, or in the northern, tropical parts of the country, you'll find Australian men *dressed up* in shorts. They are considered acceptable for many occasions and locations where they would not be at home. Generally shorter than our Bermudas, shorts are usually called "stubbies." They are more or less the length of American walk shorts, but virtually always worn with long socks. (You can take your walk shorts along for this uniform, but you'll probably have to buy the socks on the scene.) With a short-sleeve shirt, tie, long socks, and stubbies, you're dressed to kill in many areas of Australia, particularly in the warmer climes of Queensland or the Northern Territory.

Of course if you're going to take part in athletic activities—swimming, skiing, hiking, etc.—your Down Under wardrobe requirements will be pretty much as they would be at home for those things.

The woman visitor. Decide whether or not you want to wear a pants suit. They're comfortable, flexible, and convenient for traveling in, but if you're fashion conscious it's our duty to tell you that Australian women have deserted trousers, now, except for the fancier jeans, and if you see another woman in a pants suit the chances are 99 to 1 she's another American. (Women's fashions in Australian cities seem to follow what they were wearing in London or New York, allowing, of course, for the six months' seasonal lag.)

We'd suggest taking shorts, trousers, and skirts with tops that mix and match, but keep in mind that you probably will not wear shorts as often as you do at home. (One woman wrote us that shorts are so much considered men's fashions in Australia that when she wore them she was sometimes addressed as "sir"!) You'll want a couple of dresses for evening wear, of course, and take a sweater—pullover or cardigan—as evenings can be cool any time of year.

In the winter, a medium-weight, all-weather coat would be nice, and you should certainly take some kind of casual jacket. Sara was also glad she carried her folding umbrella to Australia.

For your feet, we might mention that ladies' longstemmed boots have been very popular in Australia for the past several years. Of course you must have comfortable walking shoes for everyday sightseeing, and a pair of evening shoes. And like the men you, too, will need sneakers (and a pair of jeans) for the rougher style of Aussie Outback experiences.

Men and women. Take your favorite toiletries, of course, but with the full knowledge that you can replace nearly anything you run out of. They will often be unfamiliar brands, though, and you can buy things only during Australia's rather restrictive shopping hours.

Strangely, we find plain old bottles of regular aspirin hard to get hold of. (Plenty of dissolvables, aspirin in chewing gum, and other pain killers are available.) And we were glad we tucked in some rub-on fly and mosquito repellent.

Of course you'll take your camera. And if you have a telephoto lens, don't think of leaving it at home (too many animals way up in the trees). We also enjoyed using our miniature tape recorder to capture the cockney of the tour guides and the laughter of the kookaburra. (Film and cassette tapes are readily available.)

Believe us, if you don't take a pair of binoculars to Australia you'll be

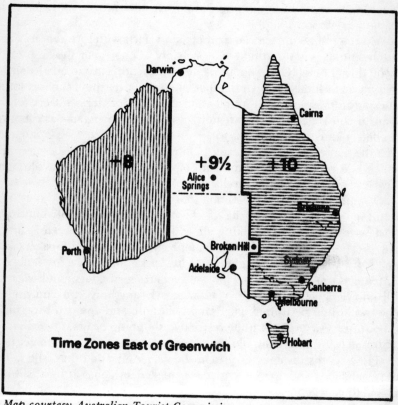

Map courtesy Australian Tourist Commission

eternally sorry, especially if you'll be traveling in the Outback. (To avoid husband-wife conflicts at crucial moments, take two.) A portable transistor radio is also good to help you keep in tune with Australia and Australians all along the way. (Their stations use the same general frequencies ours do.) And we always carry our pocket calculator, now, to check hotel and restaurant bills, exchange rates, conversion from Celsius to Fahrenheit, and a zillion other little logistical tasks that might otherwise get in the way of a dinkum holiday.

Avoiding the Crush. As in any other country, foreign visitors who find themselves casually on the go during peak periods for local traffic are due for sudden disappointment and sad inconvenience.

Look out especially for vacation times—they call them "school holidays" Down Under—when every kid in the continent seems to be traveling between boarding school and home at opposite ends of the country. Trains and planes are particularly jam-packed at the beginnings and ends of these periods.

Christmas holidays (the big summer vacation) begin in mid-December and continue until early February. Although the worst strain on public transportation appears to be at either end of that period, there will be considerable traffic by oldsters and youngsters alike throughout January. If you travel then, have your reservations firmly locked in in advance, and avoid any changes in plans.

Planes and trains are also overflowing with small fry for two other difficult periods—for about two weeks in mid-May and another two weeks at the end of August and beginning of September.

Public Holidays. Australia has about 30 public holidays, counting all the ones that are celebrated in different states on different dates. There are about 11 holidays agreed upon nearly nationwide, however. They are as follows:

January—New Year's Day; last Monday in January—Australia Day; in April—Good Friday and Easter Saturday, Sunday, and Monday (four days); April 25—Anzac Day (the national memorial day); a Monday in early June—the Queen's Birthday; first Tuesday in November—Melbourne Cup Day (official only in Victoria, but observed everywhere); December 25—Christmas Day; and December 26—Boxing Day.

Time Zones. Queensland, New South Wales, the Australian Capital Territory, Victoria, and Tasmania—states that make up the eastern third of the continent—set their clocks at Greenwich Mean Time plus 10. Since Pacific Standard Time in the U.S. is GMT minus eight, that places Brisbane, Sydney, Canberra, Melbourne, Hobart, etc., at 18 hours later than American West Coast cities. Or, since the International Date Line is between the U.S. and Australia, you can say these places are six hours earlier, but on the following day. Thus, when it is 12 noon Saturday in

San Francisco, it's 6 A.M. Sunday in Sydney—provided both are on standard time.

(Since you "lose" a day traveling to Australia across the date line, conversely you "gain" a day coming back home. Leaving Sydney Saturday evening, for instance, you'll find yourself arriving in the U.S. on Saturday afternoon.)

Australia is one of the few countries in the world to use a half-hour split time zone. But to add to the confusion, it's only in the center of the country. Therefore, it is a half-hour earlier in Adelaide than it is in Sydney.

The vast state of Western Australia is back in step with the rest of the world, eight hours ahead of Greenwich Mean Time. Of course this places Perth 1½ hours earlier than Adelaide and two hours ahead of the east coast cities.

The three time zones are called Eastern Standard, Central Australian, and Western.

During the summer months (from the last Sunday in October to the first Sunday in March), *some* states shift into daylight saving time, making those times one hour later. (Western Australia, the Northern Territory, and Queensland do not.) And because much of the U.S. also goes on daylight saving—but in the approximate opposite months—there are periods each year when Australia and the U.S. are separated by one hour more than normal or by one hour less than normal. Thus, when it is noon in San Francisco, it would be 5 A.M. in Sydney if California is on PDST, or 7 A.M. in Sydney, if N.S.W. is observing daylight saving, or 6 A.M. if neither city is on it.

But unless you're calculating airline schedules yourself, perhaps you won't have to get involved with this perplexing refinement of the clock game. American businessmen in Australia pondering when to phone the home office do find themselves performing these mental gymnastics—and usually at about two o'bloody clock in the morning!

Jet Lag. Daylight saving, Greenwich Mean, and all the king's men can hardly put you together again if you suffer from jet lag—the familiar disorientation for those who fly long distances in short amounts of time.

One of the best reasons for flying to Australia overnight, however, is that it seems to reduce the adverse effects of jet lag. You leave California after dinner, see a movie, go to sleep (if you can sleep on a plane). Then, when you awaken in the morning, you eat what might seem like a rather late breakfast, then arrive in Sydney at 6 A.M.

Nevertheless, the first effect you notice thereafter might be finding yourself famished an hour or so later and then compulsively eating again in the midafternoon. First thing you know, you're dead on your feet at six in the evening. That's midnight back in California—and much later than that in Cleveland and New York.

Some claim they are never affected by jet lag. Personally, it takes us a day or two before we stop propping open our eyes, quit yawning in everyone's face, and regain our ability to walk a reasonably straight line.

We suggest six steps to alleviate—somewhat—the effects of jet lag: (1) Sleep as much as you can on the plane. (2) Set your watch to Australian time as soon as you take off. (3) Take no sleeping pill and little alcohol during the flight, but eat when food is offered. (4) After you arrive at your hotel, pull the shades against the daylight and try for a good nap. (5) Schedule no business appointments and no demanding sightseeing your first day in Australia. (6) Eat lightly with familiar foods your first day.

Of course another good system is to break your journey for a day or so along the way. Depending on your airline arrangements you could do this, for example, in Hawaii, Fiji, or Tahiti. (Psst: We can recommend an excellent guidebook to Hawaii, which, incidentally, is our own home state.)

Metrics and Electrics

According to one story, it was the U.S.A. who convinced Australia a decade or so ago to convert to the metric (decimal) system of weights and measures. Americans said they were about to do it themselves and that, in the interests of improved international trade and communication, the island continent should quickly do the same.

Australia then set out on a well-organized program that now has the whole country easily dividing and multiplying by tens while the U.S.A. is still stumbling around with 12 inches, 16 ounces, 4 pints, and countless short and long tons.

The money came first and easiest. Pounds, shillings, and pence were smoothly changed to dollars and cents. But, steadily, the adaptable Aussies also came to accept the kilometer, the centimeter, the litre, the gram, and degrees centigrade.

To try to learn the decimal system while on vacation is, of course, absurd—and a contradiction in terms. But here are a few thoughts on how to keep from mixing your millimeters throughout Australia.

Temperature. Anybody who gets up in the morning without listening to the weather forecasts on the radio deserves to freeze or burn on the day's sightseeing. But the temperatures will be given on the Celsius (centigrade) scale.

We sometimes are a bit pedantic and take out our midget calculator, marking it with the figure the radio gives us, and then punching out

"× 9, ÷ 5, + 32 =" and coming up with the familiar Fahrenheit. If you're not carrying your own trusty LED, however, remember that the most comfortable temperatures are generally in the 20s. (20° Celsius equals 68° Fahrenheit; 29° C. = 84.2° F.) Of course the freezing point of water is zero degrees and the boiling point is 100 degrees, which is the principle behind the whole scale.

Distance. How far is it to the next town? Strangely enough, middle-aged and older Australians will still give you longer distances estimated in miles. Closer to home, where they often see signs printed in kilometers—like 32 km from Sydney to Parramatta—they may use the modern figure.

A kilometer is .621 of a mile, but for quick conversion while zipping along the highway we move over the decimal point or maybe even lop off the last digit, multiply by six, and then round off the result. In the example above, 32 becomes either 3.2 × 6 or 3 × 6, depending on how lazy we're feeling. One equation gives us 18 and the other 19. Either one we would round off to 20 miles. And if the speed limit on the road is 100 kmh, we calculate that at 60. (Of course it's really 62.1 mph, but few traffic cops are going to care much about 2.1 mph anyway.)

For small distances, well, one centimeter is about the width of your little fingernail, and there are about 2½ fingernails per inch. One hundred centimeters, of course, equal a meter, and that's about as far as a man's outstretched arm can reach from his nose—39 inches, or a little more than a yard. And since "kilo" means thousand, there are a thousand meters in the kilometer.

Volume. Gasoline and milk are sold in litres, and a litre is close enough to an American quart to our way of thinking. Therefore, four of them are darn near an American gallon. (Not the British and Canadian "imperial" gallon; that's larger.)

Now if some Digger tells you his car gets 11 km per litre of petrol, you can quickly multiply 1.1 by 6 to get 6.6 and then by 4 litres to get 26.4 miles per U.S. gallon.

Weight. Here's an anachronism. You might find Aussies still giving their body weight in stone (that's singular and plural), an old British system that amounts to 14 pounds per stone. However a kilogram, which you'll meet while grocery shopping, is 2.2 pounds, so you can double that weight quoted at the butcher shop to get the approximate weight of the meat in the system we're familiar with. You'll also hear the weight of coal or wheat given in tonnes. That's 1,000 kilograms, which works out to be 1.1 tons. Not being in the coal or wheat business, we've mentally equated the two for all practical purposes.

Area. If you think about buying land, you'll get into hectares. A hectare, which is 10,000 square meters, works out to 2.47 acres—two and a half acres is a pretty close estimate. And a square meter, if anyone wants to know, is 10.8 square feet.

Electricity. Luckily, electric current, like units of time, is *measured* Down Under the same as at home. The important thing to remember about Aussie house current is that it's powered at 240 volts, or more than twice the zap we get in the U.S.A. or Canada. This means you'll instantly cremate your Yankee razor or hair dryer if you manage to plug them in without a transformer. Lightweight transformers that will power razors and the like are practical to carry, if you want. High-watt, heat-producing devices like irons or hair dryers usually require a more heavy-duty transformer. If these devices cannot be set for 240 volts, perhaps you'd better forget them.

However many hotels do have 110-volt outlets fed by small transformers installed in the bathrooms. You can run lightduty appliances like razors from those—again, no hair dryers, irons, or the like. We do find it handy for the AC adapter for our tape recorder, pocket calculator, transistor radio, etc., when we are out of or want to save on batteries. (Take an extension cord, too, so you're not always listening to your tapes in the bathroom!) Incidentally, you can buy standard battery sizes in Australia, but it often seems you have to hunt around, the stores are closed, or whatever. So take some spares.

Australian alternating current (AC) also alternates at 50 cycles per second (versus 60 c.p.s. in the U.S.). This means that U.S. motors will run a little slower, even if the *voltage* is transformed from 240 to 110 volts. Such items as American electric clocks and phonographs, where exact speed is important, will not perform satisfactorily unless they are electrically or mechanically converted—generally a complicated process. It doesn't matter much if your razor motor revolves a little less rapidly than usual.

If you've been to Europe or England, don't think that your two-pronged adapter is going to work in an Aussie threepronged socket. If you have a 240-volt appliance like a traveling iron, and you can't find an adapter at an electrical store, go to Woolworth's or some place similar and have a look at an iron cord or an electric teakettle cord. Sometimes the American plug—or at least the European adapter—will fit into the appliance end of that cord and the other end will fit into the three-pronged "point" in the wall. One American firm sells adapters for American plugs to Australian sockets for two or three bucks. That's Traveler's Checklist, Cornwall Bridge Road, Sharon, CT 06069. We've also seen them for sale at Radio Shack stores in the U.S.

Notice that it's probably a "switched point," too. Unlike in the U.S., most electrical outlets in Australia are controlled by a switch—a darned good idea.

Changing a light bulb? Be aware that Australian light bulbs—like British ones—don't unscrew. They're held in place with two little pins, like some of our automobile and flashlight bulbs. You push in and turn to the left to take them out. And if the socket is dangling from the ceiling, for heaven's sake use two hands—one to hold the socket and the other to twist the bulb.

Money, Currency, and Prices

There is far more than a dime's worth of difference between the Yankee and the Aussie dollar. *At this writing,* the Australian dollar is worth about 70 cents American. That's the best rate for American tourists in many years. (In 1978, when we were researching the first edition of this book, each Aussie dollar cost $US1.14!) But remember that with the vagaries of international economics there can be no guarantee that the exchange rate won't take a kangaroo jump forward or backward at any time.

When writing specifically about prices, the traditional way to make things perfectly clear is to use something like "$US70," or "$A100," the "US" or the "A" indicating which country's dollars you're talking about.

In this volume, we sometimes do that, too, or make some other specific indication when it seems appropriate. But generally speaking, throughout the balance of this book, we quote and estimate prices in *Australian dollars.* This makes things easier for everyone, including travelers from other countries, to make their own conversions when calculating prices at hotels, restaurants, and other tourist facilities discussed in this guidebook. (An exception is in the earlier part of this chapter. The prices quoted there for air and sea trips to Australia from America are of course in U.S. currency.)

One thing seems clear at the present time. Your money will go further in Australia than it will in many of the expensive American or European cities that have served as traditional vacation destinations. We'll bet the price of a good steak dinner in Sydney will be about half the tab you'd pay for a comparable meal in New York, London, or Paris, for instance. And you'll do almost as well on the cost of good hotel rooms. Internal transportation, by plane, train, or bus, might be a third off what you'd pay mile per mile around the U.S. or Europe.

Be sure to pick up at least a small amount of Australian currency before you leave on your trip, so you can begin to become familiar with it. Also, it's always a good idea to land in a country with some of its currency already in your pocket. (Your bank will sell you some or will tell you where to buy it.)

Sensibly, the bills (Aussies call them "notes") are printed in different sizes and colors for different denominations, so you're not likely to find out too late that you gave the taxi driver a ten by mistake. They come in $100, $50, $20, $10, $5, and $2 versions (the $2 note is the only green one, by the way). The $1 note, a tan color like a certain Australian cookie ("biscuit") is sometimes called a "bickie," but it has now almost disappeared. The Aussies also use the term "bucks," an American influence on the lingo. But they have lost the colorful slang they had for coins before the country adopted decimal currency. A 10-cent coin is dully called a "10-cent piece." ("Tanners" and "two-bob bits" have gone the way of spats and corset stays.)

Coins are $1 (a gold-colored metal about the size of an American quarter, with a herd of roos on the back), 50 cents (a 12-sided coin about the size of the American halfdollar), 20 cents (slightly smaller, depicting a swimming platypus), 10 cents (the size and value of the old shilling but with the sheep replaced by a lyrebird), 5 cents (dime-size, bearing a spiny anteater), 2 cents (a copper coin about the size of a nickel and featuring the frill-necked lizard), and 1 cent (a small copper stamped with a feather-tailed glider).

As in most British Commonwealth countries, the profile of Queen Elizabeth (looking something like a long-necked teenager) is pictured on the obverse with the value and regional designs on the reverse sides.

Here are the personalities on the folding money: Two dollars buys you John Macarthur, the irascible settler who established Australia's wool industry. On the back is William J. Farrer, who developed the hybrid wheat grown in Australia.

The five-dollar note features Sir Joseph Banks, the scientist on Cook's voyage who catalogued much of Australia's strange natural life. On the reverse is Caroline Chisholm, who worked to improve immigrant conditions in Australia during the mid-nineteenth century.

On the $10 note is Francis Greenway; convicted of forgery in England, he became an architect in colonial Australia. Featured on the same bill is Henry Lawson, Australia's best-known writer. Sir Charles Kingsford Smith, the notable aviation pioneer, appears on the twenty. Lawrence Hargrave, who experimented with the theory of flight by using kites, is engraved on the back. And John Curtin, the wartime prime minister who defied Churchill, is honored on the fifty.

The $100 note, which was introduced in 1984, is predominantly blue and gray and pictures two Australian scientists. On the front is Sir Douglas Mawson, the geologist and Antarctic explorer, and on the back is John Tebbutt, a pioneer in astronomical studies of Southern Hemisphere skies.

Credit Cards. Visa and MasterCard are sometimes accepted in the same locations as is Australia's Bankcard. Other cards that may be used include Diners Club (often), American Express (sometimes), and Carte Blanche (seldom). We were pleased to see that the exchange rates calculated on our Diners Club bill were fair. Now, however, someone at Diners has decided that the club will charge you an extra fee for converting bills from foreign currency—a cheap trick, to our way of thinking.

Exchange Rates. Generally speaking, your best exchange rates will be at genuine banks ("trading" banks, by the way—not reserve or savings banks). You'll virtually never get good exchange rates at hotel desks, although it is handy to be able to exchange small amounts—$10 or $20 traveler's checks—there. And you'll get a slightly better rate by exchanging American traveler's checks instead of American currency, although no one has ever explained why to us.

Traveler's Checks. No problem, except you'll have to cash them at banks (or hotel desks). Don't expect a restaurant or a shop to make the current conversion to Aussie currency. (Or if they do, the chances are the exchange rate will be weighted heavily in the firm's favor.) If you want that kind of convenience, we suggest you buy your traveler's checks in Australian currency—although we've never felt the need to do this.

Unlike in Europe, incidentally, Aussie banks virtually never have asked us for a passport or other identification to cash a traveler's check, although we certainly are not well known. Apparently it was enough for most banks that our signatures seemed to match the samples. Most banks are open from 10 to 3, Mondays through Thursdays, and until 5 P.M. on Fridays.

A minor annoyance, however, is that it takes a little longer to cash checks at some banks in the hinterlands. These are ones where the tellers have no money at the windows, and all the paperwork has to be sent to a cash cage somewhere in the rear. There it waits in line with other people's requests for spending money.

This did not occur in Sydney or Melbourne, but in other cities you may as well wait it out. Sit down, and they'll call you by name when your money arrives.

Governmental Fiddle-Faddle

Your travel agent should guide you firmly through all this. But just in case, here are a few basic requirements set up by Australian authorities.

Passport. You'll need a passport and visa to enter Australia. Americans can apply directly at a passport office in major cities or at any U.S. Post Office. It now takes only a few days once you deliver or send in the filled-out form with the required photographs and fee.

Visa. You get an Australian visa—free—from any Australian consulate. Take in your passport and fill out an application, hand over a passport-size photo, and you can probably pick up the passport with visa attached the next day. By mail, send your passport, completed application, and photo to the consulate and include a stamped, self-addressed envelope. (Be sure there are enough stamps on it and that it's large enough for the thing to fit in when they send it back.)

Tourist visas are issued for a six months' stay—unless special arrangements are made with the consulate prior to your trip. Your travel agent should know which is the nearest Aussie consulate. If not, you can find out by writing to any one of them, say the Australian Consulate General, 636 Fifth Ave., New York, NY 10020, or, in Canada, the Australian Consulate General, Suite 2324, Commerce Court West, King & Bay streets, Postal Box 69, Toronto, Ont. M5L 1B9. (Other consulates are in Chicago, San Francisco, Los Angeles, Washington, Honolulu, Ottawa, and Vancouver.)

Health. Unless your situation is unusual, you won't need a health card or a vaccination certificate. But you'll have to get one if you'll be traveling in some infected countries on the way.

Immigration Officials. These fellows at the airport will want to see a few things before they allow you into the country. Your passport and visa are required, of course, and you may have to show something else. If the inspector thinks you look like someone who could become a drain on the economy, he might also ask to see evidence that you can support yourself—cash, traveler's checks, credit cards, etc. (Don't be insulted; after many years of crossing borders, I've gotten used to the fact that if an immigration official notices "writer" as my profession, he's probably going to ask to see at least my return or onward-going ticket!) If you're genuinely on vacation or on legitimate business, and are not trying to put something over on these chaps, don't worry. It'll all go smoothly.

Customs. Australian customs officials will allow you to take into Australia most normal things for your own personal use. If you're going to strain things by toting along firearms, gallons of liquor, and the like, then special arrangements will have to be sought. But you can even come in with a bicycle or motorcycle nowadays. We didn't accompany any vehicles, but we have so far managed to speed through Australian customs without incident.

Animals, fruits, and veggies are strictly controlled, however. Ask especially if you want to get into this kind of thing. One thing we might mention right off the bat: It's practically impossible to get into Australia with a live dog or cat unless your furry friends have lived all their lives in neighboring New Zealand.

Departure Tax. Australia currently levies the largest national departure tax of any country in the world, but it may not seem so much of a bummer if you're prepared for the idea ahead of time. It's $A20 for all outward-bound passengers 12 years of age or older, and no charge for the youngsters. So you might save one last picture of Sir Charles Kingsford Smith in the bottom of your shoe to fork over before you get on the plane.

3

The Land and Life
of Australia

To many travelers, Australia's dominant characteristic is also the one most difficult to grasp—its almost incredible size of just a little under 3 million square miles.

There are five countries with a greater total acreage. China, Russia, and Canada are all much bigger, and the United States and Brazil have a slight edge. But each of those countries is part of a continent, contiguous with other nations, and culturally and economically influenced by the flow of people and communication across and along their common borders.

Australia is an island unto itself and by far the largest island on earth. It is so massive and so distant from almost anywhere else that geographers have universally agreed that it should be labeled a continent in its own right. Today it is the only continent that belongs entirely to one single nation.

After its size, another ponderable for travelers from the Northern Hemisphere is that Australia is, in effect, "upside-down." The north, near the equator, is warm. In fact, 39 percent of Australia is officially in the northern tropics. The south, which looks toward Antarctica, is cool by comparison. And the seasons are also reversed in time. The Southern Hemisphere is tilted further toward the sun at the same time Europe and North America are having their deepest, darkest days of winter.

July and August, therefore, are Australia's coolest months (and in southern Australia, the wettest). Christmas Day can be boiling hot, although January and February are usually the warmest months.

In this jet age, it is possible for a person of means to spend the summer in the U.S. and then spend the summer again in Australia, year after year never experiencing winter at all—just jumping directly from fall to spring as he crosses the equator every six months. (And avid ski enthusiasts have been known to operate just in reverse: They'll spend an American winter on the slopes of Stowe, Vermont, perhaps, and then an Australian winter in the aptly named Snowy Mountains of New South Wales.

Once you begin travel to the South Pacific, strange things start to happen—events you might win bets on in future years. Sara once had 30 days in February, for instance: On a ship from New Zealand to Honolulu, she crossed the International Date Line during that month in a leap year. And both of us lay claim to experiencing the longest day of the year and the shortest day of the year on the same day: We flew from Perth to Singapore across the equator on June 22, the summer solstice. (The fewest hours of daylight occur in the Southern Hemisphere on that date and the most in the Northern Hemisphere—exactly the opposite of December 22.)

Australia, then, became known also as "Down Under." And since it was supposed to be directly on the opposite point on the earth from the mother country—the "antipode" (accent on the first syllable) to Great Britain—it also became known as the "antipodes" (accent on the second syllable), with "antipodean" (accent on the penultimate syllable) for the adjective (and for "one who lives Down Under"). The terms are also applied to New Zealand and New Zealanders. Interestingly, New Zealand is technically closer to Britain's genuine geographic antipode.

All this upside-down-ness and inside-out-ness, massive size, and distance from the sophisticated influence of the rest of the world have been addressed in sociological terms by Professor Geoffrey Blainey in his book *The Tyranny of Distance*.

But an itinerant sheepshearer downing a cold beer in the western town of Marble Bar, the hottest, dryest spot in Australia, has been credited with summing up the geographic/cultural situation in Australian terms:

"If this earth were shaped like a cow," he said, leaning back on the bar, "this country here would be its arse-end!"

Australia is often described as a very, very old land. It's true. Some of its rock was formed 2 and 3 *billion* years ago. It was already pretty much its present size and shape about 230 million years ago. And somewhere along about 170 million years later—relatively recently—it became totally separated from the Asian mainland.

The continent is also the world's flattest and dryest. The average eleva-

Australia

PLACES OF INTEREST

1. Cairns — Atherton Tableland
2. Great Barrier Reef
3. Brisbane — Gold Coast
4. Hunter Valley
5. Sydney — Blue Mountains
6. Canberra — Australian National Capital
7. The Australian Alps
8. Melbourne — Murray Valley
9. Tasmania
10. Adelaide — Barossa Valley
11. Flinders Ranges
12. Perth — The South West
13. Australia's Great Outback
14. Lightning Ridge — Gem Fields

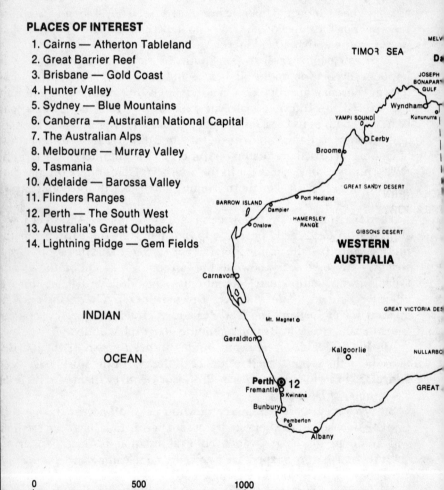

Scale of Miles

Map courtesy Qantas Airways Ltd.

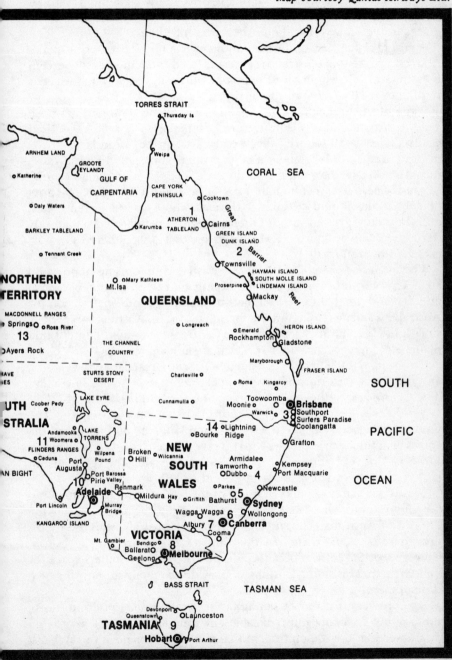

tion is about 900 feet, less than half the world's average. It does have a few respectable mountains, though. Most are in the 2,000- to 4,000-foot range, although Mt. Kosciusko, stretching up to 7,315 feet, and a dozen others in the Snowy Mountains are over a mile high.

A considerable portion of the continent is a hot and waterless plain. About 43 percent of Australia is officially "arid" and another 20 percent is "semi-arid." To emphasize the point statistically, evaporation exceeds rainfall over 70 percent of the territory.

Some of this no-man's land in the middle of the continent has been given a prosaic name—"The Centre." Sometimes it's called the "Red Centre," the "Dead Centre," the "Red Heart," or the "Dead Heart." Any of those terms refers to about a million square miles of Outback whose hub is marked by the giant monoliths of Ayers Rock (a humongous hunk of sandstone, 1,100 feet high and six miles around) and Mt. Olga, a set of elephantine mounds 20 miles to the east. Those mammoth red stones, and the sandy ground around them, are indeed red—and apparently dead, too. (The bright color, which appears only on weathered surfaces, is caused by iron oxide.)

The main use of land in The Centre is for cattle raising, though it's chancy at best; for mining; and for Aboriginal reserves. Winter is warm and dry, and the Red Centre has become a popular tourist attraction for Australians and increasingly more foreign tourists to Australia—especially since it has become apparent that The Centre is teeming with interesting plants and animals and other spectacular sights to see.

On the map you'll find three main deserts: the Great Sandy, the Gibson, and the Great Victoria, and several smaller ones in between. These and The Centre are, in the language of legend, the "Outback," the "Back of Beyond," the "Beyond the Black Stump," or the "Back o' Bourke." The Outback's rugged characteristics have often kindled and then killed the spirits of antipodean explorers—to this very day. (One dusty desert known for its lack of vegetation is called the Nullarbor Plain. The very name of that vast southern flat land means "No trees.")

This physical inhospitality of much of the land toward agriculture and seemingly toward life itself has severely limited the settlement of the interior of Australia. The size comparisons of Australia with the U.S.A. are, therefore, superficial. In the Outback, there are no Clevelands, Chicagos, or St. Louises because—despite the almost limitless space for building—there is simply nothing to provide economic support for such development.

Even in areas that receive enough rain to raise some cattle and sheep, the amount is highly unpredictable and very unreliable. There is no guarantee that the station (ranch) that managed to make it through last year won't fail because of floods or drought over the next 12 months.

This is another reason for the large property holdings. Cattle ("stock") may have to range over thousands of square miles to find enough food to remain alive, and then compete with the wild dingo and the kangaroo for the available forage.

It's often said that Australia also suffers for the lack of lakes and rivers. For such a vast land, surface water is indeed scarce.

Looking at the country on a map, you might think there is a respectable interior water supply. To travelers on foot, most of the "lakes" and "rivers" shown, even those pictured in blue ink, are cruel cartographic jokes. Lake Eyre, for instance, is seldom anything more than a 3,000-square-mile salt sump. Most years it holds no water at all. There are just vast plains of glaring, white salt—magnificent to see, but useless to any plans for human habitation.

Many of the rivers are that in name only, or at best operate only part time. The Todd River, one of the more dependable routes, courses through the Outback community of Alice Springs. The Todd is dependably dry, that is. Every August, the Henley-on-Todd "regatta" is held at Alice Springs. The "yachts" are boatshaped effigies carried by a half-dozen pairs of legs running along the dry river bed.

But even in Alice Springs no one can count on the weather. Heavy rains and sudden, unexpected floods plague the Outback. The regatta had to be canceled one year because there really was water in the Todd River—for the first time on race day in memory.

But the Outback is not all dry. Up in the "Top End" of the Northern Territory—in Darwin, for instance—they speak of two seasons. One, to be sure, is called "the Dry," and it lasts more than the winter—from about May to November. The other season, "the Wet," is a monsoon period that continues from December to February and sometimes to April. One of the wettest towns on earth might be Tully (Pop. 3,500), which manages to survive the heavy rainfalls on the North Queensland Coast. Tully often registers more than 200 inches of rain a year, and sometimes it's counted well over 300 inches.

Much of the Outback has, in the past, and even into the 1980s, proven to be rich in the minerals and other raw materials sought by man. There have been some famous gold rushes, and mining is still carried on today. But now it is mostly for other metals like iron, lead, zinc, nickel, copper, bauxite (aluminum), and uranium. Australia also has a large coal reserve and has been pumping about 70 percent of its own oil needs.

Precious stones are still mined from the dusty earth of Australia. A major diamond discovery was made in 1978 in the Kimberly region of Western Australia and rubies were discovered at a remote station northeast of Alice Springs. Other gems are unearthed regularly by amateur weekend "fossickers," particularly the opals of Lightning Ridge and Coober

Pedy. Or you can scratch around for sapphire, topaz, and amethyst near
the town of Emerald, 625 miles north of Brisbane.

The greater part of Australia may be Outback, but it is certainly not all
Outback. Most of its visitors, like most of its citizens, get no further
inland than its green and fertile coastline, site of all the big cities.

Australia on the Map

It may be confusing, but basically Australia has six states and two
territories—most of them accounting for large amounts of land—and
eight major cities. Beginning in the northeast and progressing clockwise,
Brisbane is the capital of tropical **Queensland,** home of acres of sugarcane, pineapple, and banana plantations.

Just south of Queensland is **New South Wales.** (You'll almost never see
that spelled out. It's abbreviated N.S.W., but you still *say* "New South
Wales." And if you think that's a funny name, you have to blame Captain
Cook.) Capital of N.S.W., of course, is Sydney, the largest city and perhaps the cultural leader of the country. N.S.W. boasts a population of
some 5 million, about a third the number of persons in the entire nation.

Entirely surrounded by New South Wales is the A.C.T.—the **Australian
Capital Territory**—about 750 square miles artificially carved out of N.S.W.
for Canberra, the fully planned federal capital of Australia. It was designed about 75 years ago by an American.

The southeast coast is commanded by the state of **Victoria,** whose
capital, Melbourne, is Sydney's rival in size and for influence in the
country.

Across Bass Strait, 200 miles south of Melbourne, is the island state of
Tasmania. Appearing deceptively small beside the mainland on maps of
the world, Tasmania nevertheless consists of 18,605 square miles—about
the combined size of New Hampshire and Vermont (much larger than
Denmark or Holland). Its capital is the attractive little seaport of Hobart.

West of Victoria is **South Australia,** home of most of the length of the
Murray River ("Old Man Murray") and capitaled by the well-planned
city of Adelaide. South Australia is also the home of the Barossa Valley
wine country.

The huge state of **Western Australia** is next. At 975,920 square miles,
it occupies nearly one-third the area of the entire country. (Texans and
Alaskans may note that W.A. is bigger than both their states combined,
with New Mexico thrown in for good measure.) It's not only abbreviated
W.A., but actually *called* W.A. by most of its citizens. (Incidentally, no one
has ever been able to tell us why one state is South Australia and the
other is Western Australia, and not "Southern" or "West" respectively.)

The capital is Perth, on the Swan River, and it just may be Australia's most attractive city.

The last political unit is the **Northern Territory,** sometimes called the "Top End," whose capital is Darwin. The N.T. was recently given many self-governing powers, although it will probably never support enough population to become a full-fledged state of the Commonwealth.

Living Things in Australia

Australia's land bridge to Asia disappeared millions upon millions of years ago, and so its flora and fauna began to develop and evolve in different ways from plants and animals in the rest of the world.

TREES AND BUSHES. Of Australia's trees, the most famous is the **eucalyptus.** Actually there are about 600 different kinds of eucalypts, what the Aussies commonly call "gum trees." Crush the leaves and smell them; the pungent, oily odor may help to clear out your sinuses.

Koala bears live on the leaves of certain kinds of eucalyptus, the reason you can hardly keep a koala supplied with food anywhere else in the world. (Many eucalypts are grown in other places on the earth. All originated in Australia, however.)

One type of box gum is the **coolabah tree,** sung about in "Waltzing Matilda." And another eucalypt, sometimes called the **mountain ash,** could be the tallest tree in the world. It often reaches heights of more than 300 feet, rivaling the California redwood for that honor. And among the most startling of the eucalypt family are the **ghost gums** whose bleached branches beautify the Outback. You'll see them near Alice Springs.

Thirsty Aborigines have always known they could quench themselves with gallons of water stored naturally in the trunks of **bottle trees,** of which the most famous is the "baobab," renamed the "boab" by the Australians. If you find your way to the western town of Derby, you'll see one so grotesquely swollen that it was hollowed out and used as a jail cell. The "Prison Tree" is still alive, and you can walk inside. The Aborigines say the boab tree is immortal. None have been known to die simply from old age.

You may hear a lot about **wattle trees** or acacias, of which there are hundreds of types. The yellow spikes of wattle flowers have become the official blossoms of Australia and they appear on its coat of arms. An Aboriginal word for one type of wattle is **mulga.** Early settlers called it wattle because the stems were used in "wattling," a type of thatching and packing used in making houses.

A weird-looking thing is the **grass tree.** The leaves are grasslike, but above them grow long, black, sometimes snakelike spikes, on occasion covered with white flowers. A 10-foot-tall grass tree may be 1,000 years old. After a bush fire, the blackened stalk and spike look something like an Aboriginal warrior standing with his spear. In some states they are called "black boys."

The **casuarina,** a graceful tree the Aussies have dubbed the "she-oak," has tiny, needlelike branches and no leaves. (In Hawaii, it is known as the ironwood tree or the Australian pine.) The **pandanus,** in the tropical north, has aerial roots and is the same as the Hawaiian *hala* tree. Its orange fruit is good "bush tucker" in an emergency. The **banksia,** often only a tall shrub, is named after Joseph Banks, who collected specimens on Cook's voyage in 1770. Its cylindrical flower is more familiar than the tree.

Look out: The **black bean** tree has seeds that are harmful eaten raw. Aborigines sometimes know how to prepare them safely. It's more dependable for furniture making, though. Don't eat the **cheese tree** either. Its fruit is a hollow disc and looks rather like a Dutch cheese. The red flowers on the **coral tree** are dramatic, but watch out for sharp prickles on the leaves and branches. The wood is very lightweight. **Cycads** are rather like palms or tree ferns. They are descendants of Mesozoic plants that grew 100 million years ago. The **bottle brush tree** bears a fuzzy flower that looks like a crimson version of one of Fuller's products.

Davidson's Plum trees, in Queensland rain forests, grow purple plums eaten by fruit bats and used by humans for jams and jellies. You may know **pawpaw** trees better as papaya trees. The delicious tropical fruit grows in Queensland. The **flame tree** blooms bright red overhead but is different from the flame trees (poincianas) known in other parts of the world. The **lillypilly** tree has bunches of tiny white fruit. One Australian encyclopedia says they are eaten "by Aborigines, small boys, and birds." **Paperbark** trees are well named. The bark readily peels off in thin flakes. Some produce oil used in insecticides. **Queensland nut** is the tree that produces macadamia nuts commercially in Hawaii but not much in Australia, its native habitat. And **woollybutt** is one of those wonderful, nononsense Australian names for a eucalypt with a fluffy, loose bark on the trunk.

AUSTRALIAN FLOWERS. There are thousands upon thousands of distinctive Australian flowers, and many will just have to be seen to be believed. Some, in addition to those mentioned under trees, above, are the following:

The **kangaroo paw,** official flower of Western Australia, actually looks and feels like one—but colored in red, white, and green. **Sturt's desert pea** is a large crimson flower that grows wild in dry country. **Christmas bells,** with waxy blooms, are gathered from swamps in December. **Chocolate lily** is colored purple, but it *smells* rather like a Cadbury bar. A **lamb's tail** looks just about like one, too. **Bindi-eye** is a daisylike flower, yellow and white or yellow and blue. **Birdflowers** are shaped like birds; sometimes they're called parrot flowers.

The **bladderwort** has purple blossoms but is more interesting for its ability to catch and devour insects. Some other insect eaters include the **Albany pitcher** and the **pigmy sundew.** Watch out for **blindgrass,** a type of lily that can cause blindness in cattle and sheep. **Blue devil** is a blue, thistlelike flower. **Desert roses** are found in the form of blue flowers on cotton plants. **Early Nancy** is an attractive pink flower seen all over the country. An amber flower called **fairy lantern** is rather like an iris. Each purple bloom of the **finger flower** bears five petals and five stamens. **Hairytails** are a little like hairy clover. **Ladies tresses** are a type of orchid. **Milkmaid** is a purple and white starlike lily. There are dozens of types of **orchids,** some of which grow underground, another that reaches lengths of more than 40 feet, and another (the bearded orchid) that looks like an old man with a lavender beard. **Pigface** is a bright red fruit with two "earlike" leaves. If you bother the **trigger plant,** it shoots pollen at you, no doubt figuring you'll spread some of it around. The **waratah** grows into a fantastic, 10-foot-tall plant seemingly supporting dozens of crimson cabbages.

THE MAMMALS FROM DOWN UNDER. Nearly all Australian mammals are "marsupials"—meaning their young are born immature and then develop in the pouch or pocket outside the body. Few are "placentals," like the rest of us. But when the first animals of Australia were described to the European scientific community they were called hoaxes. The learned world was not ready to accept "animals the size of greyhounds who leap like grasshoppers."

The most famous Australian marsupials are the **kangaroo** and his smaller cousin, the **wallaby.** They seem to come in all colors and sizes, ranging from big red or great gray kangaroos—seven-foot-tall "boomers," weighing as much as 200 pounds and able to hop over the plains at 30 mph—down to the tiny quokkas, rat kangaroos, and narbaleks.

Among other types are tree kangaroos, pretty face wallabies, agile wallabies, short-tailed pademelons, red-bellied pademelons, ringed-tail rock wallabies, banded hare wallabies, and one whose name seems to come from both the kangaroo and wallaby, the wallaroo. There are supposed to be 45 kinds of "roos" all together, all native to Australia.

A marsupial now almost as famous as the kangaroo is the **koala,** Australia's "Teddy bear." Once an endangered species, koalas have been preserved in sanctuaries, and chances are you'll be able to pick one up and give him a hug (a "cuddle," they call that) somewhere in Australia. (The Lone Pine Sanctuary in Brisbane is a good place.) According to one theory, the slowmoving koala is constantly drunk due to the intoxicating powers of the eucalyptus leaves he eats. They spend most of their time in trees, and because of their slow movements many have perished in the frequent Australian bush fires.

Other interesting marsupials include the **wombat,** a chunky, fuzzy fellow of perhaps 50 pounds who burrows underground and sleeps during the day; the **numbat,** a slow-moving creature incredibly possessing 52 teeth for a diet of termites; the **bandicoot,** a small critter who lives in trees and likes both meat and veggies; the **Tasmanian devil,** a small, black beastie who can tear through a hen house in nothing flat, but (they say) can still be tamed; and the **native cat** and **tiger cat,** neither of which, of course, is a cat. Actually they're tough fighters and related to the aforementioned Tasmanian devil.

Other marsupials include several kinds of possums or "phalangers" who live in trees. Some, like the **feather-tail glider,** stretch out flat like a four-pawed magic carpet to swoop gracefully from one branch to another. The **sugar glider** and the **greater glider** are also numbered among the arborial acrobats. The **brush-tailed possum** loves to chomp on mistletoe, considered an undesirable wood parasite in Australia. The **honey possum** has a long, sharp tongue for picking up nectar and pollen directly from flowers. Our favorite phalanger, though, is the **cuscus,** a white, fuzzy tree-dweller, drowsy by day but adventurous and fun-loving after dark.

Although most mammals in Australia are marsupials, there are a few notable ones that are not. Australia's most famous zoological enigma, of course, is the **platypus.** European scientists refused to believe that this animal, furry and amphibious, with a bill like a duck and a tail like a beaver, who lays eggs but still suckles its young, was anything but a monstrous fake. As late as 1884, it was still debated as to whether the platypus—of a group called monotremes—really laid eggs. Then a young English zoologist named W. H. Caldwell came to Australia at just the right time to find some eggs in a pregnant platypus. In a famous laconic telegram to the British Association for the Advancement of Science, then meeting in Montreal, he managed to report that the animals were indeed egg layers and to say just exactly what kind of egg it was: "MONOTREMES OVIPAROUS, OVUM MEROBLASTIC," Caldwell cabled.

Platypuses are almost impossible to keep in captivity because of their appetite for more than a thousand earthworms, 50 crayfish, and oodles of other edibles per day. In the wild, the platypus is in danger of extinction due to pollution in the rivers along the east coast. You can see one either at Taronga Park, a ferry ride from Sydney, or at the Mackenzie Wildlife Sanctuary at Healesville, near Melbourne.

The platypus's fellow monotreme is the **spiny anteater,** although they seem different at first glance. Note that this one also has a bill, although much thinner. He was first described in a ship's log by Captain William Bligh. Both monotremes are considered previously missing links between reptiles and mammals.

You may hear of the **flying foxes**—or hear from them directly, because there's practically a whole island of them setting up quite a ruckus a few miles upstream in the Brisbane River. Well, they don't fly and they're not foxes. They are not much different than large fruit bats. Australia has a few smaller bats around, too. (Incidentally, there is another type of "flying fox," which is a mechanical device for hanging onto while crossing a river or chasm on a suspended wire.)

Two animals have been the scourges of the nation. **Rabbits,** carelessly introduced to the country in 1859, practically devoured all vegetation on sheep and cattle stations before they were brought (relatively) under control by germ warfare—the introduction of myxomatosis, or rabbit fever. A rabbit-proof fence running more than 1,100 miles blocks off a considerable piece of Western Australia.

The other is the much-maligned **dingo,** a distinctive type of wild yellow dog domesticated and used for hunting by the Aborigines, but hunted down by sheep graziers. Dingoes are officially classified as "noxious vermin" in Australia, but recently a few have been trained for drug detection. (The dingo is not supposed to bark—only howl—but we've heard a couple barking during a disagreement and have taped the sound in case anyone is interested.)

Two other familiar wild animals are hunted in Australia. **Brumbies,** or wild horses, are sometimes shot for pet food but on occasion brought in alive to be broken as riding animals. **Buffalo** (actually water buffalo) are considered wild in the tropical Outback up north. **Camels,** first brought to Australia in 1841 to help open up the interior, were later allowed to go wild. Some are now considered pests. Some others are raised for export—even to Arabia!

Australia also has a goodly share of **seals** and **sea lions.** Although these are not unusual to North Americans, it is unusual to be able to mingle with them. You can do just that on Phillip Island, near Melbourne, and on the beaches at Kangaroo Island, near Adelaide.

The country's two most economically important animals, of course, are **sheep** and **cattle.** There are about 150 million sheep in the country, producing nearly a third of the world's wool. Australian sheep have been developed from the Spanish merino type, to suit different climate and grazing conditions found over the continent.

In the past decade, cattle have become a major industry. The nation is now the world's leading beef exporter, not to mention the producer of some of the best and most affordable veal, chops, and steaks for consumption right at home.

REPTILES OF THE OUTBACK. Australia boasts a number of **snakes,** easily as many deadly ones as in North America, although they tell us none will attack a human unless provoked. The most poisonous is the **taipan** (fortunately an antitoxin has recently been developed). The **tiger snake** and the **death adder** are also widely known. Perhaps the most dramatic snake is the **amethystine python,** which can reach about 25 feet in length and has been known to gulp down whole wallabies. The **black whip snake,** slightly poisonous, is known for its speed. It can outdistance a running man in the desert. (Luckily for the man, it is usually speeding in the opposite direction.) Of the harmless snakes, farmers encourage the **carpet snake** and the **children's python,** keeping them around the station even after they become seven feet long. They prey on rats and rabbits.

Not really snakes, of course, but none the less dramatic are the **giant earthworms.** About 3/4 inch in diameter and several feet long, they can sometimes be heard munching, gurgling, groaning, and sucking their way under the swamps in the Bass River area of Gippsland, on the route between Melbourne and Phillip Island.

There are several different kinds of **lizards,** including **monitors,** which can reach a length of six or eight feet. The monitors and their smaller cousins, the **goannas,** are the only creatures known to stagger away victorious in a fight to the finish with Australia's most poisonous snakes. They use their tails like lethal whips. Goannas have also been known to mistake horses—and humans—for trees. In the face of danger, they might just scramble up the nearest leg!

The **mountain devil,** which out-horns our horned toad, is fierce looking but harmless. The **skink,** often called the "blue-tongued lizard" in Australia, does indeed have a bright, cobalt-colored tongue. All types are harmless. **Crocodiles** (with the exception of one supposedly gentle fellow) can be counted on to be as dangerous in Australia as anywhere else in the world. There are saltwater and freshwater species.

THE WORLD OF INSECTS. Australia has all the common insects—and more. Flies, particularly **bush flies,** are most bothersome, even though they don't bite. In the warm Outback, frequent brushing is the only way to keep them away from eyes, noses, and mouths:

"I see you've learned the Barcoo salute, your highness," said the bush-roughed Australian to Prince Philip, who was visiting the Barcoo area of the Outback.

"Oh? What's that?" asked the prince, wiping away yet another squadron of flies that had settled on his face.

"That's it!" the man replied.

Not all Aussie flies are as languid, however. The assassin fly or robber fly, for instance, grows up to 3½ inches long and is able to catch and devour other insects on the wing—even bees and dragonflies. (Some beetles have now been imported from China in an attempt to cut down the breeding of Australian flies.)

As with every other living thing, there is also a strange selection of insects alive and well in Australia. One innocuous fellow, the **giant stick,** grows to be a foot long. Other outsize insects include the Australian **dragonfly,** with a wingspan of 5½ inches and the ability to fly a mile a minute; an **earwig** that can grow to be two inches; and **ants** and **termites** that grow up to an inch long. (Some kinds of termites are called "white ants" in Australia.) Some termites build nests up to 24 feet high; some flat ones are called "magnetic anthills" because they point directly north and south. They are built so the termites can take advantage of the heat from the sun as it proceeds from east to west.

There are quite a few **spiders** in Australia. Huntsman spiders are encouraged to settle in Outback homes to catch flies and mosquitoes. Black widows exist, and are called the "redback." Another deadly poisonous variety is called the funnel-web. The country's largest is the barking spider, with a *body* up to two inches in length. It has been known to kill chickens and drag them into its nest. **Scorpions** live in the Australian desert. Although they sting, they are not considered deadly to humans.

The only insect we know of that is honored by a memorial is the **cactoblastis.** This moth was introduced to Australia, where it successfully began to blast the cactus called the prickly pear from the face of the nation. The prickly pear is no longer the pest it was, and the Cactoblastic Memorial Hall was erected at Boonarga in Queensland.

The **fungus gnat** acts as a kind of glowworm in its larval state, lighting up the caves of Bundanoon in N.S.W. and the Mole Creek caves in Tasmania. Of the many **grasshoppers,** the interesting ones are more often heard than seen. One sounds like someone winding up a cheap pocket watch. Australia has more than 20,000 separate species of **beetles,** several of them, like the jewel beetle, with such startlingly beautiful colors that they are sometimes actually set in jewelry.

Of course there are also hundreds of brightly colored **butterflies** throughout the country, many of which are found nowhere else. Some Aussie butterflies, incidentally, wear a perfume as strong as the flowers they visit. You probably won't see this one, but one of the many **moths** is the giant atlas-moth of northern Queensland. Its wingspan has been reported up to 10½ *inches.* Another type of moth, the cossid moth, is more famous in its larval state. Found at the base of the witchety bush, these are the "witchety grubs" enjoyed by Aborigines as a delicacy. Raw, they taste like heavy cream. Cooked, they're compared with sweet pork rind!

AUSTRALIAN BIRDS. There are 736 species of birds in Australia, about twice the number in North America. Two of the country's most famous birds are flightless. First is the **emu,** a five- to six-foot-tall creature, weighing about 120 pounds, inquisitive but generally as dumb as they come. lts feathered body looks like a Phyllis Diller wig. Emus have been clocked running at speeds of up to 40 mph, though, and have a habit of crashing into fences at those velocities. Fully emancipated, the female emu does the courting. She changes partners each season, and leaves the male to sit on and hatch the eggs. The emu also shares with the kangaroo an honored place on the Australian coat of arms.

The **cassowary,** almost as large, also never gets off the ground, spending most of his time in Queensland rain forests. He runs with his head lowered, and he wears a permanent bony "crash helmet" to assure him a clear channel through the jungle.

Australia's most famous bird is the appealing fuzzy creature with the flattened head called the **kookaburra.** Also known as the "laughing jackass," he is the largest in the kingfisher family (although he doesn't fish). Some call him the bush alarm clock because he wakes up farmers with a long call much like mocking laughter. As a predator of reptiles and rodents, he is a welcome resident in the agricultural lands of Australia.

Until the Dutch captured some **black swans** near the present site of Perth in 1697, it was axiomatic in Europe that all swans were white. They helped to further establish Australia as a land of paradox.

The most interesting bird for our money is the **lyrebird** (pronounced "liarbird"). In addition to creating some beautiful songs of his own, he imitates other sounds—other birds, barking dogs, or even objects like a squeaky wheel, a buzz saw, a violin, a crying baby, or an old truck. Virtually nothing is beyond this feathered Rich Little. One story is told about a lyrebird who used to let everybody off work an hour early when he "blew" the factory whistle. He also has some fascinating courtship habits; that's when he shapes his two tails into a classic lyre shape. Listen to the lyrebird at the Taronga Park Zoo in Sydney or in the Sherbrooke National Forest in the Dandenong Hills near Melbourne.

There are about 50 families of **parrots** native to Australia, many of them so garishly colored they almost hurt your eyes. The **galah** is pink and light gray and often seen in flocks of 20 or more; his name is also the slang word for a loud, ignorant person. That's an anomaly because galahs can be kept as pets and will even learn to talk. A magnificent pink and white bird, the **Major Mitchell** is named after the early inland explorer who discovered it. **Cockatoos** are also parrots. You might find the sulfur-crested cockatoo wild even in a city park. (We once watched them frolic from tree to tree right in the center of Canberra.) In farmlands, look for the startling red, yellow, blue, and green **rosellas.** Also the **budgerigar,** now known throughout the world as "parakeets," "budgies," or "lovebirds," are native to Australia.

The activity of the male **bower-bird** makes him a curiosity. He builds a fancy bachelor flat, furnishing it with many flashy objects—beads, coins, maybe even a wrist watch—and if the female likes the place, she moves in with him. The most ubiquitous Australian birds surely must be those big, black-and-white **magpies.** You'll see these crowlike monsters and hear them everywhere. They are not related to European or American magpies.

Another favorite bird of ours is the **willy wagtail.** In a world of uncertainties, he can be counted on to bob his head and wag his tail every time he lands—always. Last, but certainly not least, are the wonderful **fairy penguins.** They put on a penguin "parade" nightly at Phillip Island in Victoria, returning to their nesting burrows come people or high water. No visitor to Melbourne should miss them.

LIFE IN THE WATER. There are no fewer than 180 kinds of freshwater fishes in Australia, of which the best-known is the **Queensland lungfish,** an air-breather found in the Burnett and Mary rivers, growing to a length of five feet. The lungfish is protected as a scientific curiosity, but the **barramundi** is a delicious freshwater fish popular on the plates of Australian homes and restaurants.

Much of the world's saltwater life is attracted to Australian shores, some of the most interesting specimens to the 1,250-mile strip of coral called the Great Barrier Reef, off the coast of Queensland.

Everyone asks about **sharks,** and it's true that Australian beaches have a sharky reputation, although all public ones are now protected by shark nets during warm weather. According to Sidney J. Baker, an Australian with a penchant for statistics (in the *Ampol Book of Australiana*), shark attacks are most common in January, between 3 and 6 P.M., in about 4 to 6 feet of water, between 10 and 50 yards offshore.

When an Australian talks about **crayfish,** he means big fellows—what we would call lobster. In fact, tails exported to the U.S.A. are marketed as Australian lobster tails. There are also delicious freshwater crayfish called **yabbies.** Australia's most famous shellfish, however, are the Sydney **rock oysters**—some of the most succulent bivalves in the world. Other Australian fish considered delicacies and often found on restaurant bills of fare include snapper, whiting, John Dory, gemfish, jewfish, silver bream, pearl perch, and flounder.

Big-game fishing for marlin, tuna, etc., is popular along the east coast, particularly along the Great Barrier Reef in Queensland.

The barrier reef itself, of course, qualifies as sea life since it has been built from the skeletons of millions of tiny coral polyps over thousands of years. When an Australian oil company wanted to drill along the reef one year, public indignation drove them away with red faces. Unfortunately the reef, which harbors many beautiful and intricate forms of marine life, has been under attack by the crown of thorns **starfish,** an animal that feeds on the coral. Recently, however, the threat to the reef seems to be receding.

4

Who Are the Australians?

Australia's convict beginnings were once said to be the source of a continuing national inferiority complex, and among a few Aussies that may still be true. But in the latter half of the twentieth century this has largely given way to a new sense of pride in a national character stimulated by early adversity. It is this temperament that developed a talent for building both a modern nation and "the good life" for most of its citizens.

Among Americans who know nothing about Australia, it's often criticized for "lack of tradition" and "paucity of culture." If these snobs paused from peering down their noses, they could look around and see Britain and Europe laughing over their shoulders. To those whose history runs to a thousand years or more, what is the difference between countries like the U.S. and Canada, whose formative steps were taken in the 1600s and 1700s, and Australia and New Zealand, who got a later start—by fewer than one hundred years?

What is not true in America, then, is equally false Down Under. Australia's character was shaped by experiences very much like those that shaped the United States. In fact, Americans and American history often played key roles in the formation of Australia, and they are still doing so.

"Australian history," said Mark Twain, "does not read like history, but like the most beautiful lies. And all of a fresh new sort, no moldy old stale ones. It is full of surprises, and adventures, and incongruities, and contradictions, and incredibilities; but they are all true; they all happened."

This description, in his book *Following the Equator,* is always quoted in writings about Australia for the rest of the world. Allowing for typical Twain hyperbole on the one hand, and the fact that Twain's visit to the country might be considered only halfway through Australia's history on the other, we are certainly left at least with something worth finding out about. Here is a brief synopsis of the country to date.

Voyages of Discovery—to 1770

Australia was named, and it appeared on the maps of the world, long before it was even found by modern man. Terra Australis Incognita, they called it: "Unknown Land of the South." It was daubed in a misshapen blob on the charts just because someone had theorized that it just had to be there—something to do with balancing the weight of the rest of the earth.

Fifteenth- and sixteenth-century Portuguese and Spanish navigated much of the Pacific, and it seems almost incredible that such a large hunk of *terra firma* could have been overlooked. Indeed, on a series of surviving French maps, produced between 1536 and 1567 and based on Portuguese travels, a land called "Jave le Grand" bears a definite resemblance to a portion of the Australian coastline.

China is reported to have explored part of Australia as early as the sixth century B.C. and there is some strong evidence that a Chinese landing was made near Darwin in 1432.

All this notwithstanding, the first written record of a landing on Australia was provided by the Dutch ship *Duyfken* ("Little Dove") commanded by Willem Jansz in 1606. The point of discovery was the red bauxite cliffs along the western shore of the Cape York Peninsula. The ship's log described the area as "for the greater part desert, with wild, cruel, black savages." Bauxite and its product, aluminum, were unknown, and Jansz dismissed the land saying there was "no good to be done there."

The blacks mentioned by the captain had been the human inhabitants of Australia for some time. Recent discoveries indicate that the first ancestors of the Aborigines migrated over a now-submerged land bridge from Asia about 130,000 years ago.

The Aborigines had no weapons, except for sticks and the boomerang—not an Aborigine invention, by the way, but a holdover from the stone age on other parts of the earth. They became a short, lean, and tough people, with excellent teeth from their habit of chewing sand and ashes along with their food.

They remained nomads, and although they developed a rich culture they did not learn to read and write, keeping no history of their background. Even today, confronted with the beautiful and artistic evidence of his past, the Aborigine is apt to say the images were drawn in the "Dreamtime." Dreamtime has religious significance, as well. That's when the world itself was created in Aboriginal song and story.

Throughout the 1600s, the Dutch made several landings on the island continent, without realizing it was such, virtually always followed by a negative report on the area's potential worth. One such explorer was Abel Tasman, who discovered what is now Tasmania in 1642. He called it "Van Diemen's Land," a name that lasted for 214 years, and he didn't know it was an island.

Most of the Dutch encounters with Australia were made by accident when unfavorable winds carried their ships off their established trade routes between the mother country and the rich colonies in Indonesia, and perhaps their perception was colored by these misfortunes. Some vessels were wrecked off the western shores of Australia, and even today archeologists and treasure hunters are discovering and exploring the remains of Dutch ships.

The contemporary view of the poverty and uselessness of the land was echoed by at least one Englishman, the buccaneer William Dampier, who spent three months on the northwest coast of Australia in 1688. He wrote a best seller about his travels and then returned in 1699. Dampier, too, had little good to say of the land which by now was called New Holland. He also wrote of the native inhabitants, calling them "the miserablest people in the world."

Due to this kind of bad press, Australia was virtually ignored for nearly a century. No European seemed to admit making any more landings until its east coast was explored for the first time by Lieutenant (later Captain) James Cook of the British Royal Navy, in command of the H.M.S. *Endeavor* in 1770. Cook made his historic landing at Botany Bay, near the present Sydney Airport, on April 28 that year.

The British commander found a green, more pleasant landscape on this eastern shore, and apparently more friendly, self-sufficient natives than were seen 100 years previously in the west. After making his way up the entire east coast, and almost coming to grief on the Great Barrier Reef, Cook named the entire area after South Wales, a countryside he was familiar with back home. "New South Wales," then, had as undefined a boundary in the east as New Holland did from the western aspect.

Cook didn't know it, of course, but Possession Island, on which he stood while declaring New South Wales to be British evermore, bore riches under his feet. A century later it was found to contain considerable amounts of gold, an irony at least equal to the disparaged bauxite cliffs of Jansz and his "Little Dove" a century and a half before.

The First Penal Colonies—1788 to 1810

American history sparked the development of modern Australia. The 1775 revolution of the 13 colonies not only robbed Britain of tobacco and other products but also took away the traditional New World dumping ground for England's convicted criminals. For the next decade, convicts who were formerly banished to Maryland and Virginia at the rate of 1,000 a year were instead sent to overcrowded British prisons to await the end of the American uprising.

Decommissioned ships became "prison hulks" where the only deliverance from cruelty and disease occurred when the wormridden old vessels began to sink at their moorings. Clearly some more humane treatment was called for.

A decade and a half after Cook's discoveries, someone got the idea that the countryside around Botany Bay was the answer, and King George III approved. Under the command of Captain Arthur Phillip, what is now called the "First Fleet" of 11 ships, carrying 1,486 persons, about half of them convicts, arrived in New South Wales on January 18, 1788, to begin the settlement of Australia.

The town was built at Sydney Cove, on what was accurately described as "the finest harbor in the world," and Phillip was declared the first governor of the colony.

Australia served its original purpose well. In the 80 years it accepted convicts, about 157,000 were sent there—three times as many as had ever been sent to America.

The first year in Sydney was equally unpleasant for convicts, guards, and settlers. There was little food, crops failed, sheep died, the weather was cold, the first buildings were crude, and supply ships from England were wrecked. Also relations with the Aborigines were difficult, and, most of all, the land looked so different and was so far away from England that some people literally died of homesickness.

One of the interesting early residents of Sydney Cove was an intelligent and friendly Aborigine named Bennelong, befriended by Phillip so that the colony could learn something of Aboriginal culture and language. Bennelong turned out to be something of a tragicomic character, especially when dressed in English formal wear. He was even given his own brick hut on what is now known as Bennelong Point—site of the Sydney Opera House. After Phillip, however, he became an outcast from both British and Aboriginal society. He drank heavily and was finally killed in a fight.

Conditions began to improve after two or three years, but back home in England "Botany Bay," as it was called there, held a worsening reputation. Convicts would almost choose death over "transportation," as the sentence was termed. (In Australia and Britain the word "transportation" seems still to carry the same meaning. For public transportation, they use the word "transport.")

Once in Australia, however, some of the first convicts seem almost to have taken on a philosophical resignation—to make the best of a bad job. A line of verse said to have been written for the opening of Sydney's first theater in 1796 is now famous:

True patriots all, for be it understood,
We left our country for our country's good!

Although rough by today's standards, life for the convicts became at least on a par with and often better than that of honest common laborers in eighteenth-century England. Few of the first convicts spent any time behind bars in Australia. They were just too busy building houses, barracks, and the like, and learning to raise food. And it wasn't long until a few of the best-behaved ones were pardoned—"emancipated"—and, like the marines who guarded them and other free men, were given plots of land on which they might begin to scratch out a living in the colony.

Meanwhile two explorers, George Bass and Mathew Flinders, used Sydney as a base to begin detailed examinations of the coast. They proved that Van Diemen's Land (Tasmania) was an island. The intervening channel is now called Bass Strait.

Van Diemen's Land became a penal colony in 1803, initially for incorrigibles from Sydney. Macquarie Harbour and Port Arthur were perhaps the most hated prisons in the colonies. (You can visit the peaceful ruins of Port Arthur today.)

Things became a little difficult with the appointment of the hot-tempered Captain William Bligh—of H.M.S. *Bounty* fame—as governor in 1806. A complicated series of stormy events took place, culminating in something called the Rum Rebellion. While guns were trained on Government House, Bligh was arrested and deposed by army officers in 1808. The Army was in the alcohol importing business on the side, something opposed by Bligh. The governor was later exonerated in London, but the rebels received only light sentences.

Sadly, no structure remains in Sydney today from the first two decades of the colony. But an honest approximation can be seen at Old Sydney Town, a theme park 44 miles north of the city at Somersby. Many of the events of day-to-day life in pre-Macquarie Sydney are acted out daily.

Exploration, Expansion, and Emancipation—1810 to 1850

Both the new governor, Lachlan Macquarie, and his archenemy, rancher John Macarthur, were in their own ways fathers of Australia. Macquarie encouraged the emancipation of convicts, exploration of the unknown territory to the west, and the creation of small farms. Macarthur opposed him on much of this, undermining Macquarie considerably by writing letters to sympathetic and influential friends in London.

But Macarthur, the first to import the hardy Merino sheep, is credited with establishing the wool industry in Australia. Until very recently, wool was the country's most important export.

Macquarie tried to resist the growing class system in which the soldiers and free settlers attempted to hold themselves above the emancipists. Macquarie once opined that the colony then consisted of "those who had been transported and those who ought to have been!"

Several public buildings were constructed under Macquarie, including the "Rum Hospital," put up entirely without funds. It was built by a trio of emancipists in exchange for a three-year rum import monopoly. Many of the finest buildings, some of which have managed to survive, were designed by the convict Francis Greenway, still thought of as Australia's greatest architect. Today his picture is on a ten-dollar bill, quite an honor for a man transported for forgery.

The Blue Mountains, the barrier along the Great Dividing Range, were finally crossed in 1813 in an expedition led by journalist William C. Wentworth, and lands began to be developed on the other side. Free immigrants and the offspring of prisoners were becoming important settlers of the country. John Bigge, sent out from London to inspect the running of the colony, was amazed at the second generation: "The class of inhabitants who have been born in the colony affords a remarkable exception to the moral and physical character of their parents," he wrote. The population passed 30,000 in 1819, and only about half were convicts.

In the north, settlers around Sydney were attempting, without much success, to establish some churches and schools for Aborigines. In Van Diemen's Land, however, the colonialists and the natives continued at loggerheads with clashes destined eventually to wipe out the entire race of Tasmanian Aborigines.

Elsewhere, similar attempts at genocide were unsuccessful, but for a significant period of the colony's history English settlers and the Aborigines were engaged in constant guerrilla warfare. This had all the brutality seen in fights with the Indians in America and elsewhere where the haves and have-nots, usually speaking different languages and following different cultural drums, have come into conflict.

Through it all, however, the Aborigine seems to have been reacting more than he was on the offensive. He did not understand, for instance, why white men could kill his kangaroos but he was not allowed to kill their sheep. And if he was a little slow at math, it was understandable. On one typical occasion, in reprisal for a raid on their tribe, Aborigines massacred 19 settlers at an Outback station. Then they saw 70 Aborigines—any Aborigines—killed in counter-reprisal by righteous "police" forces.

When the Aborigines developed a taste for bread, some colonials left poisoned flour where they knew it would be stolen. The white man's guilt toward the natives is no less a burden in Australia than it is anywhere else in the world.

In the 1830s and 1840s, several excursions were made into the immediate interior, often by following rivers that flowed westward from the formerly formidable Dividing Range, including the 1,609-mile Murray and the 1,702-mile Darling rivers. They were charted in 1827–29 mainly by Charles Sturt, a journey then difficult enough to make him temporarily blind. In 1844 Sturt also became the first man to explore central Australia in a vain search for the long-rumored "great inland sea." (He thought he would find it where two great bird migrations crossed.) There was no sea, and the desert nearly killed him.

In 1841 Edward Eyre *walked* the entire south coast of Australia, finding to everyone's amazement that there could be 1,500 miles of coastline with not a single river or stream to break it. And Paul Strzelecki, a Pole, explored the Snowy Mountains, naming the tallest peak after Tadeusz Kosciusko, the Polish nobleman who served under George Washington at Yorktown.

In a series of explorations on foot, Freidrich Leichardt, a Prussian, mapped out the land between Sydney and Moreton Bay and then explored from Brisbane across to the Gulf of Carpentaria and Arnhem Land, which is still as wild today. In 1848 Leichardt set out upon a transcontinental crossing but was never seen again, one of the many Australian disappearances that have never been solved to this day.

The city of Melbourne was founded in 1835 by John Batman after he "bought" 600,000 acres of land from the Aborigines for a collection of tomahawks, knives, scissors, mirrors, and blankets. Adelaide was laid out with military precision—and considerable vision—by Colonel William Light in 1838. Perth was founded entirely by free settlers in 1829. It remained generally poverty-stricken until convicts were shipped in to provide badly needed labor 20 years later. Brisbane grew out of the repressive 1824 penal colony at Moreton Bay. Like Tasmania, it was for particularly intractable convicts. It had a justifiably fearsome reputation until the cruel regime was finally ended after the military commander was killed by Aborigines in 1830.

As hopeless a situation as existed in many of these penal institutions—where the mere possession of a fishhook was worth 100 lashes—the convicts began to try to escape at all costs. Confronted by impenetrable jungle and hopeless odds, they seemed to have developed a stubbornly optimistic "give-it-a-go-mate!" philosophy that has continued in the Australian character up to today.

Some of the same attitudes may have caused a certain resignation, or an acceptance of the outcome even if things just don't work out very well in the end: "It'll do, mate." Or, "She'll be right!" (Even when it won't "do" or "be right.") Today these feelings are cited by some as evidence of a sort of national intellectual laziness—almost a Latin-style tendency toward inefficiency in general.

By 1850 Australia had become four colonies. Besides New South Wales, the massive area of Western Australia was already delineated. Van Diemen's Land also governed itself and was thinking about changing its name to Tasmania, and South Australia had been carved out of New South Wales. Three groups dominated political life—first, the government party; second, the landowners ("squatters," a respectable term in Australia, and other wealthy settlers); and last, the merchants and workers in the cities. From these three groups evolved the Liberal, Country, and Labor parties of today's Australia.

Bushrangers, Booms, and Busts—1851 to 1900

The 1849 discovery of gold in California attracted many from the people-poor colonies of Australia. (In California, they were called the Sydney Ducks, and achieved an unsavory reputation.) This in turn led alarmed colonial officials to reverse a government policy that had formerly suppressed gold information in Australia.

But no one thought there was much gold anyway until the big strike was made by Edward H. Hargraves. He was an Australian who became a forty-niner in California but returned after he noticed that the California gold country geologically resembled his own home in the Bathurst area of New South Wales. He panned gold in Summerhill Creek on his very first try, February 12, 1851. And the rush was on.

Convict transportation to eastern Australia was immediately halted. As the governor of Van Diemen's Land noted, "There are few English criminals who would not regard a free passage to the gold fields...as a great boon." Transportation did begin to the west, though, where the poor settlements on the Swan River badly needed the labor. (Western Australians hadn't discovered *their* gold yet!)

Labor was short everywhere else as servants and masters alike caught gold fever and became "diggers" (a word that came to mean Australians to much of the world). Miners from California and other areas began pouring into Australia, along with thousands of Chinese. Some of the gold lumps found were gigantic, and more diggings were soon opened up further south, in Victoria.

The Chinese, who did not bring their women to Australia, and largely kept to themselves, were soon the target of racial enmity among the diggers—the unwitting formation of a national philosophy that continued until very recently.

As in America, some diggers got rich, but most remained poor. Like the explorers, they put up with incredibly difficult physical hazards far from civilization. But many were turned against their government by the imposition of gold-digging license fees to be paid monthly whether or not the digger ever found any gold. Police stopped nearly every man they saw—sometimes several times a day—and asked to see his license, marching him off to jail if he couldn't produce it immediately.

Australia's most notorious clash between police and diggers, now known as the Battle of the Eureka Stockade, took place December 3, 1854, at Ballarat, Victoria, 70 miles west of Melbourne. Under a flag depicting the Southern Cross, 500 miners lined up against 100 police. Forty people, mostly miners, were killed in the resulting melee. Only then were the licensing laws finally relaxed, but the average Australian's distrust of authority (particularly of the police) today may be caused in some part by the memory of this event.

A battle almost as well remembered as Ballarat is the incident in which the fiery dancer Lola Montez publicly horsewhipped the editor of the Ballarat *Times* after he panned her famous Spider Dance. (Today there is a nearby re-creation of the Ballarat of that day called Sovereign Hill. Tourists pan for gold in the stream that runs through the park and see performances on a stage like the one used by Ms. Montez.)

Travel during the period was still considered only comfortable and practical by ship, even though there were dramatic disasters among both coastal steamers and transoceanic ships. One of the best-remembered tragedies was the wreck of the *Dunbar*, which took the lives of 121 persons, mostly wives and daughters returning from England. The event is well worth reading about in Mark Twain's book *Following the Equator:* "... Not one of all that fair and gracious company was ever seen alive again..." To look at the dramatic, sheer cliffs of Sydney Heads today is to imagine easily enough a cruel sea pounding the Dunbar to pieces against the unyielding rocks.

Some inland travel was accomplished via riverboats, although not to the extent they were used in America. Many rivers were just not dependable enough, drying out one year and flooding another. One that was consistently navigable, however, was the Murray River, which still keeps a few riverboats sentimentally in service. (You can even book passage on one.) A famous riverboat captain of the day was George Bain Johnston, who pulled so many nearly drowned colonials from the water that he was dubbed the River Murray Spaniel. At the height of the river trade in the

1870s, more than 200 paddle-wheelers operated over 4,000 miles in the Murray and Darling rivers.

Railroads were slow to become established in Australia, partly because of the bickering between the separate colonies. (This resulted in trains being run on no less than six different track gauges, a legacy that plagues Australian rail travelers to this day.)

The country first turned to America for a practical means of traveling long distances between the far-flung cities and towns of the colonies. Freeman Cobb and a group of fellow Yanks imported the plains-proven Concord coach to Australia and started a highly successful service called Cobb & Co. It became every bit as famous as Wells-Fargo in the U.S.A.

The drivers became characters almost as famous as the leading political, entertainment, and commercial figures whom they carried jolting and bouncing over the rough landscape. One, named Mike Dougherty, was known from Brisbane to Ballarat as possibly the most prolific bush liar in Australia, and one *grande dame* of the day is said to have booked a seat atop his coach especially to test the veracity of that appellation.

For 50 miles, though, Mike would hardly speak to her. But late in the afternoon, when the coach was traveling deep in the country, he dropped a few casual remarks about a kangaroo he had trained to meet the coach. The roo would catch the mailbag, sort through the letters, and then deliver them to settlers who lived on some widely scattered stations in the area.

Mike fell silent again, and the woman wasn't sure she took much stock in the story—not even as a respectable lie. She had almost forgotten it, in fact, when the coach rounded a curve. There in the middle of the road stood a large, "old-man" kangaroo, pausing intently in that special way of kangaroos and staring inquisitively at the approaching vehicle.

Mike didn't hesitate a second: "Nothin' today, Red!" he shouted, and then cracked his whip. Whereupon the kangaroo turned and bounced easily off into the spinifex, apparently on his way to take care of some other important business.

The coaches carried gold and other cargo, of course, as well as passengers. And these and other means of travel were occasionally stopped by another prototype of the American West who had his counterpart in the wilds of Australia. Outlaws Down Under were known as "bushrangers," and all through the nineteenth century they were an inescapable fact of colonial life.

The most famous—not to say notorious—bushranger was Ned Kelly, a murderous blackguard who nevertheless is still worshipped today by schoolchildren and elders alike as a genuine folk hero. His story has been told countless times in prose, poetry, drama, canvas, and song.

More revered by Aussies than Jesse James ever was by Yanks, Kelly led police a merry chase for two years, from 1878 to 1880.

Like many misfits in the latter half of the century, he was the son of an English-hating Irish exconvict. He made friends among and was abetted by some poor settlers in what is now called Kelly Country, northeast of Melbourne. At the final shootout, Kelly and some members of his gang donned some crude homemade armor, which was saved and may still be found in the museums. His jail cell, death mask, the armor, and other appurtenances are still popular tourist attractions.

The explorers, too, were still active throughout the late nineteenth century, building up genuine tales of dedication and sacrifice that should—but often didn't—far outweigh the somewhat trumped-up importance of the bushrangers.

One of the most successful, but certainly the most tragic, of the later explorations was the expedition led by Robert Burke and William Wills in a south-to-north continental crossing from Melbourne to the Gulf of Carpentaria in 1861. Nearly everyone died, including Burke and Wills, many of them because of a bizarre series of events that left help and food close at hand but hidden from the principals involved. To touch on the story briefly is a literary injustice. It is early Australia at its most heroic and most tragic, and the entire account should be sought out by anyone who wants to know something of how this adventure was stamped into the character of the country.

The Australian's love of horse racing and other sports also developed during this period. The Melbourne Cup, the derby for which all Australia still comes to a halt, was first run in 1861. An early style of football came in with the first settlers. But after rugby was invented, a unique Australian form of mayhem called Australian Rules football was developed during the 1850s. (It requires an oval-shaped field and no less than four goalposts!) Soccer matches were first held in Sydney during the 1880s. And two types of rugby are still played in the country.

Golf and tennis were introduced during the last years of the century. Cricket, of course, was played by the earliest settlers, but not seriously until after 1856. The first Australian team to visit England in 1868 was composed entirely of Aborigines, perhaps insuring a good attendance by its shock value alone. But English-Australian cricket rivalry became intense with a famous Australian victory in England in 1882. Prompted by a sports pundit's claim that English cricket had just died, the two countries have played for the "ashes" of that sport ever since. (The trophy is in the shape of a funeral urn.)

Although sport (as well as gambling, which is intimately related) became supreme in the occupation of Aussie leisure time, the finer arts were not completely ignored. Landscape painters who could capture the unique (and to the Englishman, strange) panoramas of Australia achieved some deserved fame. Abram Louis Buvelot is considered the father of that field, after beginning works in Victoria in 1865. John Glover also proved adept at capturing the charm of the elusive eucalyptus. The first native-born landscape artist was W. C. Piquenit.

Some artists were also peculiar Australian characters, of course. Frederick Garling developed an expertise in marine painting reportedly while painting every single vessel that tied up in Sydney Cove between 1830 and 1870!

While the French were developing impressionism in Europe, a group of Melbourne artists called the Heidelberg School was exhibiting similar works with Australian subject matter.

Victorian sentimentality did not escape Australian art and literature, but in still-wild Australia such emotionalism was more real, less contrived. Frederick McCubbin's painting of *The Lost Child,* relating to a common tragic occurrence in Australian frontier life, is as stark as Marcus Clarke's realistic story on a similar horrible theme, *Pretty Dick:* "They looked for him for five days; on the sixth, his father and another came upon something, lying, hidden, in the long grass at the bottom of a gully in the ranges. A little army of crows flew heavily away.... Pretty Dick is lying on his face, with his head on his arm...."

Clarke, more famous for his convict-era novel, *For the Term of His Natural Life* (1874), was one of Australia's important nineteenth-century writers. He was a member of a Melbourne literary group that included the poets George McCrae and the melancholy Adam Lindsay Gordon. Gordon wrote a wide variety of pieces, from masterful poems to simple homespun proverbs popular with—and often embroidered by—even the most unpoetically minded Outback Australian:

> *Life is mostly froth and bubble,*
> *Two things stand like stone*
> *Kindness in another's trouble,*
> *Courage in your own.*

It was a fine thought, but one apparently lost on the author himself. Faced with loneliness and financial problems, he killed himself in 1870.

"Bush ballads" became the folk songs of Australia, and many of them are still sung today, long after the authors have been forgotten. "Waltzing Matilda," written by "Banjo" Patterson in 1895, has been voted in and out several times as Australia's national anthem in recent years.

At that date, a new gold rush was on in Western Australia, and back east the colonies were on their way to setting up a new nation—not by revolution, as it might have been formed by the flag-bearing diggers at the Eureka Stockade, but by a Federation of the formerly separate colonies. One final impediment to the union was the continued rivalry between Sydney and Melbourne, the capitals of New South Wales and Victoria respectively and the two most populous cities. This thorn was only plucked for good when it was agreed that a new capital would be formed. It would be in New South Wales (to satisfy that state), but it could not be less than 100 miles from Sydney (as demanded by Victoria).

Canberra and the Commonwealth—1901 to the present

The Commonwealth of Australia came into being on the first day of the new century, January 1, 1901, with the approval of Great Britain and still very much under its protective wing. Australia was not then a fully independent nation. That status was developed gradually, but is in some doubt even today.

The flag adopted in 1901—what the Sydney *Bulletin* called a "bastard flag"—bears the Southern Cross, inspired by the Eureka diggers' banner. But a quarter of the field is the British Union Jack, a prominent symbol of crown power.

Parliament met temporarily in Melbourne, and one of the first new items of governmental business was the building of the permanent capital. Two Americans figured prominently in the project. One was the colorful King O'Malley, who was elected to parliament and there led the land acquisition program for the new city. He also helped conduct the international design competition for it, a contest won in 1911 by a young Chicago architect, Walter Burley Griffin. (Virtually unknown in his own country then and now, his name is probably a household word in Australia— certainly known in every schoolroom.)

Griffin eventually resigned in the face of bureaucratic meddling with his designs. And with World War I, the Great Depression, and World War II, the growth of Canberra was very slow. ("A good sheep paddock, ruined," one early cynic called it.) But today it stands as one of the loveliest and most successful of the planned capital cities of the world.

The form of government adopted has both British and American elements. The federal parliament consists of a House of Representatives and an upper house called the Senate. Each of the six states elects 10 senators for six-year terms, and the house membership (about 124) is based on population. Representatives are elected for three years at the most. But there the system turns British, for the prime minister, if defeated on a vote of confidence, must call for new elections in the house.

In Australia, it still seems like there's an election every time you turn around—perhaps appropriate enough in the country that actually invented the ballot box (in 1856). And if you are Australian, you must vote or pay a fine. It's the law.

As in Britain, the prime minister is not elected by the voters at large. The leader of a political party, like all other nominees, runs for representative (or M.P.—Member of Parliament) in his own district. If he and his party are elected, he will then become prime minister. He will pick his cabinet from the members of the House of Representatives, and perhaps a few from the Senate. The cabinet then meets in secrecy, but their proposals are enacted publicly by the parliament.

Parliament is stronger than the individual prime minister, and the federal government is also much stronger than the U.S. federal government in relation to the states. (Australian federal government has the only power to borrow money, it controls all social services, and it is the only government that can set income taxes. It does have a revenue-sharing program with the states.)

But standing in the wings of the Australian government is the Queen (or King) of England. The Crown is the only true head of state, and when push comes to shove it still holds the ultimate executive power. This was made painfully clear in 1975 when the governor-general, an appointee of Queen Elizabeth, was so opposed to the Labor government policies that he dismissed the prime minister and his party from office.

From the start of her Commonwealth status, Australia remained loyal to Great Britain. Beginning with the Boxer Rebellion and the Boer War, she began a policy of sending off her sons to fight and die in British campaigns.

Commonwealth status also formalized the White Australia Policy, designed at first to keep Queensland plantations from capturing Chinese, Kanakas, and Pacific Islanders as cheap labor. But beyond this humanitarian motive, it remained in effect as a political and philosophical policy against nonwhite—mainly Oriental—immigration. It began to fade from the scene after World War II, but only disappeared entirely less than a decade ago.

Contrary to some world opinion, it was never a repressive practice like the racial laws in the American South or the separation-by-color system of South Africa. Some Chinese families, for instance, have been citizens of Australia since the 1850s.

With some regional exceptions in attitudes toward the Aborigines (the "bloody abos" or the "boongs"), the Australians seem to be generally free of racial prejudices, although some of the exceptions have been highly visible. The conservative prime minister, the late Sir Robert Menzies, once became the only delegate at the United Nations to defend South Africa's policies toward its blacks. He was soundly condemned for this attitude in his own country, but the damage on the world stage was done.

During World War I Australia's troops, together with New Zealand soldiers, formed the Australian New Zealand Army Corps, known from

Main Eastern Cities

QUEENSLAND

Lightning Ridge

Barwon River

Bourke

Narrabri

Coonabarabran

Tenterfield

Grafton

Armidale

Coffs Harbour

Tamworth

Port Macquarie

Broken Hill

Wilcannia

NEW SOUTH WALES

Darling River

Dubbo

River Parkes

Bathurst

Newcastle

Mildura

Lachlan

Griffith

Leeton

Cowra

Blue Mts. Nat. Park

SYDNEY

Hay

Murray

Wagga Wagga

Wollongong

Kiama

River

CANBERRA

VICTORIA

Albury

Narooma

Merimbula

Eden

TASMAN SEA

MELBOURNE

Scale

0   300 kilometres

0   200 miles

BASS   STRAIT

Map courtesy Australian Tourist Commission

its initials as the ANZACs, and they sailed off to Europe to help England fight the Hun. They distinguished themselves in several fights, but their most famous campaign was their first—the disastrous attempt to land on the impregnable Turkish coast at Gallipoli on April 25, 1915, along with British, French, and Indian troops. Beachheads were held and a few temporary, small, costly gains were made from April to December, when the soldiers, decimated by the battles, were successfully withdrawn.

The famous British war correspondent Ellis Ashmead-Bartlett then wrote of the ANZACs scaling their first, nearly perpendicular cliff on April 25: "Here was a tough proposition to tackle in the darkness, but those colonials, practical above all else, went about it in a practical way...this race of athletes proceeded to scale the cliffs without responding to the enemy's fire... I have never seen anything like these wounded Australians in war before. Though many were shot to bits, without the hope of recovery, their cheers resounded throughout the night.... They were happy because they knew that they had been tried for the first time and had not been found wanting...."

The number of ANZACs killed in the campaign was 8,587. Some 25,000 were wounded. April 25, "Anzac Day," is now the solemn memorial day national holiday in both Australia and New Zealand.

The attack, incidentally, was ordered by Winston Churchill, then First Lord of the Admiralty, despite considerable advance doubts on the practicality of the tactic. This resulted in Churchill's general lack of popularity in Australia throughout World War II and for the rest of his life.

Between the wars Australia, like the rest of the world, embraced automobiles, airplanes, radios, and moving pictures, and many modernists fought the increasing "wowserism" or prudery that burgeoned incongruously along with drinking and gambling. (The latter was abetted by racing news that now came by "wireless.") Despite the censorship, art and literature were very much alive, largely centered around novelist Norman Lindsay (*Saturdee*, 1933). The motion-picture industry developed to the point where Australia could boast the largest number of cinemas per capita in the world.

The nation's two great aviation pioneers were Charles Kingsford Smith and Charles Ulm, who mapped the routes that eventually became the nation's aviation network—a formidable task in a continent so large and sparsely settled. In 1928 Smith and Ulm made the first flight to Australia across the Pacific, flying from Oakland, California, via Honolulu to Fiji and thence to Brisbane in a Fokker trimotor named the *Southern Cross*.

The *Southern Cross* may still be seen in a special museum hangar built for it just outside the passenger terminal in Brisbane. Both Ulm and Smith gave their lives for flying, however, disappearing at sea in different incidents in 1934 and 1935.

On a very different level, Australia became well known during the 1920s and 1930s for developing a strain of confidence men who played on the world's rich and gullible—often English or American—and bilking them out of millions. One of the most flamboyant was James Coates, who traveled the world first class, pretending to be whoever he needed to be to conduct his elaborate swindles. But whether it was the advent of the Depression or of war, the flashiest Australian con men had nearly faded from the scene by 1950.

Less harmful, surely, was the literary prank played on Max Harris, the editor of a poetry magazine. He received in the mail a set of modern poems said to have been written by a deceased telephone lineman named Ern Malley. Harris devoted an entire issue to the writings. Two real poets then revealed that they had deliberately written nonsense lines taken from miscellaneous newspapers and technical manuals to expose the "pretentiousness" of contemporary poetry. Harris insisted the "poems" had literary merit, but ironically he was later prosecuted and fined for printing some of the "obscenity" in the works. Today the term "Ern Malley" is sometimes applied to any unorthodox literary effort in Australia.

Severely underpopulated, Australia suffered greatly during the Great Depression, although it maintained its world reputation as a nation of athletes with gold medals won at the Olympics and with tennis titles awarded at Wimbledon and elsewhere.

In the 1930s Australians worried about a Japanese invasion, but when war came in 1939 they dutifully sailed off to help the British fight the Germans again. They distinguished themselves from 1940 to 1942 in the North African campaigns against Rommel, becoming the famous "Rats of Tobruk" who defended that post from March to December 1941. Churchill, now British prime minister, would not withdraw them from the siege.

After the Japanese attack at Pearl Harbor and the Philippines in December 1941, Australian troops began to return home to the Pacific. More than 15,000 Aussies were captured at Singapore in February 1942. During the same month Japanese air raids were carried out on Australian soil at Darwin. Later Broome, Derby, and Wyndham were also hit.

The same year, Australia took another step toward independence from Britain. When Churchill wanted to move the Seventh Division, on its way back home from the Middle East, to Burma, Australian Prime Minister John Curtin refused. A plan by the Japanese to capture Port Moresby, the capital of the then-Australian territory of New Guinea, was thwarted when Australians joined with Americans to fight the naval Battle of the Coral Sea off Australia's northeast coast. It became a major turning point in the war.

American and Australian friendships were firmly sealed during World

War II. General Douglas MacArthur moved his headquarters from the Philippines to Melbourne, and later to Brisbane for most of the balance of the war. Yanks and Aussies fought together in New Guinea and in the island-hopping campaigns toward Japan. Thousands of American troops were stationed in Australia, and although the battles at the pubs for booze and girls were highly publicized, by and large the Diggers and the Yanks became mates in the common effort to "beat the Japs."

By the end of the war, 29,400 Australians had been killed in action. An amazing total of 31,000 became prisoners of war, of whom nearly 8,000 died while held by the Japanese.

In appreciation, the electorate kept Labor in power for a few years after the war, and Prime Minister Ben Chifley was credited with seeing that the veterans all received jobs, getting automobile manufacturing in gear (with the Holden car), opening new universities, and beginning an immigration policy to bring thousands of "New Australians" to the country, most of them British, Italian, Greek, Dutch, German, and Polish. (Due to this postwar policy, a quarter of the Australian population today are immigrants and their children.)

But an attempt to nationalize the banks, the rising influence of labor unions, and the fear of communism brought Chifley's government down. In came the forceful, conservative, and arrogant Robert Menzies, destined to guide Australia from 1939 to 1941 and 1949 to 1965. (In Australia, remember that the liberal party is called Labor—or the ALP The principal conservative party is the Liberal party, and there's also a rural party called the Country party, which usually rules in conservative coalition with the Liberals.)

Australian troops took part in the Korean War, under American command, from 1950 to 1953. During the fifties, Australia's wool profits reached all-time highs, and mineral prospecting and mining were increased throughout the country. Oil was discovered in 1953 and commercially pumped beginning in 1964. Iron ore and other natural resources have continued to be found ever since. A major diamond strike occurred in Western Australia as late as 1978. Some new oil wells were also brought in.

In 1952 Australia, New Zealand, and the United States joined in a mutual defense treaty called the ANZUS pact. Each country would come to the aid of the others in case they were attacked in the Pacific. Originally it was considered mostly an alliance protecting its signatories against a resurgent postwar Japan. Gradually, however, it has come to be thought of as anti-Russian, and the pact has in recent years become controversial in Australia and New Zealand.

Over two dozen U.S. bases have been established in Australia. Two of the best-known are the U.S. Naval communications stations at North

West Cape, W.A., and at Pine Gap, N.T. (near Alice Springs). They are supersecret installations, concerned mainly with communicating with nuclear submarines worldwide. Missile bases were also built, and in cooperation with the National Aeronautics and Space Administration in the U.S., Australia set up several satellite tracking stations and played an important role in the American space program.

The authoritarian Menzies continued as prime minister through 1965 before retiring. The founder of the Liberal party, he had served nearly 20 years as P.M., the final 17 consecutively. To much of the world, he had become almost Mister Australia himself. He was extremely loyal to the monarchy, yet he worked hard for increased trade and friendship with the U.S. An imposing figure until his death in 1978, he is remembered for his oratory and his wit. (A reporter who once began his interview with, "I'm from the *Daily Mirror*, Mr. Menzies" received an immediate response: "You have my deepest sympathy!")

He was succeeded by Harold Holt, the Menzies protege who did not return from an ocean swim in 1967.

Somehow it seems that Australia has always suffered more than her fair share of natural disasters from floods, droughts, cyclones (hurricanes), locusts, and especially bush fires. Bush fires have been endemic to Australia for thousands of years; some kinds of seeds have evolved to the point where they will not germinate until after a fire has passed over the area. Most bush fires that occur far from human habitation are just allowed to burn themselves out.

One of Australia's worst bush fires took place in February 1967, when a blaze with a 90-mile front destroyed part of Hobart, Tasmania, and killed 62 persons. (See the gripping account by one of the survivors, Patsy Adam-Smith, in her book *Footloose in Australia*.)

In February 1983, bush fires over a wide area of the states of Victoria and South Australia made headlines around the world when 72 people were killed and several small towns were wiped off the map. The toll included 2,031 houses destroyed along with 82 businesses (including 9 hotels and restaurants). Also damaged were 1,238 farms, and 52,000 cattle and 319,000 sheep were killed.

In 1974 Australia was the victim of two weather extremes. The first, a massive January flood in Brisbane, killed a million sheep and 11 people, and left 8,000 persons homeless. But this was eclipsed by the horror of the Christmas Day strike of Cyclone Tracy in Darwin. It destroyed 90 percent of the town and killed 50.

The Liberal/Country party coalition held the country into the seventies, during which time America's influence and the fear of Asian communism were so strong that Australia took part in the Vietnam War (474 died), despite growing civilian protests. As in America, much of this dissent was centered in the universities and contributed to the students' disillusion about the country and its values. They began to refer to the nation as "Oz," and to heavily criticize the materialistic, militaristic, and narrowminded tendencies they saw in much of Australian society.

By this time it had already long been fashionable to "rubbish" (heap abuse on) Australia. One of the first to do it with bitter effect was Donald Horne, editor of the newsmagazine the *Bulletin*. In 1964 he published a book criticizing Australia's attitudes toward almost everything. He called the book *The Lucky Country*. Strangely the irony of that title has been generally lost, and now many Australians have come to accept the idea that they are really the Lucky Country. If so, it is certainly more true today than it was in 1964.

The Australian Labor party adopted a promise to bring home the troops from Vietnam. The withdrawal had already begun, however, before Labor was returned to power in 1972—for the first time in 23 years. Party leader Gough Whitlam became the P.M.

Under Whitlam, Australia immediately declared itself to be antiapartheid in South Africa and said it would no longer play segregated athletic teams. It also adopted sanctions against Rhodesia, due to its racial policies, and announced plans to reform the Aborigine educational system at home. For the first time the emphasis was on saving what was left of Aboriginal culture.

The government also upheld measures to give equal pay to women on the job. It recognized mainland China, and it granted full independence to Papua New Guinea after it had been ruled by Australia for more than 90 years.

In one of the first acts of 1973, "skin color" was officially barred as a factor in admitting immigrants, thereby dissolving almost the last shades of the White Australia policy. Many more Asians began to immigrate. The government also further reduced ties to Great Britain.

The world economic situation in the early 1970s, an unusual condition combining high unemployment and high prices, took its political toll in Australia. The Liberals heaped the blame for this "stagflation" on the governing ALP, and this led to political confrontation late in 1975.

Australia's most dramatic political event since the formation of the Commonwealth was on November 11 of that year. The governor-general, Sir John Kerr, used his previously untested royal powers to dismiss Prime Minister Whitlam and the Labor party from office.

Kerr said he did it because Whitlam had refused to bow to long-standing tradition and call for new elections himself, even though a budget bill passed by the House had become stalled by the Liberal majority in the Senate. It was later suggested that Liberal leader Malcolm

Fraser had led blockage of the bill in an attempt to force just such a new election.

No matter how roundly some Australians condemned Kerr's autocratic action, the Australian electorate has traditionally voted the dictates of their pocketbooks more than their consciences. When the elections *were* held the following month, the Liberals, helped by the Country party, routed the ALP The London *Economist* labeled the whole affair a "political earthquake."

Entire books have been written about November 11, 1975, and arguments still burn in pubs and parlors from one end of the country to the other. Some Aussies still blame the American C.I.A., saying it probably acted in concert with Britain behind the scenes after Whitlam threatened actions against the U.S. intelligence post at Pine Gap. In any case, when Queen Elizabeth visited Australia in 1977 she was booed and jeered by antiroyalists. (Bless her heart, she probably didn't know anything more about the fuss than anyone else. Even though Kerr was a "royal appointee," his name ironically had been put forth by Whitlam, the man he later fired.)

During the worst years of the economic slump, Australia cut back on her immigration quota, but later raised it again. She now accepts about 70,000 "New Australians" annually. About 90,000 refugees from Indochina have arrived in the country in the past decade, many of them in crowded, derelict fishing junks after a hazardous 2,500-mile trip to Darwin Harbor. The humanitarianism toward the Vietnamese "boat people," admitted outside usual immigration channels, has not been universal. Some politicians and headline writers have referred to these destitute refugees merely as "queue jumpers."

Orientals in general are becoming more and more a part of the mainstream of Australian life. As Australian journalist Fia Cumming wrote recently, "Scarcely a week goes by without a high school or college announcing that its top awards have gone to an Asian student. Often the boy or girl is a Vietnamese or Cambodian who arrived here only two or three years ago in a leaky boat." Despite Australia's apparently increasing percentage of Orientals, though, rules for their immigration are still tighter than they are for Europeans—a controversial policy, to be sure.

While much of the rest of the earth appears to be threatened with depleting natural resources, Australia continues to find more wealth under the ground. Recent discoveries of diamonds mean that Australia will soon be the biggest producer of these gems. Also there were large gold finds not long ago when such unlikely prospectors as housewives, retirees, and boy scouts with metal detectors came up with some of the largest nuggets ever found. More important in an economic sense are the deposits of alternate energy sources—coal, oil shale, natural gas, and uranium—being uncovered all over the country.

Uranium mining is highly controversial, with objections centering on the apparent lack of safeguards and the difficulty of safe radioactive waste disposal. Another aspect of the situation is that much of the uranium has been found on Aboriginal reserves, for which the tribes have traditionally not held the mineral rights. At first the government virtually gave the land to the mining companies. In response to Aboriginal protests and public opinion, however, some royalty payments are finally being made to the descendants of the original residents of the country.

Despite the natural resources boom, which began to create a demand for skilled labor, unemployment was rising during the late 1970s. High taxation and soaring interest rates also plagued the government. Fraser tried to hold down the inflation rate with strict wage controls and other unpopular measures, but with increasingly severe unemployment the opposition Australian Labor party (ALP) began to gain strength quickly. Meanwhile the population of Australia climbed over 15 million—over twice the number living in the country at the end of World War II. (About 1.2 percent of today's Australians are Aboriginals.)

The Australian work force is highly organized. Over 60 percent of workers are union members, as compared with 20 percent in the U.S. Labor has been struggling to achieve the 35-hour work week and other gains beyond the automatic cost-of-living escalators the unions have already won. However the country has a penchant for sudden, disruptive, and widespread strikes, a union characteristic that severely hampers business negotiations with Japan and other foreign countries.

A whirlwind of political activity in 1983 saw silverhaired Robert J. Hawke, the charismatic former president of the Australian Council of Trade Unions (ACTU) elected to Parliament and then chosen leader of the ALP. When special elections were called that year, the ALP was swept to victory, putting Hawke into office as the new prime minister. Hawke, now 56, has taken several steps toward solving the country's economic crisis, but with the extreme devaluation of the Australian dollar in 1985 his successes have not been as dramatic as they might have been. Unemployment is down, however, and Hawke and his party were recently reelected, although by a smaller margin than previously.

The prime minister has met twice with U.S. President Ronald Reagan, assuaging any worries that his government might work against long-established joint Australian-American military activities and objectives. There is a growing antinuclear lobby in the country, however, and the government did refuse to take part in a controversial major test firing of the American MX missile in 1985. Nevertheless Hawke has strongly reiterated the country's commitment to the ANZUS mutual security treaty, and he has been trying to help repair that alliance after policy differences between the U.S. and New Zealand seemed to threaten it in 1985.

"Australia is not and cannot be a nonaligned nation," said Hawke in a Washington speech. "We are linked with the U.S. by a whole range of common interests, attitudes, aspirations, institutions, and perceptions."

As the country begins to plan for its 200th birthday in 1988, the mood of its 15½ million people seems particularly optimistic and generally pro-American, although as competitive as ever. In 1983 an Australian boat and crew from Perth won the coveted America's Cup, taking it away from the New York Yacht Club for the first time ever. The win sparked spontaneous, nationwide celebrations in Australia. Sports-minded Aussies are now gearing up physically and psychologically for the spirited rematch in 1986 and 1987, when the races will take place in the waters off Fremantle on the West Coast. (See more details in chapter 10.)

A List of Notable Aussies

The best way to enjoy any new country, especially an English-speaking nation, is to keep up with who's doing what via its newspapers, magazines, television, and radio.

This may be a little easier, however, if you have a ready reference to some of the well-known people of the day who are active in different fields.

An exhaustive list would be prohibitively long. But here is an alphabetical roster of "names" in Australia today, whether they are famous in politics, sports, the arts, or science, or are just current darlings of the press. All were chosen somewhat capriciously from a list twice as long.

You'll be surprised at how many Aussies you already know and how many you'll learn about even in a short visit to the country. We believe all these folks are living, but some of them—particularly the few politicians and sports figures we've included—may have had a change of professional fortune by the time these words appear in print.

ACTON, Prue. The best-known dress designer in the country.

ANDERSON, Dame Judith. One of Australia's greatest dramatic actresses. Now lives in the U.S.A.

ANSETT, Sir Reginald. Self-made transportation magnate. Founder of bus services, airlines, and related industry.

ANTHONY, Julie. Popular singer and actress.

BADEN-POWELL, Frank. Highly successful restaurateur and former actor. Ended up buying the theatre-restaurants he played in.

BAKER, Tom. Trumpet player and singer. Leader of Tom Baker's San Francisco Jazz Band.

BARASSI, Ron. A top Australian Rules football coach. (A former star himself.) Also gives motivational lectures.

BJELKE-PETERSEN, Joh. Authoritarian and strong-willed premier of Queensland.

BOND, Alan. Head of the *Australia II* syndicate that won the America's Cup race for the Royal Perth Yacht Club in 1983.

BONNER, Neville. A former carpenter, he was the first Aborigine to be elected to parliament.

BURKE, Brian. Tough, colorful, and socially conservative young Labor premier of Western Australia. An ex-TV journalist and a sharp dresser.

BUZO, Alexander. Young, Sydney-born playwright. His plays have also been produced in the U.S.

CARLTON, Mike. Radio personality and newspaper columnist known for his satirical humor.

CAWLEY, Evonne (Goolagong). Tennis star with two wins at Wimbledon to her credit.

CLARK, Charles Manning. Eminent and sometimes controversial historian.

CLEARY, Jon. One of the country's most successful novelists. Several of his books have been made into films and TV serials.

COURT, Margaret. Outstanding tennis player. She won her first tournament at 13, and has won at Wimbledon four times.

DALRYMPLE, Rawdon. Australia's ambassador to the United States.

DARGIE, Sir William Alexander. Portrait painter of many famous persons.

DART, Raymond. Doctor and anthropologist. Found and named the Australopithecus in Africa.

DAVIDSON, Robyn. Sydney fashion model known as "The Camel Lady" after her trek across the Gibson Desert in 1977.

DAVIS, Judy. Prominent actress. Was nominated for an Oscar for *A Passage to India*.

DRYSDALE, Sir Russell. Internationally known artist, famous for his harsh Outback themes.

DUNSTAN, Don. Intellectual former premier of South Australia and author of several books. Now the Victoria State Tourism director.

DUNSTAN, Keith. Melbourne-based writer and columnist. Has written several excellent books on the Australian character.

ECCLES, Sir John. A neurologist and a winner of the Nobel Prize for medicine. Now lives in the U.S.

EVANS, Len. Sydney restaurateur and leading wine writer in Australia.

FOWLES, Glenys. Operatic soprano. Formerly with the Metropolitan in New York, now with the Australian Opera.

FRASER, Dawn. One of the best swimmers Australia has produced. She won 100-meter Olympic gold medals in 1956, 1960, and 1964.

FRASER, Malcolm. Prime minister from 1975 to 1983.

GALLOWAY, Sue. Hostess of the national "Today Show" on TV.

GIBSON, Mel. American-born actor who won fame as a star in Australian films, including *Gallipoli* and *Mad Max.*

GREER, Germaine. Writer and outstanding Women's Liberation activist. Now lives in the U.S.

HANCOCK, Lang. Millionaire industrialist and the man most responsible for the development of iron ore deposits in W.A.

HARDY, Frank. Novelist, playwright, and TV personality.

HARRIS, Rolf. Well-loved songwriter and entertainer. Famous for his "Tie Me Kangaroo Down, Sport" of the 1950s.

HAWKE, Robert. Leader of the Labor party, and prime minister of Australia since 1983.

HAYDEN, Bill. Former leader of the ALP, and now foreign minister.

HELPMANN, Sir Robert. Internationally acclaimed ballet dancer, choreographer, actor, and producer.

HIBBERD, Jack. Contemporary and prolific playwright.

HOGAN, Paul. A rigger on the Sydney Harbour Bridge who shot to fame as a comedian. Known in the U.S. for his "Wonder Down Under" TV commercials made for the Australian Tourist Commission.

HORNE, Donald. Author and social critic. Editor of the *Bulletin,* a newsmagazine. Wrote *The Lucky Country* and other books.

HUGHES, Robert. Art critic for *Time* magazine in U.S. who occasionally returns to Australia for TV appearances, etc.

HUMPHRIES, Barry. Actor, comedian, artist. Played in several British and Australian films. He has several regular characters.

KENEALLY, Tom. Prolific and award-winning novelist.

KENNEDY, Graham. Nationally known television personality.

LAWS, John. Controversial and independent radio and TV personality. Also writes music and poetry.

McCULLOUGH, Colleen. Author of *The Thorn Birds* and other novels.

McKERN, Leo. Australian Shakespearian actor who has performed often in England, on stage and film.

MATTIOLI, Rocky. Boxer who became world light-middleweight champion.

MICHELL, Keith. Lead actor in countless Shakespeare plays in London. Returns occasionally for Australian appearances.

MOOREHEAD, Alan. Beginning as a journalist for Australian and British papers, he became the author of many books.

MURDOCH, Rupert. The head of an international publishing and television empire. He lives in Australia, the U.S., and the U.K.

NEWTON-JOHN, Olivia. Now a top singer in the U.S., she returns to her home in Australia from time to time.

NOLAN, Sidney. Painter, now living in the U.K., who became famous for illustrating Australian historical events.

PACKER, Kerry. Millionaire magazine publisher and TV mogul. Also agolf and cricket promoter.

PATE, Michael. Australian actor who has appeared in many American movies—often as an Indian chief.

PEACH, Bill. TV host, remembered for "This Day Tonight," a public affairs program, and "Peach's Australia," a travel show.

PEACOCK, Andrew. Leader of the Liberal party and therefore the head of the opposition (shadow prime minister).

PUGH, Clifton. Painter who has done the royal family in London. Also known as a conservationist.

REDDY, Helen. Pop singer who has lived in the U.S.A. for several years.

RIGBY, Paul. Internationally known cartoonist.

SANG, Samantha. Another Aussie singer who has made it big in the U.S.A. Often returns home to Australia.

SCHEPISI, Fred. Movie producer, director, and screenwriter. Known for 1978's prizewinner *The Chant of Jimmie Blacksmith.*

SINGLETON, John. Advertising executive and radio personality who became a millionaire at 36. Married to a former beauty queen.

SMITH, Dick. Flamboyant business tycoon, dog sledder, mountain climber, helicopter pilot, practical joker, and author.

STEPHEN, Sir Ninian. Governor-general of Australia.

STRETTON, Major General Alan. "The Hero of Darwin," he led the reconstruction there in 1975–76 after a horrendous cyclone.

SUTHERLAND, Dame Joan. "La Stupenda," as the Italians called her, is Australia's most widely acclaimed opera singer.

TAYLOR, Rod. Hollywood actor who sometimes comes home to Australia.

THIEL, Colin. Author of several books, including *Storm Boy* and *Blue Fin,* which have been made into films.

WALSH, Mike. A popular television host and personality.

WARBY, Ken. The fastest man on water. Holds the water speed record now at more than 300 mph.

WEIR, Peter. Film director, now working in the U.S., too. Directed *Gallipoli* in Australia and *Witness* in America.

WEST, Morris. Prolific author. Wrote *The Shoes of the Fisherman* and other novels made into films. Now lives in Europe.

WHITE, Patrick. In 1973, became the first Australian writer to receive the Nobel Prize for literature.

WHITELEY, Brett. Enjoys worldwide fame as one of Australia's most talented contemporary painters.

WHITLAM, Gough. Prime Minister of Australia from 1972–75 before being dismissed by the governor-general.

WILLESEE, Mike. TV investigative reporter with a style and flair.
WILLESEE, Terry. Brother of Mike, he is now his competitor on a different network.
WILLIAMSON, David. Award-winning playwright whose works (*The Removalists* and others) are performed in London and New York.
WILLIAMSON, Malcolm. Musician and composer, known for operas and orchestral works in Australia, Europe, and the U.S.
WRAN, Neville. Charismatic Labor premier of New South Wales.

Picturesque Patterns of Speech

Entire books have been written on the Australian language. Just as there are differences between British and American speech patterns, Australia also occupies its own separate, very large, and quite special niche in a corner of the English-speaking world.

Besides mere differences in vocabulary, there are several other peculiar aspects to Australian speech. One, of course, is that it is somewhat affected by the Aboriginal languages—perhaps more so than the Indians ever influenced the American idiom. The boomerang and the kookaburra are Aboriginal words for things that have no English equivalent. Mulga is a popular Aboriginal word for a type of plant called wattle or acacia in English.

But the most interesting characteristic of Aussie speech is that many of its speakers take the language as a game to be played. There is a large, expressive group of regular slang words, most of which occupy a more or less permanent place in an informal lexicon. These include flip abbreviations like "mozzie" for "mosquito" and "Paddo" for the Sydney suburb of Paddington.

Beyond that is the rhyming slang and variations on that theme that create a fluid form of speech that seems to be invented and changed almost daily.

Rhyming slang is supposed to have begun with the Cockneys of London, and many travelers in England are familiar with some of the old chestnuts—"me trouble and strife" is "my wife." And "a bag of fruit" is a "suit."

The versatile Aussies have added many more examples of this. And in recent years they have taken it a giant step further with *abbreviated* rhyming slang, which almost becomes a secret code among the linguistically initiated. Thus "trouble" becomes wife and "bag" becomes suit, using the previous examples. "My shoes" can be expressed as "me kangaroos" or even just "me kangas."

Another aspect of the language Down Under is the peculiar pronunciation and enunciation of many words. Also similar to the street talk of London, the sound "A" becomes the sound "I," or at least so close to it that perhaps only another Australian could tell the difference—when "mate" becomes "mite," for instance, or "daisy" becomes "dicey."

The degree of this degradation of the "A" varies so completely in the country as to be completely nonexistent among some who carefully cultivate their speech in the mold of the Queen's English to the other extreme of the "A" and the "I" being virtually indistinguishable. This inconsistency even confuses the Australians themselves. The town of Mackay, for instance: Is it pronounced Mac-*kay* or Mac-*eye*? (We couldn't find anyone who could tell us for sure.)

Another part of the same problem is the fact that Aussies, in common with many other citizens of British Commonwealth countries, have troubles traceable to the use of a softer *R* than is used by most Americans. (Not all, though; when Bostonians and some others say "Cuba" it may come out "Cuber.") The Australians sometimes seem to leave *R*s out where they ought to be. (My wife Sara, a New Zealander who is afflicted with a slight touch of the same Down Under disease, occasionally talks about an "S.L." blanket. She means "air cell.") Or else they seem to insert *R*s where they ought *not* to be. (There are numerous examples, like maybe "Jack" who often becomes "Chairk.")

Combine this with other idiosyncracies such as the sound "ou" as in "hound," which begins sounding like nothin' but a "hand-dog." And condense things to the point where a twosyllable word like "power" sometimes becomes "par," "pair," or "pah." Now you have what one Australian writer labeled "Strine," a compressed form of shattered Australian spoken by many in the country today.

Some of the examples in the book *Let Stalk Strine* by Alistair Morrison are hilarious. Thus an "egg nishner" is a machine to cool down a room with, a popular nursery rhyme begins "Chair congeal went up the heel," and "furry tiles" always begin "One spawner time . . .'"

One of my favorite Strine sentences is quoted in John Gunther's *Inside Australia:* "Hazzy gairt non wither mare thorgan?" Try it first before peeking. Give up? It's translated, "How is he getting on with the mouth organ?"

If you get a chance to pick up a book on Strine, do so. (Some of the examples won't work as well with an American accent, remember, partly because of those harsh *R*s we Yanks have. Neither Strine speakers nor non-Strine speakers in Australia are cursed with those.)

For technical reasons, we've had to leave Strine out of the following list. There are also only a few examples of rhyming slang or abbreviated rhyme. We have confined ourselves generally to popular, semipermanent Australian slang and other terms familiar to Australians and Britishers and not considered slang by them at all, but just plain good English.

Many Aussies are surprised to hear that we don't call a black-top road "bitumen," or that "ringer" means something different in America than in Australia. British readers, I hope, will pardon us. For the benefit of other confused Yanks, we have included some of the essential Pom terms like "petrol" in this lineup. Students of this sort of thing will also want to have a look at the list in our New Zealand guidebook. Many of the Kiwi expressions numbered there are also in general use in Australia.

You won't run into all these on a short stay. However, we have taken the liberty of marking with asterisks the words and phrases that you are most likely to encounter. It would be a good idea to learn them before arriving in Australia.

Some of these words and terms are not universally used throughout Australia. Instead of "bowser," for example, you may hear something simple like "petrol pump."

Incidentally, we have attempted to use a certain amount of Strine, slang, rhyme, and other Aussie lingo from time to time throughout the rest of this book. They include some of the terms from this list as well as others that came up in the course of writing the text of the volume. The idea is that if you finish the book, you'll be much better acquainted with the language of Australia than 99 percent of the other visitors to the country.

Australian—A to Zed

A

ABC. Abbreviation of Australian Broadcasting Corporation.
ACT. Abbreviation of Australian Capital Territory (Canberra).
ACTU. Australian Council of Trade Unions.
ALP. Australian Labor Party.
AWU. Australian Workers Union.
Accommodated tour. Fully guided tour (with hotels, etc.).
Accommodation. Hotel room.
Airy-Jane. Airplane.
Alf. Stupid person.
Antivenine. Antitoxin.
Amber. Beer.
*Anzac. Member of the Australian and New Zealand Army Corps in World War I.
Arvo. Afternoon.
Auntie. The Australian Broadcasting Corporation.
*Aussie. Australian.

B

BHP. Abbreviation for Broken Hill Proprietary, a mining corporation.
Back of beyond. Far away in the Outback.
Back of Bourke. Same meaning, used more in N.S.W.
Back chat. Impudence.

Bail up. To rob, hold up.

Banana bender. Queenslander.

Banana land. Queensland.

Barrack. To cheer at a sporting event.

Bathers. Swimming suit. (See "togs.")

Battler. Person who struggles hard for a living.

Beaut. Short for "beautiful." (Very good.)

Belt up! Shut up!

Bible basher. Minister.

Bickie. Paper dollar (originally short for "biscuit").

Bike. Promiscuous woman.

Bike, to get off your. To become angry.

Bikey. One who rides bikes or motorcycles.

Billabong. Water hole in a semidry river.

*Billy. Tin container used for boiling water to make tea.

Biscuit. A cookie (sweet biscuit) or a cracker.

Bitser. Mongrel dog ("bits a this and bits a that").

Bitumen. Asphalt or black-top road.

Black stump, other side of. Same as "back of beyond," etc.

*Bloke. Man, used like "guy" in the U.S.

*Bloody. All-purpose adjective, once thought to be profane.

Bludge. Live off someone else, "sponge."

Blue. A fight, usually (has many other meanings).

Bone, point the. To hex or jinx (Aboriginal ceremony).

*Bonnet. Hood of a car.

*Boomer. Anything large—a lie, a kangaroo, etc.

Boong. Derogatory term for an Aboriginal. (Don't use it.)

*Boot. Trunk of a car.

Bo peep. Quick look, peek.

Bowser. Gasoline pump.

Brissie. Brisbane.

Brumby. Wild horse.

Buckley's chance. One chance in a million.

Budgie. Parakeet.

Bullock. Heavy manual labor.

Bulldust. Fine, powdery dust found on Outback roads.

Bundy. Time clock.

Bunyip. Mythical animal (Australia's yeti).

Burl, give it a. Give it a try.

*Bush. Countryside outside cities and towns.

Bushranger. Bandit, outlaw.

Butcher. Five-ounce beer glass in S.A.

C

Casket. A type of lottery (in Queensland).

*Chemist. Pharmacist.

*Chips. French-fried potatoes.

*Chook. Chicken.

Chuck. Throw.

Chunder. To vomit.
Cleanskin. Unbranded cattle.
Clue. Used like "idea," as in "I haven't a clue."
Coach. Long-distance bus.
Cobber. Friend.
Cockie. Small farmer.
Come a guster. Make a bad mistake.
Commercial traveler. Traveling salesman.
Compere. Master of ceremonies; moderator.
Concession (or concessional). Discount, special rate.
Cooey. An attention-getting cry in the bush.
Coolabah. A type of box eucalyptus tree.
Corroboree. Aboriginal dancing.
Crook. Broken, sick, or no good.
Cuppa. Cup of tea.

D

Daks. Trousers (in Australia; in New Zealand, undershorts!).
Didjeridoo. Aboriginal droning instrument.
Digger. Australian soldier, but used by foreigners to mean any Australian. (Australians prefer "Aussie.")
Dill. Fool.
Dillybag. Small bag for carrying things.
Dinkie-die. The whole truth.
Dinkum. Genuine or honest.
Drongo. A born loser.
Duffer. Cattle thief, rustler.
Dunny. Toilet.

E

Enzedder. New Zealander.
Evo. Evening.

F

Fair dinkum. Same as "dinkie-die" above.
Fair go. A good, reasonable chance.
Facilities. Toilets, lavatories, etc.
Fannywhacker. A marble.
Fill-up station. Gasoline service station.
Flaming. Like "bloody," another all-purpose adjective.
Flash. Fancy or ostentatious.
Flat out. As fast as one can go.
Flog. Sell or hock.
Fluff. Attractive woman.
Flyswisher stew. Oxtail stew.
Footpath. What the British call the pavement and the Americans call the sidewalk.
Fossick. To prospect or rummage. Search for gold, shells, or other goodies on or under the ground.

G

Galah. Fool or idiot (after the parrot by that name).
Gaol. Australian/British spelling of jail.
Gear. Clothing or equipment.
Getting on. Moving up in the world.
Gibber. Stone or boulder.
Gin. Aboriginal woman.
Give way. Yield to oncoming traffic.
*Good on ya! Term of approval (sometimes ironic).
Goods. Freight (as in "goods train").
Greenies. Environmentalists.
Grizzle. To complain.
*Grazier. Sheep or cattle rancher.
*Grog. Popular term for any alcoholic drink.

H

Hard case. Amusing person.
Have on. To take a challenge.
*Hire. To rent (you "hire" a car).
Hire purchase plan. Time payment plan.
*Hotel. Sometimes means only a pub.
Hottie. Hot-water bottle.
Humpy. Small hut or shack.

I

Identity. A well-known person.
In yer boot. Expression of disagreement.

J

Jackeroo. An apprentice cowboy, station hand.
Jilleroo. Female of the above.
*Joey. Baby kangaroo (in the pouch).
Jumbuck. Sheep.

K

Kanga. Abbreviated rhyming slang for "shoe" (see below).
Kangaroo. Rhyming slang for "shoe."
Kerb. British spelling of "curb" (side of the street).
Kick. Pocket or wallet.
Kip. Bed.
*Kiwi. New Zealander.
*Knock. Criticize.

L

Lady's waist. Five-ounce beer glass.
Lair or *larrikin*. Ruffian, hoodlum.
*Licensed. Legally permitted to sell beer, wine, and liquor.

Lob. Arrive.
Lolly. Lollipop, money (several meanings).
*Loo. Brit./Aus. slang for toilet.
Lot. The whole thing, bunch, mob, group.
Lubra. Aboriginal word for woman.
Lucerne. Alfalfa (in the U.S.).

M

*MP. Abbreviation for Member of Parliament.
Mad. Crazy (seldom means angry).
Marjie. Marijuana.
*Mate. Your best buddy or comrade (does not mean spouse).
Matilda. Belongings carried by swagmen, wrapped in a blanket.
Medibank. Aus. public health plan.
Middy. Ten-ounce beer glass (in N.S.W.).
*Mob. A group of persons or things (not necessarily unruly, etc.).
Mozzie. Mosquito.
Mum. Mom (almost a school of philosophy in Australia).

N

*N.S.W. Abbreviation for New South Wales.
Nark. Spoilsport, unpleasant person.
Naughty. Euphemism for sexual activity.
Never never. Desert land far away in the Outback.
Never-never. Time payment ("hire purchase") plan.
Nick. Steal.
Nipper. Small child.
Nit. Fool, idiot.
No hoper. Same as above, but worse.
No worries! "She'll be right!" (everything will come out fine).

O

Ocker. Australian hillbilly or country bumpkin.
Offsider. Follower, helper, sidekick.
*Oil. Accurate information.
Old boy. Alumnus.
Old man. Adult male kangaroo.
On the beach. An unemployed sailor.
*Outback. The bush; uncivilized, uninhabited country.
Oz. Australia or Australian (ironic term coined by university students).

P

PTC. Abbreviation for Public Transport Commission.
*PM. Abbreviation for prime minister.
Paddo. Paddington.
*Paddock. Field or meadow.
*Parcel. Package.
Packet. Envelope (as in pay packet).

Pastoralist. Similar to grazier.
Perve. To watch a woman with admiration (does not mean "perverted").
Peter. Cash register.
Petrol. British term for gasoline.
Pig's ear. Rhyming slang for beer.
Pimple squeezers. Singers of popular songs.
Pinch. Arrest.
Plonk. Cheap wine.
Plug hat. What they call a "bowler" in Britain and a "derby" in the U.S.A.
Poddy dodger. One who steals unbranded calves.
Poker machine. Slot machine.
Pom or Pommy. Englishman.
Poofter. Homosexual.
Pot. Ten ounces of beer in Victoria, twenty in N.S.W.
Prang. Accident, crash.
Proprietary (usually abbreviated "Pty"). Company (Co.).
Pub. "Public house," bar, drinking establishment.
Pud. Pudding, dessert.

Q

Quack. Slang for any kind of doctor.
Quaky Isles. New Zealand.
Qld. Abbreviation for Queensland.

R

RSL. Abbreviation for Returned Servicemen's League.
Ratbag. Eccentric character.
Raw prawn. "To come the raw prawn" means to try to deceive someone. (Honest!)
Razoo. Fictitious coin ("I haven't a brass razoo.").
Repositioning fee. Rental car drop-off charge.
Ringer. Fast sheepshearer.
Ripper. Something particularly good.
Road train. Tractor with two or more trailers.
Roo. Kangaroo.
Rum. No good, "crook."

S

S.A. Abbreviation for South Australia.
STD. Abbreviation for subscriber trunk dialing (same as direct distance dialing in the U.S.).
Sack. To fire, dismiss from employment (also as in "get the sack"—be fired).
Scheme. System or method (no nefarious connotation as in U.S.).
School. A group of drinkers, each of whom is expected to buy a round.
Schooner. 15-ounce beer glass in N.S.W., seven ounces in S.A.
Score. To inscribe.
Screamer. Noisy drunk.
Scrub. Bushland.
Sealed. Surfaced road; tar-sealed, paved.
Sheila. Young woman.

She'll be right! Don't worry.
Shoot through. Leave unexpectedly.
Shop assistant. Salesclerk in a store.
*Shout. Buy someone a drink.
Shove off! Go away!
Silk shirt on a pig. Something wasted.
Silvertail. Member of high society.
*Smoke-oh. Short break in work time.
Snoot. Disagreeable person.
Sort. Type or kind.
Square off. Apologize, make amends.
*Squatter. Large landholder.
*Station. Large farm or ranch.
*Stockman. Cowboy, station hand.
Strewth! An all-purpose exclamation ("It's the truth!").
Strides. Trousers.
Sundowner. Rural tramp.
Surfies. Young men who like to surf.
Swag. Bedroll and all worldly goods of the swagman.
*Swagman. Vagabond, rural tramp.

T

TAB. Abbreviation for Totalisator Agency Board, legal offtrack betting shop.
Take-away food. Takeout.
Tariffs. Rates (hotel).
Tattersall's. A type of lottery in some states.
Tazzie. Tasmania.
Technicolor yawn. Vomit.
Telecom. The phone company.
Telly. The TV, also the *Sydney Daily Telegraph.*
Terrible turk. Rhyming slang for work.
Thimble and pea game. Same as U.S. shell and pea game.
*Togs. Swimming suit (sometimes called a "bathing costume").
Toney. Modern, up to date, slick.
Too right! Absolutely!
Track. Country road.
Trunk. Long-distance telephone call.
*Tucker. Food.
Twit. Fool, simpleton.
Two-pot screamer. Somebody who can't take his liquor.
Two up. Popular gambling game involving two pennies thrown in the air.
Tyke. Dog.
Tyre. Brit./Aus. spelling of tire (automobile).

U

U.K. Abbreviation for United Kingdom (Great Britain).
Uni. University.
Up a gum tree. In a quandary.

Up-market. Higher-priced.
Up the Cross. At King's Cross, a section of Sydney.
*Ute. Short for utility truck—a pickup truck or similar vehicle.

V

Van Dyke. Country outhouse.
Vegemite. Yeast-based bread spread, rich in vitamin B.
Vic. Abbreviation for Victoria.

W

W.A. Abbreviation for Western Australia.
Waddy. Billy club.
Warder. Jailer or guard.
Walkabout. Traveling on foot for long distances, an Aboriginal tradition.
Wallopers. Policemen.
Waltz Matilda. Carry a swag.
Westralia. Western Australia.
Whack. Fair share.
Wharfies. Longshoremen, stevedores.
Whilst. Brit./Aus. version of "while."
*Whinge. Complain.
Willy-willy. Small dust twister.
Wog. Minor disease; also a derogatory term for a foreigner.
Wopwops. The Outback, the "sticks."
Wowser. Bluenose, prude, killjoy.
Wurley. Aboriginal shelter, "humpy."

Y

Yabber. Chatter.
Yabbie. Small crayfish.
*Yank. American.
Yankee shout. Drinking school where everyone pays for himself.

Z

Zed. Australian and British pronunciation of Z.

The National Bush Ballad

Here are a set of verses from "Waltzing Matilda," *the* song of Australia (voted in and out from time to time as the nation's national anthem, in competition with a more formal composition called "Advance Australia Fair"). By the way, we have seen several slightly different printed versions of "Waltzing Matilda" in Australia, and you may, too.

(1)
Once a jolly swagman camped by a billabong,
Under the shade of a coolabah tree;

And he sang as he watched and waited 'til his billy boiled,
Who'll come a-waltzing Matilda with me?

Chorus:

Waltzing Matilda, waltzing Matilda,
You'll come a-waltzing Matilda with me;
And he sang as he watched and waited 'til his billy boiled,
You'll come a-waltzing Matilda with me!

(2)
Down came a jumbuck to drink at the billabong,
Up jumped the swagman and grabbed him with glee;
And he sang as he stowed that jumbuck in his tucker bag,
You'll come a-waltzing Matilda with me!

(Chorus)

(3)
Up rode the squatter, mounted on his thoroughbred,
Down came policemen, one, two, and three;
Whose is the jumbuck you've got there in the tucker bag?
You'll come a-waltzing Matilda with me!

(Chorus)

(4)
But the swagman he up and he jumped in the water hole,
Drowning himself by the coolabah tree;
And his ghost may be heard as it sings in the billabong,
You'll come a-waltzing Matilda with me!

(Chorus)

5

Sydney
and New South Wales

1. The General Picture

Sydney is where it all began. Downtown, in an area called "The Rocks" just west of Sydney Cove, the first colonials and convicts built houses and barracks. The neighborhood still emits a creaky, old-world charm.

But today central Sydney is also a bright city of tall towers, as busy as any of the world's major metropolitan areas, its population of three million apparently all on the go at once. Big blue buses—both single and double-decker models—wind through the crowded streets. A fleet of ferryboats is constantly nosing into the piers of Circular Quay and then springing back out again into the bay, en route to the many waterside suburbs. They seem to pass in constant review before the concrete sails, frozen in mid-billow, of the grand opera house, symbol of Sydney and now one of the world's most recognized public buildings.

"Sydney-siders" say theirs is Australia's liveliest city, and perhaps it is. Something always seems to be happening in its skyscrapers, in its leafy green parks, or along the sparkling, watery shores. There are few vacant lots in Sydney, for the land is taxed as much as a hotel would be in the same spot. This may make parking expensive, but by the same token it maintains the viability of inner-city areas.

Today's Sydney flows over an area of 1,500 square miles, much of it in

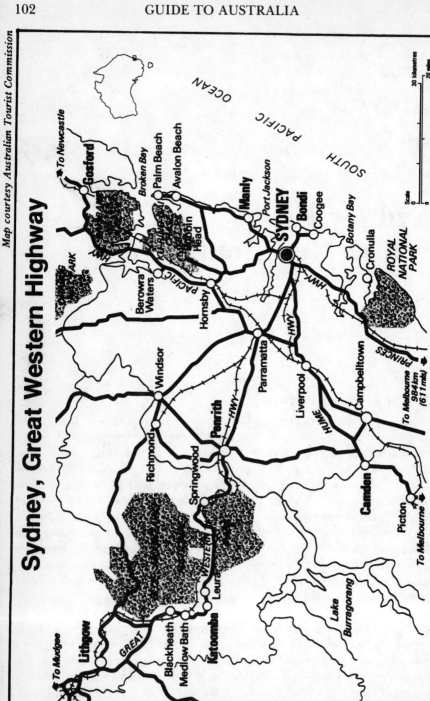

Map courtesy Australian Tourist Commission

Sydney, Great Western Highway

a suburban sea of red roofs along both sides of Port Jackson, an almost incredibly lovely crenulated estuary that cuts deeply inland from the shores of the Tasman Sea.

To experience Sydney Harbour for the first time, and perhaps to try and fail to take in all its splendor at once, is to empathize with the English writer Anthony Trollope, who saw this 21 square miles of sheltered water as a pictorial dilemma:

"I know the task would be hopeless were I to attempt to make others understand the nature of the beauty of Sydney Harbour. I can say that it is lovely, but I cannot paint its loveliness."

The next major inlet south from Port Jackson is the storied Botany Bay, an infamous name by which the early colony was feared in England for more than a hundred years. But the body of water discovered by Captain Cook was originally not part of Sydney at all. Today the metropolis has indeed sprawled out to encompass Botany Bay. Along the shoreline where the crew of the *Endeavour* picked up specimens of strange plants and trees in 1770 is Sydney's international airport.

Sydney has always been the capital of New South Wales, even when N.S.W. included all the known and unknown parts of Australia. Since much abbreviated, the state still spreads over 300,000 square miles, adding two million more souls to Sydney's three million. Shaped like a four-sided wedge, N.S.W.—like all Australian states—includes both urban areas and bushland. You'll find opera houses and shopping centers as well as billabongs and jumbucks.

The green strip along the shore is neatly lined with the viewful Highway 1. Going west, there are the tablelands, the peaks of the Blue Mountains, then the plains country, and finally the farming and mining areas.

Inland, too, are the mighty Murray and Darling river systems, important highways through the bush a century ago. In the northwest you can take a train as far as Bourke. "Back o' Bourke" begins the traditional Outback. Lightning Ridge, where amateurs still scratch up an occasional black opal, is out there, too.

New South Wales is not all of Australia, to be sure, but to the visitor who explores it well it offers a surprising percentage of the items the entire country is famous for, from the wines of Hunter Valley and the kangaroos of Dubbo, to the silver city of Broken Hill, and back again to the 34 golden beaches of Sydney.

2. The Airport and Long-Distance Transportation

If you're lucky, you'll fly into Sydney from the north, beginning your descent over the city itself. Request a window seat on the left of the airplane, so you can recognize the famous "coat hanger"—Sydney Harbour Bridge—and just beyond it the opera house.

Landing at Botany Bay, you'll enter the **Kingsford Smith Airport,** better known as "Mascot" by locals, named after the suburb in which it sits, about six miles from the city center. There are two main terminal areas at the airport—one for international arrivals and departures, and a mile or so away a separate pair of buildings for domestic flights. You can take an occasional bus between the international and domestic terminals for under $1, or hire a taxi, of course.

The **international terminal** is arranged so arrivals are handled on the ground level and departures are made from one escalator flight up. Near the departure gates are several gift shops, a newspaper stand, pharmacy, etc. Prices in these shops are relatively high compared to those in the city, and the exchange rates given for foreign currency are not as good. (Even the duty-free shops, for outgoing passengers, we thought not as good a bargain as others—say the shop in Auckland, New Zealand, for example. And the selection is limited.)

There's also a **cocktail bar and buffet** in the departures concourse. For a ten-cent piece in the turnstile, you can take in the Airport Observation Deck. Nearby is that wonderful institution, the "Mother's Room," a place where women and their offspring can be alone with others of the same persuasion. (Seriously, it's a good place for feeding, changing "nappies," etc.)

There are two large **check-in areas** on that upper level. First Class and Business Class check-ins for all airlines are located on the relatively quiet left side. At the opposite end, near the Au Revoir bar, snack bar, and coffee shop, are the Economy Class check-in counters. This part is a new system, and the area was an absolute zoo the last time we saw the place on a busy day. We can only hope more facilities will be added to ease the crush in the immediate vicinity.

Down the escalator you'll find the bank and currency exchange, the post office, rental cars, taxis, buses, etc. Waiting for a loved one to come out of customs? Believe it or not, you have to keep your two eyes on about five doors, all of which are marked "A." Coming through yourself? Be sure to look for a luggage cart to pile your bags on before they begin coming up the conveyor belt. Or you can use a porter, if you can find one.

Finally a public bus has been put on the route between both the international and domestic terminals and Sydney's Circular Quay. If you want that one, look for a yellow-and-blue bus labeled No. 300 and called the Airport Express, which costs about $2. It makes several stops along George Street and terminates at Circular Quay. Somewhat more convenient is the commercial outfit usually operating minibuses between town and the international terminal. It's called the **Kingsford Smith Airport Bus Service** (Tel. 667–3221 or 667–0663). The service has recently improved, and the fare is now $3 or so for the 40-minute ride. It will deposit and pick up passengers at several hotels, and its Sydney terminus is near the Wentworth Hotel. By taxi, the airport-to-Sydney trip will probably run a little under $10.

The **domestic terminal** at Mascot is generally divided into an Ansett wing and a Trans-Australia Airlines (TAA) wing, representing the two big interior airlines. East-West Airlines is also near TAA. You'll find covered accesses, moving sidewalks, escalators, TV-screen arrival and departure information (plus live loudspeaker announcements, a luxury that is fading from U.S. airports), and a selection of the usual restaurants, bars, coffee shops, etc.

Tip: Some of the gates are a l-o-n-g way from the central services, particularly the Ansett gates. Get your coffee and newspaper and allow yourself plenty of time. You can use it up if necessary in the departure lounge right at the gate. (And that's usually where you get your seat allocation, too—another reason for showing up in plenty of time, especially if you care whether you sit in the smoking or nonsmoking section.)

In the city, **Ansett Airlines** (Tel. 268–1111) has an airline terminal at Oxford Square, which is not far from the hotels in the King's Cross and Darlinghurst neighborhoods. And **TAA** (Tel. 693–3333) has one in the high-rise district at Chiffley Square, which is more convenient to the downtown hotels.

Some other important airline addresses in Sydney include the following (to our knowledge, none provide bus service to the airport): Air New Zealand (Tel. 234–4111), 10 Martin Place; British Airways (Tel. 233–5566), 64 Castlereagh St.; Continental Airlines (Tel. 232–8222), 7 Bridge St.; CP Air (Tel. 233–5711), 62 Pitt St.; and Qantas (Tel. 436–6111), Qantas International Centre, George Street.

Arriving in Sydney by sea? If you're lucky, your cruise ship will nuzzle up to the **Sydney Cove Terminal** and tie up next to The Rocks, just across the cove from the opera house. It's where all the action is, and we can't imagine a more beautiful way to enter a beautiful city.

For travel by train, the main Sydney terminus is the large **Central Railway Station** (Tel. 2–0942), just across the street from Belmore Park on the opposite side of the city center from Sydney Cove. Railway bookings can be terribly complicated in Australia. We'd let the **N.S.W. Government Travel Centre** (Tel. 231–4444), at the corner of Pitt and Spring streets, or the **SRA** (State Rail Authority) **Travel & Tours Centre** (Tel. 29–7614), 11–31 York St., take that off our hands. Generally speaking, a train will cost you about the same as a bus between any two given points, these days.

Sydney

1. Art Gallery
2. Government House
3. Opera House
4. Parliament House
5. Cenotaph
6. Australian Museum
7. Museum of Applied Arts
8. Kings Cross
9. Town Hall
10. Mitchell Library
11. Anzac War Memorial
12. St. Mary's Cathedral
13. St. Andrew's Cathedral
14. Circular Quay
15. Sydney Harbour Bridge
16. Argyle Art Centre
17. Observatory
18. Wentworth Hotel
19. The Rocks
20. Australia Square
21. Botanical Gardens
22. Garrison Church
23. Cadmans Cottage
24. General Post Office
25. QANTAS

Map courtesy Qantas Airways Ltd.

Many short-distance trains, particularly in Economy Class, are not very comfortable, and sometimes they are not very clean. Scenery is usually delightful, however, and we enjoyed our own rail trip up to Gosford to see Old Sydney Town. Between some destinations within New South Wales you'll find some express "XPT" trains operating today. Although the old tracks will not support true "high-speed" trains in Australia, these are considered faster than the usual service, anyway, and Austrailpasses are accepted.

There are five separate railway systems throughout Australia—four state-government services and one federal-government service. A few still operate on different-size track gauges, which means a change of carriage at places you've never heard of. What with shunting and waiting for single tracks, etc., it often takes a long time to make a medium-length interstate trip.

One of the most dramatic exceptions to this rule is the famous *Indian Pacific,* the proud coast-to-coast service between Sydney and Perth. Currently that costs about $500 First Class or $400 Economy fare, although you can save a lot if you purchased the Austrailpass outside of Australia (see chapter 2). A new train called *The Alice* runs from Sydney clear through to Alice Springs.

Other important Sydney train services include the *Southern Aurora,* the *Spirit of Progress,* and the *Intercapital Daylight* runs between Sydney and Melbourne. All three are daily. The first two are overnight trips and offer sleeping accommodations for about $35 extra in First Class. Travel time is scheduled at about 14 hours.

Monday to Friday, the *Canberra Monaro Express* runs from Sydney to Canberra in five hours. And the *Brisbane Limited Express* has an overnight run between Sydney and Brisbane every day. (Again, it's about $35 extra for a berth in First Class.) That trip runs about 16 hours.

Rates will be going up, but we'll make a guess on the fare from Sydney to the following places: Brisbane—$90 First Class, $70 Economy. Canberra —$30 First Class, $25 Economy. And Melbourne—$90 First Class, $70 Economy. (To repeat, please don't hold us to these.)

If you're traveling by **interstate bus,** you'll find the Sydney Coach Terminal at Oxford and Riley streets. Both Ansett Pioneer (Tel. 268–1881) and Greyhound (Tel. 268–1414) are now housed there.

Rental cars. The principal outfits in Australia have the following headquarters in Sydney, all almost within honking distance of each other near King's Cross: **Avis Rent-A-Car** (Tel. 357–2000), 214 William St.; **Hertz Rent-A-Car** (Tel. 669–0066), nearby at the corner of William and Riley streets; and **Budget Rent-A-Car** (Tel. 339–8811), 93 William St. They may cost from $40 to $90 a day, unlimited distance.

You may do better financially from **Thrifty Rent-A-Car** (Tel. 357–5399), a nationwide firm at 85 William St. in Sydney or at **L.R.C. Rent-A-Car** (Tel. 331–3099), a smaller firm, at 118 Darlinghurst Rd. (it also has offices in some other cities). A local place is **Kings Cross Rent-A-Car** (Tel. 33–0637), 169 William St., corner of Forbes. Finally, for perhaps the best rates in town, you can rent veteran vehicles from **Rent-A-Wreck** (Tel. 808–2888) at the corner of Windsor and Victoria streets in Baulkam Hills. (Be sure to see our remarks on renting and driving in chapter 2.)

3. Local Transportation in Sydney

We covered rental cars in the previous section (and in chapter 2), because we think of them as a mode of long-distance travel. In the city and around the immediate suburbs, "public transport" is usually safer and more convenient. (Note that sightseeing excursions are also not covered here. You'll find those in section 7.)

Get **taxicabs** either by hailing, telephoning, or hopping into one at a cab rank. They look like normal cars except for the light on top.

At last report, rates were comparable to familiar fares at home. There are a few extra charges—perhaps a telephone charge of about 60 cents, if you called them, and 10 cents a bag if you're carrying suitcases. And here's a convenient plus: *Many Sydney taxis accept credit cards.*

There's some debate about this, but we normally never tip a taxi in Australia. It's usually not expected, except in special situations. You may, in fact, sometimes find a driver in effect tipping *you*—rounding off the fare with a jolly, "That'll do, mate!" just to make the change even. (*That* kind of tipping, we do too.)

Taximen usually typify the Australian's determinedly egalitarian nature. In fact, *a man taking a cab alone is considered a "regular bloke" if he sits up front beside the driver.* If you're a woman, or there are two or more of any sex, it's all right to sit in the back.

With all the "New Australians" and students working their way through the university, and even the occasional woman driver, there may be no such animal as the typical Australian cabbie anymore. But if you get the kind we remember most fondly you'll probably have an enjoyable trip as well as pick up a little homespun philosophy with the latest slang and Strine along the way.

Even when such a driver isn't particularly cooperative, he may mitigate his obstinacy with a sardonic sense of humor. John O'Grady, who wrote Australia's all-time best seller about an Italian immigrant and his new Aussie mates—called *They're a Weird Mob*—once told another writer that when he returned from Europe he was so pleased to be home that he hopped in the first taxi he saw and asked to be taken to his home in the suburb of Oatley, about 15 miles outside of Sydney.

"Oatley!" the driver exclaimed. "Gawd, I wouldn't go that far on me holidays!"

A couple of radio-call cab companies we've called successfully include **Taxis Combined** (Tel. 339–0488) and **Legion** (Tel. 2–0918). One more curious thing about Sydney taxis: The radios "sing" following each transmission. Drivers are so accustomed to it that they generally don't know what it is, but the "toodle-oodle-oo" apparently has something to do with the computer back at home base. (If you find out something more specific, we'd like to know, too, please!)

There's nothing wrong with the taxis, but you'll save more, of course, if you take advantage of the excellent **bus services** run by the Urban Transit Authority of New South Wales (the UTA, and not to be confused with the airline by that name). Be sure to pick up an official map, which shows bus as well as train and ferry routes. (It's available at the UTA offices at the corner of York and Margaret streets or at any newsstand or bookstore.) If you stay "up the Cross" (in the King's Cross neighborhood), you'll probably find yourself catching No. 324 and 325 via William Street and George Street to Circular Quay, and returning on those numbers via Pitt and William either to the Cross or, if you're feeling adventurous, on out to Watson's Bay.

You pay by how far you go, at 50 cents an increment, and it seems to work out that most trips are between 50 and 90 cents. If there's a sign saying "pay as you enter," you hand your money to the driver. Otherwise you wait for a conductor to come around, and you tell him your destination. *Yes, the driver or conductor will make change.* Things haven't yet come to the stage where they won't do that in Australia.

There's also a free bus (No. 777) that meanders through the central city area. The public buses are all big, blue Mercedes diesels, by the way, and sometimes they are double-deckers, too. If you want to know how to get somewhere, phone the UTA's special bus information number (Tel. 2–0543).

You'll make better time under and above the ground on the electric **Sydney Rail Transport System,** covered by the same map as above. There are seven lines: the North Shore Line, the Main North Line, the Western Richmond Line, the Southern Line, the Bankstown Line, the East Hills Line, and the Illawarra-Cronulla Line. In the center, all travel through the Sydney underground system, connecting with stations on the City Circle Line. Determine which platform serves the line you want, and then watch the lighted signboard by the platform to find out if the next train is heading for the station you want to reach.

The City Circle Line is a handy loop that runs mostly under the surface from Central Station through the city center with stations at Town Hall, Wynyard Park, Circular Quay, St. James Road, and the

Australian Museum, then back to Central Station. You may now travel between any two stations on the circle for 50 cents. (You can often buy 50-cent tickets from an automatic machine.) Underground train stations bear a remarkable resemblance to New York City subways—except they're safer and are not decorated with graffiti.

A long-delayed success is another suburban line called the Eastern Suburbs Railway, in the works since the 1870s. They finally introduced a bill to build it in 1915, passed the bill in 1946, began construction in 1948, ceased work in 1952, and began work again in 1968. Then things came to a halt again for awhile. (A Sydney bus driver who keeps up with N.S.W. politics explained it all to us: "When the Liberals are in, they stop work on it; when Labor is in, they start work on it.")

Finally, in 1979, the Eastern Suburbs Line opened for business; it runs from Central Station, with stops at Martin Place, King's Cross, Edgecliff, and Bondi Junction. Fares run from about 50 to 90 cents.

Probably the most fun division of the UTA is made up of its **ferryboats,** which seem to leap into the water every few minutes from Jetties 2 through 6 at Circular Quay. There are some special cruises we'll cover in section 7, but here are some of the main ferry services used by Sydney's commuters and shoppers, which may be enjoyed as cheap cruises by visitors, too. Fares generally run a dollar or so. All leave from Circular Quay.

● *Manly Ferries.* Depart Jetty No. 3 for a 30-minute, $1.20 ride to Manly. Check the map; it's a long voyage for your money. Some of these vessels date back to before the war—World War I, that is!

● *Manly Hydrofoils.* Depart Jetty No. 2 for a 15-minute, $1.75 ride to Manly. (Avoid this fast one during rush hours. You may queue up for a longer time than you would use if you took the old ferry.) The spray may keep you from seeing the harbor as well as you might like from the windows. There's an open deck topside, if you can take the wind. *Tip:* You may enjoy taking the ferry over to Manly and then the hydrofoil back to Sydney.

● *Mosman Ferry.* Departs Jetty No. 5, stopping at Cremorne Point, Musgrave Street, Old Cremorne Wharf, and Mosman.

● *Taronga Park Zoo Ferry.* Departs Jetty No. 5. Note that there is a combination ferry/bus/zoo admission ticket available, for perhaps $8 or $9.

There are several more ferries. For most, information is available from the UTA (Tel. 27–9251). All newcomers to the capital of New South Wales who've been out on the water—including us—agree: To leave Sydney without making some kind of trip on the harbor is to have gone to Sydney without seeing it at all.

One last word for bargain hunters. For compulsive UTA users there are several special discounts available for heavy ɔcal travel. Most of these are of interest only to commuters, but one or t o others stand out. One is the **Day Rover** ticket, which allows you to trav l all day on anything the UTA runs (except hydrofoils) for $4.

There's also something called the **Awayday** ti ket, for $6, allowing you a much wider radius into the countryside of N. .W. on Sundays. Stop by the UTA or call its Customer Service Bureau to recheck these prices, 7 to 7, Mondays through Fridays (Tel. 290–2988).

Long-term visitors or new residents of Sydne y may want to pick up the comprehensive $5 manual called *Gregory's Sydney by Public Transport,* sold at bookstores and magazine stands.

4. The Sydney Hotel Scene

If you get into correspondence or conversation with Australian hotels, express your needs quite specifically and look out for problems in terminology. A tub is a "bath" to most Australians. If you want a bathtub and shower, be sure to say so. Otherwise you'll more likely get one or the other.

Remember that if you want a baby's crib, you have to ask for a "cot." A "double" to Australians will mean a double bed. If you want twin beds, ask specifically for them. (But in this book we generally use the terms "double" or "twin" interchangeably to mean a room for two, regardless of the number of beds in the room.) "Facilities" in Australian is a rather sappy euphemism for bathroom. "Tariffs" is a synonym for room rates.

Here's a confusing point for many American travelers: *The word "hotel" in Australia is often taken to mean merely the local pub,* and many buildings you see labeled with the word "hotel" are nothing more than drinking establishments. (You may see a sign on these hotels that says "no accommodation.") Under the old laws they were required to rent out at least a few rooms in order to have a liquor license. Although that has been repealed, in most states a hotel for staying in is still not allowed to call itself a hotel unless it does have such a license. When it is unlicensed, it will use the term "private hotel," "guesthouse," "lodge," "inn," or something similar. The term "motel," of course, means that automobile travelers are catered to, although in recent years the word has been going out of style in favor of terms like "motor hotel" or "motor inn."

Some hotel miscellany:

● All opinions in this book are based on our own inspections and investigations of the establishments. We could be wrong, and probably are in some places.

● On checking out, leave enough time to look over your bill carefully. Australians seem to be scrupulously honest but often very sloppy in accounting. (Many hotel workers, too, are recent immigrants. The weakness in English may account for some confusion.) Frequent sources of difficulty are those "prestocked" fridges from which you pay for the beers and mixes used; sometimes the room maids have been given the job of counting the bottles. We try to avoid succumbing to this expensive temptation (drinks can cost 2½ times what they would in a bottle shop), although it is certainly a convenience.

• Phone calls from hotel rooms are usually expensive—30 to 50 cents, even if you dial yourself. (We have to make so many calls in every city that we sometimes stock up on 20-cent pieces and move our office into phone booths in the lobby.) If you are dialing out from your room, invariably you dial "9" to reach the hotel operator and "0" to get an outside line.

• If you're *driving* throughout Australia, be sure to pick up the Accommodation Directory published by the National Roads & Motorists Association, even if you have to join the NRMA to do it. In Sydney, they're at 151 Clarence St. (Tel. 236–9211). In Melbourne, you can pick up a similar directory from the Royal Automobile Club for about $5, without becoming a member to do it. (See the Melbourne chapter.) Both publish separate directories for budget travel and for trailer parks ("caravan camping").

• Throughout this book we estimate the price for two in a room in Australian dollars. To convert these double prices into single rates, deduct maybe 10 percent, although some hotels charge the same for singles or doubles. You will have to multiply these prices times the exchange rate to get the approximate amount in your own currency. (For example, if a hotel room costs $100 and if the current exchange is 70 U.S. cents for the Aussie dollar, the hotel will set you back $US70.)

• If you don't want to spend all your time staying at hotels, you might consider several days in a private home, either in town or on a station (farm or ranch), where you are usually invited to take part in farm and family activities, outings, etc. Some readers have reported to us that they enjoyed this kind of thing immensely in Australia. A good travel agent should have the material, or you can write for details to Bed & Breakfast International, P.O. Box 442, 18–20 Oxford St., Woollahra, N.S.W. 2025. (In the Sydney area you can telephone them at 33–4235.)

• Also, over much of Australia there are caravan (trailer) parks where you can often rent an "on-site" caravan for a minimal charge—from $20 to $30 per night for two people (although many sleep five or six). These are usually equipped with all kitchen needs, and you can rent sheets and blankets for a small additional charge if you're not traveling with your own. In Sydney and other large cities, of course, these are set up in the suburbs. Some readers report they don't mind driving or taking public transportation into the city for shopping and sightseeing.

• In Sydney, some women traveling alone say they are not comfortable staying at any hotel in the King's Cross neighborhood, and for a few that might include nearby Darlinghurst and Potts Point. Although the Cross sometimes looks much more unsavory than it really is, one woman said she felt like a prisoner in her hotel room after nightfall and said that she would only stay in the downtown area next time. Perhaps that's a good idea, but we also have letters from young couples, for example, who say they like the Greenwich Village atmosphere in the neighborhood and wouldn't stay anywhere else in town.

EXPENSIVE HOTELS

These are Sydney's top accommodations, and prices begin at something over $100 per night for two. (Like all our quotes, these are in Aussie dollars, remember.) Unless otherwise noted, all these "international-standard" establishments will have luxury amenities, including central air conditioning and heating, color televisions, refrigerators, room service, a free newspaper in the morning, etc.

For a nearly perfect combination of luxury, convenience, beauty, and dramatic vistas, our top-ranking Sydney hotel has to be the supersleek 620-room **Regent of Sydney** (Tel. 238–0000), a massive landmark commanding George Street near The Rocks, Circular Quay, the opera house, and most of the points of interest in downtown Sydney. The $80-million structure is Australia's largest hotel, and here's the way we saw it:

Two ground floors, the lower on George Street, the other level with Harrington Street at the rear; dramatic skylit pink-and-polished three-story atrium lobby, alive with the hum of conversation; a grand granite staircase to the interior balconies; a profusion of potted plants; several bars and restaurants, including the Lobby Restaurant for people watching, the American-style Club Bar, the black-and-brass Kable's featuring nouvelle cuisine on the mezzanine, and Don Burrow's Supper Club, open until 3 A.M. and named after Australia's favorite jazz flautist; attractive wine cellar on display; semisheltered, large, angular outdoor swimming pool, surrounded by health-club facilities and another bar; a verandah full of shops on Level 3.

Well-appointed rooms throughout the 34-floor tower; great views from the corner junior suites overlooking the water from the bridge to the opera and now renting for about $250 per day; standards from about $125 to $175 daily, depending more on location than anything else, the less expensive units viewing the Darling Harbour instead of Sydney Cove; all rooms trimmed in light Tasmanian oak; many in unusual shapes; all with couches, writing tables, and telephones everywhere; king-size bedrooms with full bath but some twin-bed accommodations with shower only; several homey touches like cuddly bathrobes and the like.

We have thoroughly explored the premises twice but haven't yet checked in ourselves, so we can make no comment on service standards. But reader reports have been excellent. (Reserve through the Regent organization or write to the hotel at P.O. Box N 185, Sydney 2000.) For luxury at any price, the Regent is "it" for 1986–87.

Not far away, the **Sheraton Wentworth** (Tel. 230–0700) has been a personal favorite for the past eight years. This American-designed house, which has undergone some massive and intelligent refurbishment, occupies the block from Phillip to Bligh streets, just off Chifley Square. Established in the government and financial district, the 448-room, 20-year-old structure with the semicircular façade is also within walking distance of Circular Quay, the opera house, and several historic sites:

A lighter, livelier place these days under its Sheraton management; large, wine-carpeted lobby with comfortable leather furniture and unusual 60-bulb chandelier; several nice shops tucked away in the ground-floor arcades; slick dining areas including the bright, garden-style Joseph Banks, the Club Grill (a wood-paneled, English-style restaurant), and the Garden Court, sometimes featuring a Sunday brunch; several bars; no swimming pool; good parking facilities; tastefully appointed bedrooms in either gray, blue, or green; a few with tiny balconies; all with openable windows, a welcome plus when the "southerly buster" blows through the city; well-furnished suites running $200 to $300; other doubles from about $110 to $135. We've stayed once and thoroughly enjoyed the experience. (Reserve through the Sheraton chain or write to the hotel at 61–101 Phillip St., Sydney, N.S.W. 2000.) Still a top choice, and much improved over the past four years.

Many travelers will logically choose the 13-year-old, 43-story **Hilton International Sydney** (Tel. 266–0610), our own headquarters in 1985, and it is truly a superb hotel: Convenient site running between George and Pitt streets in the middle of the shopping and theater district; massive, marble-floored upstairs lobby reachable by escalators from the street or from the serpentine underground shopping complexes; heated outdoor nineteenth-floor swimming pool; gymnasium, including an open-air jogging track; particularly lavish convention facilities; large number of dining, drinking, and entertainment locations including the gourmet, black-white-and-gold San Francisco Grill (eight kinds of oysters), the Terrace Cafe, the Market Place steak house, the 24-hour Hilton Coffee Shop, Juliana's supper club and discotheque, and a large collection of pubs, among them the 1893 Marble Bar reassembled inside the structure, the George Adams Bar, the heavy-timbered, brick-lined Henry the Ninth Bar, and the brassy Americas Cup Bar.

A total of 619 accommodations, with all sleeping rooms above the 20th floor, effectively reducing traffic noise; very comfortable bedrooms with thick carpets, double draperies, and all the top amenities; good, high-pressure showers over genuine bathtubs; lowest rates at around $110 on up to more than three times that for the sumptuous suites; new 36th-floor Executive Club providing a "hotel within a hotel" for high rollers at premium prices. (Reservations through the Hilton reservation system or from the hotel at 259 Pitt St., Sydney 2000.) The Royal Automobile Club and similar organizations give the smooth-running Hilton five stars, an opinion in which we heartily concur.

Conveniently next to Wynyard Gardens (and the Wynyard Station) is the traditional businessman's favorite, the 14-story **Menzies** (Tel. 2–0232). Its roots go back to the 1850s, although it has been rebuilt top to bottom several times and frequently refurbished. It's the kind of a place where your shoes will be shined if left in the hallway overnight, and you'll find some fresh fruit in the room after checking in: Lots of heavy leather, timber, and warm colorings; large reception area with patterned carpet and comfortable sitting room; 17 bars and several restaurants on the premises, including Archibald's, an intimate "fine dining" room, the Keisan Japanese Restaurant, and the Buttery, a coffee shop; pleasant rooms, some appearing small when the drapes are drawn; 8th through 14th floors slightly higher in price than 3rd to 7th; excellent tub/shower combinations. (Booking through the MFA Homestead organization, Utell International, or from the hotel at 14 Carrington St., Sydney 2000.) An efficient, comfortable choice.

Opening after our final deadline is the brand-new **Hotel Inter-Continental Sydney** (Tel. 230–0200), which cleverly incorporates the stone façade and other features of the 100-year-old former treasury building in front of a modern 31-story tower of guest rooms. The official address is 117 Macquarie St., but another entrance is at the corner of Phillip and Bridge streets—an excellent location, in any case.

Sorry, we haven't been inside to inspect at this writing, but the plans are certainly intriguing. The ground floor incorporates an atrium and a series of vaulted sandstone arcades that fully exploit the structure's historic roots. Restaurants and bars include The Treasury for gourmet meals, the Cafe Opera for more informal dining, the Cortile, offering light snacks and cocktails, the Tavern Bar for local dishes in a pub atmosphere, and the Harbour Room, a rooftop cocktail lounge next to a glassed-in indoor swimming pool and exercise facilities. Most of the 545 air-conditioned guest rooms, including 60 suites, are said to overlook commanding vistas of the city and harbor. Units are to be equipped with the usual luxury facilities, even down to hair dryers in the bathrooms. Again, we don't have specifics on the rates, but they will surely be competitive with the Regent, the Sheraton, etc. (Reservations through the Inter-Continental chain or the hotel at Sydney, N.S.W. 2000.) Maybe we'll meet you there in '86 or '87!

Just as professionally polished as any other topflight establishment is the prestigious **Boulevard Hotel** (Tel. 357–2277). We would have ranked it higher if we liked the immediate neighborhood better, but 90 William St. is somewhat of a no-man's land in the auto sales district (and, conveniently, the auto rental district) between the city and King's Cross (there was once a plan to turn the thoroughfare into an antipodean Champs Elysées, a hope the hotel may have counted on): Large chandeliered lobby in reds and purples; marble-lined reception desk; front doors often bolted against the gusts; garage entrance then open for guests; expensive Cafe Terrazzo at lobby level; well-regarded Palmer Room one flight up; The Loft, a viewful cocktail and dancing club on the 25th floor; several other bars; indoor heated pool also way upstairs. Total of 280 colorful, well-designed bedchambers, in the $100 range; some wonderful overlooks to all of Sydney, the Botanic Gardens, the opera house, bridge, harbor—the whole lot. (Reservations through the Travelodge system in several countries, including the U.S.A., or by writing the hotel at Sydney 2011.) The boulevard outside may not be the greatest, but the Boulevard inside is one of the handsomest in Sydney.

The next two in the category are "up the Cross," and despite its huffy-puffy, hilly location, we far prefer the **Sebel Town House** (Tel. 358–3244) where general manager Henry Rose keeps his staff hoppin' like kanga-roos to make things happen for his guests. All together, the hotel proba-bly has more of a distinct personality than many others in its price range: Past the little Japanese garden and waterfall to a small lobby; inviting Town House restaurant to one side (crepes a specialty); cocktail bar with 8 × 10 glossies of local celebs who've come to call; sunny rooftop swim-ming pool with excellent panoramas of the skyline; poolside food and drink service; large guest rooms, also with good views (usually); excellent furnishings; patterned wallpaper; some king-size beds; children under 12 free in their parents' room; draperies and blackout curtains (handy for jet-lag recovery); well-arranged bathrooms with lots of shelf space, unusual in Australia. (Reservations from the hotel, 23 Elizabeth Bay Rd., Sydney 2011.) The Town House may seem just a bit out of town, but she's just as sophisticated as her big-city cousins.

The **Hyatt Kingsgate** (Tel. 357–2233) has two strong points. One, its location at the very gate to King's Cross is a plus for those who want to dip their toes daily into the spicy sauce of the neighborhood. Number two is the availability of some of the best and most dramatic views over the city. We spent an hour gazing and photographing the wide-angle northwestern exposure from our room. The room itself, however, was no more than just okay. To be fair, there are many refurbished units in the hotel that are better (next time we'd ask specifically for one of those). Prices may begin at slightly lower rates than the others in this group, but the place is also too group-happy for our FIT souls.

We are also not very fond of the **Park Regis** (Tel. 267–6511), where we felt cramped in a rather threadbare apartment. The new **Southern Cross Hotel** (Tel. 2–0987) at the corner of Elizabeth and Goulburn streets, south of Hyde Park, is nice, but the neighborhood is marginal at best. Its glass-walled lobby gives an excellent view of the peeling paint across the street. We'd skip this one, too.

The **Hilton International Sydney Airport** (Tel. 597–0122), not to be confused with the similarly named downtown hotel, also has not been inspected by us. Catering principally to businessfolk, it offers a swimming pool as well as tennis and squash courts.

MEDIUM-PRICE HOTELS

The following establishments, which will run about $70 to $100 for two, are generally comfortable for everyone. The TV may or may not be in color, some have fridges and some don't, and views can be relatively limited. Australians might class some of these as "motor hotels" and "apartment hotels," a distinction perhaps less important to international travelers.

The top choice in the category, as long as they keep the prices reasonable, has to be the new **Telford Old Sydney Inn** (Tel. 2–0524) at 55 George St., probably the first genuinely new hotel in a century to be located smack in the historic Rocks district: Unimposing red-brick façade in key with the neighborhood; interior boasting a surprisingly attractive six-story atrium created partly by using the remnants of two old warehouse buildings; huge skylight above it; overstuffed wicker chairs and circular stairway off the lobby; nearby fireplace and lounge; reportedly very good Snooty Fox Restaurant on the balcony, plus a bistro named Carriages; open-air swimming pool with glimpses over rooftops to Sydney Cove and the opera house; 176 well-equipped rooms with color tellies and other features of more luxurious houses; views of the historic neighborhood with its gaslights and brickpaved streets; 24-hour room service. The rates for this new find have been holding at around $80 for two, but don't count on it forever. (Reservations from the hotel in The Rocks, Sydney, N.S.W. 2000 or through the Telford or Flag Inns groups.) By far the best bargain in town at these more modest rates.

Now don't be confused, because our next choice is a second one in The Rocks area. **The Russell** (Tel. 241–3543) is an unusual and very special small hotel that could be ideal for certain clients, and perhaps anathema for others. This former sailors' flophouse at the corner of George and Globe streets, which will be exactly 100 years old in 1987, was taken in hand by a trendy fashion stylist inspired by family hotels she had stayed at in Europe. She converted it into a *tres chic* and homey haven of just 18 individually decorated rooms, mostly in styles reminiscent of the 1930s. Go upstairs and say hello to manager Maggie Bell, who greets you from behind a jar of jelly beans. You'll find no TVs here, but there are writing desks and direct-dial phones, and some rooms have interesting views. In most cases you must leave your bedchamber to go to the bathroom, but then robes are provided for all. Rates, which include continental breakfasts, are in the $60 to $80 range for two, a little less for a single. (Reservations direct from the hotel at 143A George St., Circular Quay, Sydney 2000.) Some may think the decor runs to the frilly, but it's a success of its type, and certainly unique in Sydney.

Back in Sydney proper, and behind the façade of an old building at No. 4 Bridge St., is the **Cliveden** (Tel. 235–1333), an apartment building run as a hotel and one of the first of a new type of Sydney accommodation: Good site just off George Street; tiny, well-kept reception area; adjoining licensed French restaurant; small rooftop pool and spa; five sizes of apartments on each of 11 floors; color TV and radio; direct-dial phones; full kitchens with all equipment; garbage disposals; washing machines and dryers; bamboo and rattan furnishings; some with those Aussie showers without curtains; no views to speak of; full hotel maid service. Apartments vary in price between $70 and $100, depending on size and position. (Reservations from the hotel at the address above.) A good location if they can hold the line on prices.

At least three other establishments are now similarly equipped apartment/hotel operations like the Cliveden: The **Hyde Park Plaza** (Tel. 331–6933) at 38 College St., near Liverpool and Oxford streets, with very nice housekeeping digs for $80 to $90; **The Park Apartments** (Tel. 331–7728) at 16 Oxford St., which has living units running around $70 to $80; and **The York** (Tel. 264–7747). Not to be confused with the later-mentioned York *Hotel*, this newer York, at 5 York St., offers some snazzy flats with good views of the Harbour Bridge for about $90 and up, but cheaper by the week. Unlike many "condo" operations in the U.S., Sydney apartment hotels generally will have a restaurant on the premises for those who don't want to cook all meals at home.

Back into conventional hotels, now, the well-equipped **Wynyard Travelodge** (Tel. 2–0254) is up a steep slope at York and Margaret streets: Small lobby in black and orange, sometimes too crowded for comfort; pleasant coffee shop–style restaurant and Howzat Bar; Outrigger Restaurant on the roof next to the pool; some of the 211 units with excellent views; all with color TVs and several extras; rates now nearing $100 for two, which just about puts it out of the category. (Reservations from the hotel at 7–9 York St., Sydney, N.S.W. 2000.) The Wynyard is perhaps still a wynner, although some think it's priced too high to remain competitive.

In the King's Cross environs, a cylindrical hotel called the **Gazebo Ramada** (Tel. 358–1999) has been a favorite for the past decade: Pleasant, open location next to Fitzroy Gardens and its fuzzy fountain at the opposite end of Darlinghurst Road from Kingsgate; bustling reception area in bright colors; attractive Pavilion Room restaurant with some outdoor tables; heated rooftop pool with liquor and food service; all rooms air conditioned with TV, radio, fridge, coffee- and tea-making equipment, etc.; each room with a walkout balcony and many with excellent views (north and northwest the best); specify bath or shower. The manager told us his house is large enough to offer all the modern conveniences while still small enough to be friendly. Most doubles are in the $80 to $90 range. (Reservations from the hotel at 2 Elizabeth Bay Rd., King's Cross, N.S.W. 2011.) The Gazebo is a charming garden retreat.

There are three nice choices up Macleay Street from King's Cross in the Potts Point area, all relatively comfortable. The baronial, seven-story **Chateau Sydney** (Tel. 358–2500) attempts to bring the flavor of Europe to Potts Point in the middle of a tree-lined residential block at a bus stop: Small, dark-wood lobby guarded by suits of armor and crowned by heavy chandeliers; two restaurants spanning culinary gulfs—from the Caves de Montparnasse to Marty's Steak House; Grecian swimming pool on the roof; bedrooms in solid colors; nicely designed showers (apparently few tubs); few vistas, but pleasant aspects from the semicircular balconies. Some rooms are priced higher than the category. (Reservations from the hotel at 14 Macleay St., Sydney 2011.) A chateau it's not, but it's still *tres joli.*

Down the street, the pool-less **Sheraton Motor Hotel** (Tel. 358–1955) boasts a tiny, uncomfortable, and too-purple lobby, but nicer rooms upstairs than you might have suspected: A few good views from the upper floors; showers but no bathtubs; all rooms with color television; some with small balconies. (Reservations through the Flag chain or the hotel at 40 Macleay St., P.O. Box 149, Sydney 2011.) Respectable, but not really a Sheraton.

Some people will prefer the nearby (and slightly cheaper) **Macleay Street Travelodge** (Tel. 358–2777), a nine-story entry with a rooftop pool. Many rooms have an excellent panorama north to the opera house, etc., and they are generally well equipped, although some may seem a little sterile. Most doubles were about $70 at last report. Try for units on the ninth floor. (Reservations from the hotel at 26–34 Macleay St., Potts Point, N.S.W. 2011.) Not bad for the outlay.

We've heard nice things about the **Clairmont Village Inn** (Tel. 358–2044) at 5 Ward Ave., but haven't managed to check out this King's Cross address ourselves. With such things as an *indoor* pool, color tellies, and the like, its rooms rent in the $60 range. It just may be pretty good. And Susan Klimley of Manhattan, U.S.A., said she and her husband liked the "funky" **New Crest Hotel** (Tel. 358–2755) at 111 Darlinghurst Rd. in King's Cross. Their room, at least, had a view and was convenient to the suburban train station. Rates now run about $65 for a pair of pillows.

BUDGET ACCOMMODATIONS

We hope there will still be several hotel rooms in Sydney selling for under $50 for two. The best in this minimum-outlay group might be the **Canberra Oriental** (Tel. 358–3155), up the Cross, *if* they can hold the line on their rates, and *if* you draw some decent digs. The best doubles are already up to $65 or so, but we include it here for the lower-price models, down to something less than $50: Convenient location at 223 Victoria St.; generally older clientele; smallish, light-wood lobby with breakfast room off to the side; fresh flowers here and there; a cantilevered stairway to the upper regions; about 300 rooms hither and yon, some still without private bathrooms (although they at least have washbasins and hot and cold water). The rooms *with* private "facilities" also have televisions, telephones, coffee- and tea-makers, etc. (In other rooms you can rent TVs for an extra charge.) There's a roof garden for sunbathing and a nice panorama toward the harbor. This hotel may still offer single rooms at prices around $25, including breakfast. (Rates may change, so ask them for up-to-date price sheets. Reservations from the above address at Sydney 2011.) A usually smooth operation for the tariffs asked.

Another King's Cross address (or actually Potts Point) is that old GI R&R favorite, the **Texas Tavern** (Tel. 358–1211) at 44 Macleay St.: An amazing roundup of restaurants, bars, and discos on the property, catering to drop-in and nighttime trade; friendly folks at the reception area; 130 bedrooms scattered higgledy-piggledy through the building; many of them renovated with TVs, fridges, air conditioners, etc., but perhaps a few shilling-in-the-slot electric heaters remaining; doubles around $50, singles around $40, both with breakfast. The Texas Tavern seems always in transition. Good luck, pardner.

If you must have a low-budget address near the city center, the logical choice may be the **Gresham** (Tel. 267–1266) at the corner of Druitt and York streets, across from Town Hall. More than 110 years old, its basic structure is protected by the National Trust. The rooms are simple but clean, with no TVs (there's a separate lounge with a telly), but perhaps a Flit gun at the ready atop the wardrobes. Some chambers with private baths, some without; short on heaters, but electric blankets provided when needed. We liked No. 26, a large, sunny corner room, but we suspect that light sleepers might find the traffic disturbing when the windows are open. If you're lucky, you'll snag a double for $40, with breakfast, or a single at around $30. You'll carry your own luggage, of course, but the tiny elevator will help. (For reservations, write the hotel at 147 York St.) Though no longer young, Grandma Gresham holds her own at the price level.

Paul W. St. Anthony, a Minneapolis lad with an eye for value, wrote us glowingly of the **Maksim Private Hotel** (Tel. 358–6008), at 40 Darlinghurst Rd.: "The room was spartan but very clean, had two beds and TV, tea and coffee, etc. . . . A good value with nice staff." Maksim-mum rates are now about $35 for two, $30 for one, according to our records, although we've never set foot inside.

The **York Hotel** (Tel. 29–2613), at 48 King St., was our mistake. We had one depressing inside room there once, and only once. It has a nice pub downstairs, but that's as far as we'll go next time. Virtually last and least there is the Salvation Army chain hotel, called in Sydney, as it is over most of Australia, the **People's Palace** (Tel. 211–5777). It's at 400 Pitt St., near Central Station. You may still get twins for under $40 and singles for $20 there. Some call it a bargain, but we call it very basic.

Youth hostels. You must be a member, of course, and if you haven't taken care of that detail, apply to the Australian Youth Hostels Association (Tel. 929–3407), Eagle House, 118 Alfred St., Milsons Point, N.S.W. 2061, just over the bridge. The **Sydney Youth Hostel** itself (Tel. 692–0747), which will set you back about $5 a bed, is a century-old mansion at 28 Ross St. (corner of St. Johns Road) in the western suburb of Forest Lodge, near the university.

Rooms in New South Wales. Since we have not been able to inspect these personally, we'll mention some based on recommendations made to us and other sources in section 6, Sightseeing. (Also, see our note on the NRMA Accommodation Directory at the beginning of this section.) Ski lodges in the Snowy Mountains, however, will be found in our Canberra chapter, since they're much closer to that city than they are to Sydney.

5. Dining and Restaurants in Sydney

Once was a time that the cuisine of Australia was the cuisine of Liverpool and Houndsditch. There were certain local variations like carpetbagger steak (beef with those wonderful Sydney Rock oysters), meat pies (with a dash of ketchup squirted under the crust), and Pavlova (a rich meringue dessert). These still exist, but today the kitchens of Australia are the kitchens of the world, brought to the country by the tremendous wave of "New Australians" who have immigrated over the past 40 years. Today, Australian cosmopolites can dine on authentic cuisine from all parts of the world, at least in the large cities.

Australian wine. A few words about the fermented grape, which now belongs to Australia as much as it does to France, Italy, and California. Wines are very good and very reasonable, and we think no serious meal can be enjoyed without one. The whites are particularly excellent, world-class wines. The reds, though some are a little earthy as compared to their U.S. and French counterparts, are nevertheless inexpensive and absolutely enjoyable—certainly much better than the average *vin ordinaire* served in restaurants in France.

Wineries are in three main areas in Australia:

• The Hunter River Valley, near Pokolbin and Rothbury, 60 miles north of Sydney in New South Wales.

• Throughout much of the state of Victoria, particularly at Rutherglen on the N.S.W. border.

• And the best grape-growing area of all, South Australia, mainly in the Barossa Valley (Clare, Coonawarra, etc.), not far from Adelaide. About three-fourths of Australia's total wine output is produced here.

(Some wines are produced along the Swan River in Western Australia. There are also small operations in Queensland and Tasmania.)

White wines. Look for these types: Rhine Riesling (and other Rieslings, which vary from slightly sweet to dry), Sauterne, Grave, Pearl, Moselle, Mosel, White Burgundy, Semillon, Traminer, the drier Chablis and Hock, as well as Champagne and several other sparkling varieties.

Red wines. The best reds are Claret, Cabernet Sauvignon, Shiraz (Hermitage), and Pinot Noir. (Red Burgundies sometimes seem a little harsh to foreign palates.)

There are also a few nice appetizer wines including varieties of sherry and vermouth, several dessert wines including Port, Muscat, Madeira, Frontignac, and Tokay, and of course some brandies, which are wine by-products.

Some of the more outstanding wineries are represented by the following well-known brands: Elliott, Hardy's, Hungerford Hill, Huntington, Leo Buring, Lindeman's, McWilliam's, Mildara, Orlando, Penfolds, Rosemount, Rothbury, Seppelt, Stanley, Tulloch, Tyrrell's, Wyndham, Wynns, and Yalumba. (There are many more good small operations tucked here and there throughout the country.)

Prior to World War II Australia was almost strictly a beer-drinking country. Many oenophobic Aussies looked down on any wines, all of which they lumped together as "plonk." (Probably after learning of *vin blanc* during two wars in France.)

The beers are also excellent (we discuss those further on in our own "pub crawl" in section 11). But now that Australian wines have come into their own in the past few years, you'll even find them stocked in limited quantities in Canada, England, and the U.S.

The BYO scene. Many Australian restaurants are not "licensed"—i.e., they cannot serve alcohol. These are known as BYO restaurants, allowing you to "Bring Your Own." Even when a Sydney restaurant does receive its license, it may still invite you to cart in your favorite wine if they might not have it in their own cellar. In some BYOs you place your order and then run next door to the pub or wine shop to choose your bottle while your meal is being prepared. (Most Australian wine in the shop will cost you from $4 to $6 a bottle. The markup will be about 80 to 90 percent in licensed restaurants.)

AUSTRALIAN AND COSMOPOLITAN RESTAURANTS

One of the most fun of the old-style Australian restaurants is the **Argyle Tavern** (Tel. 27–7782), at 18 Argyle St. in the historic Rocks district. In the rough-brick and candle-lit atmosphere, you might try Convict Broth and then roast beef while joining in the Australian bush ballad singalongs. Dinner will run around $16 and a one-price lunch may be available for $5 or so. (Closed Sunday evenings.) Fun for the right crowd.

Also in The Rocks, a special place for those who want to broil their own steaks or roast pork is **Phillip's Foote** (Tel. 27–2585) at 101 George St. North. For a price of about $8 you get the meat and a glass of wine. In good weather, sit in the brick-walled garden at the rear. A somewhat similar place not far away is the **Orient Hotel** (Tel. 27–2464) at the corner of George and Argyle streets, which also offers some made-to-order sandwiches. It's deservedly popular at lunchtime. Nearby is another tourist favorite, the BYO **Gum Nut Tea Garden** (Tel. 27–9591), up some narrow stairs at 29 Harrington St.

For breakfast at any hour (they never close) in the same general neighborhood, look into **Pancakes on the Rocks** (Tel. 27–6371) at 10 Hickson Rd. There are a lot more than pancakes on the menu, of course, many items with a bizarre touch. Would you believe Buckwheat Mignon with Hollandaise Sauce? (We haven't tried that, and aren't likely to.)

Another pancake breakfast we enjoyed once was at the **Bourbon & Beefsteak Bar** (Tel. 358–1144) at 24 Darlinghurst Rd. in King's Cross. The service was excellent, but with Australian-style bacon, of course (you have to cut off the rind). We haven't tried the beefsteak and bourbon available at the Bourbon & Beefsteak in the evenings.

A reasonably priced choice for lunch (weekdays) and dinner (any day but Sunday) is the **Woolloomooloo Woolshed** (Tel. 357–1978) in a nineteenth-century terrace house at 132 Forbes St. in Woolloomooloo. The decor is supposed to evoke a typical woolshed, where Australian sheep are shorn, and the atmosphere is casual and relaxed. Some nights feature a singalong. The emphasis is on lamb and seafood. Figure about $40 for two, with the house wine.

A high-quality luncheon choice is not far from Circular Quay down a tiny alley called Bulletin Place. There at No. 16–18 is Len Evans Wines Pty. Ltd., and almost in a secret upstairs hiding place is the **Beef Room** (Tel. 27–4413, and *do* reserve; we didn't, but were uncommonly lucky). Apparently furnished and equipped with the castoffs from a fleet of old sailing ships (the sandstone brick walls were carried as ballast), the Beef Room offers a one-price lunch—perhaps $14 by now—including two glasses of Evans's own wine. There's a serve-yourself fruit and cheese bar as well as sailor-size helpings of succulent roast beef, Yorkshire pudding, and lots of other trimmings. The "business lunch" is only served Monday to Friday. (Men, wear a tie in here.) Evans himself is a wine writer of considerable note. We never met him, but we'll be back to his Beef Room again.

One of Australia's highest restaurants—in altitude as in charges—is the 47th-story location of the **Summit** (Tel. 27–9777) at Australia Square. It revolves, of course, once around in an hour and 45 minutes. A la carte, you'll leave with a bill of around $35 each. The one-price smorgasbord may be a better deal. Book a table—windowside or nothing—for a half hour before sunset for the most scenic go-around.

Newer, but also high up and also rotating are the restaurants at the **Sydney Tower** (Tel. 233–3722) above the Centrepoint shopping center. The self-service section is usually the better deal; the panorama is unsurpassed at either.

A nice little casual place for lunch-only downtown is the below-street-level **South Australia Wine Bar** (also known as the Adelaide Wine Cellar, Tel. 232–8521). Designed as public relations for that southern state, the tiny niche has several nice quiches, sandwiches, etc. on the blackboard menu in the $3 to $5 range. We had our quiche with the house white, then a half-litre of Hardy's Riesling. Go in at noon to avoid the crush (which begins at about 12:30 in Sydney).

Last, if you're looking for Yankee food, you might check out the bustling **New York Deli** (Tel. 327–4537) at 459 New South Head Rd. in Double Bay. Also you'll now find **McDonald's** and **Kentucky Fried Chicken** in several locations. Even **Pizza Huts** have mushroomed and pepperonied all over Australia.

CHINESE AND ORIENTAL FARE

The most flamboyant and most flavorful Chinese restaurant is the **Imperial Peking Harbourside Restaurant** (Tel. 27–7073), carved into an historic waterfront warehouse at 15 Circular Quay. Besides the delicious views of the harbor, the opera house, etc., the place also offers reasonably spectacular and spicy cuisine. Try the Burning Iron Emperor Chicken. The *Sydney Morning Herald* calls this the finest Chinese restaurant in town.

One of the dependable, more modest Chinese entries is **Yick On Yuen** (Tel. 212–5958), a family operation at 17 Campbell St., almost next door to the Capitol Theatre. Try the fresh fish in ginger or the roast pork with pickles. No credit cards. Otherwise, just wander the three blocks of Dixon Street and pick one of the dozens of Chinese establishments there. The **Hingara** (Tel 212–2169) at No. 82 is good for the hungries—and cheap, too.

A favorite activity for Chinese-food fans in Sydney is the *yum cha* lunch. You sit down, order a drink, and then wait for goodies to be shown to you on a tray or a cart. You pick from such choices as spring rolls, chicken pies, *dim sum,* and the like. You'll find *yum cha* available at several Chinese restaurants, including the **Pearl Palace** at the corner of Sussex and Little Hay streets, the **Shanghai Village** at 65 Dixon St., and the **Peking Duck,** 738 George St. **Nine Dragons,** however, is off our list.

A sleeper for most out-of-towners is the **Fortuna Court** (Tel. 438–4604) at 24 Falcon St., in Crows Nest, a popular dining neighborhood on the North Shore. This is often confused with another restaurant by the same name, but which we haven't tried, in Sydney proper.

For Korean food, look for **The Korea House** (Tel. 358–6601) at 171 Victoria St. in King's Cross. As our friend Sue Gallie says, the decor is ghastly purple and generally awful, but the Korean barbecues and other specialties are delicious. Some tasty Thai cuisine will be found at the **Siam** (Tel. 331–2669), 383 Oxford St. in Paddington. Try the prawn and lemongrass soup. Right downtown, however, Dutch Indonesian dishes are offered at the **Warung Indonesia** (Tel. 267–1539). Order the spicy beef curry for around $7, or the full nine-course *rijstafel* for around $13.50.

CONTINENTAL AND FRENCH CUISINE

The little **Le Cafe Nouveau** (Tel. 33–3377), which you'll find at 495 Oxford St., near Moore Park Road in Paddo (but which you won't find in the Yellow Pages), was once sought out and praised by the late James Beard. It's superelegant, superexpensive, and has a very changeable menu. Beard wrote lovingly of the steamed fresh tuna with poached oysters and champagne sauce, the cold lamb with pistachio dressing, and the fillets of beef and veal in a watercress-flecked marrow sauce. He didn't say how it all added up, but we'll guess you won't see the door again without leaving $45 per person—plus the wine.

Almost as top-drawer, but slightly less pricy, is **Pegrum's** (Tel. 357–4776), a family operation at 36 Gurner St. in Paddington. There are both lamb and seafood specialties, all served well and expensively. Reserve well ahead of time. You can't beat the atmosphere at **Pavilion on the Park** (Tel. 232–1322), opposite the Art Gallery in the Domain, and the food is good too. Uninhibited diners may find themselves toting up $30—even for a noonday meal!

On our latest Sydney visit, **Kinsela's** (Tel. 331–3100) was all the rage. Actually it's two restaurants in one, both set up in a former funeral parlor at 383 Bourke St. in Darlinghurst. The main restaurant is the "brasserie" (try the roast duck with pickles) and the second part is a theatre-restaurant offering two shows nightly along with your meals. Something with a little more conventional decor is **Breheny's** (Tel. 922–5601) at 123 Blues Point Rd. at viewful McMahon's Point on the North Shore, about a 10-minute cab ride from downtown Sydney. Food and service are generally excellent, and the tables are not crowded either.

Another newish establishment, becoming a culinary champion, is **Chanterelle** (Tel. 660–6050) at 461 Harris St. in Ultimo, east of the railroad station. Owner/chef Paul Elser lays out a long menu featuring fish, but we might opt for the veal in a light cream and chive sauce or the beef with creamed scallions. Always reserve, and then take a taxi, for Chanterelle may be the only bright spot in this rather run-down neighborhood.

In the same general area, at Taylor Square, we had a happy meal at **The French Restaurant** (Tel. 331–3605), 379A Bourke St., not far from Kinsela's. Candles reflect off the stucco walls, and there may be a live accordionist in another niche someplace. The house pâté is fine, they trot out excellent French-style steaks with Bearnaise sauce and le works, and an excellent half chicken is the Spatchcoq au Vin Bourguignon. We experienced friendly and efficient service and emerged with our wallet not badly dented, either.

Not to be confused with the above is the similarly named **French Tavern** (Tel. 27–7740), which we also recently enjoyed. It's in a somewhat hard-to-see location at 1-B Hamilton St., a tiny alleyway off Bridge Street or Pitt Street, not far from Australia Square right downtown. There was live music in French "cave"-like surroundings. It's a bit commercial in some ways, but we enjoyed Veal Cordon Bleu and several other dishes.

A dependable Gallic address not far from King's Cross is **The Yellow Book** (Tel. 358–6121) at 1 Kellett Way, Potts Point. Actually it's two restaurants, the cheaper one featuring light and heavy meals in an open garden. Besides the full bill of fare, you might even be able to get some unusual sandwiches here.

At 9 Albion Place, just around the corner from the movie palaces on George Street, is a usually sharp little bargain called **La Guillotine** (Tel. 264–1487). They specialize in dozens of kinds of omelettes, but there is also a *plat du jour* that we've never heard anything but praise for. You'll dine from $5 to $10 per person here and still have enough time and money left to catch the show. Almost next door, at No. 1, there's a popular new Spanish entry named **Don Quixote** (Tel. 264–5903). The house specialty is suckling pig, but it must be ordered in advance when you make your reservations. Most dinners will run about $40 for two here.

ITALIAN RISTORANTES

Not far from the Australian Museum, and no less an institution in Sydney, is **Beppi's** (Tel. 357–4558), 29 Yurong St., which has been dishing out *cucina Italiana* for more than a quarter century. If you speak the lingo as well as you like the linguini, you'll feel especially welcome here. If not, you'll probably still enjoy it. Then there's **Darcy's** (Tel. 32–4512) at 92 Hargrave St. in Paddington. It has also been around a few years. Among other things, the seafood platter is famous.

Less expensive, but probably equally good, is the little **Mario's** (Tel. 331–4945) at 73 Stanley St. in Darlinghurst. It's a "trendy" place, as the Aussies say; you'll often find it filled with the fashion and advertising folk of the city. (Closed Sundays.) A California reader has also just praised the **Italo-Australian Club** (Tel. 211–5150), an inexpensive entry at 727 George St.

Buona fortuna was waiting for us in the **Arriverderci** (Tel. 357–6809) at 77 William St., downstairs under the chassis of one of the automobile shops there. Walk past the dramatically presented antipasto spread to your red-and-white checkered table. The stucco walls bear the inevitable mural of the harbor at Naples (or was it Sorrento?). Unlike most of the previous entries, this is an inexpensive *trattoria* where you can keep the bill even lower by choosing only the entrees. We enjoyed our *scallopine al burro e limone*. (Closed Sundays.) *Molte bene!*

When everything else is closed, the family-run **Natalino's** (Tel. 358–4751) is open at 1 Kellett St. in King's Cross. In good weather you may prefer the garden. Three other budget Italian entries were recommended by Leo Schofield, the knowledgeable Sydney food writer, in an article in the *Bulletin:* **Bill and Toni** (Tel. 357–4702) at 72 Stanley St., offering basic Italian *piattos* for low *prezzos;* the **No Names** (also no phones), 2 Chapel

Lane, which is often crowded (Bill & Toni's takes the overflow); and **La Rustica** (Tel. 569–5824), somewhat far out in the western suburb of Leichardt at 435 Parramatta Rd. (go early; closed Sundays).

Much further out, in more ways than one, is **The Abbey** (Tel. 660–1211), a northern Italian–style entry carved out of an old church in Glebe, just east of Ultimo. The architecture and interior decorations have been written up everywhere. The fare is pretty fair, they say, although some dishes have been rather tastelessly named after some local celebrities. If you're driving, you'll have to look for the place at 156–60 Pyrmont Bridge Rd.

Finally, we're not sure if you can call it Italian, really, but the pasta is cheap, hot, and some say good at the **Old Spaghetti Factory** at 80 George St. on The Rocks. There's a fascinating collection of Victorian antiquerie, including a genuine old Bondi tram.

GREEK CUISINE

Recently opened is the **New Hellas** (Tel. 264–1668) at 287 Elizabeth St., near the corner of Market. It specializes in large, inexpensive portions of delicious dolmades and the like. Reserve early for a view over Hyde Park. Another lively choice with good-size dishes is **Diethenes** (Tel. 267–8956) at 336 Pitt St. Try the eggplant in garlic sauce. (Closed Sundays.)

The **Ethnic** (Tel. 264–7081) is at 349 Pitt St., not far from the YMCA. Chef Tassos specializes in lamb and souvlaki and other Hellenic delights. (Recheck this address before going.) And an old reliable on the Greek scene is the **Iliad** (Tel. 267–7644), not far away at 126 Liverpool St., off Pitt. Try the Arista—spinach, cheese, and pine nuts in filo.

INDIAN RESTAURANTS

We hope that Sydney, like London, will eventually be blessed with an abundance of Indian restaurants. There are a few, however, led by the **Mayur** (Tel. 235–2361) at Level 8 of the MLC Centre at Martin Place. In a decorous setting you can watch your tandoori bread being prepared at the oven. There are lots of excellent curries, and most Sydney-siders agree this is now the best place of its type in town. Your final bill may be about $50 for two (plus wine).

A tiny place we tried awhile back, **The Bombay** (Tel. 358–3946), was quite tasty. There are just nine tables in a weensy spot at 33 Elizabeth Bay Rd., near the Sebel Town House hotel, and when every chair is occupied service can be frenzied. But the selection of curries may make it worth it. A complimentary glass of sherry comes with every meal. We might go again. Some readers have also enjoyed the **Peacock Curry Cellar** (Tel. 232–2298) at 398 George St., near American Express. And a higgledy-piggledy address, at perhaps half the price of the Mayur, is **Gulu's** (Tel. 211–5442) at 340 Elizabeth St. This modest BYO accepts no credit cards but is deservedly popular for the cash crowd. (Closed Sundays.)

LEBANESE FARE

There are several of these around, but one of the best is out at Bondi at 100 Campbell Parade. **Ya-Habibi** (Tel. 30–4526), which means "Oh My Darling," has spit-roasted lamb and things like that. On Saturday nights it features a belly dancer, Ya-Habibi Clementine.

An old favorite a little closer in is **Emad's** (Tel. 698–2631), at 298 Cleveland St. in Surry Hills. The decor is undistinguished, but the skewered meats are usually delicious and inexpensive. **Ala'din** (Tel. 212–5939) is at 651-A George St., just south of Goulburn. We haven't been in yet, but it rubs most people the right way.

SEAFOOD RESTAURANTS

Sydney's two top ocean restaurants are both named Doyle's and today they're right next door to each other at 11 Marine Parade out at Watson's Bay. First, there is **Doyle's on the Beach** (Tel. 337–2007), a century-old BYO, and, a few yards away, **Doyle's on the Wharf** (Tel. 337–1572), which is licensed. It's hard to imagine a trip to Sydney without a lunch or a dinner at a Doyle's. This is the place to try the fine Australian fish John Dory (known as Peterfisch in Germany), and a lot of other things for that matter. Or you could opt for platter feasts of steamed mussels, mud crab, blue swimmers, and prawns. Go for an open-air lunch "On the Beach" or for an early dinner at either to enjoy the waterside view. Unless the policy has changed, there are no reservations and there's certain to be a queue at popular hours. Nevertheless, we call the Doyles worth waiting for. (No credit cards.)

The **Waterfront Restaurant** (Tel. 27–3666) has been making quite a splash during the past year at 27 Circular Quay West. You couldn't want a more beautiful site—a reconditioned old building with views over the harbor, the opera house, etc., and the tucker is pretty good, too. If the Waterfront suffers from anything it is simply TMT—too many tourists. Go on a nice day or evening and ask for an open-air table under the awning. A reader who loved the Waterfront strongly recommends against the **Pier One Hotel** in the same area. We haven't seen it.

In the center of the city, the **Backstage Restaurant** (Tel. 233–2116), at 350 George St. near the General Post Office, has a good local reputation for seafood. Less expensive but just as good is the **P and S Cafe** (Tel. 212–1241) at 410 Pitt St. A $6 dinner will probably include soup, salad, today's fish, french fries, and bread.

Another atmospheric winner for breakfast, lunch, and dinner is **Micha's** (Tel. 969–9827), right on the sand at the Esplanade at Balmoral Beach, a 15-minute cab ride from town. Many have liked the "Sole of Sweden" filets. Sunday brunch is especially popular. Two excellent choices just across the bridge from Sydney are **Sails** (Tel. 920–5998) at McMahon's Point (2 Henry Lawson Ave.) and the much more modest **Eric's Fish Cafe** (Tel. 43–4907) in the restaurant-laden suburb called Crows Nest (316 Pacific Highway). The latter especially wins high praise from Sydney public-relations executive and seafood *savant* Jan Lee Martin.

6. Sightseeing in Sydney (and in N.S.W.)

Sydney is a city where it's relatively easy to organize sightseeing excursions, at least to most of the musts. Two important areas—The Rocks and downtown Sydney—can be efficiently encompassed in walking tours, and ones where you can mercifully cut out those "points of interest" that are not very interesting to you.

THE ROCKS

Sydney's oldest commercial/residential neighborhood, west of Sydney Cove, has a laconic name that belies the rich historical and cultural significance of the area. In a very real sense it is Australia's birthplace, since it was here in this winding, hilly area—and against its stone cliffs— that soldiers and convicts splashed together the first wattle-and-daub structures of the new colony 200 years ago.

Later it became the squalid slum that eventually fostered the disastrous plague on Sydney in 1900. Scoured and whitewashed from top to bottom, The Rocks then went through a series of other adventures. It was both the haunt of rollicking sailors and the home of wealthy families; then the area fell on hard times again until a decade or so ago.

Now the Sydney Cove Redevelopment Authority has restored The Rocks to a position of elegant rusticity, and it's a fascinating place to twist and turn through tiny streets and up and down stairways, peeking into the windows and doorways of the past.

There's only one place to start, at the museum and the **Rocks Visitors Centre** (Tel. 27–4972) at 104 George St., an old court building near the Overseas Passenger Terminal. They'll have suggested walking tours, maps, and all sorts of information available. Don't miss the excellent sound and slide show in the back-room theater, which will give you some dramatic feeling for the area's significance.

Other spots in The Rocks include the nearby little **Cadman's Cottage,** an 1816 stone house that is now the oldest existing structure in Sydney. There's a small maritime museum inside.

At **Argyle Terrace** is the largest restored area of The Rocks. Wander through the arcade of shops that wind around and about the **Argyle Arts Centre** (Tel. 241–1853). Guided walking tours of The Rocks are given four times daily from Cleland Bond in the center of the Centre. It's a hefty climb, but some say well worth it, under the expressway and up Observatory Hill to Fort Philip and the **Observatory** (Tel. 241–2478; tours by appointment only). It was built originally to observe incoming ships, but now it's pointed toward the stars.

From here, as well as from many locations in The Rocks below, you can see Sydney's favorite old "coat hanger," the **Sydney Harbour Bridge.** Opened in 1932, it was to have had the longest single span in the world at 1,670 feet, but some more obscure bridge in the U.S.A. bettered it by about five feet just before the Australian project was completed. More than 140,000 vehicles a day now cross the bridge, most of them inch-by-bloody-inch during rush hours.

A monument to deficit spending, the bridge's price tag once read $9.5 million, but what with interest, inflation, etc., millions are still owed on it! Built during the Depression, the bridge was also known as the "iron lung" because it kept thousands of construction workers and their families breathing through those hard times.

Be sure to wander through **Pier One,** a newish shopping and "leisure" complex under the southern pylon of the bridge. (Enter from Lower Fort Street or Hickson Road, or take the free bus that leaves every 15 minutes from Circular Quay.)

CENTRAL SYDNEY

What Americans would call "downtown," Sydney-siders generally refer to as "The City," the compact core area that is officially Sydney. Beginning at a terminus for train, bus, and ferry transportation, right at the end of Sydney Cove, we are at **Circular Quay.** Ruth Park calls it "Sydney's doorstep" in her delightful and exhaustive *Companion Guide to Sydney.*

The quay is no longer circular, however, having long ago been squared off and then fitted out with five ferryboat wharves. It is here that you go to board the boats to the zoo or to take the hydrofoil to Manly.

Very much a part of the background, and easily approachable after a 10-minute stroll, is the famous **Sydney Opera House** (Tel. 2–0588). Designed by the Danish architect Joern Utzon, the opera house took 14 years to build and was finally completed in 1973 at a cost of $102 million. (The original estimate was $12 million.) Incredibly, it's all paid for, due to a unique and very Australian system of financing via public lottery. Still a controversial structure (some say it's more a piece of sculpture than a building), it made architectural history by overcoming seemingly insurmountable construction problems. Some like to speak of the opera house as sails billowing in tile. Unkind critics are apt to call it an orgy of turtles. In any case, it's not a single theater but a huge complex for the performing arts. There are four main rooms—the Concert Hall, the Opera Theatre, the Drama Theatre, and the Music Room. Besides that, add several exhibition areas, two restaurants, and six theater bars.

You may not wander the 4½-acre opera house unaccompanied. At this writing, guided tours are given every half hour between 9 A.M. and 4 P.M., seven days a week, for about $3. Be ready to register several kilometers of stair climbing and to carry away baskets of facts and figures. (Most visitors to Sydney say it's worth every step.) On good-weather Sundays you'll find free outdoor entertainment there beginning around noon and continuing for two or three hours.

The opera house sits on **Bennelong Point,** named for an Aborigine befriended by Governor Philip. Bennelong had just a little hut here when he lived on the site.

Walk from Circular Quay up Loftus Street to **Macquarie Place,** a cool triangle-shaped patch of green that features the 1818 obelisk from which all Australian roads were once measured. There, too, is the anchor from the *Sirius,* the flagship of the First Fleet.

If you move up Bridge Street to the end, you'll have partly penetrated the **Royal Botanic Gardens.** You might save the vast gardens and the wonderful collections of statues, flowers, palms, ponds, and swans for another day, but have a look at least at the castlelike **Conservatorium of Music.** Designed by Francis Greenway, the convict father of Australian architecture, the 1817 alabaster structure was to be a magnificent stable for the governor's horses. Lunchtime and twilight concerts are often given at the school today. **Government House,** the official mansion of the Queen's representative to New South Wales, may not be visited, but you'll glimpse its ghostly towers and garrets from several locations in the area.

Strolling south along **Macquarie Street,** an old thoroughfare laid out and named by Governor Macquarie himself, you'll pass many of the historic buildings of Sydney. One of the few elegant century-old town houses left is now the headquarters of the Royal Australian Historical Society. On the eastern side of the street is the **Mitchell Library** (or the State Library of N.S.W., Tel. 21–1388), the center for Australiana research, then **Parliament House.** One wing of this building and part of the next-door **Old Mint** were sections of the famous "Rum Hospital," built from 1811 to 1816 at no charge by three emancipists in exchange for a lucrative license to sell rum. And next door to that is the present **Sydney Hospital,** a late Victorian building. Past the law courts and **Hyde Park Barracks** Macquarie Street ends at **Queens Square.**

Two full blocks of **Hyde Park** are filled with fountains and shady trees. To the east rise the Gothic Revival spires of **St. Mary's Cathedral.** Also bordering the park, just past William Street, is the free **Australian Museum** (Tel. 339–8111), open daily until 5 P.M. Most of the exhibits seemed rather humdrum to us, with the exception of the Aboriginal and South Pacific rooms.

Walk west on Bathurst Street or Park Street to George. The **Town Hall,** flanked by St. Andrew's Cathedral, is one of Sydney's great civic buildings, constructed like many from local sandstone in true Victorian style. In the next block north on George, across from the Hilton, is the recently reburbished façade of the 1893 **Queen Victoria Building,** which creates an entire Byzantine block between Druitt and Market streets.

Near here (at Market and Pitt streets) is the dramatic structure called the **Sydney Tower.** This nine-floor steel basket—sometimes nicknamed the "wine goblet," the "golden pagoda," and other terms by irreverent Sydney-siders—has been jacked up to a height of 1,000 feet and is now the country's tallest structure by far. It costs about $3.50 to take the elevator up, but the view over the entire Sydney region is well worth it. Go through the Centrepoint shopping arcade to find the entrance, then take the elevator to the two observation decks. There are also two restaurants for the public and five floors reserved for telecommunications use (these are not available to sightseers). Weekdays the tower is open until 9:30 P.M. for night viewing. Nobody carrying a camera should miss it, day or night.

Continuing north for a couple of blocks you will arrive at **Martin Place,** a wide thoroughfare now converted to a majestic mall for pedestrians. The large and ornate **General Post Office** is there, an Italianesque creation Australians seem strangely proud of.

Another couple of blocks along Pitt or George streets is the round building incongruously called **Australia Square,** which rises 50 stories above the street. (Don't confuse this with the eight-sided MLC Building.) You can zip up to the deck called the Sky Walk at the top. Until the Sydney tower was built, Australia Square was the place to go for a bird's-eye view.

ELSEWHERE IN SYDNEY

The following are listed in alphabetical order, since it would be impractical to design a tour to encompass them all on a logical circuit.

Southeast of the city, **Bondi Beaches** are the most famous in the area and one of several sites for that strange display of shoreline masculinity called the surf carnival, held in the summertime (December through March). The precision march by lifeguards wearing full bathing attire—including color-coded caps—may seem ridiculous, but the launching of the surf-boat contests is difficult and thrilling. (The lifeguards are also excellent at their job.) If you're not going into the water, have a seat and a drink at the Bondi Hotel. (Bondi—now pronounced "bond-eye," was originally an Aboriginal onomatopoetic word—*"Boondee"*—the sound of a heavy surf breaking on the shore.) It's 25 minutes from Sydney by buses No. 380 and 389, or faster via the new Eastern Suburbs subway to Bondi Junction and thence by bus.

Botany Bay, as we mentioned before, is the site of the international airport. It was also the port of call of James Cook in 1770. Today you can visit the Captain Cook's Landing Place Museum (Tel. 668–9923) here; it's in the park at Kurnell on the southern peninsula, if you want to "have a Captain Cook" yourself. (That's "take a look" in rhyming slang.) Also, there's a fort on Bare Island built during a Russian invasion scare in 1885. You can reach that via the suburbs of Chifley and La Perouse (Bus No. 394).

Back near the city—actually between it and Woolloomooloo—lie the **Domain** and the **Art Gallery.** The grassy common is open to all ("public domain," to be sure), and it's a favorite spot for weekend soap-box orators. Within its green surroundings is the Art Gallery of New South Wales (Tel. 221–2100), which has an excellent collection of late-nineteenth and early-twentieth-century Australian paintings, plus examples of Aboriginal and Melanesian art. It's open daily for a small admission charge. The restaurant is also pleasant.

And while we're thinking about nearby Woolloomooloo for a moment, be prepared for "double-talk" in Australia. The Aussies sometimes seem to bubble with doubles when reciting numbers or letters. Would you believe it's spelled "double-U, double-O, double-L, double-O, M, double-O, L, double-O"? The same goes for phone numbers; thus, 299–2211 becomes "two, double-nine, double-two, double-one." Try to say it any other way, and a telephone operator may correct you!

At the very end of the Domain is Mrs. Macquarie's Chair, an enormous piece of sandstone where the early governor's wife supposedly liked to sit at the end of the three-mile road that also bears her name.

About a quarter mile north of this point, out in the harbor, is **Fort Dennison** (Tel. 2–0545, Ext. 292), more popularly known as Pinchgut Island, supposedly nicknamed in honor of ill-fed convicts who were once confined there. You can visit the island and its little museum, but you must book in advance at the phone number above.

Far across the bay, and accessible by ferry from Jetty No. 5, is **Hunter's Hill,** a mid-nineteenth-century settlement of cottages along a narrow peninsula. The streets are a popular stroll on a sunny Sunday.

At the head of William Street begins the neighborhood of **King's Cross,** which for years has had the reputation of being Sydney's Greenwich Village (or Sydney's Soho, if London is the city of comparison). Much of it is, indeed, Sydney on the seamy side. Here are the strippers, the female impersonators, and the like. Ruth Park's poetic description of the Cross is unsurpassed:

"It is a weird, electric place by night, exorbitant, often as bent as a bicycle wheel, offering venal and dubious pleasures as well as four-cornered ones. It swims out of the dusk like a blob of spilled oil, all rainbow and reflections, and gamesome groups of middle-aged tourists, noosed with cameras and excitedly speculating whether the epicene youth in an exoskeleton of painted leather is a drug pusher.

"Upon these aliens, the austerely clad old voluptuary spidering in the coffee bar smiles his abstracted scholar's smile; the adolescent prostitute heaves up her Luxaflex eyelashes and looks right through them. The boy sitting on his kidneys beside the El Alamein Fountain, soaked with the spray, does not even glance their way as they boldly shoot off their flashes and take his picture for a souvenir."

The Cross also has many good restaurants and an often interesting night life, and it is a pleasant walk by day, too. At night, keep to the main, well-lighted drag. (There are several buses from the Quay to the Cross, including Numbers 311, 312, 324, and 325.)

The former working-class suburb of **Paddington** ("Paddo," in local parlance), south of King's Cross, has become the height of fashionability in the 1980s with the revival of the "terrace houses" with their wonderfully intricate and lacy wrought-iron balconies. The streets now host little art galleries, coffee bars, and specialty shops, and the atmosphere is somewhat similar to Washington's Georgetown. Also in Paddington is the 1841 Victoria Barracks (Tel. 31–0455, Ext. 517), on Oxford Street, where the public watches the changing of the guard at 11 A.M. on Tuesdays. (Buses 379 and 380.)

Southwest of the city, where Broadway becomes the Parramatta Road, is **Sydney University.** Busily sculpted in Gothic Revival style, the university buildings were begun in 1854. The ornate sandstone docs provide a welcome relief from the miles and miles of monotonous bungalows that otherwise pave the precinct. Two free museums there are popular browsing spots on rainy days.

You'll take a delightful 15-minute ferry ride from Circular Quay to get to the **Taronga Park Zoo** (Tel. 969–2777), but be prepared for lots of walking on hilly pathways. In fact, after your boat docks be sure to climb on the waiting bus (No. 237 or 238) to the *uphill* zoo entrance to allow you to accept the aid, not the hindrance, of gravity while wending your way down to the lower entrance/exit near the dock. Nearly 100 years old, the zoo is about the only dependable location for seeing many of Australia's animals. Even if your itinerary will take you deep into the bush, there are birds and beasties at the zoo that you probably won't see in the wild.

There's a special koala enclosure, a Platypus House (open daily only between 11 and 12 and 2 and 3—and this could be your lifetime chance to catch the creature in action), and the Animals of the Night exhibit (where day and night are switched for Australian nocturnals; it's only open from 10 to 4). Also, don't miss the Rain Forest Aviary, where you walk in the cage with the birds. The main part of the zoo is open from 9:30 A.M. to 5:00 P.M. and costs about $5. There's an all-inclusive excursion rate (perhaps $8) that throws in the ferry and the bus. In our book, the Taronga Zoo and its delightful inhabitants are personal prerequisites for Australian Animal Appreciation 101.

Far out toward the ocean, past Rose Bay to Vaucluse, is **Vaucluse House** (Tel. 337–1957), the home of William C. Wentworth (1790–1872), the first Australian-born citizen to achieve high political office. The colony's first constitution was drawn up in the house of this patriot and explorer. It's an ideal example of colonial architecture and a pleasant site maintained by the N.S.W. National Parks and Wildlife Service. *Hint:* There's a 50-cent booklet sold at the door; buy it *before* you go in so that you can read about the significance of the rooms and furnishings. (Open daily until 4 P.M.; take Bus No. 327.)

A little past Vaucluse is **Watson's Bay,** an attractive body of water that boasts the Macquarie Lighthouse, designed by the prolific Francis Greenway in 1816. (It was destroyed and then rebuilt in 1883.) Also nearby is the anchor from the *Dunbar,* which was wrecked spectacularly here. Have a look at the sheer cliffs of The Gap, which the ship's captain mistook for Sydney Heads on that fateful night in 1857 (see chapter 4).

NEW SOUTH WALES

Again in alphabetical order, here are a half-dozen sites of historic or scenic interest around the state. (The Snowy Mountains, though part of N.S.W., we'll cover in our Canberra chapter.)

The Blue Mountains. They really are blue, too, due to a thick distance haze caused by oil evaporating from the milliards of eucalyptus leaves and the refraction of light through it. The popular recreation area, about 60 miles from Sydney, includes the resort towns of Katoomba (where you can see the Three Sisters rock formation from an aerial cable car, Tel. 047 + 82–2699), Leura, Blackheath, and Wentworth Falls. (For local atmosphere, stay in the Carrington Hotel in Katoomba or the palatial Hydro-Majestic in Medlow Bath. And don't miss the historic Paragon Restaurant in Katoomba.) By train the once-impenetrable Blue Mountains can be reached in a little over two hours for about $8.

Dubbo is a busy city of 21,000 on the Macquarie River, 200 miles northwest of Sydney, and a popular air excursion from the state capital. There visitors see sheepshearing demonstrations and visit the Western Plains Zoo. The town is also proud of the local jail, now restored as a tourist attraction. (It costs 50 cents to get in.)

Hunter Valley. This is the wine-making district near the town of Pokolbin about 120 miles north of Sydney. You can tour the wineries, including Tyrrell's, Lindeman's, Penfolds, Hungerford Hill, Rothbury Estate, etc. Tastings are included, of course. A recommended lunchtime restaurant in Pokolbin is The Cellar. An interesting hotel in nearby Cessnock is the Bellbird, furnished with Australian antiques. Sylvester Bakery is famous for its damper bread.

Incidentally, the wine country is also the beginning of Australian coal country. If you drive up the road to Mount Wingen, you can see the smoke from "Burning Mountain," an underground coal fire that has been burning steadily out of control for thousands of years.

Lightning Ridge, of course, is the home of the world-famous black opal, 475 miles northwest of Sydney. You can inspect a "walk-in" mine, watch the opal polishers, or even arrange to "fossick" for gems yourself in some of the old mullock heaps. Better not buy an opal from someone on the street, however. In theory, you can get a good bargain from some down-on-his-luck miner. But recently thin slices of black opal were being mounted behind a convex crystal and being returned to Lightning Ridge where unscrupulous types would sell them as solid opals, a difference between a product worth $5 and one worth $50. Buy opals, and any other gems, only from established dealers, and you'll still get a good price. (The Mine and Spectrum are good bets.) We've always wanted to try the Tramway Hotel in Lightning Ridge, made by a man named Harold Hodges from a series of old Sydney trolleys. (A set of Hodges's teeth, a bite of solid opal, are on display at the Diggers Rest Hotel in Lightning Ridge.) The Wallangulla Hotel also has a good reputation as a place to stay for about $40 for twins. All in all, Lightning Ridge is only about $175 round trip from Sydney, and it's a good way to see something of the closer-in Outback.

Old Sydney Town (Tel. 043 + 40–1104), near Gosford, is one of the most intriguing ideas in theme parks we've seen. In a natural setting very much like that of Sydney in the early nineteenth century, a period that predates any building existing in the real Sydney today, they have tried to re-create the colony as it was about 1810—the "pre-Macquarie" period.

Authentic construction methods and materials were used, and the towns-people—convicts and free settlers—are all in costume. There's an all-inclusive train/bus/admission ticket, or you can drive to the location about 54 miles up the Newcastle Expressway (take the Gosford exit). Admission at the gate is about $6. Unfortunately, O.S.T. has been having a tough time of it financially, and we wonder if it will continue to be viable in the years ahead. (Recheck at the tourist office before going.)

Parramatta was founded in 1788, 15 miles inland, less than a year after Sydney. It was once slated to be the state capital. The most interesting building is the Elizabeth Farm House, built by John Macarthur, whose face is on the $2 bill. Old Government House (Tel. 635–8149), Lancer Barracks, and St. Johns church are also traditional sights in Parramatta.

7. Guided Tours and Cruises

If we look on bus tours with a jaundiced eye in other areas of the world, we view them much more kindly in Australia. Reason: This is simply a delightful way to meet the Aussies themselves.

Your fellow passengers will usually not be merely a group of other foreigners. Australians are heavy travelers around their own country, and the friendly folk you meet on a bus tour in Sydney might be from Melbourne, Adelaide, Perth, or some other city, large or small. And if their hometown is on your later itinerary, well, you just might make some new friends to look up when you get there. (No promises, of course!)

Short bus tours, naturally enough, are not nearly as merry as longer ones. The driver and the passengers can't get to know each other very well in two or three hours. An all-day excursion, or one that includes a meal, is generally the best deal—and the most fun.

Some of these trips will be operated daily, others only from Monday to Friday, so you'd better check on the scene. If your travel agency hasn't already booked them, you can reserve any seats at the New South Wales Government Travel Centre (Tel. 231–4444), 16 Spring St., Sydney, N.S.W. 2000, or at any of their other locations. Several guided day tours leave from Circular Quay West. With the exception of the Sydney Explorer, these tours will be operated by several different companies, including Ansett Pioneer, AAT, Australian Pacific Tours, and Deane's Clipper Tours. We haven't tried to explain which company runs which; those plans change almost monthly. The fares listed below are approximate and are listed for comparison purposes only.

Note: In Australia many tours do not pick you up at hotels, unless you are part of a large group. Generally you have to meet at the point from which the bus departs. Be sure to find out from the operator just exactly when to be where in order to catch your tour.

BUS (COACH) TOURS

The Sydney Explorer. An excellent excursion run by the N.S.W. Government Travel Centre. Bright red buses leave every 15 minutes through the day to cover a couple of dozen points of interest on a 10-mile route. Buy a daily pass for about $7 or $8, and you can step off the bus and back on the next one whenever it's convenient.

Sydney Opera House, The Rocks, and the Inner City. 3½ hours, usually in the morning. About $15.

Sydney and the Southern Beaches. 3 hours, usually in the afternoon. About $13.

Sydney in a Day (includes the Captain Cook luncheon cruise). 8 hours. About $38.

North Shore Suburbs, Manly, and the Beaches. 3 hours, usually in the morning. About $16.

Sydney by Night (usually includes dinner and floor shows, but recheck). 5½ hours. About $52.

Parramatta, Katoomba, and the Blue Mountains. 7½ hours. About $23.

Hawkesbury River, Koala Park, and Pittwater. 7½ hours. About $21.

Hunter Valley Wine Tasting Tour. Saturdays (or in some cases Sundays) only. 11 hours. About $32.

Bush Barbecue. Sheepshearing demonstrations, etc., and visits to Woolongong, Berrima, Bowral, and Moss Vale, including lunch. 9 hours. About $37.

AIR TOURS

A helicopter operation called **Heli-Aust** (Tel. 267–6262) has been launched in the Sydney area. We know little about it, but it looks like fun. It lists tours from a $25-per-seat overview of the harbor and city center on up to $80 or so covering a much wider area.

Jolly Swagman Tours. There are several operated by Air New South Wales (Tel. 268–1893), and for most you'll have to get up before dawn. One is the *Jolly Swagman to Dubbo,* a 14½-hour tour for about $250 that includes rural activities like sheepshearing, a sheep-dog demonstration, boomerang throwing, barbecue lunch, and a visit to the zoo and the historic old jail. We rather enjoyed the trip, but suggest it could be more fun with a large gregarious group rather than the few along on our wintertime visit. There is also a lesser-known *Jolly Swagman to Lightning*

Ridge. This 11-hour, single-day trip costs about $200, but may be available to groups only. Other trips last two, three, or four days.

CRUISES ON SYDNEY HARBOUR

It sounds clichéd, but it's true: No visit to Sydney is complete without getting out on the waters of Port Jackson at least once, even if it's only taking the ferry to the zoo or the hydrofoil to Manly. In addition to these, we also enjoyed the **Captain Cook Cruises** (Tel. 27–4416). We sailed on the 2½-hour *Coffee Cruise* (adults $14, children $12), and were amazed at how well our attractive, red-uniformed leader knew her harbor lore. There is also a 1½-hour *Luncheon River Cruise* (about $16, including lunch), which explores narrower areas farther up the estuary. A shorter *Sydney Harbour Budget Cruise* lasts an hour and costs about $8. And dinner cruises with a live band and dancing are offered for around $35 aboard the **John Cadman Cruising Restaurant,** now also operated by the folks at Captain Cook. All except perhaps the dinner cruise depart from Pier 6, Circular Quay. (Call the above number to reserve or use the aforementioned N.S.W. Government Travel Centre, Tel. 231–4444.) If you go, let us know.

And the **Urban Transit Authority** (Tel. 290–2988) has set up some attractive-looking 2½-hour harbor and river cruises on certain restricted days, all still around $5 at this writing. Bookings are not necessary, but you'd better call to see from which slip and exactly what time they leave for where.

8. Water Sports

Sydney is for swimming and for surfing, and that's a fact that has become known among the outdoor brotherhood in Hawaii, California, and South Africa. The beaches are divided into "Northern," from Manly to Palm Beach, and "Southern," from Bondi to Cronulla. The opening at Sydney Heads provides the dividing line between the two areas.

Unless you're driving, the **Northern Beaches** are best reached by ferry from Sydney to Manly and thence by bus to other beaches. The beaches (going north) include Manly's Ocean Beach, one of the world's best for surfing; Harbord, favored by body surfers; Curl Curl, good for the youngsters; Dee Why, also a good surfing beach; and Collaroy, now being spoiled by sea erosion. One small nude swimming area near Manly is called Reef Beach.

The **Southern Beaches,** between Bondi and Malabar, anyway, are better established than any north of the Heads except Manly itself. In fact, Bondi, Bronte, and Coogee on the southern coast have been famous for

100 years. You can travel by bus to these magnificent strips of sand. When the big-name strands are overcrowded, look for smaller beaches like Tamarama, Clovelly, and Malabar. There is a beach in the buff on the southern shore, too. That's Lady Jane Beach, near Watkins Bay.

Sharks? There certainly are some, especially between December and February. And in the same way that visitors to San Francisco are afraid of earthquakes, it may not help much to know that your chances of being struck by a shark in Sydney are one in a million.

Where sharks are most likely to appear, such as in the calm waters of Port Jackson, there are metal nets to protect the swimming areas. Along the ocean beaches there are shark patrols by helicopter and by land observers. When a shark is spotted, everyone is quickly shooed out of the water. Then boats close in on the "nasty brute," relentlessly pursuing it until it is killed or driven far away. On no account—never-ever—enter the water anyplace other than a designated, guarded official swimming area!

More likely dangers at the beach would be the occasional riptides, but then the highly trained lifeguards are ready for those. Perhaps no beaches in the world are guarded better than those of Australia. And last, watch out for the sun. Somehow it seems to burn more quickly and more severely Down Under than it does many other places in the world.

For most of us, **yachting** is more a spectator sport than one in which we can readily join. The sailboat season in New South Wales starts in September and ends in May, with races and regattas held on the harbor nearly every weekend. Some like to watch the 18-footer races while taking the ferryboat to Manly and back.

The best **deep-sea fishing** is not in New South Wales but in northern Queensland (see last chapter). One popular site in the state, however, is at Coffs Harbour, about 360 miles north of Sydney, where Spanish mackerel and occasionally marlin are taken. Other fishing sites include Port Stephens (marlin from January to March) and Lord Howe Island, if you want to call that dot 325 miles out in the ocean part of N.S.W. Supposedly some of the country's best fishing is there, with dozens of denizens of the deep practically yours for the asking.

9. Other Sports

Perhaps no people in the world are more sports-crazy than the Australians. Indeed, they are often criticized for this love, usually by visiting English writers who express scant appreciation for the influence of a beautiful outdoor climate that fosters more athletic activities than it does cold cultural pursuits like reading and the enjoyment of classical music.

SPECTATOR SPORTS

Australians have two big seasons, cricket in the summer and football in the winter. There are four types of football, all of which are faster-moving than the American version. Play is continuous and there are no substitutions.

Football. The two kinds far preferred in New South Wales (and Queensland) are Rugby League and Rugby Union. Union (sometimes called "rugger") is the older, dating from 1864. It is played with 15 men on a side and is strictly an amateur sport.

League dates from 1907 and is a professional spin-off from Union, with only 13 men per team and a few more rule changes. Rugby League is the big sport in this part of the country from about March to September. Although invented in Australia, League is also played in England, France, New Zealand, and South Africa, so teams from these countries often come to give an international flavor to the sport. (However the famed New Zealand All-Blacks are a Union team, so they play the amateur Wallabies in Australia rather than the professional Kangaroos.)

In Sydney, Rugby League can be seen at the Sydney Sports Ground at Moore Park (south of Paddington) or at Redfern Oval in South Sydney.

Soccer. The game has been widely promoted by Australia's recent British and European immigrants and is gaining ground all over the country. It is sometimes called "Association Football." There are 11 on a side, and each team tries to kick or "head" a ball through the opposing goal. Unlike other forms of football, no hands are used. You might catch a soccer match at Marks Field.

Australian Rules football is a big Victoria/South Australia game. Although it is sometimes played in Sydney, too, Sydney-siders will likely put it down in some way. Anyway, we cover it in section 9 of our Melbourne chapter.

The summer activity is **cricket,** played from October through February all over the country. If the crowds seem smaller, it's only because it must compete with the siren calls of the beaches on the weekends. Australian state teams compete for the Sheffield Shield (one home game, one away game for each team). Each of those matches is four days long, usually starting on a Friday or Saturday. Later, England and Australia compete for the coveted trophy called The Ashes in a series of five matches. International games in either cricket or rugby are generally called "test matches."

Cricket in Australia dates back to the earliest days of the colony. It involves bowlers and batsmen, attempts by the bowler to propel a ball at—and to knock down—one of two wickets, and attempts by a batsman to keep that from happening. There are many refinements to the game, all of which are mysterious to nonplayers. In Australia, as in England, the importance of cricket is thought to be much beyond that of a game. It is considered an important factor in the development of good character and is an integral part of a child's schooling. (Schoolchildren also have national and international contests in cricket.)

You may catch this gentlemen's game in Sydney at the Sydney Cricket Ground in Moore Park. If you want to make sure you get a seat at a test match, contact the N.S.W. Cricket Association, 55 George St., Sydney 2000.

Some would say that although every Australian male is a football and cricket fan, his absolute passion is **horse racing.** In truth, it may be much more the gambling instinct that attracts the Aussies to the nags. (Australians are said to love betting on anything, even two flies climbing up a wall.) During the running of the Melbourne Cup, the first Tuesday of November, practically the entire country comes to a halt while the race is run, the citizens glued to radios or televisions.

The Australian satirical poet Alec Derwent Hope once addressed this equestrian obsession in some witty lines that recall a popular assertion that Gulliver's mythical travels took him to a modern Australia:

Far in the South, beyond the burning line,
Where Gulliver, that much-wrecked mariner,
Described their customs, such as they then were,
And found them, like their manners, somewhat coarse,
The yahoos live in slavery to the horse . . .
A sort of costive English, too, they speak,
And sweat and drink and quarrel round the week;
And what they earn in their own time, they spend
On their four-footed masters each week-end.

All over Australia you can bet on the ponies without going out to the track, quite legally, at the special shops labeled T.A.B. In Sydney, if you want to experience the roar of the horseflesh and the smell of the mob, you can go out during the week to Randwick Racecourse on Alison Road in Randwick or the Rosehill Racecourse on Aston Street in Rosehill. (Take the Carlingford or Sandown train.) Others holding races on Saturdays and holidays include the Canterbury Park Racecourse on King Street in Canterbury and the Warwick Farm Racecourse on Hume Highway at Warwick Farm. (Several trains run on race days.)

Greyhound racing is also becoming popular. You go to the dogs in Sydney at Glebe—either at Harold Park on Minogue Crescent (Bus 433) or Wentworth Park on the Wentworth Park Road nearby.

PARTICIPATION SPORTS

Some may think the Australians invented **tennis** because of the championship players that have come up from Down Under to win big tournaments all over the world. In fact spectator tennis has sparked interest in playing tennis among all Australians, both on paved courts and on grass. You'll find "hard courts" at Moore Park, Prince Alfred Park, Rushcutters Bay, and White City. If you want to find some courts in your neighborhood, call or visit the N.S.W. Lawn Tennis Association (Tel. 31–7144), 30 Alma St., Paddington 2021. Also, have a look in the Yellow Pages under the category "Tennis Courts for Hire." You'll find lots in every city.

Golf courses in Australia are often on private clubs and not generally open to the public. However, if you are introduced by a member, or perhaps even can prove you are a member of a similar golf club in another country, you may be admitted. Greens fees are around $7, and club rental is about the same.

One good 18-hole public course in Sydney is the **Lakes Golf Club** (Tel. 669–1311), King Street, East Mascot 2020. The top course, however, is the **Royal Sydney** (Tel. 371–4333), which overlooks the harbor at Rose Bay. Unfortunately it's terribly exclusive. You might have better luck at the **Australian Golf Club** (Tel. 663–2273) in Kensington or the beautiful **N.S.W. Golf Club** (Tel. 661–4455), a magnificent site on Botany Bay at Matraville.

Australia's biggest participant sport is **lawn bowling,** which doesn't come as naturally to much of the rest of the world. If you're into this sport, however, you'll get a friendly reception at the Royal N.S.W. Bowling Association (Tel. 29–2475), 95 York St., Sydney.

Running is Australia's newest sport, in common with many other countries. The big event is the August "City-to-Surf" fun run over nine miles from Sydney to Bondi.

Snow skiing is big during the winter. Although the best resorts are officially in New South Wales, they're closer to Canberra and the A.C.T., so we report on the *schussing* scene in the next chapter.

10. Shopping in Sydney

Sydney has the smart shops and clever emporia of all types that you would expect in any of the world's major cities, plus the added accents provided by things specifically antipodean like Aboriginal "X-ray" artworks, Australian gemstones, wool products, and so forth.

Here are some of the things you might look for in Sydney:

Aboriginal arts and crafts. You can buy boomerangs at any price from one dollar on up, depending on wood, decoration, etc. Didjeridoos, those one-note droners, are from $10 or so for small ones up to about $500 for the deep-throat monsters. Spears run from a short $10 up to a long $40. Woomeras, a type of Aboriginal throwing stick, begin at about $8, and woven baskets and mats cost $15 to $50. The best watercolors in the Namatjira style run from around $100 to $200. Other Aboriginal creations range from simple bark paintings at around $15 on up to large works sold for $100.

Australian paintings. You can get mass-produced oils of Ayers Rock, the opera house, etc., starting from around $20 (try the store at 163 King St.), but no really good works for less than $75, and they're more likely to average around $200.

Here is a list of commercial galleries, some offering works by contemporary Australian artists, others specializing in Aboriginal art, and several displaying both. Many of these grace the fashionable Paddington neighborhood: **Hogarth Galleries** (Tel. 357–6839, also known as the Gallery of Dreams), 7 Walker Lane, Paddington, shows largely Aboriginal work from all over the nation. The **Collectors Gallery of Aboriginal Art,** 40 Harrington St., near The Rocks, and **Barry Stern,** 19 Glenmore Rd., Paddington, both have extensive collections of Australian art. **Artarmon Galleries,** 479 Pacific Highway, Artarmon, has realistic Australian works. **Macquarie Galleries,** 204 Clarence St., is one of the best-known galleries for Australian artwork, and the **Holdsworth Galleries** (Tel. 32–1364) has new exhibitions by well-known Australian artists every three weeks at 86 Holdsworth St. in Woollahra.

Ceramics. Some of these are of Aboriginal themes, but not made by Aborigines. Others are just Australian art in their own right. Prices range from $2 for a small pot up to nearly $1,000 for sculptured Australian pottery. We found some of the inexpensive ones to be good last-minute gifts sold at the airport. (You'll pay more out there, though.)

Leather goods. Look for wallets at $10 and up or handbags at $50. Jackets zip up to more than $100, now, with coats over $150. The department stores may be your best bets.

Opals and gemstones. Don't just go out and buy an opal. Look in several stores first and talk to the salespeople about the product. There are two main types mined in Australia—"white" opals and the more valuable "black" opal. Of course neither is really white or black, but the white opals seem to have their vivid blues and greens splashed over and through a sort of milky background. Black opals flash fiery reds and yellows and even dark greens and violets on a natural black background.

You can invest in solid opals, or for much less money you can buy thin slivers made into doublets (a layer of opal attached to a special backing) or triplets (the same as a doublet but with a clear crystal dome fastened above it to protect the opal and slightly magnify the color patterns). Opal products are sold at almost any price from about $5 for a key ring on up to hundreds of dollars for the very best mounted stones. But you may get a very nice triplet ring for $50 or so.

Some reliable stores for buying opals and other jewels include **Percy Marks** (Tel. 233–1355), 79 Castlereagh St., **Flame Opals** (Tel. 27–3446), 119 George St., near Circular Quay, **Gemtec Australia** (Tel. 267–7939), 250 Pitt St., and **Allison's Opals** (Tel. 267–7133), 15 Park St.

Skin products. Most of these items are made either from sheepskin or kangaroo skin. (Stuffed koala toys use kangaroo skin, generally, because koalas are a protected species.) Sheepskin rugs are a soft, fuzzy bargain from around $35 on up to $75. Sheepskin seat covers for your car are another good idea. They keep you warm in the winter and cool in the summer. Some drivers like the steering-wheel covers, too. You may get the best bargain on either at a good hardware store. (Try **B.B.C. Hardware,** 422 George St.)

Coats will run $200 to $400, slippers from $25 to $30, and the stuffed toys (kangaroos, koalas, lambs, rabbits, etc.) from $15 to $50, depending on their sizes. Try **The Sheepskin Shop** (Tel. 27–1599) at 139 George St. in The Rocks.

Souvenirs in general. Besides the other categories mentioned here, there are things like small silver souvenir spoons from around $10, pressed wildflower pictures for about $10, and cork table mats with Australian scenes for perhaps $19.95 for a set of six.

Some general souvenir shops in the center of the city include **The Koala Bear Shop** (Tel. 267–3187), 133 Castlereagh St., and the **Koala Center** in the Tank Stream Arcade. Souvenirs and jewelry are sold at **Prouds** (Tel. 233–4488) at the corner of Pitt and King streets. For some offbeat objects try **Christies** (Tel. 264–6751) at 248 Pitt St. They have strange T-shirts and obscure military insignia.

Wool products. Besides the aforementioned sheepskin rugs, there are many finished wool items that are less expensive and better made in Australia than what you're likely to find at home. Cardigans and other sweaters may run $25 and up. You may find some hand-spun pullovers for $60 or so. Wool blankets could cost about half what you'd expect to pay in the U.S.

Shop hours. Visitors to Australia have an easier time making the rounds of the stores than Australians on the job, due to the generally repressive shopping hours. Throughout the country businesses are usually open from 8:30 to 5:30, Monday through Friday, and from 8:30 to 4:00 on Saturdays, with one late night per week—on Thursday in Sydney the shops stay open until 9:00 P.M. Recently some merchants in Sydney began challenging the closing-hours law and staying open until 5:00 P.M. on Saturdays, creating quite a furor. It looks now like the state law will be changed to allow those late closings. On Sundays, forget it! They roll up the footpaths all over the country, and only a very few specialty places are allowed to keep their doors open.

Department stores. The largest in Sydney is **David Jones,** with entrances on Elizabeth, Market, and Castlereagh streets and a branch at George and Barrack, followed closely by **Grace Brothers** with entrances on Pitt, Market, and George streets. Both are worth a big browse and offer a surprising variety of goods, generally well displayed. (We've seen Aboriginal art at David Jones for lower prices than in Aboriginal country at Alice Springs, although the selection was more limited.)

Other department stores (Aussies say "departmental," by the way) include **Winns,** Oxford and Riley streets, and **Waltons,** 2 Park St. at George.

Shopping arcades. Melbourne might claim the ancestorship of Australian shopping arcades, but Sydney has taken the concept into the twentieth century—tunneling, twisting, and turning through the commercial blocks with modernistic gusto. A good example is the superslick **MLC Centre,** which burrows a modern route under the octagonal skyscraper between King Street and Martin Place. Besides its chrome- and mirror-lined shops, it features an unusual circular fountain. (You can walk to its center and never get wet.)

Another is **Centrepoint,** where there are at least 200 shops in the four levels under the pedestal to the dramatic Sydney Tower. With its bridges and tunnels, it connects the Grace Brothers and David Jones department stores, too. The **Royal Arcade,** underneath the Hilton, is also popular.

But a beautiful refurbishment of an old Victorian shopping complex is the 1883 **Strand Arcade,** lined with wrought iron and polished mahogany. The narrow, four-floor balconied passageway runs between George and Pitt streets (No. 193 Pitt is the official address) in the block bounded by Market and King. You can miss it, so do search it out. It's a minor masterpiece from an architectural viewpoint, anyway, but don't lean on the railings!

Another unusual set of shops is the **Argyle Arts Centre** at 18 Argyle St. in the historic Rocks district under the approaches to the Sydney Harbour Bridge. The complex winds around a series of 1829 warehouses, which may have been dreary a century and a half ago, but today seem to possess a genuine, old-world charm. In the Centre, a pleasant stop is the **Argyle Opal and Gem Centre** (Tel. 27–9125), where A. C. Geary is knowledgeable and helpful on the subject of opals—even if you don't buy. He also sells a few nice souvenir minerals with several kinds of rocks fastened on a souvenir card for $5 or so.

While we're considering the Rocks area, there is an attractive souvenir shop across the courtyard from the Argyle Centre. That's the **Voyagers Cottage,** and it's actually at 25 Playfair St. Not far away is a somewhat famous address for malacologists—Lance Moore's **Marine Specimens** (Tel. 27–7357) at 27-A George St. It's also known as "The Shell Shop," but they have more than that, branching out into mounted butterflies, minerals, etc. And at 81½ George St., across from Cadman's Cottage, is **Left-Handed Products** (Tel. 27–3674), a special store for southpaws. **Australian Craftworks** sells pottery, jewelry, wood, leather, and other goods from its address in an old police station and jail at 127 George St. And a short stroll away from The Rocks look for **Pier One,** a complex of specialty shops and restaurants in an old wharf. It's especially crowded on weekends.

Boutiques at Double Bay. Some call Double Bay "Double Pay," but be that as it may these are the smart, exclusive shops in a suburb about five miles to the east of Sydney, for—as our friend Alexandra Piechowiak puts it—"all the Guccis and the Puccis." A few samples: **Gianni Boutique** (Tel. 327–6687), 27 Knox St., specializes in imported shoes, some designed for them especially. **Courrèges,** (Tel. 32–0215), Bay Village, 28 Cross St., is the only Courrèges boutique in Australia. And **Michal** (Tel. 328–6355), 12 Cross St., stocks exclusive jewelry designs.

Men's wear. You can be outfitted well at the department stores, of course. But sartorial-minded blokes who want top fashion may head for either **Richard's** at 41 Castlereagh St. or **Richard Hunt,** 107 Pitt St.

Dime stores. Of course there are no "dimes" in Australia, but the local equivalent to *our* Woolworth's is *their* **Woolworth's.** The main store is at 320 George St., opposite Town Hall. (There's no connection, incidentally, between the Yank and the Aussie "Woolies.") **Coles** is another chain with similar goods all over the country.

Bookstores. Considering that Australians are supposedly always at the beach, in the pubs, or glued to the telly, Sydney has an amazing number of bookstores racking up a large number of sales. At least three should not be missed. **Angus and Robertson Bookshops** (Tel. 265–1188), 168 Pitt St. (down below the Imperial Arcade) and R27, MLC Centre, Martin Place, generally has a good stock. One of a smaller national chain is the **Mary Martin Bookshop** at 47 York St. And for concentrated Australiana, try **Henry Lawson's Bookshop** (Tel. 267–1487), 127 York St., named in honor of Australia's best-known writer. At some bookstore, incidentally, you should pick up a good map of Sydney for finding your way around the city. One of the best we've seen is Gregory's City of Sydney, Map No. 11 (about a dollar). For maps of an earlier day, look into **Antiquarian Maps and Prints** (Tel. 31–2745) at 247 Victoria St., Darlinghurst. And here's a hint for obtaining extremely inexpensive Australian publications produced by the Australian Government Publishing Service: Buy them over the counter at the **AGPS Bookshop** at 309 Pitt St. Most of these, of course, are of dull reports and the like. But there are some good maps and a few beautiful pamphlets on Australian nature, history, etc., in full color, and at a fraction of the price you'd expect to pay.

Duty-free shops. We're not very impressed with the many special duty-free shops. If you know the product you're interested in, how much it costs at home, etc., then have a look in a duty-free shop. (You can only order things for planeside delivery if you have a ticket out of the country.) You'll probably find that booze is your best buy.

A last thought: The local equivalent of the flea market is **Paddy's Market** on Hay Street, featuring hundreds of stalls and carts selling anything you can imagine, and lots that you can't. It's an ideal Saturday excursion (open from 7:00 to 4:30, and to perhaps 9:00 P.M. on Thursday).

11. Entertainment and Night Life

With its beautiful opera house, a healthy number of theaters, and a multitude of discos, Sydney is certainly Australia's entertainment capital.

On some street corners, weather permitting, you'll find the "buskers"—musicians, jugglers, and other performers doing their thing for whatever passersby will throw in their hats or violin cases. Free outdoor concerts may also be enjoyed, notably those given weekdays from 12 to 2 P.M. in Martin Place.

In the evening the action shifts to a few downtown theaters as well as up to King's Cross, of course. Neither qualifies as an antipodean Las Vegas; nevertheless, the after-dark scene in Sydney is certainly a few shades brighter than, say, Wagga Wagga, Murrumburah, or Dunedoo.

Nightclubs. There are few in the traditional sense. The most ambitious of the genus is probably **Bull 'n' Bush** (Tel. 357–4627), now in new and better quarters at 113 William St.

Similarly, the **Town & Country Dance Hall** (Tel. 358–1211) swings in that burgeoning entertainment complex at the Texas Tavern Hotel.

But much of the action in Sydney actually takes place at the **private social clubs,** sometimes known as "leagues clubs" or "sports clubs." There are dozens upon dozens of these, all supposedly open to members only. Most you can hardly call "exclusive"; they may have an active roster of more than 50,000! They are generally joined only by men, incidentally. Women are admitted as wives or girl friends of members. These clubs are supported not by dues, but by the earnings of their own poker (slot) machines, which, under N.S.W. law, may be installed on such premises. That painless Down Under Way of building an opera house has thus been successfully transferred to keeping the clubs solvent, too!

Several social clubs are more than happy to welcome overseas travelers as "complimentary" members. Just take your passport to the door and you'll get in for a fair admission charge. A good one for that is the **Mandarin** (Tel. 211–3866) downtown at 396 Pitt St., not to be confused with the restaurant by the same name (although the Mandarin Club also reportedly sells delicious and cheap Chinese meals, we haven't sat down there yet ourselves). There's generally a good cabaret show and dancing— besides that wonderful opportunity to help finance the club treasury while exercising your biceps at the same time. The one-arm bandits, by the way, show poker hands instead of oranges, lemons, bells, and the like.

You may hear a lot about the **N.S.W. Leagues Club,** 165 Philip St., but we call it one of those for the local "rugby, racing, and beer" set, interesting perhaps only sociologically. The **St. George League's Club** (Tel. 587–1022), on the other hand, welcomes foreigners with open cash drawers. It's at 124 Princess Highway in Kogarah. You might catch a topflight comedian there, and it may feature a full-length musical comedy extravaganza on other occasions.

When name entertainers come to town, it is often the social clubs who can afford to hire them. Otherwise they must attract a sizable audience to a large hall, something that hardly exists anymore. The opera house's Concert Hall seats only 2,600. When Bob Hope came to town, he performed again in the barnlike **Anthony Hordern Pavilion** (Tel. 33–3769), which he dubbed "Sydney's Garage." (Hope and Australia have a genuine affinity for one another, however, which dates back to World War II.) Until recently the Hordern Pavilion also hosted all the big indoor rock concerts in Sydney. But now the **Sydney Entertainment Centre** (Tel. 212–4100) has opened on Harbour Street in Chinatown. It seats up to 12,000, but take your binoculars.

Discotheques and rock clubs. The disco scene is alive and well in Sydney, although the choices are smaller than in some major cities—due partly, at least, to the proliferation of the social clubs. By the way, many discos are not true to the original definition, often bringing in live bands and singers drawn from Australia's large stable of rock performers or visiting artists.

One of the city's premier sites for Monday-to-Saturday-night fever is **Juliana's** at the Sydney Hilton, associated with the famous Juliana's of London. Other popular discos include **Arthur's,** a polka-dotted dive Up the Cross, **Williams** in the Boulevard Hotel on Williams Street, **Tivoli,** 652 George St., the **Cauldron,** 207 Darlinghurst Rd., **Jamison Street,** 11 Jamison St., and **Sheila's,** 77 Berry St. in North Sydney.

Notable Australian pop/rock groups currently on the charts include the following, some of whom are also well known to American music fans: Men at Work, Midnight Oil, the Little River Band, InXs (pronounced "in excess"), Moving Pictures, the Angels, Mental as Anything,

the Divinyls, Jimmy Barnes' Band, Goanna, Moving Pictures, Kids in the Kitchen, and Dragon. (Air Supply has permanently moved to the U.S.A.)

Jazz. Jazz has been gaining in popularity in Sydney the past few years. Look for some of the best in modest restaurants like **The Basement,** 29 Reiby Place, near Circular Quay, or the **Rocks Push,** 109 George St. in The Rocks.

Three cheers for beer! Before an idealized pub crawl, we should address Australian beer as the Australian does—very seriously. A marvelous, frothy, honey-silk brew, it's a delicious fluid we've had nowhere else. And Australia is somewhere between the third and the fifth biggest beer-drinking country in the world on a per-capita basis. (The U.S.A. is about twelfth.)

The nation has two dozen breweries, which produce more than brands of beer. To avoid argument, you'd better drink a beer of region you happen to be in at the moment. Most Aussie beers are r lagers, by the way, even though some may be called "ale" or "bitter

Sydney's many beers are brewed by two corporations with si names—Toohey's and Tooth's. Among the Toohey entries are Stag (its best), Pilsener, New Special Draught, Hunter Ale (the coal m favorite, also called Toohey's Old), a dark beer named Flag Ale Miller's Oatmeal Stout. Tooth's has Resch's KB (Sydney's best s Resch's D.A. (Dinner Ale, which we like better), XXX (prono "Three-X"), Special New, and a genuinely bitter Tooth's Sheaf S

Besides these traditional favorites, there are now a proliferating ber of "light" beers in Australia—not reduced in calories as in t but drastically cut in alcohol percentage, some down to 2.2 percei is a result of crackdowns by police "booze buses" against drunk with random breath tests ("Will you blow in the bag please, si severe fines against those found guilty.

There are several different sizes of beer glasses, all with in names. These vary from state to state, but in New South V "pony" is 5 ounces, the "glass" is 7, the "middy" is 10 ounces "schooner" sails in at 15. You'll occasionally find a "pint," wh ounces. (Not all pubs will have all sizes.)

The pub crawl. As explained earlier, pubs are more often c tels," and they often sell only specific brands of beer. In Sy means that there are Toohey pubs and there are Tooth pubs which usually will be easily determined by the advertising on th of the establishment.

Until recently pubs in Australia had a sort of antiseptic loc will still find a few that seem to be paved with bathroom tile. I ly made them easier to hose down after the madding mob home. But this has evidently gone out with the "six o'clock sv

practice of declaring drinking illegal when it was time for the men to go to dinner and their long-suffering wives. Now the women themselves are coming more to the pubs, and they are insisting on good decoration and carpeted floors.

Some pubs, however, are still for men only. There is no sign to tell you such; it's just a matter of long local custom in certain neighborhoods. In general, women or couples might tell whether or not they'll be welcome by taking a "bo peep" into the bar first. If there are other women in there (other than the occasional hard-bitten local character who may be only technically female), okay. Otherwise, see if the pub has a separate area labeled the "lounge." If so, that's central headquarters for distaff and mixed imbibing.

To confuse things still further, many pubs in the country have several different "bars," often all with their own separate names—perhaps served from the same back bar and perhaps not. Some have dress codes, but the "public" bar may only require that you wear pants.

Fear not. Even Australians often become befuddled and walk into the wrong bar themselves in an innocent attempt to hoist a glass of "the amber." This is especially true today when many of the old customs and standards are being challenged and are in a state of flux.

Here are a brewer's dozen pubs in Sydney, some of which are also open for lunch and dinner: **Australian Heritage,** a century-old watering hole at the corner of King's Cross and Bayswater, has a baby-blue exterior and two or three comfortable bars inside. The **Bondi Hotel,** 178 Campbell Parade in Bondi, an ornate building from the twenties, is popular with the young folks. The **Centrepoint Tavern** on Pitt Street is a new pub with five bars representing different operatic themes. The building is on the site of Sydney's first opera house. **The Clock,** at the corner of Foveaux and Crown streets in Surry Hills, is a formerly rough, workingman's pub now converted to a chic "in spot." **The Grand,** at 30 Hunter, off Pitt, appeals to members of the stock exchange. The **Grand National Hotel,** 161 Underwood St. in "Paddo," is a friendly local pub with an outdoor garden. The famous old **Hero of Waterloo,** at the corner of Windmill and Lower Fort Street in The Rocks, was built in 1817, and is the oldest pub in town. **The Marble Bar** today is technically part of one gigantic "pub" called the Sydney Hilton. The marble walls and pillars were dismantled from the 75-year-old Adams Hotel and then erected in all their glory in the Hilton after it was built on the same spot. Don't miss it! **The Royal Hotel,** at Broughton and Heeley streets in Paddington, also has an outdoor beer garden. Several bars and a restaurant are featured in this 1889 establishment. The **Steyne Hotel,** at the corner of The Corso and Manly Beach, is a Manly landmark. There's a smashing ocean view and an inviting open courtyard. The **Tilbury Hotel,**

at 22 Forbes St. in Woolloomooloo, is also known as Louis at the Loo. It's open 6:30 to 6:30. That's A.M. to P.M. It sometimes features modern jazz on Saturday afternoons.

Theater-restaurants. These are catching on in Sydney, and they are fun with the right show, the right crowd, and the right meal. One of the most popular today is **Kinsela's** (Tel. 331–3100) at 383 Bourke St. at Taylor Square in Darlinghurst. Another featuring a floor show is **Dirty Dick's** (Tel. 929–8888), with a medieval motif, at 313 Pacific Highway, Crows Nest. Also there is the "Jolly Swagman" show at the **Argyle Tavern** (Tel. 27–7782) at 12–18 Argyle St. in The Rocks.

The **Les Girls** (Tel. 358–2333) theater-restaurant, formerly the Carousel Cabaret at 2 Roslyn St., King's Cross, features all-male reviews, and may appeal to Sydney's large population of homosexuals as well as to many others. To some, it's merely a drag.

Other theaters. There are dozens of professional theaters with constantly changing cards featuring Australian, British, and American productions. Check the newspapers, like the *Sydney Morning Herald*'s Saturday amusement classified section for the latest on who's playing where, from *Hair* to Shakespeare.

Some of the well-known Sydney theaters include the **Theatre Royal** at the MLC Centre, **Her Majesty's Theatre** at 107 Quay St., the **Drama Theatre** in the Sydney Opera House, the **Genesian Theatre** at 420 Kent St., **Seymour Centre** (in the round) at Cleveland Street and City Road, the **Ensemble Theatre,** 78 McDougall St., Milsons Point, the **Old Tote Theatre,** Anzac Parade, Kensington (opposite the University of N.S.W.), the **New Theatre,** 542 King St., and the new **Sydney Theatre Company** theater at Pier Four, Walsh Bay.

Australian theatrical standards are indisputably high, and some modern drama by accomplished local playwrights is outstanding. Unfortunately for Australia, some of the country's best talent soon flies to London, New York, or Hollywood—and stays there.

Movies. Sydney has cinemas all over the metropolitan area, many of them in Pitt Street and even more in George Street, most showing British or American productions.

There are three large cinema complexes, each of which screens a half dozen or more films simultaneously. All are timed to break at different moments, which tends to keep a relatively steady demand out at the refreshment stands.

The first of these was **Hoyts Entertainment Centre** at 505 George St., near the Town Hall. Two new emporia are the **Village City,** not far away at 545 George St., and the **Pitt Centre Cinema** at 232 Pitt St.

There are four film classifications. R is more or less like the American X—no one under 18 admitted. Then there's M or SOA, suitable for

persons 15 and over ("mature"). Then NRC or A—not recommended
for children under 12 (*Star Wars* received this classification in parts of
Australia!), and finally G, suitable for all ages.

Just as you should try to catch an Australian play while Down Under,
you should also see at least one Aussie film production. The number and
quality of Australian films is far out of proportion to the country's population, with an amazing number of features produced in recent years.

Opera. As we mentioned, opera is only performed in one of the four
main halls at the Sydney Opera House, the **Opera Theatre,** which seats
1,547 patrons. There are periodic program guides to everything going
on in the opera house, by the way. The Australian Opera company, based
there, also performs in all other state capitals and in Canberra. The box
office is open daily from 9:30 A.M. to 8:30 P.M. for tickets (Tel. 2–0588).

Again, Australian opera singers go on to enrich the culture of the rest
of the world. Harold Rosenthal, the editor of the British magazine *Opera,*
wrote, ". . . Not only London, but most of the leading opera houses of the
world would, if not actually forced to close their doors, be very hard put
to perform certain operas if it were not for the existence of Australian
singers."

Ballet. It's also performed at the Opera House, usually in the same
Opera Theatre. The Australian Ballet not only handles the classics, but it
has also commissioned dozens of new works from Australian and foreign
choreographers. One of the recent Australian ballets is "The Display,"
which is based on the life of the lyrebird. And "Corroboree," of course, is
inspired by Aboriginal ceremonies.

Classical music. Often performing in the Concert Hall, the Music Room,
or the Recording Hall of the opera house are the Sydney Symphony
Orchestra, the Elizabethan Sydney Orchestra, and the Australian Broadcasting Commission orchestra, performing works by classical artists as
well as those of many contemporary Australian composers like Ahern,
Banks, Brumby, Butterley, Conyngham, Dreyfus, and Pemberthy.

The orchestra and choir of the N.S.W. State Conservatorium of Music
sometimes perform in the opera house. The number to call for information on all opera house events is 2–0588. For some inexpensive Sunday
noon performances, no advance reservations are taken.

Television and radio stations. If you're staying home, you can be elec-
tronically entertained at least as well as in cities back home. There are
five TV channels in Sydney—the government-owned Australian Broadcasting Commission station at Channel 2; the three commercial channels, 7, 9, and 10; and the ethnic Channel Zero. Color transmission is
technically superior to the American system. And there are at least nine
radio stations, including three run by the government. The commercial

stations are generally devoted to popular music, news, and talk-back programs.

12. The Sydney Address List

Airlines, International—Air New Zealand, Tel. 234–4111. British Airways, Tel. 233–5566. CP Air, Tel. 233–5711. Continental Airlines, Tel. 232–8222. Qantas, Tel. 436–6111.

American consulate—T&G Towers, Park and Elizabeth streets (Tel. 264–7044).

Australian Tourist Commission—5 Elizabeth St. (Tel. 233–7233).

Bank—Westpac Banking Corp. (formerly Bank of New South Wales), 60 Martin Place (Tel. 233–0500).

Barber—The Stallions Stable, 398 George St. (Tel. 233–2521).

Beauty salon—Clark & Ireland, 61 Market St. (Tel. 267–7328).

British consulate—1 Alfred St., Circular Quay (Tel. 27–7521).

Camping and ski equipment rental—Paddy Pallin, 69 Liverpool St. (Tel. 264–2685).

Canadian consulate—AMP Building, 50 Bridge St. (Tel. 231–6522).

Dental Hospital of Sydney—14 Chalmers St. (Tel. 211–4322 or 211–2120 after hours).

Dry cleaners—Lawrence Dry Cleaners, Town Hall Station Concourse.

Emergency (police, fire, ambulance, etc.)—Telephone 000 (no coin is required).

Fishing supplies—The Compleat Angler Pty. Ltd., 428 George St. (Tel. 241–2080).

Florist—Town Hall Florist Shop, Town Hall Station (Tel. 264–5709).

Hospital—Emergency medical attention at Sydney Hospital, Macquarie Street (Tel. 230–0111).

Legal Aid Office—140 Phillip St. (Tel. 233–0233).

Library of New South Wales—Macquarie Street at Hunter Street (Tel. 221–1388).

N.S.W. Government Travel Centre—16 Spring St. (Tel. 231–4444).

New Zealand consulate—60 Park St. (Tel. 267–3700).

Pharmacy (all-night)—Blakes Pharmacy, 28 Darlinghurst Rd. (Tel. 358–6712).

Police station—General business Tel. 2–0966, but dial 000 for all emergencies, no coin required.

Post Office—G.P.O., Martin Place, between Pitt and George streets.

Theater tickets—Mitchell's Bass Box Office, 54 Park St. (Tel. 266–4922).

Tourist Information Service—Sydney Convention and Visitors Bureau, 100 Market St. (Tel. 232–1377).

Travellers' Aid Society—Central Railway Station, 358 Elizabeth St. (Tel. 211–2275).
Weather forecasts—Tel. 2071.
Women's Amenities Centre—Park and Elizabeth streets (Tel. 264–2061).
Youth line—Tel. 264–1177.

6

Canberra
and the A.C.T.

1. The General Picture

Because of the intense rivalry that has existed between Melbourne and Sydney from the earliest days of the colonies, it was someone's brilliant idea that, on federation, Australia should develop an entirely new national capital that would be far enough away from the influences of both ambitious cities.

Canberra was designed about 1910 by an American, Walter Burley Griffin, then a landscape architect in his mid-thirties and a former associate of Frank Lloyd Wright. Some of his inspiration may have come from Washington, considering his use of patterns of circling streets and broad thoroughfares that radiate from various points on the map.

Because of two world wars and a Great Depression in between, plus the inevitable bureaucratic controversy over the grandiose plans, Canberra took its time getting off the drawing board and onto the ground. Nevertheless in the past 30 years the city has come into its own and developed largely into the beautiful swirling patterns envisioned by Griffin. Its burgeoning population today is about 250,000, and it's preparing for half a million by the end of the century.

Canberra is still unfinished. There are empty lots all over the place, but even those help carpet the city with a sort of shaggy green between the spaced-out buildings and the more manicured lawns. And when

autumn comes in late April and early May, Canberra with its four million imported trees and shrubs changes colors more dramatically than any other metropolis in Australia. In the crisp, cool climes at 1,500 feet, the leaves are reflected in rust and golden symmetry in the artificial lake that bears the name of the young Chicagoan who first drew its banks.

Canberra is more than a political capital. It is also an important intellectual and scientific research center. The Australian National University was established here, as well as the National Library of Australia and the prestigious C.S.I.R.O. (Commonwealth Scientific and Industrial Research Organization).

As Washington has a D.C., Canberra has the A.C.T.—the Australian Capital Territory. It covers an area of nearly 1,000 square miles, an elongated patch carved right out of—and surrounded on all sides by—the state of New South Wales. There are dozens of Canberra suburbs they call "new towns" winding between the hills, all built on government leasehold land in order to protect the environment, plus a few other villages that predate the A.C.T. The territory includes an animal reserve in a rural bush setting, and it borders N.S.W.'s Kosciusko National Park, home of the Snowy Mountains.

All together the Australian Capital Territory turns out to be a lovely bucolic area. If it seems without roots or a distinctive personality, it also appears to be far from the cares of the governmental and political world for which it was created.

2. The Airport and Long-Distance Transportation

Canberra's modest airport is about four miles out Morshead Drive. Strangely, considering its capital status, it is not an international facility. (Everyone destined for Canberra must go through customs and immigration somewhere else.) Like most airports in Australia, it is basically divided into areas for **Ansett Airlines** (Tel. 45–1111) and the government-owned airline, **TAA** (Tel. 68–3333). **East-West Airlines** (Tel. 95–3677) is tucked into a corner. In the terminal's center you'll find a small bar, newsstand, etc., beside the waiting room. There are no baggage carousels; you pick up your bags outdoors right off the trolley. There are several flights daily to and from Sydney (about 30 minutes away) and Melbourne (about 60 minutes).

By train, you take either the InterCity "XPT" or the *Canberra Monaro Express* from Sydney all the way to Canberra in about five hours. Tickets are about $25, unless you have the Austrailpass. From Melbourne it's longer, less convenient, and more expensive. The all-day trip (leaving 8:40 A.M. last we checked) goes first only to Yass. There you change for a bus for the final hour into Canberra via **Yass-Canberra Bus Coaches** (Tel. 26–1378), arriving at 6:15 P.M. That's around $60, all together.

Canberra

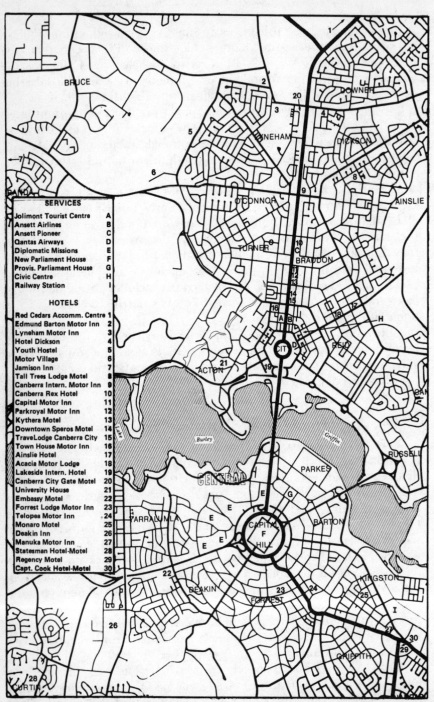

SERVICES

Jolimont Tourist Centre	A
Ansett Airlines	B
Ansett Pioneer	C
Qantas Airways	D
Diplomatic Missions	E
New Parliament House	F
Provis. Parliament House	G
Civic Centre	H
Railway Station	I

HOTELS

Red Cedars Accomm. Centre	1
Edmund Barton Motor Inn	2
Lyneham Motor Inn	3
Hotel Dickson	4
Youth Hostel	5
Motor Village	6
Jamison Inn	7
Tall Trees Lodge Motel	8
Canberra Intern. Motor Inn	9
Canberra Rex Hotel	10
Capital Motor Inn	11
Parkroyal Motor Inn	12
Kythera Motel	13
Downtown Speros Motel	14
TraveLodge Canberra City	15
Town House Motor Inn	16
Ainslie Hotel	17
Acacia Motor Lodge	18
Lakeside Intern. Hotel	19
Canberra City Gate Motel	20
University House	21
Embassy Motel	22
Forrest Lodge Motor Inn	23
Telopea Motor Inn	24
Monaro Motel	25
Deakin Inn	26
Manuka Motor Inn	27
Statesman Hotel-Motel	28
Regency Motel	29
Capt. Cook Hotel-Motel	30

Map courtesy Canberra Tourist Bureau

There is also a train from the Canberra station to Cooma, the gateway to the Snowy Mountains recreation area.

Ansett Pioneer (Tel. 45–6624) and **Greyhound** (Tel. 49–8630) offer trips from the major cities to Canberra at prices close to the train fares. Or it's a pleasant 200-mile ride in a rented car from Sydney. Take the Southeastern Freeway to Goulburn, and then the Federal Highway (No. 23) to Canberra. You can make it easily in about 3½ hours today. A longer route would be the Princes Highway along the Illawarra Coast (Route 1) to Bateman's Bay and then a local road via Queanbeyan to Canberra. From Melbourne it's at least an eight-hour drive to Canberra.

3. Local Transportation

In spread-out Canberra you may be better off renting a car than relying on local transportation. **Avis** (Tel. 49–6088), **Budget** (Tel. 48–9788), and **Hertz** (Tel. 49–6211) are at the airport as well as downtown. If you get a car at the airport, you'll begin by saving the $5 taxi (or $2 bus) fare into town. A less expensive local agency is **Rumbles Rent-A-Car** (Tel. 95–0019) at 5 Bramble St., Red Hill. There's a branch of **Thrifty Rent-A-Car** (Tel. 47–7422) at the corner of Mort and Girrawheen streets.

Taxis (Tel. 46–0444) are banded into a monopoly and are sometimes difficult to find.

The orange-and-blue government bus service run by **ACTION** (Tel. 47–6185), an acronym for Australian Capital Territory Interurban Omnibus Network(!), is allegedly good, but although the service is frequent and convenient for commuters, it's not as well designed for visitors. Rates are drastically reduced on Sundays, however, and some readers say they've used them for a good, cheap overall view of the city then. You can also take ACTION buses to a point to catch the Canberra Explorer (see section 7).

In any case, don't try to take ACTION seriously without picking up a copy of their Route Map and Passenger Information folder. Note that there is a free bus service (Route 301) over a small circuit in the commercial area generally around London Circuit. And if you see a man in green, he's a bus inspector and available to answer rapid-transit questions.

Bicyclists know that Canberra is supposed to be the best two-wheel town in the country. You may be able to rent your bike down by the ferry terminal near the "Uni," or out at the youth hostel. Cost is about $5 per day. You can pick up a special bicycle map for the city at the A.C.T. Government Tourist Bureau.

4. The Hotel Scene

There are several excellent hotels in Canberra among the group that charge about $70 to $100 a night for two. (These are followed by others

Canberra—Kosciusko National Park

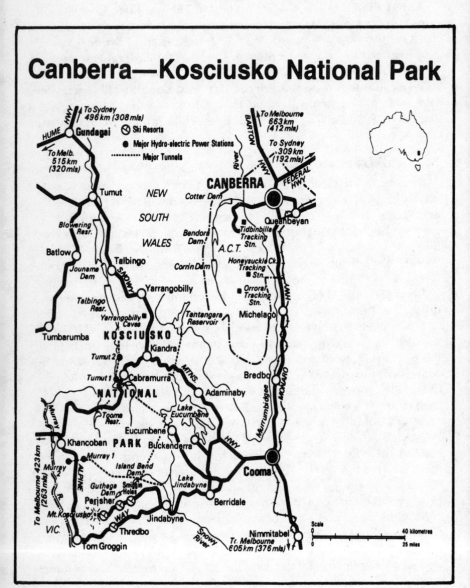

Map courtesy Australian Tourist Commission

that are certainly acceptable for the budget range—anything under $50 in Canberra.)

EXPENSIVE HOTELS

Like many new hotels in Australia, the **Canberra International** (Tel. 47–6966) has the requisite central atrium, and it carries off this architectural technique very well: Conveniently located at 242 Northbourne Ave., near Wakefield; main portico in a red, sail-like design; pleasant lobby in greens and browns; atrium/courtyard practically a forest of trees and plants; unusually roofed in fabric, softening the effect no matter how harsh the daylight outside; two-tier Garden Terrace restaurant; the Lemon Tree coffee shop; an outdoor pool for dedicated splashers and sun-soakers. A total of 150 rooms in this three-level low-rise; those we saw in greens and blues with wicker furnishings; all the mod cons, as they say, including in-house movies on the color tellies, international long-distance-dialing phones, clock radios, etc.; also about 36 suites with kitchens or spa baths; 24-hour room service; most doubles in the $100 range as 1986 begins; a few with kitchenettes or hot tubs for around $150. (Reservations from the hotel at Canberra, A.C.T. 2602.) Perhaps the most prestigious address currently in this prestige-conscious town.

Some prefer the **Lakeside International Hotel** (Tel. 47–6244), sometimes called Noah's, a high-rise right on London Circuit at City Hill, and it is the only really high-class address within strolling distance of the original Canberra business section: A proud-looking structure with the flags of eight nations out front; acres of green, in effect, for a front yard; broad, tasteful lobby; cozy if a little confusing bar to one side (that fellow bustling about picking up glasses is doing all he does; you place your own order at the bar); top tucker at the viewful Burley Griffin Room on the roof; coffee shop with tipsy chairs on our own stay; a windy swimming pool out back. Good, rosewoodlike furnishings in the bedchambers; subtly striped wallpaper; many nice vistas over the lake; blackout curtains a thoughtful extra; prices for two *starting* at around $110. Ask for a room in the front for the best panoramas. (Reservations through the Noah's organization or the hotel at Box 1450, Canberra, A.C.T. 2601.) A good choice for the lake side.

The four-story **Canberra-Rex** (Tel. 48–5311) on Northbourne Avenue and Ipima Street is a dependable old standby, although we can't go into much detail this edition. On our recent revisit, the hotel had changed hands and was about to begin massive renovations that will restructure the place almost from top to bottom, incorporating the headquarters of Ansett Pioneer in the process. Many rooms in the house continue to have a view of Mount Ainsley, of course, and facilities throughout should rival other establishments on the avenue. Longtime Romanian bellhop Ron Vatavalis may tell you about the time President Lyndon Johnson stayed here, if you let him. (Reservations from the hotel at Canberra, A.C.T. 2601.) Somewhat of a "?" due to circumstances beyond our control, but worth checking out and probably checking in.

The **Canberra Parkroyal** (Tel. 49–1411) is officially a motel (or "motor inn"), although here, as in most of Australia, we can discern little or no difference between good hotels and good motels (this one is owned by the university): Entranceway flanked with flags and fountains at a convenient covered bus stop; over the moat to the purple welcome mat; attractive modern lobby with complimentary coffee; handsome blue-and-silver Silver Grill and adjoining Swizzle Stick bar; spacious rooms in the $100 to $110 range; patterned walls; units with walkout balconies overlooking the pool. (Reservations at the Parkroyal, 102 Northbourne Ave., Canberra, A.C.T. 2600.) A royal choice.

The **Canberra City Travelodge** (Tel. 49–6911) at Northbourne and Cooyong Road may be more modest, but it's within walking distance of the city center, and we found friendly, competent young women in charge. There's a small lobby, but the sleeping rooms are sizable. Grounds include a swimming pool and mini golf course. It's perhaps a little less pricy than some of its prestigious sisters up the avenue. Recommended for the more modest outlay.

The **Canberra City Gate** (Tel. 47–2777) and the **Capital Motor Inn** (Tel. 48–6566), both further up on Northbourne Avenue, are not bad. But with tariffs at around $75 per twin-bed night they don't provide much of a saving over the top spots on a one- or two-night stand.

BUDGET-PRICE ACCOMMODATIONS

If you don't have a lot of luggage, the nicest nest in the category is the tiny, friendly **Downtown Spero's Motel** (Tel. 49–1388), which sits almost alongside the big boys right on Northbourne Avenue at No. 82: No lobby to speak of, but an attractive French restaurant on the premises; no pool either (perhaps that's the reason for the reasonable prices); compact rooms, each as neat and as well designed as a ship's cabin, with lots of extras like color TVs and free coffee- and tea-making materials; a self-service laundromat on the premises; new wing open but unseen by us so far; perhaps some larger units in there. We liked this tidy operation by John Spero Cassidy, and if he can keep his tariffs to $50 or so for two, it probably will remain the biggest little bargain in the capital.

Some other budget establishments are all right, too, even if they didn't strike us as solidly. The **Kythera** (Tel. 48–7611), just up the street at 98 Northbourne Ave., will do. There's a pool, and it has some good, large family units. The **Hotel Dickson** (Tel. 49–6711) in the Dickson Shopping Centre (across from McDonald's) has a lot of fancy facilities, but may be a little overrated locally. Choose the room before signing up; we thought some were a little rough on our inspection tour, although twin rates of less than $40 might make up for a lot.

Youth hostel. Canberra's hostel is the **National Memorial Youth Hostel** (Tel. 48–9759) on Dryandra Street in O'Connor. (Take Bus 29 to Scrivener Street.) Members only may get a bed here for $7. Also, the **YWCA Hostel** (Tel. 47–3033) at 2 Mort St., downtown, has dormitory beds beginning at about $15 per person.

Accommodations in the snowfields? See section 9, Sports, for everything relating to ski fiends.

5. Restaurants and Dining

There are supposed to be more than 250 restaurants in Canberra, but we know of none that stands out as an unforgettable gourmet experience. Reportedly the embassy crowd keeps things cosmopolitan, but we wonder if that isn't just wishful thinking. Few restaurants outside your hotel will be within walking distance of it, but we believe all listed below are within practical taxi distance.

Certainly one of the most elegant salons is the **Burley Griffin Room** (Tel. 47–6244) atop the Lakeside International Hotel. We found it dark enough to enjoy the panorama of lights out the window, but still bright enough to see the menu and the food. There are purple and red upholstery and white tablecloths, with formal French service by professional waiters. The Chicken Kiev was very nice. The Veal Cordon Bleu had a rather Italianized tomato accent, but we wouldn't complain. Music (organ and drums) began at 8 P.M. A well-planned dining choice. In the same hotel the **London Grill** (same phone number for reservations) has a good local steak-and-chops reputation, but we haven't cut in yet.

For that kind of fare, we enjoyed the friendly atmosphere at the **Charcoal Restaurant** (Tel. 48–8015) at 61 London Circuit. The narrow room is relieved by a wall of mirrors that reflect the open kitchen. Most steaks are in the $9 to $10 range, and you can get a baked potato here—called a jacket potato in local parlance. The house red wine was also good.

Somehow we've not yet made it to the attractive **Carousel** (Tel. 73–1808). It's a French-style salon perched atop the Red Hill lookout. You can order a dinner as late as 10 P.M. here, but like most nonhotel restaurants in Canberra it's closed Sunday. **The Lobby** (Tel. 73–1563) is the traditional gathering place for M.P.s (not counting Parliament House itself, which is right across the street). It's an elegant place for lunch or dinner. (Try the creamed fettucine with smoked chicken and prosciutto ham.)

Another top-drawer establishment, almost at the hub of everything, is **Le Rustique** (Tel. 48–6514) at 24 Garema Place, where the cuisine of southern France is lapped up by a loyal local clientele. (Reserve always.) Another elegant entry with innovative international recipes is **Peaches** (Tel. 49–7333) at Blamey Crescent in Campbell. (One Canberran we know says he reckons it's the best restaurant in town.)

We tried the **Red Door** (Tel. 49–6911) in the Canberra City Travelodge for lunch. It's a pleasant-looking place, but the service and selection were poor. Maybe it's better for dinner.

Chinese food is popular in Canberra, and the most mentioned spot is the **Peking,** formerly the Mandarin (Tel. 82–3393). Specializing in northern Chinese cooking, it's open Tuesday through Sunday at the corner of Townshend Street and Dundas Court in Phillip, up above the Singer Sewing Centre. Other Chinese choices include **The Emerald Gardens** (Tel. 54–7939), which serves seven days a week in the Hawker Shopping Centre, and **Lotus** (Tel. 47–6318), 100 Northbourne Ave., next to the Kythera Motel.

The **Taj Mahal** (Tel. 47–6528), an Indian entry at 39 Northbourne Ave., is pretty good. The **Shalimar** (Tel. 49–6784) is newer but reportedly gaining ground. It's in the Tasman House at Hobart Place.

The **Private Bin** (Tel. 47–3030), at 50 Northbourne Ave., is informal, cheap, and fun for chicken, steaks, beer, and wine from Monday to Friday.

A gregarious Greek style is apparent at **Zorba's** (Tel. 51–2357) in the Belconnen Mall shopping center, but it is not limited to Hellenic fare. Not too surprisingly (if you remember that old movie), it's open "Never on Sunday."

For light snacks, pizzas, etc., wander down Garema Place and the little plazas adjoining. Several small cafes are there, some of which will no doubt change their owners and menus again before this perishable research finds its way into print.

Last, and perhaps least, Canberra, too, may be making a bid for recognition as a dinkum big city at last; it now has its very own revolving dining room. The **Tower Restaurant** (Tel. 48–6162) turns around the new telecommunications tower crowning Black Mountain. The view is wonderful. The buffet lunch isn't bad, although we haven't tried the evening fare. To tell the truth, our experience throughout the world is that the quality of the food has always been in inverse proportion to the degree that the restaurant moves. Let's hope, however, that this one is the exception.

6. Sightseeing in Canberra (and the A.C.T.)

On wheels, you can make the Canberra itinerary described here in the suggested order. If you're busing, taxiing, or jogging, consult the map and cut in and out, depending on what seems interesting and practical. You may want to pay a visit first to the **Canberra Tourist Bureau** (Tel. 45–6464). This is the official government tourist office in the Jolimont Centre on Northbourne Avenue. There's also a **Visitor Information Centre** farther out on Northbourne Avenue near Morphett Street. Both are open weekends.

Most itineraries suggest starting at Parliament House, but the best beginning for foreigners, at least, is the **Regatta Point Planning Exhibition** set up by the National Capital Development Commission (NCDC) on the lakeshore near the northern end of the Commonwealth Avenue Bridge. See the displays, scale models, etc., explaining the capital's design and development, and don't miss the audiovisual production in the theater. It's open daily from 9 A.M. to 5 P.M.

Just outside, of course, is **Lake Burley Griffin,** the seven-mile-long artificial lake that was finally created in 1963. It was named after the American designer of Canberra, Walter Burley Griffin.

Near the Planning Exhibition, and just 550 feet offshore, is the 250- to 450-foot-high (depending on the winds) jet of water called the **Captain Cook Memorial,** modeled after the taller *Jet d'Eau* of Geneva. Perhaps symbolic of Australia's strict labor laws, even the fountain takes time out for lunch. It shoots generally from 10 A.M. 'til noon, and then again from 2 to 4 P.M. (It also turns off automatically on windy days so it won't spray traffic on the nearby bridge.) On shore, the Terrestrial Globe indicates the routes of Cook's travels.

Driving across the Commonwealth Avenue Bridge and then along Commonwealth Avenue, you pass on the right the Commonwealth embassies of Great Britain, New Zealand, and Canada, respectively. (The American embassy is also nearby, just off State Circle at Perth Avenue.) Many foreign legations are in the area, and most have been inspired by their own native architecture, sometimes to the point of caricature. The American embassy looks like something lifted from Colonial Williamsburg, for instance, and it's true that all those red bricks were imported from the U.S.A.

Construction is still continuing on the dramatic **New Parliament House** in Capital Circle, and the structure that received so much initial criticism is now emerging as an architectural *tour de force*. You probably won't be able to go inside until 1988, when the building will be opened as part of Australia's bicentennial celebrations. Nevertheless there are several vantage points from which you can watch the progress of the building as well as a special **exhibition center** (Tel. 70–5237) on State Circle (almost across the street from St. Andrew's Church, between Brisbane and

Canberra avenues) that explains with models and other exhibits just what is going on.

Although a unique curvilinear effect is visible, those involved with the design take offense when the plan is described as merely a couple of giant boomerangs. With intelligent landscaping, the Parliament Building should blend well into a setting that apparently will even put some grass on the roof.

Meanwhile the "temporary" **Parliament House,** which was built in 1927, is the long, low building on King George Terrace. If the lawmakers are in session, you can see much of the old-world froufrou that Australia inherited from Great Britain—the robes, wigs, swallowtail coats, ruffled shirts, knee britches, and buckled shoes, as well as convoluted ceremonies like the pointing of the mace and other rigamarole that will seem more than slightly incongruous to Americans.

You can watch parliamentary proceedings when the Senate or House is in session (normally Tuesday, Wednesday, and Thursday, March through June and August through October), but the free, 25-minute tours are conducted only when sessions are not being held. They're conducted throughout the day from 9:00 A.M. until 4:30 P.M. King's Hall in Parliament House contains a 1297 issue of the Magna Carta, preserved under a sea of argon gas.

You may notice the Parthenonlike building down by the water. That's the **National Library.** A handsome structure, it's supposed to file everything written on Australia, and we can only hope there's another copy of this modest volume there by now among its 2 million works. Not far from the library, along King Edward Terrace, are two new structures, the High Court of Australia (the supreme court) and the **Australian National Gallery.** (Art exhibits, including a surprising number of works by Europeans and Americans, are open from 9 A.M. daily; closing hours vary considerably. Photography is allowed but large bags must be checked.)

Across King's Avenue Bridge to the left, on little Aspen Island, is the three-column tower housing the **Canberra Carillon,** which merrily plays with 53 bells, a 1963 gift from Great Britain. In addition to the automatic "Westminster Chimes" played throughout the day, there are live recitals Wednesday and Sunday afternoons. (By the way, the Australian pronunciation of "carillon" rhymes with "pavilion.")

At the end of King's Avenue you'll see the **Australian-American War Memorial,** a 258-foot-tall aluminum spire with the American eagle roosting on top. (It's so tall that the eagle with the upswept wings sometimes looks more like a scared rabbit. Some locals call it "Bugs Bunny.") It commemorates American aid to Australia during World War II.

Drive north a few hundred yards along Russell Drive, then Constitution Avenue, if you want to look in at the 1858 **Blundell's Farmhouse,** one of the few old buildings around that predates all the rest of the city. (Open daily, 2 P.M. to 4 P.M. except Wednesday, 10 A.M. to noon.) In any case, it's on the way to **Anzac Parade,** a broad thoroughfare finished in 1965 and honoring the 50th anniversary of Anzac forces landing at Gallipoli. It's lined with Australian blue gum trees and New Zealand veronica shrubs.

At the head of the Parade is the fortresslike **Australian War Memorial,** by far the most popular tourist site in Canberra. Filled with relics (including a vast collection of old aircraft and historic weapons), pictures, and dioramas of Australia's many foreign campaigns, the copper-domed structure is sometimes criticized for seeming to glorify war more than it laments those who died. The memorial is free and open from 9:00 A.M. to 4:45 P.M. daily. Be sure to get a floor plan to find your way around, or take the guided tour. Parts of the memorial are being renovated and they show no signs of being completed for years to come.

About a mile east on Fairbairn Avenue a drive leads up to **Mount Ainslie Lookout,** one of three giving an excellent panorama of the city. (The others are Red Hill and Black Mountain.) From here there are several choices. We recommend returning to the city to have a quick look at the exterior of the **Academy of Science** (you can't get inside). The copper umbrella at Edinburgh Avenue and McCoy Crescent is at least of architectural interest. (The 150-foot-in-diameter igloo shape has been called the "Eskimo Embassy" by Canberrans.) In any case, the **National Film and Sound Archive,** just across the street, *does* invite visitor exploration. The Art Deco–style building holds public screenings and exhibitions from its collection of films, television shows, and recorded radio programs. (Open 10 to 4 daily.) This building was formerly the National Institute of Anatomy, and the last we checked you could still go in there to see the heart of Phar Lap, if you have a mind to do so.

These latter two buildings are on the fringe of the 358-acre campus of the **Australian National University** (see the Visitor Information Centre on Balmain Crescent, opposite University House). It was founded in 1946 and now has about 7,000 students.

Behind A.N.U. on Clunies Ross Street just past the C.S.I.R.O. is the **National Botanic Gardens** (Tel. 47–3822) on the lower slopes of Black Mountain. There are several trails through its 100 acres. They attempt to grow as many species of Australian plants and trees as is possible in the temperate climate.

Farther up the winding road, and crowning Black Mountain itself, is the lancelike **Telecom Tower,** completed in 1980. It's a huge antenna that spears into the sky for 640 feet. It also includes three viewing platforms (worth the $1 per view charged) and the obligatory revolving restaurant (merry enough for a lunchtime go-round). Pray for a clear day. Although Canberra doesn't really suffer from air pollution, things can get quite hazy sometimes, especially in the summer, due to distant bush fires in the countryside.

THE AUSTRALIAN CAPITAL TERRITORY

Ten miles out of town the Cotter Road leads to the **Mt. Stromlo Observatory.** (Like lots of things in Australia, it's the largest "in the Southern Hemisphere," a specious comparison you may hear repeatedly all over the country.) There's a visitor center at this telescopic site, open from 9:30 A.M. to 4:00 P.M. On the same highway you can visit the **Tidbinbilla Tracking Station**—one of two active satellite stations in the A.C.T., but the only one that is open to the public with a visitor center, etc.—and then the **Tidbinbilla Nature Reserve,** a highly recommended 13,617-acre piece of protected bush only 25 miles from the national capital. In this forested mountain region are several kinds of native trees growing among massive boulders. Also living there are possums, swamp wallabies, a colony of koalas, wombats, and spiny anteaters. And you can enter large fenced areas to see the emus and red and gray kangaroos who live there. Some of the roos have room enough to "kanga" along at speeds up to 30 mph. Catching anything out in the open during the cold months of April through October would be pretty chancy, though.

Just south of the A.C.T. the Monaro Highway (No. 23) leads to **Cooma,** gateway to the Snowy Mountains, headquarters for the giant Snowy Mountains Hydro-Electric Scheme, and an interesting town in its own right. Drop in to the Visitors' Centre (Tel. Cooma 2–1108) on Sharp Street to (a) check on road conditions in the mountains and/or (b) see how best to experience some of the massive dams, underground power stations, man-made lakes, etc. The almost incredible water system, completed in 1974 after 25 years abuilding, basically diverts water that once flowed to the Pacific from the Snowy River into various other reservoirs and outlets. This allows it to irrigate more than 1,000 square miles of normally dry land to the west and at the same time to run seven power stations producing as much as four million kilowatts of electricity.

From Cooma you can drive over sometimes difficult road (but through lovely alpine scenery) to **Kosciusko National Park** and its fields of snow or wildflowers. It's ideal ski country (see section 9).

7. Guided Tours and Cruises

Don't hold us to these, but here was what was available the last time we checked and our estimate of what prices might be by now.

Ansett Pioneer (Tel. 45–6624), the Gray Line franchisee, offers three half-day trips. *The National Gallery, Australian Mint, and the Library* leaves about 9 A.M. daily and may cost around $12. But we would choose one of the afternoon tours for around the same price; it's called simply *City Sights Tour* and it leaves about 1 P.M. and lasts a little over three hours. The same company also has its *Canberra in a Day*, which combines the points of interest from the morning and afternoon tours for a seven-hour, 45-mile trip. We'll guess the price at over $22 now. Lunch is extra.

Murray's Australia (Tel. 95–3677), an excellent local outfit, offers several good tours every day except Sunday for similar prices. We like their half-day *Highlights* leaving at 1 P.M. and covering about what Ansett does for about $10. They also have an all-day *Grand Slam* tour leaving at 10 A.M. It costs more—perhaps $30, by now—but it includes the launch and lunch on the lake. This is pretty good if you can take a whole day of regimentation.

Both companies offer tours that include a visit to a nearby country sheep station. We took the approximate equivalent of the Murray's *Aussie Barbecue* tour, and enjoyed meeting the Colverwell brothers (Ray and Rhuben) on their station (ranch) and watching them at work, herding, shearing, dipping, etc. Equally impressive is their sheep dog who rounds up the "woolies," even running across their backs when necessary.

Following Sydney's lead, the new **Canberra Explorer** buses run hourly during daylight hours over a 15-mile route, making 22 stops. You hop off at any that interest you, then reboard the next red bus an hour later. Watch out, though, because there are two separate routes. Route A is a short one that mainly features the Telecom Tower. Route B is much more comprehensive. Both make stops near the hotels on Northbourne Avenue, and daily tickets were $7, the last we looked—or you could get one that will keep you rolling all week for $14.

We haven't tried Canberra's famous **Radio Motorcades** (Tel. 95–7082), where the commentary is given by a tour guide who broadcasts to a convoy of cars. Cost is around $15 per car. Frankly, we'd like a tour guide we could talk back to. If you try it, let us know how you like it.

You'll pay top dollar of course, but some prefer a personalized car and driver/guide. **Canberra Hire Cars** (Tel. 49–7844) is one we found to be good, especially if Ken Appleby is your driver. Rates are around $25 an hour.

Get the latest on all tour itineraries by contacting the tour companies or the **Canberra Tourist Bureau** (Tel. 45–6464) in the Jolimont Centre, which can book you on these and a lot more, including fishing trips, tours to Mt. Kosciusko, and ski trips to the Snowy Mountains.

BOAT CRUISES

Murray's (see above) also runs 1½-hour cruises for around $5 and luncheon cruises of about the same length for $15 or so on Lake Burley Griffin aboard the *Lady Claire* or the *City of Canberra*. (There's also a new dinner cruise for around $35.) If the boat isn't too crowded (ours was), it's nice to get out on the water on a hot day, but remember that you can't get very close to anything. The ferry terminal is at Acton Park on the West Basin, easily walkable from the Lakeside Hotel, and there's ample parking if you drive down.

8. Water Sports

Canberra and the Capital Territory are the only major land-bound settlements in Australia, so there are no ocean-oriented activities in the immediate area. (It's about 100 miles to the surfing beaches at Batemans Bay.) We don't recommend swimming in Lake Burley Griffin, whose waters are fed by the polluted Queanbeyan River. Prudent folks take different strokes in the Olympic Swimming Pool and other clean, rectangular waters in the area.

There are a few good swimming holes on the Murrumbidgee River (from November to April only in these colder climes) outside the city at Casuarina Sands, Kambah Pool, Cotter Reserve, and Uriarra Crossing— all popular picnic spots, too, incidentally.

You can rent a paddle boat, canoe, windsurf board, rowboat, or aquabike for your own private trip on Lake Burley Griffin from **Dobel Boat Hire** (Tel. 49–6861), casting off in these floaters down by the ferry landing in Acton Park. Catamarans rent for around $12 per hour. (Powerboats are generally not allowed on the lake.)

Trout fishing is allowed in the lake from about October 1 to May 31. No license is needed, but the bag limit is 10. Some fisherfolk prefer taking trips to nearby trout streams, something the Canberra Tourist Bureau will be happy to arrange.

9. Other Sports

Spectator sports are often held in **Bruce Stadium,** seating 20,000, put up for the 1977 Pacific Games. In 1985 it was the setting for the International Amateur Athletics Federation's World Cup.

There are two 18-hole public golf courses, **Gloucester Park** in Narrabundah on Jerrabomberra Avenue, off the Cooma Road, and the **Belconnen Public Golf Course** (Tel. 54–6740) at the end of Drake Brockman Drive, Holt. You'll also find four private golf clubs in the

territory: the **Royal Canberra,** where you need some sort of good introduction to get on the greens; and the **Federal** (at Red Hill), the **Yowani**
(on the Federal Highway at Lyneham), and the **Queanbeyan** (at Queanbeyan, N.S.W., nine miles away), all of which readily welcome out-of-
town players.

There are tennis facilities in several areas. Call the A.C.T. Lawn Tennis
Association. If you're into backpacking and hiking, you might want to
check with the **Canberra Bushwalking Club** (Tel. 47–3064). Skaters,
whether on blades or wheels, look in at the **Paradice Ice and Roller
Skating Rink,** in the showgrounds off the Federal Highway (at Flemington
Road).

SNOWY MOUNTAIN SKIING

Canberra is a good staging area for the ski country that is actually
headquartered about 100 miles away in the Kosciusko National Park in
the Snowy Mountains. Although this area is part of the state of New
South Wales, the Canberra Tourist Bureau will help you set up tours or
make bookings. There are three main alpine villages on the slopes of Mt.
Kosciusko—Thredbo, Perisher Valley, and Smiggin Holes.

Thredbo is Australia's snazziest ski resort, although Perisher Valley
certainly gives it a run for its money. At Thredbo there are 36 miles of
trails, plus three double chair lifts, seven T-bars, and some poma lifts.
Perisher Valley boasts three triple chair lifts, one double chair lift, 19
T-bars, two J-bars, and three pomas. The ski season generally runs from
June through September.

We've never skied in the area, but friends who have tell us snow conditions are often unstable on the lower half of the mountain, but that at the
top, actually a plateau about 6,500 feet above sea level, the snowfields
stretch for miles and are bigger than many in Switzerland.

Thredbo, popular with a young singles crowd, has about 15 hotels,
some with outdoor heated pools. Other activities in the area include ice
skating and soaring (gliding). Night life is centered at "The Keller" (a live
band and lots of lively young folks) or at the Schuss Bar, both in the
Thredbo Alpine Hotel. At either the most popular winter beverage is a
hot, spicy "gluhwein." Perisher Valley and Smiggin Holes are more family resorts than party communities.

You can get Thredbo snow reports from Canberra by dialing 47–0686,
from Sydney at 2–0510, or from Melbourne at 1–1544. Several companies run ski tours to the area from Sydney and Canberra.

In addition to the traditional Snowy Mountain ski centers, there is also
a new ski facility right in the A.C.T. and less than half the distance away

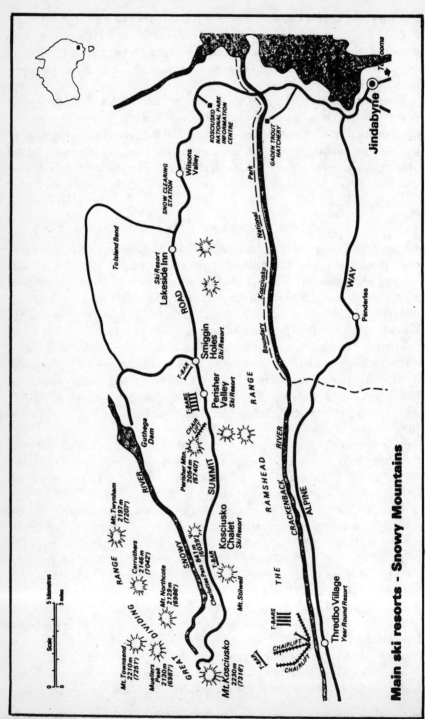

Main ski resorts - Snowy Mountains

Map courtesy Australian Tourist Commission

called **Corin Forest.** All-day lift tickets were under $10 there, the last we heard. A snow-making machine ensures slick schussing.

10. Shopping in the A.C.T.

Shopping is largely decentralized among the several suburbs in Canberra. There is one shopping nexus in the Civic Centre, near the bottom of Northbourne Avenue. Some of those Italianesque, arcaded shops are among Canberra's first buildings, built in 1926. A branch of the **David Jones** department store is there.

The big shopping centers are Belconnen Mall and Woden Plaza. There are also popular shopping areas at Weston Creek, Manuka, and Kingston. All shopping is carried out during the usual Australian hours, except that late-night shopping in the A.C.T. is permitted on Friday. On Thursday night, capital residents go over to Queanbeyan for the bargains and the bright lights.

Save your serious shopping for Sydney, Melbourne, and other large cities, if you can. But for die-hard shop hounds, here are a few things you might find in the A.C.T.

Souvenir shops. Right downtown, **The Opal Studio** (Tel. 47–5474) in the Cinema Centre Arcade has loose opals, rough opal specimens, opal and other gemstone jewelry, and Australian sapphires. **Lakeside Gifts** (Tel. 48–0956) in the Lakeside Hotel offers leather goods, sheepskins, and suede items. **The Shearing Shed** (Tel. 95–9754), 52 Giles St., Kingston, specializes in leatherwork but also has sheepskin car seat covers and coats and vests made to order. **The Handcrafters Centre** at Paragon Mall in Fyshwick has Australiana craft materials plus hand-spun wool for knitting.

Galleries. In Manuka, **Marunari Aboriginal Arts** on Franklin Street has a large number of native works for sale. **Beaver Galleries,** 81 Denison St., Deakin, features works by Australian artists, printmakers, and sculptors, and **Narek Galleries,** Naas Road, Tharwa, offers pottery, leather goods, jewelry, and paintings. (Arts and crafts enthusiasts should pick up a special Crafts Council brochure on A.C.T. galleries from the tourist bureau.)

Books. There are several bookstores. One where we found some Australiana we needed was **Dalton's Bookshop** (Tel. 49–1844) on Garema Place. Amazingly, it's also open for Sunday browsing.

11. Night Life and Entertainment

Canberra is not what you would call a swinging town, but there are enough activities to keep things interesting for a city of its size.

The closest things to nightclubs are **Juliana's** in the Lakeside Hotel and the **Queanbeyan Leagues Club,** just over the state line in Queanbeyan, N.S.W. As in Sydney, leagues clubs usually welcome foreign visitors.

Several discotheques have spun into action in the past couple of years. Four of them are in the city center—**Cafe Jax,** the **Manhattan, Tipperary,** and the **Private Bin.** Also there is **Starburst** in the Captain James Cook Hotel in Griffith, **Honey's** in Phillip, and **The Hut** in Oatley Court, Belconnen.

You'll find drinking and entertainment, too, at **Kimbo's** (Tel. 82–3585) and the **Contented Soul** (Tel. 82–1263) in Phillip; **Blind Beggars Inn** (Tel. 51–1965) and **Pot Belly** (Tel. 51–4530) in Belconnen; the **Boot and Flogger** (Tel. 95–8425) in Kingston; the **Royals Football Club** in Weston; and **Bustles** (Tel. 47–6139) right in the city.

There's often rock music or something else going on at the Australian National University campus, usually upstairs in the Union bar (on North Road).

The main theater in town is the **Canberra Theatre Centre** (Tel. 49–7600) in Civic Square. There's a 1,200-seat auditorium and a 310-seat playhouse, playing host to traveling theater, ballet, or opera companies, or the Canberra Symphony Orchestra.

The Canberra Repertory Society, dating from the 1930s, performs in its own **Theatre 3** (Tel. 47–4222) at Ellery Crescent in Acton or at **Bard's** (Tel. 82–2983) at Adelaide House in Woden Plaza.

There are movie theaters in several shopping centers, including those around Mort and Bunda streets in the Civic Centre.

12. The Address List

Ambulance—Tel. 49–8133.

American embassy—State Circle and Perth Avenue, Yarralumla (Tel. 73–3711).

Automobile club—NRMA, 92 Northbourne Ave. (Tel. 49–6666).

British embassy—Commonwealth Avenue (Tel. 73–0422).

Bus information—Tel. 95–0251.

Canadian embassy—Commonwealth Avenue (Tel. 73–3844).

Emergency calls—Dial 000; no coin required.

Flower shop—Christine's Flower Boutique, Canberra Arcade (Tel. 47–0426).

Hospital—Canberra Hospital, Edinburgh Avenue, Acton (Tel. 48–9922).

New Zealand embassy—Commonwealth Avenue (Tel. 73–3611).

Pharmacy (after hours)—City Health Promotion Center, Clark Street (Tel. 49–1919).

Police station—Knowles Place and London Circuit (Tel. 49–7444).

Post office—G.P.O., adjoining Jolimont Centre at Alinga Street.

Queanbeyan Information Centre—Farrer Place (Tel. 97–4602).

Secretarial service—Western Girl (Tel. 49–7777), 99 London Court.

Tourist information—Canberra Tourist Bureau, Jolimont Centre, Northbourne Avenue (Tel. 45–6464).

7

Melbourne, the Victorian Capital

1. The General Picture

Melbourne at first appears to suffer from an inferiority complex, constantly comparing herself to Sydney and feeling the need to count out one by one the reasons why she is better than—or at least as good as—the N.S.W. capital up north.

Seen from a foreign perspective, she needn't do this at all. But Melbourne, with a population of some three million, just doesn't seem to have confidence in herself as a major, significant, and attractive metropolis. And that's too bad.

Melbourne saw flamboyant Sydney get the extravagant opera house—pushing the flashiest kid on the block onto the stage of the world—-and for some years she has been hoping to build an international landmark of her own. There's an ideal site available if designers can roof over the 74 acres of railway yards that now scar the area between the Cricket Ground and the Yarra River.

The Yarra, which winds to the south of the main part of the city, is often said to be Australia's only river that "flows upside down"—i.e., with all the mud and silt on top. It's an unkind exaggeration. Seen from some of the miles of green parkland skirting the city, the Yarra is a shiny, silvery ribbon reflecting the city's tallest buildings. Yet it's true that you wouldn't want to swim in it.

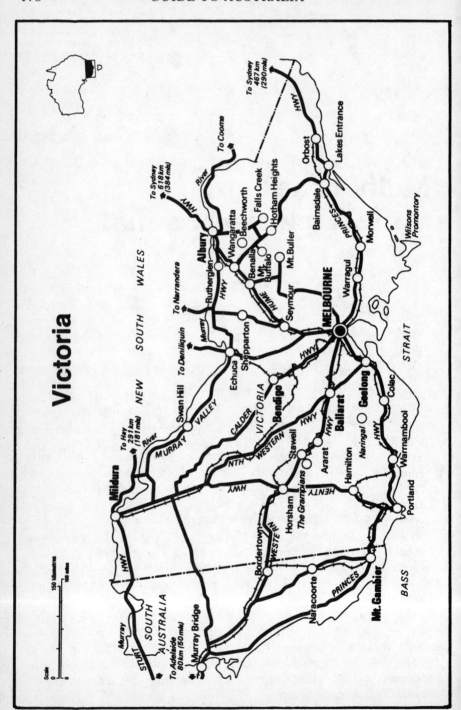

The Yarra flows to Port Phillip Bay, a body of water too far away to be considered part of the city itself, although the suburban trams and trains eventually roll their way to some handsome beaches at South Melbourne, St. Kilda, and Brighton.

In the other direction, Melbourne's outskirts now brush up against the Dandenongs, the attractive mountainlets that provide so many viewful weekend drives.

At a distance, Melbourne seems to be a small forest of skyscrapers, an appropriate configuration for a city known as "everyone's home office." It is definitely a business center, but it also has an historical dignity, seen best in a street-level view of the scores of Victorian-era public buildings. These filigreed structures, legacies from the gold-rush days in the latter half of the nineteenth century, give Melbourne its "English" look. However, a walk along upper Collins Street, under the speckled patterns created by the leafy trees along the city's proudest thoroughfare, seems more like a stroll along the Rue Madeleine in Paris.

If Sydney-siders think about Melbourne at all, it is usually as the slightly amusing home of that form of formalized mayhem called Australian Rules Football. Or they know it as the city where it might decide to rain with no prior warning at all. It's true that Melbourne's weather has a "sudden change" quality about it—but statistics prove that more total rain falls on Sydney than on Melbourne.

Whether skies are clement or not, Melbourne shoppers may keep dry and warm by browsing their way through the famous glass-covered arcades, many of which date back more than 100 years. And speaking of shopping, much of Sydney would agree that Melbourne is "fashion central" in Australia. Some of the country's best-dressed women parade along Collins Street or attend civic functions at the quietly wonderful Arts Centre. Though less grandiloquent than Sydney's opera house, its beauty is one of thorough character.

A European living in Australia who travels between its two largest cities might confirm that it is indeed possible to love both Melbourne and Sydney. Sydney, of course, is an attractive and carefree mistress, full of fun and convivial sensuality. But Melbourne may be your wife, the neat, sensible, and loving mother of your children.

A most practical, comfortable, and even lovable life's companion, she is perhaps made even more attractive by her jealousy toward that "other woman who lives up north."

2. Airports and Long-Distance Transportation

The Melbourne International Airport, universally known as **Tullamarine,** is excellently designed, although unfortunately located a good 12 miles' drive northwest of the city.

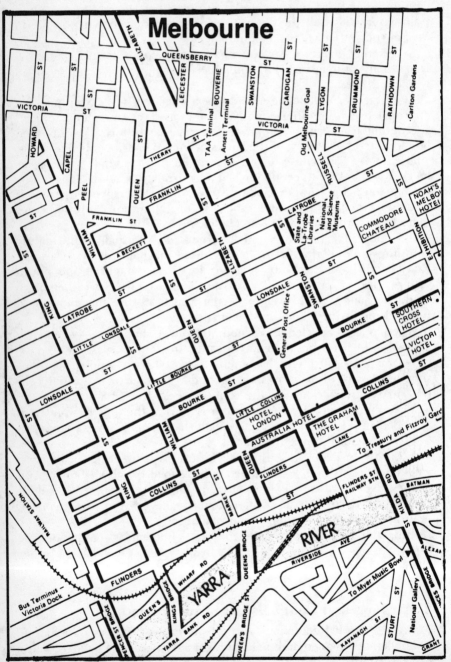

Map courtesy Victorian Government Tourist Bureau

The airport terminals are designed in a shallow U, with the international section at the middle and the two main domestic airlines, **Trans Australia Airlines** (Tel. 345–1333) and **Ansett Airlines of Australia** (Tel. 342–2222—be sure to say "double-two, double-two!") taking up space on the north and south arms respectively—a long walk if you're switching between Ansett and TAA. Headquarters for the up-and-coming **East-West Airlines** (Tel. 63–7713) is near TAA.

In the international terminal, departures (Gates 1 to 6) are on the second level. There's a duty-free shop, a newsstand, etc., and you can visit the observation deck by dropping a ten-cent piece in the turnstile. The large Top Air restaurant and cocktail bar are up one more story, also providing a view over the runways. Arrivals are handled on the bottom floor, which is the location of the bank for currency exchange and the site for rental cars, buses, and taxis. On the sidewalk outside the domestic terminal is where you'll find the most convenient transportation into town. That's the **Skybus Bus Shuttle Service** (Tel. 347–8977), which leaves every 30 minutes and drops off and picks up at the Ansett and TAA buildings on Franklin Street. A smaller bus will pick you up from the major hotels and will meet the shuttle service at Franklin Street, but on a more restrictive schedule. The fare is about $6.

The two split-level **domestic terminals** are also arranged for check-in on the upper level and arrivals down below. After checking in, wait for your flight in the middle-level departure lounges (TAA Gates 1 to 10, Ansett Gates 1 to 11). Boarding calls are no longer broadcast throughout the building. Both terminals have cafeterias, small bars, gift shops, and newsstands. On the Ansett side you'll also find a pharmacy, a post office, a florist, and a "Mother's Room." On the TAA side there is also a jewelry shop and a hairdresser.

If you don't take the bus, remember that it's a long way between the terminal and town. A cab will set you back at least $20. Avis, Hertz, Budget, and Thrifty cars are available at the airport, ready to hand over the keys seven days a week.

All interstate and most country trains arrive at the **Spencer Street Railway Station** (Tel. 62–0771 for reservations) at the foot of Bourke Street. (For information, look for the "Man in Gray" near the main entrance.) Daily expresses to Melbourne from Sydney include two overnight services, the *Southern Aurora* and the *Spirit of Progress* (about $60 for an Economy seat), and the *Intercapital Daylight* service from Sydney and Canberra. Adelaide runs are made on the daily *Overland* (about $50 Economy).

Ships to and from the island state of Tasmania dock at Port Melbourne, near the mouth of the Yarra. Just after our recent visit the old *Empress of*

Australia was retired. A new vessel, the *Abel Tasman,* launched by **T. T. Lines of Tasmania,** has taken over the 14-hour trip across the Bass Strait. Fares range upwards from about $60 each way (maybe $120, if you want a stateroom). Further information is available from **Tasbureau** (Tel. 63–6351), the Tasmanian Government Travel Office at 254 Collins St. in Melbourne.

Coach (bus) trips come into Melbourne on either **Ansett Pioneer** (Tel. 342–2422), 465 Swanston St., or **Greyhound** (Tel. 614–4240), Bourke Street near Spencer, at prices comparable to train fares.

You can drive to Melbourne on good roads from Sydney and Canberra or from Adelaide. The most scenic route from any of those cities to Melbourne (or vice versa) is via the coastal Princes Highway—Route 1, which goes nearly around the entire continent. Via this route it's about 660 miles from Sydney, two or three days' trip. On a circular tour, to or from Sydney, it would be more fun to take Route 1 one way and drive the other way via the Hume Highway, shorter at 580 miles. Or you can take the scenic route over the Victorian Alps via Corryong.

3. Local Transportation in Melbourne

Before you rent a car in Melbourne, consider that the city has one of the finest systems of public transportation in the country. Trolleys and suburban trains run nearly everywhere, although a car is ideal for exploring the countryside around the state of Victoria. We once tried to tour the Dandenong Ranges in a bus and were bitterly disappointed. The large vehicle just can't make the tight turns and park in the small areas we wanted to get to.

Although **Avis Australia** (Tel. 689–7777) is the biggie at 400 Elizabeth St., there are several other reliable U-drives to choose from. These include **Astoria Rent-A-Car** (Tel. 347–7766), 630 Swanston St.; **Thrifty Rent-A-Car** (Tel. 663–5200), 390 Elizabeth St.; **Morley Ford Rent-A-Car** (Tel. 62–0321), 29 Yarrabank Rd., across the river; **Hertz Rent-A-Car** (Tel. 347–3322), 97 Franklin St.; and **Budget Rent-A-Car** (Tel. 320–6331), 21 Bedford St., North Melbourne. Avis, Budget, Hertz, and Thrifty also have airport counters.

Taxis cost about the same as in other Australian cities. Extra charges include 30 cents to telephone them (versus hailing them on the street), small extra charges for suitcases, and higher rates after business and shopping hours. Some phone numbers that will get you taxis in Melbourne: 62–0331 (Taxi Combined Services), 347–5511 (Astoria), 345–3455 (Silver Top), and 567–3333 (Black Cabs).

Melbourne's streetcars—they call them "trams," though—are legendary. They are run by "the Met"—the **Metropolitan Transit Authority**

(Tel. 618–3333 for information). In the city center, at least, there always seems to be a tram approaching that will take you pretty near where you'd like to go, and the chances are that you'll get there for $1 or less. (Hold onto your receipt; inspectors often board the cars to have a look at them.) Careful when running for the trolley stops; although partly protected by guardrails, they are often out in the street, and Melbourne always has lots of out-of-town drivers who are unsure how to navigate through the tram system.

You might pick up a Public Transport Map for about 70 cents at most tram and bus depots and at train stations. It includes color-coded descriptions of all tram, bus, and suburban train routes.

Those trains all used to leave from the **Flinders Street Station** (Tel. 602–9011 or 6–1001 for information). That's the multigabled antique garage with the 10 clocks on the front. (It's traditional for some Melburnians to "meet under the clocks.") Now, however, you may also catch most of these same trains at several new and supermodern stations around the "City Loop." This includes the **Museum Station** at the corner of LaTrobe and Swanston streets, **Parliament Station** on Spring Street, and the new **Flagstaff Station** at the corner of LaTrobe and William streets.

We would consider using this cheap, convenient transportation out to such interesting destinations as Ballarat, the Healesville Sanctuary, and the venerable "Puffing Billy," as well as to catch the boat for Tasmania at Port Melbourne or some of the beaches on Port Phillip Bay (see later).

However, be prepared for some walking in Melbourne. Not only is it interesting, but the straightforward street pattern, at least in the central city, makes it a snap to find your way around.

4. The Melbourne Hotel Scene

Be sure to see our general comments on Australian hotels under this same section in the Sydney chapter. If you're driving around the country, you may want to get hold of a copy of the Royal Automobile Club's *Tourguide.* You can buy it for around $5 at RAC headquarters (Tel. 607–2211), 123 Queen St. in Melbourne.

EXPENSIVE HOTELS

Rates will change, of course, but this category generally covers hotels charging more than $80 a day for two. (Again, check the exchange rates, which may make these prices seem less painful.) Unless otherwise noted, all have "international-class" amenities like color televisions, air conditioning, a room refrigerator, coffee- and tea-making equipment, etc.

The high, wide, and handsome **Regent Melbourne,** formerly the

Wentworth (Tel. 63–0321), commands the top end of Collins Street, its rooms occupying the top 15 floors of one of the twin 50-story towers (some guests report they have found it sunny in their room, but cloudy and rainy at ground level!): Enclosed, glass-domed driveway bordered year-round by trees and flowers; open mezzanine-style lobby and reception area overlooking an indoor "Great Space" patio with its outdoorsy restaurant; several bars, etc., down there, too; six elevators whisking up to the first stop after the lobby, the 35th floor, where most of the hotel begins; the dining room on this floor with a view over Melbourne to the Blue Dandenongs; grillroom to one side, specializing in beef; also a pleasant piano bar; same level, actually the "bottom" of a 17-story cylindrical atrium lounge decorated with a hanging acrylic fabric some irreverent Melburnians have dubbed "the shredded shower curtain"; no swimming pool.

Total of 377 rooms from the 36th to the 50th floors, including 52 commodious suites; normal doubles totaling about 300 square feet; dramatic but perhaps nerve-rattling floor-to-ceiling bay windows in each unit; shutters to close if the altitude makes you shudder; modern furnishings; all luxury amenities, including international-dial telephones (there's even one of those in the loo!); northern aspect the nicest for our money—and speaking of money, rates beginning at about $130 for two, then continuing as high as the view. Once we got used to sleeping in the clouds, we enjoyed our own stay in this proud tower, although we haven't checked in since the management did its switcheroo. Certainly for opulent and dramatic architecture nothing else around matches it.

Back down to earth, relatively speaking, the 21-story **Hilton International Melbourne** (Tel. 419–3311) is certainly still a challenger, and it is just as expensive: Nicely situated next to Fitzroy Gardens and the Melbourne Cricket Ground; large, marble-floored lobby; overhead glass sculptures glittering by spotlight; a swirling staircase up to the mezzanine; elegant Cliveden Room restaurant with stained-glass windows; less formal Gallery (open daily); the Hacienda coffee shop (with Latin American specialties); the MCG Public Bar, an old-fashioned Aussie pub attached to the newer building; Juliana's of Melbourne, a disco for Tuesday to Saturday terpsichore; heated swimming pool (pool bar open on the terrace in warm weather).

Outback-sized elevators to 41 suites and 387 spacious, excellently equipped bedchambers, all with standard luxury amenities (color TV, direct-dial phones, etc.); other special touches like the self-service fridge/bar; terrific views from the higher floors; some units available right next to the pool; reportedly excellent service everywhere (or as the locals say, "spot on!"). We looked high and low for anything critical to say about the Hilton. The only thing we could come up with is that some folks think it's a little far to walk to shopping, theaters, etc.—a very small penalty to pay, especially with the ubiquitous taxis and trams available. (Reservations through the Hilton organization or from the hotel at 25 Collins St., East Melbourne 3002, Victoria.) We call it "spot on" indeed!

A special place in the hearts of Melburnians has been reserved for the venerable **Hotel Windsor** (Tel. 63–0261), whose century-old plant has been restored and refurbished by the Oberoi organization to recapture its authentic grand-hotel aura. (Even the staff uniforms duplicate those of the 1880s.)

We have been through the Windsor three times. Once we stayed there before its renaissance, finding its leaky and creaky interior decidedly unlovable. Then we explored again while it was still in the midst of its heroic major surgery. Since then we have seen the hotel after it reopened to great fanfare, receiving deserved praise from all quarters for its renewed elegance.

It's a wonderful location opposite the State Parliament House on Spring Street. The lobby has the traditional grand staircase. (The elevators are new, but note the old lifts now converted into open-cage telephone booths!) The 1883 dining room with its stained-glass dome lights is considered an architectural *tour de force,* and readers report they had some excellent fare there, too. The best bedchambers have been redone in Queen Anne style. The five Victorian suites feature atmospheric fireplaces. Nightly tabs for two now begin at around $110. (Reservations from the hotel at 115 Spring St., Melbourne, Vic. 3000.) Readers have been universal in their opinion that the Windsor is as comfortable as it is historic.

In recent years, new Australian hotels have been going "atrium-crazy" in their bids for architectural recognition. Something similar has happened at the **Menzies at Rialto** (Tel. 62–0111), but this time a novel approach was used. Here they have taken two neo-Gothic nineteenth-century structures, façades full of filigree and froufrou and garnished with turrets and gables, partially degutted them, and then created a roof of glass 10 stories over the cobbled delivery lane in between. It sounds weird, but it works wonderfully:

Entrance into the alley between the old Rialto and Winfield buildings; white-marbled lobby to one side; two floors below, the Portego lounge, piano bar, and Cafe Rialto restaurant forming the visual focus of the atrium; other dining in the somewhat more intimate Chandelier Room or the Tavern Bar; several cocktail lounges; enclosed, heated swimming pool and sauna on the roof; some specialty shops tucked here and there; 243 living rooms, some in unusual designs dictated by the exterior architecture; most with balconies directly overlooking the lounge and within easy earshot of the flute or piano music echoing below; all units with today's set of standard luxuries, plus extra phones, a writing desk, in-house movies on the telly, etc.; bathrooms in Italian marble; most rooms with king-size or queen-double beds; doubles beginning around $110; 24-hour room service available.

Managed by the well-known Federal Pacific Hotels group, the Menzies is pretty far down Collins Street at No. 495, and it is the only hotel located in what might be called the bank and business end of town. This logically makes it a favorite with the traveling stock-exchange set and a little less convenient for dedicated vacationers. Otherwise we would have placed it further up on our list. But on its own merits, at least, the Menzies brings credit to a grand old name in Melbourne and it deserves to succeed.

Another re-creation of the past, seemingly inspired by the above, is the more modestly sized **Gordon Place** (Tel. 663–5355) at 24–38 Little Bourke St. in the heart of Chinatown. Here, too, is a group of old buildings that have been glassed over and tastefully pulled together into a single hotel, this one specializing in apartments: Several wings connected with corri-dors and bridges on different levels; heated saltwater pool in one court-yard; Cafe Palma, an Italian restaurant, in the other one, with a giant date palm and lots of tropical greenery; cozy Gordon's Bar and Bistro to one side; 59 widely varying rooms, all with kitchens or kitchenettes; high ceilings in the top-floor units; no food room service; all with maid ser-vice, however. Rates at this writing begin at $80, with one-bedroom apartments from $110 to $120, two-bedroom units at $150, and split-level apartments at $200. There are weekly discounts of 10 percent, but you'd better recheck this information. Gordon Place is convenient to lots of theaters, and for the right kind of guest it puts on a good show.

The **Southern Cross** (Tel. 63–0221) is also a viable choice: Convenient to Chinatown and the theater and shopping district; modern steel-and-glass structure at the corner of Exhibition and Bourke streets; direct connection to a modern, two-level shopping arcade; rambling lobby with burbling, cherub-filled fountain and purple paisley-patterned carpet; several public rooms including the frond-full Palm Court Restaurant, the tartan- and brick-lined Club Grill, the Tavern Bar, the Wilawa Piano Bar, etc. No pool; free parking. Nearly all bedrooms with king- or queen-size beds; excellent decorations with patterned wallpaper or draperies and bedspreads; most rooms with tub and shower together; rates begin-ning at around $115 double. (Reservations from the hotel at 131 Exhibi-tion St., Melbourne, Vic. 3000.) The Southern Cross, like the one on Australia's flag, deserves its five stars.

A little far from the center of things, although less than ten minutes by tram, the **Telford Old Melbourne** (Tel. 329–9344) has excellent facilities even if it is somewhat overdecorated for our taste: Designed rather like an old coach house in some parts, a baronial European mansion in other areas; antiques abounding everywhere. Four- to six-story building surrounding an interior cobblestoned courtyard; small lobby with red and pink flocked wallpaper and a bust of Shakespeare (or somebody); Haymarket 1886 Restaurant with blue velvet and more statuary; Norman Lindsay Cocktail Bar (named after the late Australian author and artist); separate piano bar, lit by a piano-top candelabrum; Nellie Stewart's Bar; Benjamin's Cellar; ample outdoor swimming pool.

Well over 200 well-maintained bedrooms, 75 percent with walkout iron-railed balconies; good-quality though heavy furnishings; rates beginning now at about $85. (Reservations from the hotel at 5–17 Flemington Rd., Melbourne North 3051, or through the Commodore chain.) Maybe it's somewhat saccharin and a mash of mixes, but it's well run and popular.

With less personality, but more convenience, **Noah's** (Tel. 662–0511) attracts many to its midtown location. Nevertheless its heating difficulties, old-fashioned plumbing, substandard coffee shop, and other problems have combined to remove it from our list. No longer the dependable ark that it was, in our opinion.

Rockman's Melbourne Regency (Tel. 662–3900) should not to be confused with the similarly named Regent Melbourne, above. The 190-room hotel at the corner of Lonsdale and Exhibition streets sports a swimming pool and is popular with visiting businessmen. We missed it last trip. However one reader said facilities and service were fine except that as a late sleeper she was constantly interrupted by hotel personnel going through their daily routines. (Maybe a "do not disturb" sign on the door would have done the trick.)

Still under construction on our recent visit to Melbourne, the new **Hyatt on Collins** is due to open in late 1986, piercing the sky with an unusual curving tower behind the traditional façades in the area. Plans for the 468-room establishment look interesting—at least if Australia can stand another hotel atrium. (But then, Hyatt pioneered in this feature, so maybe they can pull it off.) The hotel will be conveniently located on Collins Street, near the corner of Russell. We'll be anxious to check in and check it out ourselves soon.

MEDIUM-PRICE HOTELS

We have only two candidates for hotels in this category for this edition. The better is the somewhat tired **Hotel Australia** (Tel. 63–0401), whose salad days began in 1939. It could hardly be more central, however, in its enviable site at 266 Collins St.: Lots of stairs to and through a multitiered lobby; browns and oranges predominating; several restaurants scattered around; some rooms with shower, others with tub; TVs (some in color) and fridges throughout; some singles at about $60; fancier doubles at around $75. It's respectable enough, and certainly a winner for location.

Then there's the **Sheraton** (Tel. 63–9961), which we hasten to point out is another of those modest hostelries, like the Marquee Sheraton in Sydney, that has somehow got hold of the Sheraton name in Australia (neither is part of Sheraton Hotels in the Pacific, which administers Sydney's Wentworth and the Sheratons at Perth and Ayers Rock): Not a bad address at 13 Spring St., across from the Treasury Gardens and a statue of Bobby Burns; small lobby; Terrace Restaurant with second-level park view; 166 generally neat rooms, some with queen-size beds, some with balcony; most in the $70 range. (Reservations from the hotel or through the Flag chain.) As we said, it's no showplace, but it's okay.

BUDGET ACCOMMODATIONS

The **Victoria of Melbourne** (Tel. 328–2880), which has rooms perhaps still running a wide gamut between $30 and $50 for two, occupies spot number one at this "Bare Bones" price level. Like the Australia, it's also the relic of another age, but one more fairly priced for its fading charms. Very central location at 215 Little Collins St.; popular with out-of-town shoppers of modest means; lobby dominated by a staircase to the mezzanine salon; TV lounge somewhere; creaky corridors; smaller, older rooms in the rear with radios about $30 single, $35 double; newer units in the east wing with color TVs about $50 for two by now. The old Vic is viable enough for the category.

A very different kind of establishment is the peaceful little **Magnolia Court** (Tel. 419–4518), far away from the bright lights at 101 Powlett St. in East Melbourne, not far from Fitzroy Gardens. This is a very clean, family-run bed-and-breakfast place, still offering rooms at approximately $35 for two (maybe $30 for one). Breakfast is extra but usually delicious. Write Mrs. Doyle, the resident manager, at the address above (Zone 3002). The Magnolia is a pleasant blossom.

Other possibilities near the center include the six-story **London Hotel** (Tel. 67–6201) at 99 Elizabeth St. with singles at $25 and doubles at $30 and the **Spencer Hotel** (Tel. 62–6991) at 44 Spencer St. with singles at $35 and doubles at $45. (Don't hold us to these rates, please.)

Also very practical, if a little sterile, is the **YWCA Motel** (Tel. 329–5188), 489 Elizabeth St., near the Ansett terminal. No frills, but it's clean accommodation for women, men, or families for about $35 double, $25 single. There's a TV lounge, a Red Phone at the end of every corridor, etc. We met one budget-minded American family who were staying here, and they thought it was great.

Hosies Hotel (Tel. 62–5521), almost above the famous painting of Chloe in Young & Jackson's pub, has some unsurpassed views of the Flinders Street Railway Station. Check out the Mile High Club on the fourth floor. It's filled with leftover furnishings from old airliners, apparently. The rooms, which take off for about $45 double, $35 single, are undramatic, often small, but fairly clean. You'll find it, if you want it, at the corner of Elizabeth and Flinders streets. Unlike Chloe, Hosie's no longer rosy. But she's friendly, willing, and probably able.

Youth hostels? There is one, at 500 Abbotsford St., North Melbourne (Tel. 328–2880), which will set you back around $6.50 a night for seniors, $3.50 a night for juniors (but bring your own sheets in any case). You must be a member, of course. If you're not, you can apply to the Youth Hostels Association of Victoria (Tel. 63–5521), Shop 11, Princes Gate Arcade, Flinders Street, Melbourne 3000 (at the corner of Swanston Street).

5. Restaurants and Dining

Melbourne has a deservedly delicious reputation for elegant dining. It is also known for changeable chefs and peripatetic proprietors who kanga from kitchen to kitchen, making it difficult to keep up with what's curently "in."

By type of cuisine, we list those dining rooms in the central area—Melbourne, with East, West, and South Melbourne, as well as Carlton (the "Uni" neighborhood) thrown in. Following that is a group in greater Melbourne and other out-of-town precincts by the name of their respective areas. Remember that some of Melbourne's best salons are indeed far out from the center—e.g., Glo Glo's in Toorak.

AUSTRALIAN AND COSMOPOLITAN

The category may sound a little modest for such an excellent restaurant, but **Petty Sessions** (Tel. 61–3854) is too varied in its ability to be called Continental. A below-street-level site in the law courts and financial district, it offers sensible fare for lunch and then superb evening-out dining later on. We can personally recommend the garlic prawns (Sara had 'em as a full meal) and the Escalope de Veau Calypso, in which the veal was cooked in a coconut and mango sauce. The beef Wellington and rack of lamb are also good. Others have praised the crayfish thermidore (that's a lobster, of course) and the supreme of chicken (either "butterfly" or "Rossini").

Most meals are in the $20 to $25 range. Two with wine and dessert will share a bill of about $60. We had excellent attention from the waiter and the maitre d', and the whole experience was one accented by candlelight and a live orchestra playing by a dance floor somewhere toward the rear. Our only grouse was that, as in many successful restaurants around the world, management tries to crowd too many tables into some narrow spaces. The official address is 456 Collins St., but look for the striped awning on a side street just a few steps south of the main drag. Petty Sessions was a Grand Session for us. (Closed Sundays.)

Fun for lunch—and we mean especially for long, drawn-out, conversational lunches—is the incomparable **Jimmy Watson's** (Tel. 347–3985) at 333 Lygon St. in Carlton. Cheap drinks, substantial food, and noisy conviviality characterize this place, which winds through an old wine shop near the university. It isn't so much what you have here (roast beef and the like) as who you have it with. Say hello to Prop. Alan Watson, jovial son of the founder and a Melbourne city councilman. We enjoyed one of Watson's own wines, a special Tokay, with our own midday munch with Stan Marks, the Melbourne author and *bon vivant* who let us in on it. Fondly recollected and recommended.

For steaks, steaks, and only steaks, the prime choice is probably **Vlado's Charcoal Grill** (Tel. 428–5833) at 61 Bridge Rd., Richmond. Vlado will bring to your table roasted red peppers and spicy Croatian sausages to go with the beef. Many respected trenchermen rate Vlado's the best steak house in Australia. Large servings will add up to about $50 for two. Bring your own wine. (Closed Sunday evening.)

Other Melbourne dining rooms currently winning critical favor include **Lazar** (Tel. 602–1822) at 240 King St.; **Tsindos Bistrot** (Tel. 663–3076), a much smaller place at 100 Bourke St.; and especially **Stephanie's** (Tel. 20–8944), a more expensive *haute cuisine* address at 405 Tooronga Rd. in Hawthorn.

For seafood, dive into **Jean Jacques** (Tel. 328–4214) at 502 Queensberry Rd. in North Melbourne. (Some compare it to Doyle's or the Backstage in Sydney.) A little closer to the center, the **Melbourne Catch** (Tel. 67–3542) at 12 McKillop St. offers a good catch of very fresh fish. There is also the **Melbourne Oyster Bar** (Tel. 67–2745), a newer operation at 209 King St., and **the Quay** (Tel. 654–1233), in a wonderfully atmospheric location overlooking the river at 1–19 Princes Walk, below Batman Avenue.

Eleventy-seven varieties of pancakes are available at the **Pancake Parlor** outlets, the oldest of which is off Bourke Street in the theater district at 25 Market Lane. There are now branches in the Centrepoint Basement off the Bourke Street Mall and at 20 McKillop St. We stayed with something mapley and conservative and enjoyed drawing up to the warm fire on a cold, wet day. (Open daily, but there's a weekend surcharge after 5 P.M. Friday.)

We know of one dependable all-vegetarian restaurant this year. That's **Gopal's** (Tel. 63–1578) at 139 Swanston St., opposite the Town Hall. The last we looked, you could dine on "all you can eat" for $6 at dinner, $2.50 at lunch—but please don't hold us to those prices. (Closed Sundays.)

ORIENTAL RESTAURANTS

Melbourne's foremost Chinese restaurateur is Gilbert Lau, justly famous for the **Flower Drum** (Tel. 663–2531), which beats a fragrant song at 103 Little Bourke St. (Try the shark's fin soup.) Some who object to being drummed to the tune of about $35 per person say they prefer several more modestly priced but still excellent family-run Chinese kitchens.

These include the **Bamboo House** (Tel. 662–1565) at 47 Little Bourke St., for spicier, Peking-style dishes; the **Confucian Inn** (Tel. 663–3200), a BYO at 11 Waratah Place (off Little Bourke near Russell), which serves *yum cha* at lunch; and especially the **Empress of China** (Tel. 663–1883) at 120 Little Bourke St., one of the best Chinese addresses around.

At least two very good Indonesian restaurants have opened in Melbourne: **Widuri** (Tel. 241–4765) is at Shop 6, 300 Toorak Rd. in South Yarra, and **Borobudur** (Tel. 82–7249) is at 159 Camberwell Rd. in Hawthorn. Neither has a wine license, but that helps keep expenses down. Bring your own, and they'll pop your cork.

A couple of Japanese entries are also making fans. The **Sukiyaki House** (Tel. 63–84201) at 21 Alfred Place is one; **Kuni's** (Tel. 63–9243), at 27 Crossley Lane, is the other. Both are in Chinatown.

CONTINENTAL AND FRENCH CUISINE

On one of our own rambles over the restaurants of Melbourne, we experienced outstanding cooking at **Cafe Balzac** (Tel. 419–6599) at 62 Wellington Parade, a short march from the Hilton. Somehow in our exuberance we lost our notes, but we remember it as an attractive, streetside cafe, with waiting room in the fountain patio. Here is the place for tender veal or roast duckling. We enjoyed the Escalope de Veau a la Savoyarde served with dry vermouth and cream sauce. There's a long, five-page menu—inspired, perhaps, by Honoré de Balzac's history of France. Almost a *tour de force*.

You won't see any advertising for **Fanny's** (Tel. 663–3017), which has consistently held its reputation as the most authentic French restaurant in Melbourne for the past several years. Try the breast of chicken with

hazelnut sauce. Find Fanny's at 243 Lonsdale St., between Russell and
Swanston. Expensive and often crowded, but with good reason. (Closed
Sundays.)

A smaller and less pricy place, a little north of the center near Carlton
Gardens, is **Tansy's** (formerly "Fives," Tel. 380–5555), apparently once
named after its telephone number and address at 555 Nicholson St. This
BYO is open daily except Tuesday, and a woman chef named Tansy
Good is reputed to be one of the best in town. We haven't been in, but it's
on our list for a personal try. (Open for lunch and dinner.)

Three more modest but well-regarded Gallic addresses this year include **La Bouffe** (Tel. 67–1047), a jolly BYO in new digs at 4 Bank Place;
La Chaumière (Tel. 328–1650), with intimate atmosphere at 36 Abbotsford
St. in West Melbourne; and **Tolarno** (Tel. 534–0521), a licensed bistro at
42 Fitzroy St. in St. Kilda.

ITALIAN FOOD

Melbourne is well-known for the cooking delights of its Italian popula-
tion, and their delight in opening it all up for everyone to enjoy. Lygon
Street, in Carlson, is known as the center for Italian cooking in Melbourne.
One good, inexpensive example is **Lentini's** (Tel. 347–6813) at No. 323.
Any veal dish is likely to be good—and cheap, too. One Italian success
for us downtown was the **Society** (Tel. 63–5378), high up at 23 Bourke
St., about 25 yards south of Spring. We loved the ravioli verdi, filled with
pâté and covered with a spicy sauce. Try the osso bucco or the spaghetti
marinara, too. The staff was attentive, and the house wine was satisfacto-
ry for an average meal. (Recheck the above number before going. Closed
Sundays in any case.) The **Metro** (Tel. 63–2094), at 41 Bourke St., has a
good Italian reputation. We enjoyed a pistachio omelet here recently for
lunch, but didn't get back for an evening meal. We feel **Florentino's** (Tel.
662–1811), 80 Bourke St., may have slipped a bit. It was once Melbourne's
premier Italian address, and it still satisfies some of its loyal customers.

Sassi's (Tel. 489–5254) is a little north of the center at 99 Queen's
Parade. An old savings bank, it has been converted to an elegant dining
room and cheaper bistro at the end of a tree-lined driveway. Amid brick
walls and blue-tiled floors, Tony Sassi and his mother dish out delicious
calamari (squid), steak pizzaola, and other recipes emanating from Milano
to Palermo. (Open daily except there's no lunch on Saturday or dinner
on Sunday.)

The **Latin Cafe** (Tel. 662–1985) at 55 Lonsdale St. is a popular gathering spot for Melbourne's communicators. We'd stick with the spaghetti
and pasta standards and enjoy rubbing elbows with the city's writers and
politicos who show up to gossip and relax. Other well-regarded and

reasonable Italian kitchens in or near the center include the following modest BYOs: **Catta Bistro** (Tel. 663–2718), at 177 Exhibition St.; **Campari** (Tel. 67–3813), at 25 Hardware St.; **Frascati** (Tel. 62–5972), at 149 Lonsdale St.; and **Pellegrini's** (Tel. 662–1503), at 66 Bourke St. (behind the espresso bar).

And not far from the Old Melbourne Gaol, where Ned Kelly met his maker, is **Toto's Pizza House** (Tel. 347–5974) at 101 Lygon St. According to Melbourne pizza cognoscente Ed Kaptein, there are great choices in these Italian pies for around $6, all served in pleasant surroundings. Then Michael Giller of La Mirada, California, wrote us that **Casa di Iorio,** also on Lygon Street, served him "one of the best pizzas in the world" for around $5.

OUT-OF-TOWN RESTAURANTS

We hasten to say that we define "town" a little more narrowly for international travelers than a Melburnian would when it comes to restaurants. Neighborhoods like South Yarra and Collingwood are fruitful gourmet districts in the metropolitan area if you have a car and know your way around.

Collingwood

The French-style **Clichy** (Tel. 417–6404) is not far from the Yarra Bend National Park at 9 Peel St. This is good French fare in quiet surroundings, and with a long wine list. (Closed Mondays, like many Melbourne restaurants.)

St. Kilda

Check out the inexpensive foreign restaurants along Acland Street, near the Village Bell (a pub). One well-known German dining room is the **Black Rose** (Tel. 534–6885) at 94 Acland St. The nearby **Fairy Stork** (Tel. 534–1936), at 89 Acland, is a popular Chinese and vegetarian address. Both of those are BYOs. A no-nonsense (but licensed) French establishment is the **Tolarno** (Tel. 534–0521), at 42 Fitzroy St. And St. Kilda is also the home of the deluxe French establishment called **The Willows** (Tel. 267–5252) in an historic building at 462 St. Kilda Rd.

South Yarra

Mention South Yarra in Melbourne, and everyone almost seems to salivate. Indeed there are several good restaurants in this close-in neighborhood. The most famous is **Maxim's** (Tel. 266–5500), at 60 Toorak Rd. It's expensive and very French, of course, although some say it's faded somewhat now in its later years.

Two Faces (Tel. 266–1547), at 149 Toorak Rd., is considered by some to be the best French restaurant in six states and two territories. We've never been in, but our Melbourne informants say it's often noisy and the quality seems to be slipping. Others strongly disagree. It does have an unusually extensive wine list, and it rates three hats in the *Melbourne Age*'s *Good Food Guide.* Not as well known is **Jardin's** (Tel. 266–4936), another attractive French entry at 123 Park St. Here the cuisine tends more toward the traditional, but many say it's just as good as its famous neighbor. Prices are about the same—about $35 for a full meal, plus wine.

A smaller and less expensive Continental choice is **Ellie's** (Tel. 240–9030), further along at 278 Toorak Rd. Try the Duckling a l'Orange.

Toorak

Among some local gourmets, **Glo Glo's** (Tel. 241–2615), at 3 Carters Ave., will always be *the* chic international dining room. We couldn't see paying the price, however—maybe $100 per couple by now. If it holds that reputation, we'll hoe into their tucker one of these days. It's open until midnight, and the "in" crowd dines late here. Our reliable informants tell us that although the place is glamorous and glossy, the cuisine is certainly excellent. (Closed Sundays.)

6. Sightseeing in Melbourne (and Victoria)

We certainly don't recommend a hectic round of "musts" in Melbourne. A couple leisurely walks might do the trick.

THE "GOLDEN MILE"

That somewhat expansive term is what Melburnians like to call central Melbourne or "Melbourne City." It's a rectangular crosshatch of about 18 principal streets north of the Yarra River. That network, in turn, is set at an angle to hundreds of other regularly spaced streets and roads. (You can get an excellent view from the new West Gate Bridge.)

If you have a map, here's a theoretical walk down Collins Street to about Elizabeth, then back up Bourke to Spring, along Little Lonsdale Street to Swanston, then over to LaTrobe and thence to Russell. We've lopped off quite a bit of the Golden Mile. You may want to add on a few discoveries of your own or to shave some more off this.

Some say that **Collins Street** has lost its ambiance of years gone by. Many of its Gold Rush Gothic and Victorian buildings have fallen to make way for the high-rise headquarters of diverse banks and insurance companies, and even a couple of hotels. Nevertheless it retains some of the all-mixed-up charm of Fifth Avenue in New York, and there are still enough trees, flagstones, and nineteenth-century structures to provide pleasant backgrounds to a walk down Collins from Spring.

Near Swanston Street is the fountain-filled **City Square** and its graffiti wall, where everyone is invited to vent his spleen on washable walls. Across the street, with its entrance on Swanston, the **Town Hall** dates back to 1867. About 3,000 can crowd in for public events, they say, but that mob has never included us.

A side-step to the left, along Swanston, leads to **St. Paul's Cathedral,** a stylistic mixture that started out with a British architect in 1880. If you're only going to look at one cathedral, however, you might want to wait for St. Patrick's. Across the street, at No. 1 Swanston, hides Melbourne's truest treasure—at least to hear some speak. There in the bar at **Young & Jackson's,** a tiny pub, is the work of art that shocked the Melbourne Exhibition of 1880. It's a large, full-length nude oil called *Chloe*—positively Australia's most famous single painting and the subject of countless toasts from Young & Jackson's to North Africa over the past 100 years.

In the next block south on Collins is the ancient **Royal Arcade,** one of several skylit shopping tunnels that burrow through the business blocks. Look for the painted statues of Gog and Magog. When fully operational, they call attention to the time of day every hour. The Arcade, built about 1870, has entrances on Collins and Little Collins streets and also to the mosaic-tiled Block Arcade. Nearby is **Victour** (Victoria) Travel Centre (Tel. 602–9444), the state government tourist office at 230 Collins St.

At the corner of Elizabeth and Bourke is the **General Post Office,** which owes its rococo design to no fewer than 65 architects. At 2 P.M. daily the clock plays several bars of the national anthem, *Advance Australia Fair.* Bourke Street between Elizabeth and Swanston is a walking street, *except for trams,* so watch out! (Motormen are pretty careful, of course, but they can't swerve.) Little Bourke Street between Swanston and Spring, now known as **Chinatown,** is the heart of the cinema and theater district.

At Spring Street, the historic old **Windsor Hotel** has been restored to nineteenth-century glory. (Peek into the dining room, lounges, etc., if you can, to see how successful it has been.) Across Spring Street is the neoclassic **State Parliament House,** which they began building in 1856 and continued working on for 36 years before giving up. Two sides of the building are still incomplete. In 1901 the National Parliament met here and liked it so much that they continued to do so until 1927 when the lawmakers moved to Canberra.

In the nearby little triangular park called **Carpentaria Place** is the seated statue of Adam Lindsay Gordon, the tragic Australian poet (1830–1870) described in chapter 4.

The corner of Spring and Little Bourke streets is taken up by the elaborately decorated **Princess Theatre,** built for Queen Victoria's jubilee in 1887. Large-scale productions are still staged here.

Not far away, in quite a different world, is **St. Patrick's Cathedral,** the triple-spired Gothic structure at Gisborne and Albert streets that every architectural enthusiast says we should see. We've yet to go in ourselves, but those in the know say it's got to be one of the best Gothic interiors in the world. Sorry, we missed it again.

The **Museum of Victoria** (Tel. 669–9888, formerly called the National Museum) at the corner of Little Lonsdale and Russell streets presents extensive natural history and ethnographic collections. But its prime exhibit as far as most Australians are concerned—perhaps rivaling the aforementioned *Chloe*—is the stuffed Phar Lap, the chestnut gelding who won 37 races, including the Melbourne Cup of 1930. He died in 1932 right after winning the Agua Caliente Handicap at Menlo Park, California. (Australians can't seem to let Phar Lap go. His heart is on display in Canberra.) The museum is open daily until 5 P.M., beginning at 10 A.M. weekdays and 2 P.M. Sundays.

Where Russell Street meets Franklin Street is what's left of the 1841 **Old Melbourne Gaol** (Tel. 654–6328), now a penal museum open daily from 10 to 5. As every Australian schoolchild knows, this was the site of the hanging of the bushranger Ned Kelly on November 11, 1880. His armor is there, too, along with the cell where his mother admonished him, "Mind you die like a Kelly!" Still in place, too, is the hangman's scaffold where, at the age of 25, he spoke his last words: "Such is life!"

Many Australians who visit Melbourne wouldn't feel they had done the town at all if they hadn't experienced the whole trinity: (1) the painting of Chloe, (2) the skin of Phar Lap, and (3) the spirit of Ned Kelly in the old jail. We agree.

THE VICTORIAN ARTS CENTRE

Rapidly becoming the internationally recognized symbol of Melbourne is a silver-white 375-foot-high spire of tubular steel. This somewhat Eiffel-like structure caps the Theatres Building, the recently opened complex of underground auditoriums that was the final stage in the three-part Victorian Arts Centre. Just across the Yarra from the Golden Mile, the Theatres Building is flanked by the cylindrical Melbourne Concert Hall, right next to the river, and the rectangular Victorian Art Gallery.

The richly decorated **Theatres Building** houses three major stages, including the State Theatre, one of the world's largest stages and designed for the most opulent productions; the Playhouse, for traditional drama and musicals; and the Studio, a theater-in-the-round for smaller, more experimental works. Together with the associated support facilities, including some spectacular foyers, art exhibitions, and a couple of restaurants and bars, the building reaches six stories below the ground.

The 2,600-seat **Melbourne Concert Hall** is also a dramatic structure inside and out. It is now the home of the Melbourne Symphony Orchestra, but it performs equally well for rock and jazz concerts. Its Grand Concert Organ, with 4,189 pipes, was built by Casavant Freres of Quebec, Canada. The building also holds the Performing Arts Museum (admission $2) and the Treble Clef, a well-regarded restaurant.

We recently took the one-hour guided tour through the Theatres Building and Concert Hall, something that no show-biz buff should miss. Buy your tickets ($2.50) at the Smorgon Family Plaza inside the Theatres Building.

A few steps further along St. Kilda Road is the Victorian Art Gallery. It's now also known as the **National Gallery of Victoria** (Tel. 62–7411), a better term, since the name Victorian Art Gallery gives the impression to an out-of-towner that it houses "Victorian" art—that is, art created during the Victorian age. (Unfortunate misunderstandings occur all over the place among foreigners like us because of things named after the *state* of Victoria, not the *era* of Queen Victoria.)

The basalt bluestone structure beckons from a rounded archway across a moat. An inner glass wall supports a sheet of running water. There's also a Great Hall whose roof is made of stained-glass panels. Three open courtyards and many halls house fine sculpture and art that ranges from Asian to European (contemporary and Old Masters), plus a large collection of paintings by the Heidelberg School, Australian artists who were strongly influenced by French Impressionism. Other periods of the nation's art—colonial, Edwardian, and contemporary—are also represented, and, in fact, the Australian collection is so large that only about a third of it can be exhibited at once.

The museum opens at 10 daily, except Monday, closing at 5 every day except Wednesday when the lights stay on until 9 P.M. (Admission is $1.) Free guided tours are often available.

MELBOURNE PARKS AND GARDENS

Somehow there always seems to be a place to sit down in Melbourne. Or almost always. (If you're a man, better note the occasional benches that are labeled sternly in stone "Ladies Only"—a genteel touch that even equal-rights advocates are not likely to erase.)

Part of the aura of relaxation in this otherwise conservative, business-like city is due to its extensive parks and gardens system. Nearly a quarter of the city's acreage has been set aside as green space. It would be impossible to cover all the parks in this chapter, but here is a

J-shaped sequence, which, if followed strictly, would keep you generally off the streets and on the grass all day.

Just across St. Kilda Road from the Victorian Arts Centre is **Alexandra Gardens,** a popular lunchtime picnic site by the Yarra River. There stands the statue of Peter Pan. A quick trot across the broad, tree-lined Alexandra Avenue brings you to the little **Queen Victoria Gardens.** A floral clock there may tell you if it's two carnations past a rhododendron.

Continuing south, crossing another avenue, you'll see the **Sidney Myer Music Bowl**—the tentlike, partially open-air amphitheater where on occasion 100,000 people listen to free concerts. It's in the park called the **King's Domain,** sometimes called the Royal Domain. You have to skirt **Government House** (where the Queen's representative lives, and not open to general peeking) to walk to the **Shrine of Remembrance,** a heavy, classical Greek–style memorial to Australian war dead.

Nearby, though, look for the statue of a donkey with two soldiers. The private leading the animal is John Simpson (Kirkpatrick), an obscure English immigrant who became an Australian hero. He rescued many wounded by carrying them to safety on a stray donkey for 25 days at Gallipoli in 1915 until he himself was killed.

Governor La Trobe's Cottage (Tel. 63–5528), the former residence of Charles La Trobe, the first Victoria governor, was prefabricated in England. La Trobe lived in the four-room unit at Jolimont while governing from 1839 to 1854. In recent years it was restored and moved to the Domain by the National Trust of Australia. Now open about 10:00 A.M. to 4:30 P.M. daily, and worth seeing.

A step across Birdwood Avenue is Melbourne's **Royal Botanical Gardens,** a total of 88 acres of lawns, gardens, and lakes, some of the best classical landscaping in the world. There are ducks and swans and examples of almost everything that will grow in Australia—some 12,000 species, anyway.

Crossing the 1899 Morrell Bridge takes you into the world of sport. Here you'll find the **Sports and Entertainment Centre** (formerly Olympic Park) with its sports arena and velodrome (for cycle racing), which was developed for the 1956 Olympic Games. Just to the north, across Swan Street, is **Yarra Park,** home of three separate cricket fields, of which the most famous is the **Melbourne Cricket Ground** (M.C.G., for short), site not only of that gentlemen's game but of rough-and-rumble Australian Rules Football during the winter season. The M.C.G. has held a crowd as large as 120,000.

Near the Hilton you can quick-march across Wellington Parade into the **Fitzroy Gardens.** On our first foray into Fitzroy, at night, we thought we saw a little wallaby waiting for us. He turned out to be one of a large family of possums who regularly freeload there after dark, and when we had nothing to offer he hopped away. Extend your hand with some food and you'll receive a warm marsupial welcome.

In the gardens, too, is what's called **Captain Cook's Cottage,** which Cook apparently never lived in. The eighteenth-century house belonged to his parents in their later years, however, and it was brought to the park from England in 1934 to celebrate the Melbourne Centennial. (Open 7 A.M. to 5 P.M.)

Across Lansdowne Street are the **Treasury Gardens.** You have to walk along the traffic of Spring Street for a few minutes, past Parliament House, etc., to get to **Exhibition Gardens,** sometimes called Carlton Gardens. These 60 acres were the site of the Melbourne Exhibition of 1880. On the grounds, look for the statue of **Burke and Wills,** commemorating the two explorers who left from Melbourne to explore the Outback and establish a land route to the Gulf of Carpentaria in 1861. After making important discoveries they died in the desert, needlessly, through an almost incredible combination of unfortunate circumstances.

About four blocks west on Grattan Street is the campus of **Melbourne University,** founded in 1853 and now enrolling about 20,000. There's a famous music exhibit in the **Percy Grainger Museum.** Others could safely skip it, but I was strongly reminded of the time I was a member of an orchestra directed by the late Maestro Grainger. We halted rehearsal in admiration when he began to conduct a passage of one of his difficult compositions—3/4 time in one hand and 4/4 time with the other, simultaneously!

Royal Park, which begins near the campus, is devoted largely to games and recreation, and includes hockey fields, a golf course, basketball courts, and a baseball diamond. In one corner of the park is the **Melbourne Zoological Gardens,** Australia's first zoo. We'd limit any exploration to the section on Australian fauna, and that only if there was to be no opportunity to see Healesville in the Dandenongs or Taronga Park in Sydney.

OUT IN THE COUNTRY

Rent a car or hop on a sightseeing bus to take a "Captain Cook" at some of the countryside sights of Victoria, particulaly the Dandenongs, Ballarat/Sovereign Hill, and Phillip Island.

The "Beautiful Blue" **Dandenongs,** a range of modest mountains about 30 miles east of Melbourne, feature fern gullies and giant eucalyptus trees, some of which reach 300 feet. The highest point in the range is Mount Dandenong itself at 2,077 feet. Unfortunately the natural feeling there is marred by Melbourne's TV towers and the Sky High Restaurant, but it's still a joy on a clear day.

Two or three sights are nestled in the hills. Three miles from Healesville, at the foot of Mount Riddell, you'll find the **Sir Colin MacKenzie Wild Life Sanctuary** (often called the Healesville Sanctuary). There in the open air are koalas, emus, kangaroos, wombats, possums, and at least one platypus. This research station, where the duck-billed critter was first bred in captivity, was named after the scientist who accomplished it. (Open daily from 9 to 5.)

Nearer Mount Dandenong, at Olinda, is the **William Rickets Sanctuary.** Rickets, an artist of around 80 years, lives there and carves his Tolkienesque figures in wood, a project partly subsidized by the Victoria Forests Commission. His statues reflect his belief that he must save the Aboriginal spirits, and nature in general, from encroaching modernization.

At Healesville, at the Rickets Sanctuary, or anyplace in the Dandenongs, incidentally, you may hear and perhaps see the lyrebird, that strange twin-tailed creature who can imitate other birds or even chain saws, trucks, and factory whistles.

A favorite diversion for kids of all ages is the little narrow-gauge steam railroad train, **Puffing Billy,** which chugs between Belgrave and Menzies Creek from time to time, especially on weekends.

About 70 miles to the west of Melbourne is the gold-rush town of **Ballarat,** famous as the scene of Australia's almost-revolution, the Eureka Stockade rebellion of 1854.

A pleasant town, today known for its begonias (we enjoyed the flower-filled park along with the busts of past prime ministers), Ballarat is also the location for the commercial theme park called **Sovereign Hill,** a re-creation of a gold-rush town much like Ballarat in its heyday. Not surprisingly it seems very similar to Virginia City or some other revived old ghost town in the American West. You can go down in a mine, and even buy a miner's right and pan for gold in the little stream. On weekends, hundreds do. (Open 9:30 to 5:00 daily, admission about $7. You can go by train, too; call VicRail at 62–0771.)

If you continue west on the same highway (No. 8), you go through the **Grampians,** a spectacular set of mountains on the way to South Australia. It's one of the few areas where the platypuses still roam free. Then the Great Ocean Road goes by way of the picturesque village of **Lorne** to Port Campbell National Park and its spectacular rock formations.

In northeast Victoria, visitors like the nineteenth-century granite look in the old gold-mining town of **Beechworth.** Bushranger Ned Kelly, the national folk hero, used to stir up trouble around here, and you'll find his statue, complete with homemade armor, in nearby **Glenrowan.** (Modest—but historic(!)—accommodations are available in Beechworth at Tanswell's, the Nicholas, or the Star.)

Our favorite trip out of Melbourne, however, has to be the 80-mile excursion south to **Phillip Island.** There are fur seals and koalas frolicking about, but the main purpose of the journey is to see the fairy penguins. About 3,000 of these protected birds come home from the sea every day of the year, just at dusk, although usually they may be viewed only from October through April. After riding in on the waves, they shake themselves a moment, get their bearings, and then begin their "parade," until they find the burrows where their families are waiting for the bacon. (No flash pictures are allowed, but we caught them in the floodlights on high-speed color film.) It's a charmer. Don't miss it!

7. Guided Tours and Cruises

Probably the easiest way to set yourself up with a guided tour is to arrange it through the **Victour Travel Centre** (Tel. 602–9444) at 230 Collins St. Other agencies include **Ansett Pioneer** (Tel. 342–3144) at 501 Swanston St. (the same as the Ansett Airlines terminal), **Australian Accommodation & Tours** (AAT, Tel. 321–3144), and **Australian Pacific Tours** (Tel. 63–1511), 181 Flinders St.

Here are a few coach tours and our estimate of their approximate cost this year. Victour will probably be able to book you on several more. (Be sure to ask where to board the bus, and note that all-day tours will probably stop somewhere for tea as well as for lunch.)

Healesville Wildlife Sanctuary. 4 hours, 2 or 3 afternoons a week. $21.

Blue Dandenongs. 3 hours, 2 days a week. $18.

Melbourne Sights and Gardens. 3 hours daily. $18.

Fairy Penguin Parade (Phillip Island). 9½ hours, 3 days a week, October through April. $32 (including dinner).

Ballarat and Sovereign Hill. 8½ hours. $32.

Like Sydney and Canberra, Melbourne has now set up a **City Explorer Bus.** Run by A.P.T. (Australian Pacific Tours), the red double-decker leaves Flinders Street Station on the hour every day except Monday and stops at Captain Cook's Cottage, the Old Melbourne Gaol, the Museum of Victoria, Queen Victoria Market, the *Polly Woodside* museum ship, the National Gallery of Victoria, and the Performing Arts Museum. You can hop off anywhere and catch the next bus later. The fare at this writing is still $3, and tickets are valid for discounts on some sights.

A new aerial tour we know little about is the *Penguin Express* run by **Maloney Aviation** (Tel. 379–2122). For around $100 they will fly you to Phillip Island to see the famous penguin parade and then back to Melbourne. Flights are 30 minutes each way, and the whole tour lasts about four hours. Sounds interesting, but we don't know anyone who's made the flight. If you go, let us know.

Melbourne is the headquarters of one of the best adventure tour outfits, **Bill King's Northern Safaris,** 108 Ireland St., West Melbourne, Vic. 3003, with four-wheel drive, bus, horseback, and tent excursions to wild Outback areas lasting from three to thirty days. We've never gone, but we have met satisfied travelers who sing their praises. Write for a brochure, or see the tourist bureau for details.

8. Water Sports

Melbourne's beaches are nothing to compare with the dramatic surfing strands of Sydney, the Gold Coast, or Perth. But they're pleasant for relaxation and gentle swimming. You can take the tram to St. Kilda or Albert Park, suburbs on Port Phillip Bay, in 15 minutes. Further down the eastern coast, avoid the polluted waters between Beaumaris and Frankston, although the beaches between Mornington and Portsea are clear and popular. Cancel at all costs any thought of swimming in the Yarra (yuck!) River.

For serious surfing and swimming in heavy wave action, you'll have to go beyond Port Phillip Bay to the ocean side of Mornington Peninsula, 50 miles from Melbourne. (Portsea and Sorrento almost at the very tip are popular, although Sorrento is unpatrolled and often dangerous.)

You can rent **sailboats** at almost any resort beach, but remember the changeable weather. It's doubly dangerous for boaters with Port Phillip Bay's sudden shifts in wind and waves. Try Black Rock, Frankston, Mordialloc, and Sandringham. If you want to make contact with fellow sailors, call the Royal Melbourne Yacht Squadron (Tel. 534–0227) in St. Kilda.

Water skiers can hire the appropriate equipment at several bay beaches as well as inland lakes. You might make contact with the Victorian Water Ski Association (Tel. 531–1388).

Deep-sea fishing boats can sometimes be had in towns on Western Port Bay, about 40 miles southeast of Melbourne. Bluefin tuna is the big catch in these waters January to March, followed by Australian salmon. There is trout fishing on several inland lakes and rivers. Get the latest on all this from the Victour Travel Centre.

9. Other Sports

SPECTATOR SPORTS

From April to September it seems difficult to get into any social conversation in Melbourne that doesn't eventually degenerate into a discussion of Australian Rules Football. Indeed, Melbourne columnist Keith Dunstan once lamented this fact over several weeks and even organized the tongue-in-cheek A.F.L.—the "Anti-Football League."

No one took it very seriously, however, including apparently Dunstan himself. But "footy" is taken *very* seriously in Victoria and other southern and western states. Melbourne's most famous Aussie Rules star and later coach Ron Barassi once said flatly, "Getting out of football is just like death."

It may be impossible for Americans—or even Englishmen or New Zealanders (or, for that matter, northern Australians!)—to understand "Rules." Sports fans from Sydney and Brisbane sniff and call it "aerial ping-pong," presumably because of the spectacular high jumps in a scramble for the ball, often photographed by the newspapers. For the same reason, others call it "ballet with blood."

As in America, football keeps many glued to the telly on weekend afternoons during the winter. In Melbourne, the Victorian Football League competes in home and away games with about a dozen professional teams. The final series, played in September, may pull in a crowd of 120,000 or so to the VFL's stadium at Waverley, 15 miles from Melbourne, or the Melbourne Cricket Ground in Yarra Park near the Hilton.

The football used is ovoid, like an American pigskin or a rugby ball, but scores are made only by kicking it through goalposts. The team receives six points for a goal, but they can also get one point for a "behind," a kick that missed the main posts but got through another set of posts stationed at either side. There's little carrying of the ball allowed. It must be kicked, pushed, or punched down the field, and the long, accurate kicks, sometimes made on the run, account for much of the game's excitement. The whole match is carried out on an oval field, an inheritance from the familiar cricket oval.

It's a rough, fast-paced game, played without padding for about two hours of nonstop action. The true Aussie Rules fan feels the other 99 percent of the world is missing out on the greatest joy in life. Supporters not only carry flags of team colors to the matches, some of them may outfit the whole house—towels, bedspreads, and whatever—in the pattern.

The other kinds of football, rugby and soccer, draw small crowds by comparison in Victoria, but soccer at least is on the rise due to the number of foreign immigrants.

Cricket, of course, is still a popular summer pastime on Melbourne weekends, and you may catch that at the M.C.G. or any of a number of suburban ovals. (One of the prettiest is at Como Park in South Yarra.)

Horse racing, too, is a local passion, one that peaks in the running of the Melbourne Cup the first Tuesday in November, the climax of the spring racing carnival. Cup Day, as a matter of fact, is a legal holiday in Victoria. With its high fashion and associated merrymaking, it's comparable to Derby Day in London or Louisville—only much more so.

The Cup is run at Flemington Racecourse, the largest track in the state

(320 acres), located on Epsom Road four miles northwest of the city center. You can travel by tram No. 57 or Bus No. 404 or by train from the Spencer Street Station. Other tracks include the Caulfield Racecourse, six miles east on Normanby Road in Caulfield, the Moonee Valley Racecourse, on Dean Street at Moonee Ponds, and the Sandown Racecourse on the Dandenong Road in Springvale.

Racing addicts who haven't had enough with horses can also take in **dog racing.** In Melbourne, the greyhounds run at Olympic Park on Batman Avenue in East Melbourne or at Sandown Park on Dandenong Road in Springvale. Betting is at the track.

PARTICIPATION SPORTS

Australian **tennis** (grass or hard court) is also a top spectator sport, with the Australian championships in January attracting the best players from all over the world, many of whom, of course, are Australians. State championships are held in December and January, and in Melbourne these would be at the courts run by the Victorian Lawn Tennis Association (Tel. 20–3333) at Kooyong. The main stadium (also the site of the Australian Open) seats 12,000 spectators.

Phone the association to get some recommendations on sports clubs or public courts that may be available to you near your hotel. There are courts in Royal Park and Albert Park. Commercial tennis courts are also listed in the Yellow Pages of the telephone book.

Just as popular in Australia as in the U.S.A., **golf** is also both a spectator sport and a playing sport for everyone. But because of the need for memberships or at least introductions by members, there are few courses where visitors can just show up for a round of 18 holes.

We know of three exceptions, however. The **Victoria Golf Club** (Tel. 584–1733) welcomes strangers. It's on Park Road in Cheltenham, Victoria (post code 3192, if you're writing first). Also check out the beautiful public golf course at **Yarra Bend National Park** (Tel. 481–0171), about four miles northeast of the Golden Mile. And there is the **Albert Park Course** (Tel. 51–1841) in Albert Park. Greens fees may be around $5 or $6—double that if you need clubs.

If you can wangle an introduction, the best course in Australia—and the top of the private club list in Melbourne—is supposed to be the **Royal Melbourne** (Tel. 598–6755) on Cheltenham Road, Black Rock. It's well known for sand traps. One of the famous courses where you share the fairways with families of friendly roos is the **Anglesea Golf Course** at Anglesea, along the coastline, about 65 miles southwest of Melbourne (near Route 1 at Geelong).

And what about **skiing?** Ski runs in the Victorian Alps are preferred by many to those in the Snowy Mountain resorts we reported on in the Canberra chapter. The season begins in mid-June and carries through August, and skiers say they like these resorts because they are uncrowded and you can often sleep above the snow line (thus almost falling out of bed and into the snow in the morning). Mount Hotham is the highest resort, so it gets the snow first, and it stays there longer. It's a four-hour drive from Melbourne. The picturesque Falls Creek area incorporates an attractive alpine village. Mount Buffalo is the oldest ski area, and Mount Buller, 150 miles from the capital, is the largest snow resort in Australia, with more lifts than anywhere else, too.

10. The Melbourne Shopping Scene

In some quarters Melbourne is known more for shopping than anything else. For the past few years it's been the trend center for women's fashions, especially, or at least the first in Australia to snap up, re-create, or adapt the latest styles seen in London, New York, and Paris, many of them then sold from exclusive little boutiques in Toorak Road or Chapel Street in the suburbs.

(It's a pity that many Melburnians still don't take advantage of the city's fashion leadership. The British actor Robert Morley—no lover of Melbourne, to be sure—once sniffed: "The inhabitants looked as if they had been clothed in some gigantic relief operation, carried out in the dark!")

Much of the serious shopping is accomplished in a 30-block portion of downtown, bounded by Lonsdale, Spring, Flinders, and Queen streets. Store hours are 9:00 to 5:30 Monday to Friday and until noon on Saturdays. There is late-night shopping on Friday night until 9 P.M. Here are some places and purchases to think about:

Aboriginal arts and crafts. Although far from the Outback and Aboriginal country, you'll find a considerable amount of native X-ray bark paintings and the like available. Some of the most authentic original pieces (and the most expensive) are at **Aboriginal Handicrafts** (Tel. 63–4717) at 182 Collins St. Also, there's the **Aborigines Artists Gallery** at 50 Bourke St.

Melbourne has become known for **antiques** dating back to its affluent period during the gold-rush era. Many shops are in the High Street between Kooyong and Glenferrie roads in Toorak, southeast of the center. Also there are several antique addresses in High Street, Malvern. (Go to one shop and they'll probably give you a brochure listing several others.)

Arcades. Melbourne is well known for its shopping arcades, covered and glassed-in malls that wind through the business area, particularly off Collins Street and Bourke Street. The oldest is the 1870 **Royal Arcade,** which runs under the watchful eyes of the two Beefeater bell ringers between Collins and Little Collins. The nearby **Block Arcade,** with entrances on Collins, Little Collins, and Elizabeth streets, has domed ceilings and old-world shop fronts. Then there is the Y-shaped **Australia Arcade,** under the Hotel Australia.

That wonderful aroma in the Block Arcade comes from a fast-pie shop called **Dinkum Pies,** in the entranceway called Block Place between the arcade and Little Collins.

Australian paintings. Some of the commercial galleries include the following (none are in the center): **Tolarno Gallery,** 98 River St., South Yarra; **Realities,** corner of Jackson Street and Grange Road, Toorak; and **Avant Gallery,** 579 Punt Rd., South Yarra.

Bookshops. There seem to be several in Bourke Street, for some reason, including the well-known **Collins Book Sellers** (Tel. 654–3144) at 86 Bourke, which offers a good range of Australiana. You might check out **Mary Martin Bookshop** at its 269 Swanston St. address and at 36 Toorak Rd. in the chic South Yarra section. They're open for Sunday browsing, too. The well-known **Angus and Robertson** chain is at 107 Elizabeth St. And don't forget the bargains you'll sometimes find at the federally subsidized **Australian Government Publishers Service** (Tel. 663–3010) at 347 Swanston St.

Department stores. One of the world's largest stores is the **Myer Department Store** (Tel. 6–6111), which takes up two blocks on Bourke Street. In addition to the standard items, check here for souvenirs, boomerangs, paintings, books, etc. It also hosts the Miss Myer Boutique, where all the best Australian designers are supposed to be represented. Look for a pretty good shoe department, too. Other department stores include the swell-elegant **George's** at 162 Collins St. and **David Jones** at 310 Bourke St. on the Mall.

Opals and gemstones. As in Sydney, there are lots of Australian jewelry stores featuring black, white, and green opals as well as other native gemstones. Australia's most famous opal dealers are **Altmann and Cherny,** 227 Collins St. Others include the **Opal Den** (Tel. 63–8385) at 17 Howey Place and **Dunklings** (Tel. 63–6611), 325 Bourke St.

Skin products. Sheepskin, kangaroo skin, etc., you might find in several department stores, souvenir shops, etc. One that specializes, however, is the **Sheepskin Rug Shop,** 235 Bourke St.

Souvenirs. The traditional leader is **Mond's Gifts and Souvenirs** (Tel. 63–7542) at 103 Swanston St. The wide range includes toy koalas, kangaroos, and the like as well as mass-produced boomerangs and barrels of bric-a-brac of one sort or another. A store of a similar persuasion, but smaller, is **Proud's,** standing tall at 339 Bourke St. And **Damman's,** a tobacconist on Swanston, just off Collins, also has a large souvenir stock.

Film? There are lots of camera shops, of course, but on our last trip we found the best discount prices on film at **Tom Schiller's Photo Services** (Tel. 67–3815) inside the Elizabeth Pharmacy at the corner of Elizabeth and Little Collins Street.

Something unusual? You can buy genuine Australian ANZAC hats at **Mitchell's** (Tel. 63–5785), an Army and Navy store at 134 Russell St. Then wander over to see the beaut fruit and veggies at the outdoor **Victoria Market** on Tuesdays, Thursdays, Fridays, Saturdays, and perhaps Sundays at William and Franklin streets. It's a good way to experience the city's multicultural atmosphere. On Sunday take the tram out to St. Kilda to browse at the open-air **St. Kilda Esplanade Art & Craft Market** on the Upper Esplanade. From 9 to 5:30, artists and crafts people display and sell their own products here.

11. Night Life and Entertainment

If you're searching for some of the far-out fun you can find in Sydney, you may have to look harder for it in Melbourne. Still, some writers have been saying for years that Melbourne is the massage parlor and escort service capital of the world. (The Yellow Pages are filled with agencies called Dial A Lady, Fly Girls, the Gentle Touch, Undercover Agents, Maiden Australia, and the like.)

Nightclubs and discotheques. Traditionally, Melbourne's nightclubs have led a precarious economic life centered around Fitzroy Street and its side lanes in St. Kilda, the closest thing the city can offer to the King's Cross neighborhood of Sydney. Lately, however, several new clubs have been opening to champagne and fanfare in the city center. One is **Madison's** (Tel. 654–1122), four floors of a former clothing factory at the corner of Flinders Lane and Russell Street. Another is **Billboard In Concert** (Tel. 663–2989), not far away at 170 Russell St., which is billed as a rock restaurant and supper club.

Discos and rock clubs are also turning up more and more in Melbourne, and some even stay spinning past midnight. The most trendy platter palace—where you have to pass inspection or they won't let you in—is the **Melbourne Underground,** below the surface of 22 King St. It supposedly cost more than a million Down Under dollars to build, and it will charge you between $5 and $10 to experience its nether regions. Also, look for **Inflation** at 60 King St., with dancing, dining, and drinking on three different levels. There's one of the **Juliana's** chain of discos in the Melbourne Hilton. Other than that, look for **The Love Machine** (Tel. 240–8373) at 14 Claremont St. in South Yarra and **Cheveron** at 519 St. Kilda Rd. The wonderfully named **Mandate,** on Carlisle Street in St. Kilda, is a gay disco.

Rock and jazz. Melbourne is considered a musical town on several different levels. It offers a lot of popular and syncopated beats at several different pubs and wine bars. The scene changes swiftly, and most of it is in the suburbs.

For rock music, check out the **Fun Factory** on Swanston Street; the **Sydenham Hotel,** 14 Elizabeth St., and the **Kingston Hotel,** 55 Highett St., both in Richmond; the **Village Green Hotel,** corner of Springvale and Ferntree Gully roads, Springvale; and **the Nicholson Hotel** (formerly the Polaris Inn, Tel. 347–1871), 551 Nicholson St., North Carlton.

You'll probably find some genuine jazz and folk music at the **Manor House Hotel** at Lonsdale and Swanston streets, the **Victoria Hotel,** Albert Park, or the **Lemon Tree,** Rathdowne and Grattan streets.

The beers of Melbourne. We're not up enough on Melbourne pubs yet to make a literary pub crawl in this edition, having confined most of our imbibing to our own hotel, restaurants, or the homes of friends. (We would welcome nominations for the most interesting pubs.) But we do have some thoughts on the excellent brews of Melbourne.

If you drank Foster's in the U.S.A. and weren't very impressed, don't let that dissuade you. Foster's is brewed by C.U.B. (Carlton United Breweries), which must make the export stuff bland or the American Feds won't let it in. Foster's in Victoria is fine, although we far prefer one of C.U.B.'s dozen other beers, one called Melbourne Bitter. (Technically it's not a bitter but a strong lager.) There's a milder version, too, called the Victoria Bitter. Similar to Foster's are Carlton Crown Lager and Abbots Lager.

A fizzier C.U.B. brand is Pilsener. We haven't tried their Malt Ale or their alleged low-calorie beer called Dietale. C.U.B. also owns the Ballarat Brewery, now, turning out Ballarat Bitter there.

The other brewery in Melbourne until recently was British, although called Courage Australia. A relative newcomer, Courage has been turning out beers since the 1960s that seem to be named to suggest that they, too, have a long history—1770 Old Colonial Ale, for instance. Their Crest Lager calls itself a pilsener, but hardly seems zippy enough. Courage Draught is nicely dry. Tankard Bitter may have more of a kick to it. In any case, most of Courage's stock has now been sold to Sydney's Tooth's. (It was bad enough being a Pom beer, but now it seems a beer sold in Melbourne is actually owned by Sydney!)

Incidentally, perhaps due to the allegedly higher alcoholic content of Melbourne beer, there are some tiny servings offered in some places. The "pony" or "small glass" holds just 4 ounces. Ask for a "glass" of beer to get 7 ounces or a "pot" for 10 ounces.

Theater. Theater-restaurants have become established on the Melbourne stage. One gaining an audience is the **Last Laugh Theatre Restaurant**

(Tel. 419–6225) at 64 Smith St., in the suburb of Collingwood ($25 might buy dinner and the show). You can also try **Tikki and John's** (Tel. 663–1754), 169 Exhibition St.; the **Comedy Shop Cafe** (Tel. 419–2869) at 177 Brunswick St., Fitzroy; **Dirty Dick's** (Tel. 266–2837) at 23 Queens Rd.; and **Bunratty Castle** (Tel. 699–2960) at 127 Dorcas St.

More than a half-dozen theaters for stage plays, opera openings, etc., are firmly established in the Golden Mile, giving credence to Melbourne's reputation as the theatrical capital of the country. Check out what's playing in the newspapers (the morning *Age*—especially the seven-day Leisure Guide in the Friday edition—or the evening *Herald*) or the weekly tourist publication *This Week in Melbourne*.

The three main stages are the **Princess Theatre** (Tel. 662–2911), 163 Spring St., **Her Majesty's Theatre** (Tel. 663–3211), 219 Exhibition St., and the **Comedy Theatre** (Tel. 662–3233), 240 Exhibition St. Notice that the **Russell Street Theatre** (Tel. 645–1100), at 19 Russell St., is known for premiering the work of Australian playwrights, along with **Saint Martin's Theatre** in St. Martin's Place in South Yarra. The two are run by the Melbourne Theatre Company. And experimental theater is up in the university area, where the Australian Performing Group tries out new things at **The Pram Factory** (Tel. 347–7133) at 325 Drummond St., Carlton. Tickets run around $5 or $6.

As reported in our Sightseeing section, the new three-stage **Theatres Building** (Tel. 617–8211) of the Victorian Arts Centre has now opened under the dramatic silver spire. Inside, the Playhouse, an 850-seat space, is designed to be used mostly by the Melbourne Theatre Company. Theater-in-the-round and other special small productions are scheduled for The Studio, which seats 400.

Movies. The cinemas are also in the theater district in the eastern blocks of the Golden Mile. You'll find many along Bourke Street, between Spring and Swanston, as well as on Exhibition, Collins, Swanston and Russell streets.

Opera. The Victoria State Opera is now headquartered in the new State Theatre in the Victorian Arts Centre. It is also the venue of the Australian Opera Company when it comes to call.

Ballet. The Australian Ballet leaps all over the country from a Melbourne base. At-home productions are now staged in the new State Theatre. The ballet, which has made many world tours, is known for its penchant for commissioning and performing newly choreographed works on Australian themes as well as the classics.

Classical music. Performances are generally given in the new Melbourne Concert Hall (reservations Tel. 60–0721) in the Victorian Arts Centre, although a few may still be scheduled for the Town Hall (reservations Tel. 63–0421). Sometimes the M.S.O. carries its instruments over to the

Sidney Myer Music Bowl in the King's Domain. You can pick up concert information from the Australian Broadcasting Commission Concert Department, 10 Queen St.

Theater tickets. Many productions sell tickets through a central bookings office called **BASS** (Tel. 11–566 or 11–500). Supposedly that stands for Best Available Seating Service.

12. The Melbourne Address List

Ambulance—Tel. 662–2533.

American consulate—24 Albert Rd. (Tel. 699–2244).

Australian Tourist Commission—324 St. Kilda Rd. (Tel. 690–3900).

British consulate—330 Collins St. (Tel. 602–1877).

Bus, tram, and train information—Tel. 602–9011.

Canadian consulate—151 Flinders St. (Tel. 63–8431).

Chamber of Commerce—60 Market St. (Tel. 611–2233).

Citizens Advice Bureau—197 Russell St. (Tel. 63–1062).

Dental Emergency Service—Tel. 347–4222.

Emergencies of all types—Tel. 000.

Hospital—St. Vincent's, corner Victoria Parade and Nicholson Street (Tel. 418–0221), one of several in the central area.

New Zealand consulate—30 Collins St. (Tel. 67–8111).

Police station—376 Russell St. (Tel. 662–0911). Tel. for all emergencies.

Post office—Corner of Bourke and Elizabeth streets (Tel. 609–4265).

Royal Automobile Club of Victoria—123 Queen St. (Tel. 607–2211).

Travellers' Aid Society—281 Bourke St. (Tel. 654–2600).

Tourist bureau—Victorian Tourism Center (Victour), 230 Collins St., (Tel. 602-9444).

8

Tasmania, The Island State

1. The General Picture

For sheer physical beauty, the water-mountain-and-sky setting for Hobart, the capital of Tasmania, actually surpasses that of Sydney.

The city seems small, almost quaint, with its mixture of Georgian, very few Victorian, and some modern buildings all wrapped together in a comfortable "hometown" feeling, apparent even on a short stay. It has a definite appreciation for its roots, too, for Hobart was founded in 1804, making it Australia's second oldest settlement after Sydney.

Like Sydney, Hobart owes its beginnings to a penitentiary. The infamous Port Arthur was constructed nearby, and between 1830 and 1877 the name was as feared in England and the rest of Australia as Devil's Island was in Europe. Today the prison city lies in mellow, romantic ruins 60 miles by road from the capital.

Hobart's population now numbers about 175,000 out of the island's total of 425,000. Shaped rather like a shield, the state is a rugged, sparsely settled, even partly unexplored area of 26,215 square miles. That's about the size of West Virginia or of Scotland. Were it not so dwarfed physically, culturally, and economically by the continent above it, it would qualify as a big, important island indeed.

Like many scenic lands, Tasmania has a violent history—marked not only by conflicts with convicts but also by struggles between the settlers

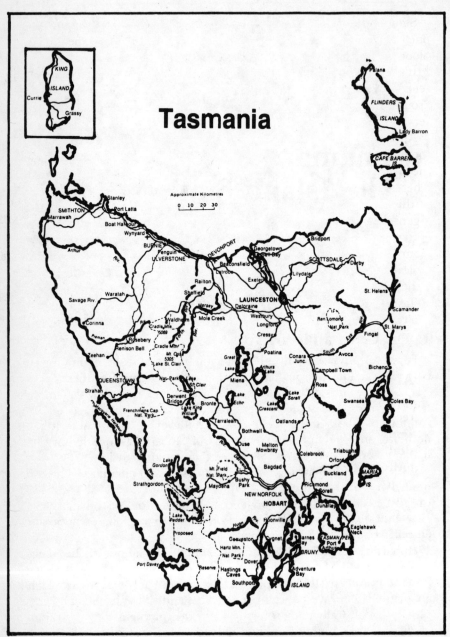

Tasmania

Map courtesy Tasmanian Government Tourist Bureau

and the indigenous population, a nation of Aborigines of completely different racial stock than the natives of the mainland.

Somehow the early English colonialists managed to slay virtually every one of them. A few older survivors were rounded up, but the last full-blooded Tasmanian Aboriginal died about 100 years ago.

It's been a similar story with nature. The Tasmanian tiger hasn't been seen since 1933, although there is some hope that a few may be creeping around the rough country on the west coast. Nevertheless, wildlife conservation is still a controversial issue in Tasmania.

Among Australians, "Tassie" is still thought of as the "Apple Isle"; some of the world's most delicious apples are grown there. Unfortunately they've been largely priced out of the export market in recent years. There is considerable industry, now, led by iron-mining activities. Much of this has been attracted by the very cheap electricity provided by an ingenious hydroelectric system.

In recent years Tasmania has come to rely more and more on income from tourism from the rest of Australia, an irony to some who note the typical Tasmanian's traditional distrust of the mainland Australian. Nevertheless, because of this new commercial interest, things move smoothly in Tasmania and facilities for visitors today are among Australia's best. If you're going between mid-December and mid-February, however, have all your reservations sewn up tight.

2. Airports and Long-Distance Transportation

Major airports are at Hobart, Launceston, Devonport, and Wynyard, all receiving frequent flights from Melbourne and Adelaide via **Ansett Airlines** (Hobart Tel. 38–1111; Launceston Tel. 31–7711) and **Trans-Australia Airlines** (Hobart Tel. 34–6644; Launceston Tel. 31–4411). TAA and **Air New Zealand** now also offer international flights between Hobart and Christchurch, New Zealand. **East-West Airlines** (Hobart Tel. 38–0200) flies direct from Sydney or Melbourne. There's also the smaller **Airlines of Tasmania** (Hobart Tel. 34–9577), which flies between Hobart, Launceston, Queenstown, Wynyard, Devonport, King Island, and Flinders Island. Hobart's airport is about a half hour out the Tasman Highway. **Tasmanian Redline Coaches** runs frequent buses to town from the airports at Hobart (Tel. 34–4577) and Launceston (Tel. 31–9177). Fares are around $3 a seat. (By taxi you would pay perhaps $15 in either city.)

By sea, you can take the new state-owned *Abel Tasman*, which sails from Melbourne Monday, Wednesday, and Friday for 14 hours overnight to arrive in Devonport. Sailings from Devonport to Melbourne leave Tues-

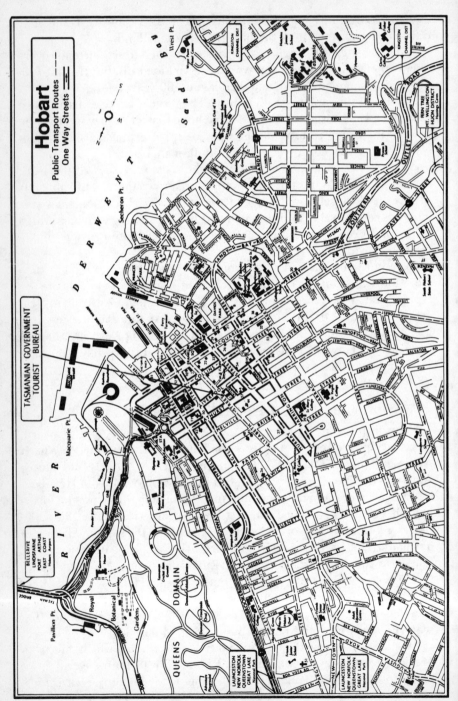

Map courtesy Tasmanian Government Tourist Bureau

day, Thursday, and Sunday. Reserve passage through the tourist bureau (Tel. 34–6911) in Hobart.

This service won't save you any significant money, however, unless you're taking your own car to the island. Fares may run from about $70 to about $180 for the best cabin between Melbourne and Devonport—a trip that costs about $100 and takes 75 minutes by air—and you will still have to rent a car or take a bus to the state capital at Hobart.

By bus, you can travel all over the island on the **Tasmanian Redline Coaches** (Tel. 34–4577), headquartered at 96 Harrington St. in Hobart. The last we heard, it cost about $20 to bus between Devonport and Hobart.

3. Local Transportation in Hobart

In Hobart and Launceston there are frequent bus services run by the **Metropolitan Transport Trust** (MTT). In Hobart these are divided between Western Shore Services—Routes 1 to 59 (Tel. 34–5670)—and Eastern Shore Services—Routes 60 to 96 (Tel. 44–1599), which run along the opposite side of the Derwent Estuary from downtown Hobart. (Notice that all the bus stops are numbered, a handy feature.) Pick up a map from the tourist bureau or the MTT office at 49 Macquarie St.

Taxis seem a little more expensive in Hobart than in other cities. You'll find them waiting at most hotels. Downtown, the biggest stand is near the corner of Elizabeth and Macquarie streets.

An amazing number of rental car companies compete fiercely all over the island. **Avis Rent-A-Car** (Tel. 34–4222) is the leader. We once rented a nice little Holden from **Hertz Rent-A-Car** (Tel. 34–5555), at 223 Liverpool St. or the Wrest Point Casino. Cheaper rates are offered by **Costless Car Rentals** (Tel. 34–3480), **Curnows Rent a Car** (Tel. 23–7336), 10 Barrack St., and **Thrifty Rent-A-Car** (Tel. 23–3577), 156 Harrington St. There may be several others, however; you can compare rates if you pick up a copy of the Tasmanian Tourism Department's newspaper, *Tasmanian Travelways*.

4. The Hobart Hotel Scene

We have stayed in or inspected hotels only in the capital. Following these we'll mention a few possibilities in the countryside, chosen on the basis of current information and personal recommendations.

EXPENSIVE HOTELS

The acknowledged leader, and candidate for the title of Las Vegas in Australia, is the **Wrest Point Hotel-Casino** (Tel. 25–0112), consisting principally of a 21-story cylinder now dominating Sandy Bay, a couple of miles along the shoreline from the city center. This was the first legal casino in Australia, and the hotel takes its razzmatazz role seriously and slickly. There's a well-regulated casino offering all the standard games plus that Australian institution called "two up." Other public areas include a cabaret showroom (often featuring lavish productons and big-name stars) and the revolving restaurant on top, offering peerless panoramas over sea- and mountainscapes. There are several bars and coffee shops, an indoor pool, tennis and squash courts, etc. Rooms in the tower, with all luxury facilities, run from around $88 up (around $180 to $300 for suites), and they are as modern as tomorrow. (Suites are decorated in Spanish, classical, or Oriental themes.) There are a few nicely refurbished chambers in the old, original hotel adjoining, now called the Derwent Lodge, renting in the $75 range for two. (Reservations from the Federal Pacific Hotel chain or the Wrest Point Hotel itself at Hobart 7005.) An added convenience is its own private bus from the airport. A thoroughly professional operation.

That out of the way, we can tell you that another hotel we liked every bit as much, but on a very different level, is the historic **Lenna Motor Inn** (Tel. 23–2911), perhaps more officially called the Innkeepers Lenna. The main building is the restored mansion originally built between 1874 and 1880 by a well-known whaling captain. (Locals like to talk of a ghost in the attic!) The wonderful collection of marble, carved wood, patterned wallpaper, gold-framed mirrors, French windows, and the like exudes the flavor of 100-year-old luxury. Alexander's, the ornate restaurant with its columns, arches, and piped classical music is one of the best dining rooms in town.

Rooms in the Italianate original building have more genuine character, but those in the unusually designed open-patio annex are also well appointed and colorful, with comfortable facilities. (There's no pool, but a self-service laundry is a convenient dip for your duds, anyway.) Doubles rent for about $85 up to $125 or so for the best suites. We happily stayed here on one visit to Tasmania and will be back again. (Reservations through the Innkeepers chain or from the hotel at Battery Point, Tasmania 7000.) Absolutely charming.

If you have a rental car at your disposal (a good idea in Hobart, anyway), the scenically sited **Hobart Pacific** (Tel. 34–6733) becomes a viable alternative at more modest rates. Formerly called the Hobart Explorer, the red-brick motel is on a street named Kirby Court, reached by driving up, up, and up in a steep residential area (just off the bottom center of our map of Hobart near Shannuk Drive, which is marked). There's a pool available. The small, attractive restaurant and some of the

52 rooms offer magnificent panoramas over the city and harbor. Standard units seem comfortable, with a fridge, color telly, and all the mod cons, and rent for around $60 or $70. During the summer the Hobart Pacific sometimes hosts live music-hall theater, but the view at night is a good show the year round.

Less original, but certainly four solid choices, would be the four **Four Seasons Hotels** (Tel. 34–6288 for central reservations). In Hobart they are the Downtowner at 96 Bathurst St., around the corner from the tourist bureau, the Town House at 167 Macquarie St., and the Westside at 156 Bathurst St., all at Hobart 7000; or the Motor Lodge at 429 Sandy Bay Rd., post code 7005. The quartet all seem much like businessmen's hotels, relying on color schemes like purple and brown, red brick, etc. They're comfortable for the tabs of around $60 to $80 for two, but relatively humdrum in spring, summer, fall, or winter.

Hatcher's Hobart (Tel. 34–2911) would do in a pinch, but we think the noise of freeway traffic nearby might hinder peaceful lodging. The historic **Hadley's Hotel** (Tel. 23–4355), of which we were not enamored, has reportedly improved considerably with its recent refurbishing. It's downtown at 34 Murray St.

BUDGET ACCOMMODATIONS

A charmer recommended to us by a reader, which we subsequently visited recently, is **Barton Cottage** (Tel. 23–6808), nested in the narrow, winding lanes of Battery Point near several good restaurants. There are just six rooms off its carpeted, creaky corridors, so you'll have to plan ahead or be awfully lucky. Old-style bedchambers are equipped with televisions, tea-makers, electric heaters, and electric blankets. No views. Rooms perhaps $45 for two and $35 for one, breakfast included. (Reservations from the cottage at 72 Hampden Rd., Hobart 7000, or through the Tasmanian Government Tourist Bureau, which also knows of some similar "colonial cottages.") Recommended—if you can squeeze in.

A downtown address where you might still check in for under $40 per pair of pillows is the **Black Prince** (Tel. 34–3501) at 145 Elizabeth St. (entrance on Melville within walking distance of the Ansett bus terminal). We found it basic but clean, and you might still get rates of $35 for a couple or $25 for a single knight. Lucy Izon, the youth travel columnist in dozens of U.S. and Canadian newspapers, told us she had a good stay in the **Good Woman Inn** (Tel. 34–9091) at 186 Argyle St. Rates are about $19 per good person, bed and breakfast.

Other inexpensive hotels in Hobart (which we haven't seen) include the **Brisbane** (Tel. 34–4920), downtown at Brisbane and Campbell streets, the **Marquis of Hastings** (Tel. 34–3541) at 209 Brisbane St., the **Motel Mayfair** (Tel. 34–1670) at 17 Cavell St., and the **Hobart Tower Motel** (Tel. 28–4520) at 300 Park St. And the youth hostel is across the river at Bellerive (Tel. 44–2552), where members may pay about $5 a bunk.

ELSEWHERE IN TASMANIA

Launceston. There are dozens of places but two are particularly interesting: One is the **Penny Royal Watermill** (Tel. 31–6699), a converted 1825 mill with a waterwheel, etc. Doubles run about $65, but at least one reader complained that the waterwheel creaked at night. Then there's the **Colonial Motor Inn** (Tel. 31–6588), an interesting place in an old, converted grammar school at the corner of George and Elizabeth streets. (Readers report it still goes by some rules and regulations even today.)

Devonport. Try the **Gateway** (Tel. 24–4922) at 16 Fenton St.

Burnie. The best bet may be the **Voyager** (Tel. 31–4866).

Port Arthur. Look for the **Four Seasons Motor Hotel** (Tel. 50–2101) and a nearby inn called the **Fox and Hounds** (Tel. 50–2217).

Eaglehawk Neck. Near Port Arthur, the **Penzance Motel** (Tel. 50–3272) is supposed to be the very first motel in Australia. Rooms are about $45 for two.

5. Restaurants and Dining

Like many vacation spots, Tasmania has a lot of restaurants, most of them somewhat volatile and changeable, depending on the time of year and the ambitions of the chefs and managers. So please take this only as an approximate guide, all of it subject to sudden change. Reserve early for dinners on Saturday night, when you'll be competing with locals out on the town. (The local winery, by the way, is Chateau Lorraine, bottling a Rhine Riesling and Cabernet Sauvignon.)

HOBART

Alexander's (Tel. 34–6288), the dining room at the historic Lenna Motor Inn at Battery Point, is one of the top choices in town. In an old-fashioned, Florentine atmosphere, with polished silver and antique china place settings, you dine elegantly in the style of the last century. We loved it and will go again. (Open daily.)

One of our choices awhile back was **Lord Monro's** (Tel. 25–1161) at 646 Sandy Bay Rd. in Lower Sandy Bay. Warmed by a fireplace and brightened by candlelight and flowers on the tables, it offers a varied Continental menu. We liked the Crayfish Strudel and Oyster Sauce and the Souvaroff "Gourmet," a beef filet flamed with vodka. We also enjoyed the Piccatina de Vitello "Quadri," veal sauteed in olive oil, tomatoes, white-wine sauce, oregano, and *fines herbes*. It can have an off night, but it's usually a firm favorite. (Closed Sundays.)

For seafood, it's **Mure's Fish House** (Tel. 23–6917), not far away at No. 5 Knopwood St. Specialties are flounder and trevally. For dessert, some praise the Creme Courvoisier. The prima Italian kitchen is **Mondo Piccolo** (Tel. 23–2362) at 196 Macquarie St. (Closed Saturday and Sunday.)

For steak, look into **Dirty Dick's** (Tel. 23–3103), near Mures, at 22 Francis St. (Closed Sundays.)

Also in the Battery Point area, the **Ball & Chain** (Tel. 23–4949), in one of those intriguing old warehouses on Salamanca Place (No. 87), re-creates the prison theme with grisly exhibits throughout the dungeonlike interior. The food is adequate, but that's not the specialty here. It also serves that great Australian favorite, the singalong, with the words to the various convict and bush ballads printed on your bib.

That revolving restaurant at the top of the **Wrest Point** (Tel. 25–0112) isn't bad, considering that no revolving restaurant in the world is ever top-notch. (You always pay more for the panorama.) The trevally, a popular local fish, was certainly okay, but service at our lunchtime meal was not. They were pleasant enough, but simply understaffed. Local residents say that things go 'round better at night.

Some other possibilities in the capital: For more Italian fare, try **Don Camillo** (Tel. 34–1006), a tiny place at 6 Magnet Court, Sandy Bay. Especially good is a newer Swiss restaurant, **Stucki's** (Tel. 28–1885), at 23 Stoke St., New Town. Fun for fondues.

KITCHENS IN THE COUNTRY

Here are a few reliable choices elsewhere around the island:

Launceston. **Rowell's French Restaurant** (Tel. 31–8026) is the traditional leader. It's at 135 George St. But go to **Dicky White's** (Tel. 31–9211) in the Old Launceston Hotel for shish kebab. Another favorite—for light meals and a heavy view—is the **Gorge Restaurant** (Tel. 31–3330) at the foot of the dramatic Cataract Cliffs. Drive there via Gorge Road, or take Basin Road to the end and board the chair lift to the restaurant. The **Quill and Cane** in the Colonial Motor Inn is also good.

Port Arthur. We weren't terribly impressed with our buffet lunch at the **Four Seasons Motor Hotel** (Tel. 50–2101) in Port Arthur, although we understand that it's improved now. Next time, though, we might eat down the road at the **Penzance Motel** (Tel. 50–3272) at Eaglehawk Neck, or at the **Fox and Hounds.**

Richmond. We had a "counter lunch" once in the **Richmond Arms Hotel** (Tel. 62–2109) in that historic community about 20 miles from Hobart. This is a typical, no-nonsense Aussie pub operation—cheap and substantial. (Place your order at the bar. They'll deliver it to your table.) It was a Monday, because we had been heading for the well-known 1830 **Prospect House** (Tel. 62–2207), outside of Richmond, which is closed Mondays. We still haven't hit it, but the old mansion is famous for excellent and gracious home cooking. Still on our list—but never on Monday!

Evandale. The leader is **Casey's** (Tel. 93–6403). *Perth.* At the **Leather Bottell Inn** (Tel. 98–2248), a country tavern on the Main Road, they may still make their own beer. *Ross.* The same is true, we think, at the **Scotch Thistle Inn** (Tel. 81–5213) on Church Street, another colonial building in an historic town. (Closed Sunday.) *Devonport.* The **Edgewater** (Tel. 27–8441), in the motel at 12 Thomas St., is a "find" reported by Bill Kline, a radio-TV station manager from Honolulu. *Burnie.* The **Chandelier** (Tel. 31–1088) shines brightest in the Burnie Motor Lodge on Queen Street. Also, try the **Martini** (Tel. 31–3408), 63 Wilson St.

6. Sightseeing in Hobart and Tasmania

Your first stop should be the **Tasmanian Government Tourist Bureau** (Tel. 34–6911), 80 Elizabeth St., to see what there is to see.

In Hobart, **Battery Point,** with its early-nineteenth-century buildings and traditions, is the local equivalent to Sydney's Rocks area. If you have the pamphlet *Battery Point Historic Village* you can follow a well-designed walking tour of this historic area.

At **Salamanca Place** a terrace of 150-year-old storehouses provides a colorful backdrop to a Saturday open-air market in good weather. And on Hampden Road look for "Narryna," which houses the **Van Diemen's Land Folk Museum** with displays reflecting colonial life in Tasmania. (Monday to Friday until 5 P.M.; admission $1.50.)

Other museums include the **Post Office Museum** on the Castray Esplanade; the **Tasmanian Museum,** 5 Argyle St., with its sad exhibits on the fate of Tasmanian Aborigines, a race that no longer exists; the **Allport Library,** 91 Murray St. (corner of Bathurst), with its books, maps, and antiques (open weekdays, 9 to 5); and the **Maritime Museum of Tasmania** at Cromwell Street, Battery Point, which has many models of ships from windjammers to modern liners (open daily from 2:00 to 4:30 P.M.).

You'll of course notice **Mount Wellington,** southwest of the city. You can drive for about 10 miles right to the top of the 4,166-foot peak, where it often snows in winter. (Wear something warm and water-resistant, and skip it if the weather is not clear.)

On the opposite side of town, the large green area is the 640-acre **Queen's Domain** and the adjoining **Royal Botanical Gardens.** Nearby the attractive $14.7-million **Tasman Bridge,** built in 1965, spans 3,364 feet over the River Derwent. In 1975 it was closed after a ship crashed into its pilings, causing part of the roadway to collapse. Counting the victims whose cars fell into the river, a total of 24 persons died. The bridge was repaired and reopened over two years later.

Also in Hobart, but a sight we've never made it to, is the **Tudor Court** (Tel. 25–1194), a miniature model village at 827 Sandy Bay Rd. (Bus Stop 30). Readers tell us they like it.

PORT ARTHUR

An absolute must is an excursion out of Hobart, by coach or car, to Port Arthur, about 60 miles from the capital. The old penal institution, which held as many as 12,000 convicts at one time, is largely in ruins but is maintained as an historical exhibit. Knowledgeable National Park Rangers and a small museum there explain the background of the famous— or notorious—prison. It's about $3 for a guided tour of the grounds. (Take Route 3 to Sorrell, then Route 7 to Port Arthur.)

THROUGHOUT TASMANIA

Elsewhere in the state are many scenic towns, historic villages, and dramatic natural features. If you're going to Launceston, by all means see **Cataract Gorge.** An attractive theme park, **Penny Royal World,** has been drawing scads of visitors there, too. On the northwest coast, the old town of **Stanley** features an unusual rock formation called "The Nut" at the end of its peninsular site. And there is some spectacular scenery on the narrow Lyell Highway into **Queenstown.**

For a detailed description of virtually every site on the giant island, pick up the *Official Visitors' Guide* produced by the Tasmanian Tourist Council and available for about $3. (Buy it at the tourist bureau to be sure of getting the latest edition.)

A last word: Tasmania has lots of distinctive wildlife, though you'll often have a devil of a time seeing it. However, since our last visit to the area, a fellow named John Hamilton has opened up the **Tasmanian Devil Wildlife Park** (Tel. 50–3230) in Tarrana, near Port Arthur. It's open daily for a charge of around $4 a ticket. And by the way, stay away from any snake in the wild. Every species in the state is deadly poisonous. (They say, however, that the snakes are shy and prefer not to bite humans!)

7. Guided Tours and Cruises from Hobart

Book all tours through the Tasmanian Government Tourist Bureau
(T.G.T.B., Tel. 34–6911), 80 Elizabeth St. (Some of these may not run
from June through November.)

Historic Port Arthur. 8 hours. About $30. *D'Entrecasteaux Channel.* Half
day. About $15. *Hastings Caves and the Huon Valley.* 8 hours. About $25.
Lake Peddar and Russell Falls (we've never taken this but have heard the
falls are spectacular). 9 hours. About $25. *Kingston and Mount Wellington.*
Half day. About $12.

Some boat cruises up the River Derwent may cast off this year. See the
T.G.T.B. for details. One that's often operating is the **Derwent Explorer**
(Tel. 34–4032), a Friday-night jazz-band cruise down to Kettering for a
fare of around $25.

Air tours? **Par Avion** (Hobart Tel. 48–5390) offers several scenic flights
(including sunset trips) over the southwest of the island. They also may
continue offering an air tour to Port Arthur and back. Check at the
above number.

8. Water Sports

Good beaches line much of Tasmania, including some sands, like Kingston and Long Beach, on the Derwent Estuary near Hobart. There are
more choices on the Eastern Shore, however.

Scuba diving is consistently popular. Rent equipment from the **Aqua
Scuba Diving Services** (Tel. 34–5658) at 54 Collins St. For boating, check
first with the secretary of the **Royal Yacht Club of Tasmania** (Tel. 23–4599)
at the Marieville Esplanade, Sandy Bay 7005. (Hobart is the terminus for
the annual Sydney-to-Hobart and Melbourne-to-Hobart Ocean Yacht
Races. The first boats usually arrive New Year's Day.)

Big-game fishing is a big sport in Tasmania during the summer, and
some of the best tuna is caught at Eaglehawk Neck, near Port Arthur.
Charter boats cost from about $250 to $350 a day. The tourist bureau
will have the names of some skippers and boats. There's plenty of trout
fishing on lakes, streams, and rivers, particularly in northern Tasmania.
Rainbows regularly tip the scales at more than 30 pounds up at Lake
Crescent, they say.

9. Other Sports

Hobart's most famous sport is indoors. The gambling casino at the
Wrest Point Hotel offers roulette, blackjack, craps, baccarat, poker, keno,
and "two up," the traditional Aussie coin toss.

The casino operates from noon to 4 A.M. If you're going to gamble, ask at the Wrest Point for the little booklet *Introduction to Gaming* and read it first. (Note that no slot machines are allowed in Tasmania.) Ostensibly for tourists, gambling actually attracts mostly Tasmanians to the tables as players. Many tourists just come to watch.

Horse races are run every Saturday, alternately at **Elwick Racecourse** on Elwick Road, Glenorchy, about three miles up Route 1, and at **Mowbray Racecourse** in Launceston.

Tennis addicts, if there are no nets at your hotel look for facilities at the **Domain Tennis Centre** in that big park overlooking the bridge. You can call the Tasmanian Lawn Tennis Association there (Tel. 34–2365); they'll help put you on a hard court.

For golfing, by far the most outstanding course is the private **Tasmanian Golf Club** (Tel. 48–5098), which spreads over a spectacular promontory surrounded on three sides by the waters of Barilla Bay, near the Cambridge Aerodrome. Then there is the **Royal Hobart** (Tel. 48–6161) at Seven Mile Beach, near the Hobart Airport, which is also good. A little closer to town and open to all comers is the **Rosny Park** (Tel. 44–6754), a public course in Bellerive (Bus Stop 7).

Tasmania is not the antarctic refrigerator most Australians think it is. Nevertheless, **skiing** is a popular sport June to September at the higher elevations in Mount Field and Ben Lomond national parks. Snow conditions are not as reliable as those in Victoria and New South Wales, however.

10. Shopping in Hobart

As the second oldest settlement in Australia, Hobart not surprisingly comes up with several antique shops, many of them at Battery Point. Also there, or more specifically on Salamanca Place, be sure to wander through the colorful and musical open market held under the umbrellas and plane trees on Saturdays.

The main department stores downtown are **Fitzgerald's** on Collins Street and a branch of the Melbourne-based chain, **Myer,** on Liverpool Street.

Also downtown, some general souvenir and antique shops worth looking into include **Ward's Gift Shop,** 114 Elizabeth St., and **Barclay's Souvenir Centre,** 24 Elizabeth St. Check out the original work available at **Aspect Design,** 79 Salamanca Place, plus the handicrafts and jams and jellies sold (for charity) at the **Country Women's Association Gift Shop** at 165 Elizabeth St.

Don't miss a walk through **Centrepoint Hobart, The Place,** or **Elizabeth Mall,** three new complexes with small, interesting specialty shops, or the little **Cat and Fiddle Arcade,** which tunnels between Elizabeth and Murray streets in the block also bounded by Liverpool and Collins. The name honors a pub that once stood there and is symbolized by some mechanical nursery-rhyme figures that are animated on the hour in an interior courtyard. Several souvenir shops are there. The **Sanitarium** features lots of Tassie goodies, including honey, apple juice, etc.

Out of town, if you get up to Hamilton, about 47 miles northwest, you'll find a good selection of local crafts at the **Old School House.** And a reader with an eye for quality woodwork has recommended a stop at the **Peppercorn Gallery** in Richmond for wood crafts.

In Launceston, check out the souvenirs and crafts at **Emma's Arts,** 78 George St., and the **National Trust Old Umbrella Shop,** 60 George St.

You may see some of the island's apples sold at roadside stands. Look for Red Delicious, Golden Delicious, Jonathan, Crofton, Cox's Orange Pippin, and, of course, the green Granny Smiths.

11. Night Life and Entertainment

The average Tasmanian doesn't much believe in a lot of fuss after dark, but the state's new reputation as "Tasmania, the Treasure Island" is forcing some changes in that attitude.

Not the least, of course, is the influence of the casino at the Wrest Point Hotel, which we covered under section 9.

Completing the Nevada image at the Wrest Point is the large **Cabaret Room** (Tel. 25–0112), which generally features a lavish, full-scale revue. The tables are well arranged in three tiers, so everybody gets a good look at the action. A dinner show is offered nightly, although it's more expensive on weekends and holidays. (Recheck exact prices on the scene.)

We liked the show we saw there, except we thought it strange that the small live band was sometimes supplemented or replaced by recordings of a big orchestra—a practice that cast somewhat of a provincial tone to an otherwise professional production.

Since we were last in town, a new $20-million **Convention and Entertainment Centre** has opened at the Wrest Point. The auditorium, seating 1,600, hosts about three international concert acts a month.

The disco in the same hotel is called **Regines,** gussied up in the grand tradition of this modern institution.

You'll find some other action scattered here and there. One theater/ restaurant, the **Cedar Court** (Tel. 23–7521), has opened up in the refurbished Hadley's Hotel at 34 Murray St. Another, the **Rampant Bear** (Tel. 23–5002), is at 13 Cromwell St.

The Hobart Repertory Theatre group as well as traveling productions often appear in Hobart. The capital is the headquarters of the Tasmanian Symphony Orchestra and a choir from the Tasmanian Conservatorium of Music. Visiting rock bands might appear at the Hobart City Hall or at the theaters.

Hobart theaters include the famous and haunted old **Theatre Royal** (Tel. 34–6266), 82 Campbell St., the **Playhouse** (Tel. 34–1536), 106 Bathurst St., and **ABC Odeon** (Tel. 30–9903), 163 Liverpool St., usually the venue for classical music. There are also several motion-picture theaters.

A few pubs feature live jazz on the weekends. Try **Tattersalls Bar & Bistro** at 112 Murray St. or the **Travelers Rest Hotel** at 394 Sandy Bay Rd. Other popular pubs are the **Red Lion** and **Winston Churchills.**

And beer? Of course! The popular Hobart brew is Cascade (Est. 1824), which now also owns its former Launceston competitor, Boag's. Both the Cascade Red Label and Cascade Blue Label are fairly mild beers. Green Label is stronger and more bitter, and there's a Cascade Stout with quite a stout kick to it. Boag's also has a Red Label and a Blue Label, each a little stronger than the direct Cascade equivalent. And both breweries produce an ale, which we haven't tried.

In the pubs, beer comes in four-, six-, eight-, and ten-ounce glasses.

12. The Tasmanian Address List

Bank—Westpac, 74 Elizabeth St., Hobart (Tel. 30–4444); 109 Brisbane St., Launceston (Tel. 31–5899).

Books and magazines—O.B.M. Newsagents & Booksellers, 36 Elizabeth St. (Tel. 34–4288).

Bus information—Western Shore buses, Tel. 34–5670; Eastern Shore buses, Tel. 44–1599.

Camping equipment—Outdoor Equipment, 212 Liverpool St. (Tel. 34–6213).

Emergencies of all types—Dial 000.

Hiking and backpacking information—Federation of Tasmanian Bush Walking Clubs, P.O. Box 106, Bellerive 7018.

Hospitals—Royal Hobart Hospital, Liverpool Street, Hobart (Tel. 38–8308); Launceston General Hospital, Charles Street, Launceston (Tel. 31–8111).

Laundromat—11 Magnet Court, Hobart.

Post office—Corner of Elizabeth and Macquarie streets (Tel. 20–7290).

Royal Automobile Club of Tasmania—Murray and Patrick streets, Hobart.

Tourist information—Tasmanian Government Tourist Bureau, 80 Elizabeth St., Hobart (Tel. 34–6911); St. John and Paterson streets, Launceston (Tel. 32–2101).

Youth Hostel Association—133-A Elizabeth St., Hobart (Tel. 34–9617).

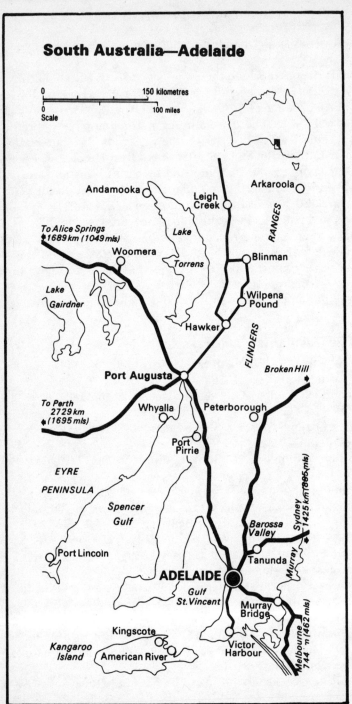

South Australia—Adelaide

Scale
0 — 150 kilometres
0 — 100 miles

Andamooka
Arkaroola
Leigh Creek
Lake
RANGES
To Alice Springs
♦ 1689 km (1049 mls)
Woomera
Torrens
Blinman
Lake
Gairdner
Wilpena Pound
Hawker
FLINDERS
Port Augusta
Broken Hill
To Perth 2729 km (1695 mls)
Whyalla
Peterborough
Port Pirrie
EYRE
PENINSULA
Spencer
Gulf
Sydney 1425 km (885 mls)
Barossa Valley
Port Lincoln
Tanunda
ADELAIDE
Murray
Gulf
St. Vincent
Murray Bridge
Kingscote
Melbourne 744 m (462 mls)
Kangaroo
Island
American River
Victor Harbour

Map courtesy Australian Tourist Commission

9

Adelaide
and South Australia

1. The General Picture

Adelaide seems to be just about the liveliest city in Australia.

They used to call her the "City of Churches." Now she seeks—and deserves—the title of the "Festival City." Since the 1970 construction of a magnificent arts complex on the banks of the Torrens River, she has hosted a biennial extravaganza that brings every kind of performer and artist from the rest of Australia and from other cultural centers of the world.

But throughout non-Festival years, too, there is a feeling of activity in Adelaide—of something going on that should not be missed.

The capital is also one of the best-designed cities in the world. It was laid out midway between the coastline and the Mount Lofty Range by its 1838 founder and surveyor, Colonel William Light. The main portion of the city today is almost completely surrounded by extensive parklands.

The town seems divided into two parts: The southern square-mile grid of 75 blocks contains nearly all the business, government, and cultural centers. To the north, across the Torrens and the wide green belt, is a city of homes, gardens, and parks.

The entire state of South Australia likewise divides itself into two different regions. Adelaide sits in the southern third of the state—fertile coastland with a Mediterranean climate and hills and valleys that provide excellent soil for olives, almonds, and especially the European grapes that have made the region famous for wine production. The 1,600-mile-long Murray River also passes its final 400 miles through southern South Australia before emptying into the Great Australian Bight.

Adelaide, though green, is also dry. It averages only about 20 inches of rain a year. But the second region, the northern two-thirds of South Australia, receives only half as much rain, and seemingly twice as much heat. These are the beginnings of the great deserts for which Australia as a whole is known worldwide.

First there are the Flinders Ranges, colorful and rugged mountains popular with "bushwalkers" and lovers of spring wildflowers. Beyond those the country is flatter and less inviting, although spectacular in a different way. Here is Lake Eyre, which most years has no water at all—just 3,000 square miles of glaring white salt. Here, too, is the opal country, where man lives underground, not just to dig out the precious stones, but to protect himself from the oppressive heat. And in this section is the shadeless Nullarbor Plain, where the *Indian Pacific* train sets out on a stretch westward that includes 300 miles of perfectly straight track.

South Australia, gateway to the Outback, has the distinction of being the most lively and the most deadly state at the same time.

2. The Airport and Long-Distance Transportation

The domestic terminal at Adelaide airport is in a T shape, with the check-in counter for **Ansett Airlines** (Tel. 212–1111) resting inside the right arm of the T and its departure lounges and gates lined along the right side of the stem. The check-in for **Trans-Australia Airlines** (Tel. 217–3333) occupies the mirror image on the left arm with the left side of the T-stem devoted to TAA gates and lounges.

Although compact, the terminal squeezes in several facilities. Across from Ansett is the Walkabout Restaurant, Coffee Shop, and Grill, and there's a "canteen" (takeout stand) nearby, too. As befits this vineyard vicinity, there's also a wine store there. Across the walkway the newsagent displays a good collection of books and pamphlets about S.A.

If you're flying out to Kangaroo Island—about $45 each way—you may look for **Airtransit** (Tel. 352–3128) or **Commodore Airlines** (Tel. 217–3333). **Airlines of South Australia** (Tel. 217–7332) also hops to K.I.

There's a small airline around called **Opal Air** (Tel. 217–7222) that offers flights and aerial tours to the gemstone areas of Andamooka and Coober Pedy, to Ayers Rock, and to other Outback destinations. Flights on **Qantas, British Airways,** and **Singapore Airlines** leave from the new international terminal, which is adjacent to this one.

Bus service between the airport and Adelaide is run by **Transit's Airport City Bus** (Tel. 381–5311), which sells seats for about $2.50 for the five-mile ride.

Daily railroad services from the rest of Australia connect with Adelaide. To or from Melbourne on the *Overland* (about $50 Economy Class, $85 for sleepers) you can ride for 12 hours all the way on the same train. Traveling to and from other major capitals requires a change at Port Pirie. This is the way to connect with the famous transcontinental *Indian Pacific* (west to Perth or east to Sydney) or the new *Ghan,* which travels overnight to Alice Springs. (It leaves Adelaide at 10:30 A.M. Thursday and Sunday and arrives in the Alice at 10:30 A.M. the following day, for a one-way fare of about $200 First Class, $150 Economy.) The modern train, which runs via Tarcoola, has replaced the century-old Central Australian route, which was plagued with dust storms and washouts until it was abandoned at long last in 1980.

Train reservations are handled by **Australian National** (formerly known as Australian National Railways, Tel. 217–4455). Interstate trains have deserted the old Adelaide Station, coming in now at Keswick Railway Station (at the lower left in our city map). For information on tracks, time, etc., "Ask the Man in Blue" (you can't miss him!). There is a bus from Keswick into the city center for about $2. Suburban train service still leaves from the old station on North Terrace.

Bus services to Adelaide are launched from Alice Springs, Darwin, Brisbane, Canberra, Melbourne, Perth, and Sydney via **Ansett Briscoes** (formerly Ansett Pioneer, tel. 212–7344), 101 Franklin St., and **Greyhound Coaches** (Tel. 212–1777) at the Central Bus Station, 111 Franklin St. Also from that station, several small feeder lines connect with destinations within South Australia.

If you're taking the ferry to Kangaroo Island, be sure to catch the new one-hour service aboard the *Valerie Jane,* which leaves from Cape Jervis, south of Adelaide. There's a special bus from Adelaide to connect with the boat. (An older ferry, which still runs from Port Adelaide, also carries automobiles and takes about seven hours.) Don't forget, however, that you can reach Kangaroo Island in about 30 or 40 minutes by plane from the airport.

Driving into Adelaide, you'll most likely wheel in on Highway 1, either the Princes Highway from Melbourne (about 600 miles) or the Eyre Highway from Perth (about 1,700 miles). Both roads are generally excellent, but plan the Adelaide-Perth excursion carefully. The section across the Nullarbor is not to be taken lightly.

People we've talked to now say this recently improved desert trek is more easily done. Nevertheless, in the past this section of road has fallen victim to an Outback bacteria that actually eats asphalt for breakfast. In

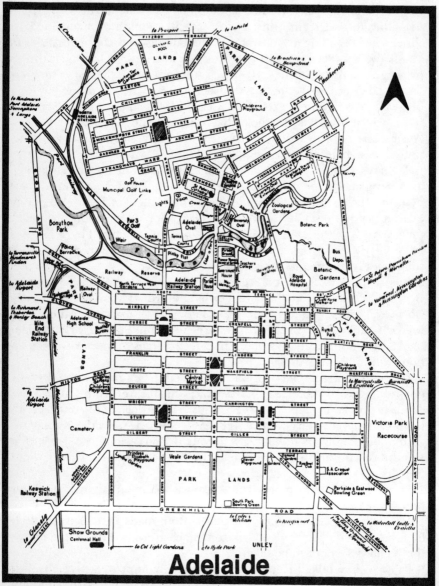

Adelaide

Map courtesy *South Australian Division of Tourism*

any case, your car should be in excellent condition, you should carry extra water, and your nightly reservations should be prebooked all along the way. We advise getting a membership in—and the latest information from—the **Royal Automobile Association of S.A.** (Tel. 223–4555), 41 Hindmarsh Square, Adelaide 5000, before making the trip. (If you're a member of another automobile club, membership will probably be reciprocal.)

One caveat about traveling to or from South Australia by any means. Remember that it's on a bastard time zone. Under normal circumstances, it's *one half hour* earlier in South Australia and the Northern Territory than it is in the eastern states. And it's 1½ hours later than the state of Western Australia.

This, of course, is when all parties are observing standard time. Western Australia, the Northern Territory, and Queensland do not observe daylight saving time, but South Australia and much of the rest of the country do. So this will obviously confuse the time picture still further for those reading airline, train, and bus schedules between South Australia and other states.

Forewarned is forearmed. Good luck!

3. Local Transportation in Adelaide

With the city's wide, easily understood streets, driving is relatively simple, and there are several rental car agencies clamoring for your business. At the moment, and subject to a sudden shift of gears, the best rates seem to be with two or three companies: **Action Rent-A-Car** (Tel. 352–7044), 280 Burbridge Rd., Cowandilla, **Koala Car Rentals** (Tel. 352–7299), 39 Burbridge Rd., and maybe **Thrifty Rent-A-Car** (Tel. 211–8788), 100 Franklin St.

Most rates will be over $40 a day, however, including those at **Budget Rent-A-Car** (Tel. 223–1400), 274 North Terrace, **Hertz Rentals** (Tel. 51–2856), 30 Morphett St., and **Avis Rent-A-Car** (Tel. 211–8000), 298 Hindley St. (All offer flat daily and weekly rates.)

If you're a pedal bicycle fan, Adelaide with its parks and gardens is one city where it might be practical to ride one. You can rent them ("push bikes," they call them in Australia) from **Super Elliotts** (Tel. 223–3946) at 200 Rundle St., and at several other addresses throughout the suburbs.

Metropolitan Bus Services (Tel. 210–1000 for information) are well described in the color-coded Public Transport Map issued by the Ministry of Transport from time to time. (Ask for one at the tourist office or the railroad station.) Maximum fare on the silvery gray vehicles is 90 cents, but note the free multicolored "Bee Line" service (99-B) shooting between the railroad station and the Victoria Square tram terminal, and the "City Loop" service (99-C) from the railroad station, which is also gratis.

There is now only one trolley left. That's the little chocolate car called the **Bay Tram.** You get it at Victoria Square and it takes about a half hour to get to the seaside suburb of Glenelg on the Gulf St. Vincent. (Other Adelaide streetcars were retired years ago, but the Glenelg line had its own right-of-way so it never had to war with motor vehicles.)

4. Hotels in Adelaide

You'll pay at least $90 for two in most rooms at Adelaide's top hotels. All have the standard luxury features—color tellies, fridges, air conditioners, tea-makers, newspapers, etc. Following those, we'll list a few possibilities at lower rates.

EXPENSIVE HOTELS

An absolutely perfect location goes a long way to recommend the 21-story **Gateway Hotel** (Tel. 217–7552) at 147 North Terrace, across from Parliament, the Festival Centre, the river, and a grand view of North Adelaide—and also around the corner from the business section. Lots of central facilities, including laundry, dry cleaner, swimming pool, the Chelsea Restaurant, Portico Grill, cocktail bar, travel agency, etc.; colorful, well-lighted, nicely designed bedrooms (notice the little breakfast-tray hatch accessible from the hallway); convenient bathrooms with good showers and tubs. We experienced friendly, efficient service. Our only small criticism of the Gateway is that if you travel a lot between Adelaide, Perth, and Brisbane, you may have to look out the window in the morning to be reminded which of these cities you're in, because the three links in the chain look like identical triplets inside. (Reservations through Ansett, of course, or write to the hotel.) There's little in Adelaide today that matches it.

Now coming on strong, however, the 379-room **Hilton International Adelaide** (Tel. 217–0711) is open and breathing some life into somnolent Victoria Square:

A marble-lined lobby features check-ins beside a waterfall. Public facilities in the 18-story hotel include two restaurants, three bars, a disco, five shops, a health club (complete with gym and sauna), a tennis court, and a heated outdoor swimming pool.

Rooms with all the mod cons begin at around $110 and then move rapidly upwards. All rates include the old-world overnight shine, if you leave your shoes outside. (Reservations through the Hilton chain or the hotel at 233 Victoria Square, Adelaide, S.A. 5000.) We haven't seen the establishment since its opening, so we cannot specifically recommend it. Still, except for its lackluster site, quite removed from the action, the new Hilton has been receiving high marks from its first guests.

Also very nice, if a little inconvenient, is the **Oberoi Adelaide** (Tel. 267–3444), north of the green belt at 62 Brougham Place. This was the old Hotel Australia, which fell on hard times but was finally rescued by the Oberoi hotel chain of India: Two buildings now joined in a single operation; spacious, two-story reception area in rich reds and growing greens; cocktail bar in the lobby; some eastern artwork in evidence; stairway to the balcony above; small outdoor swimming pool in the rear; two sets of elevators; a pair of good dining rooms, the silver-service Brougham Restaurant and the unique (for Adelaide) Rang Mahal Indian restaurant; 150 generally spacious bedrooms with all luxury amenities; pleasant, classic furnishings with wallpaper, patterned carpets, etc.; excellent views over parklands and city lights; normal twins in about the $80 range; pleasant folks attending on our own recent stay. (Reservations from the hotel address at Adelaide 5006.)

MEDIUM-PRICE HOTELS

The venerable old **Grosvenor** (Tel. 51–2961), a few doors down the street from the aforementioned Gateway, has been brought fairly smoothly into the 1980s. The hotel was first built in 1918 by a farmers' cooperative organization who wanted a decent place to take their families when they came to town, and it still fulfills that role nicely. Modernized, wood-paneled lobby with blue-and-gold monogrammed carpet; Coolibah Room and new Sables Restaurant; cozy Pioneer Bar; no pool; no views to speak of; free parking; 280 widely varying bedchambers, but most with air conditioning, stocked refrigerator, color TV, tea-maker, subdued colors. Rates run from around $50 here, and it's a good bargain. (Reservations from the hotel at 125 North Terrace, Adelaide 5000.) An admirable job of preserving an ancient model.

Some will prefer the **Town House** (Tel. 211–8255), a modern candidate around the corner at the conjunction of Morphett Street and "swinging" Hindley Street: Red-brick façade; covered porte cochere; reception area with some unusual lamps and a certain amount of clutter; Lipizzaner Dining Room reflecting the manager's love of horses; bar and coffee lounge open to guests only; large, heated pool on the roof, with wind-protected sun deck; several conveniences catering to businessmen. Amply proportioned bedrooms and many suites; some with walkout balconies; good, full bathrooms; color TVs and many luxuries in all units; some with views over the rooftops. Prices, beginning at about $60 for doubles, are perhaps a little steeper than we think they should be. (Res-

ervations through the M.F.A. chain in Australia, or from the hotel at
Adelaide 5000.) Certainly comfortable.

If you can't get into any of the above, you might try the recently
renovated **Adelaide Parkroyal** (Tel. 223–4355), inconveniently situated
at 226 South Terrace (it's fine with a car): Imposing façade with fountains playing; large, outdoor pool in the back garden; pleasant restaurant; well-arranged rooms, many with balconies. The Parkroyal is one of
a pair of Travelodge-owned hotels established next door to each other.
The second, which was once two hotels itself, is the **Adelaide Travelodge**
(Tel. 223–2744). We judged it clean, neat, and dull.

BUDGET-PRICED ACCOMMODATIONS

"Absolutely charming" is the comment we keep hearing about one of
our favorite low-price bargains in the entire country. That happens to be
the **Newmarket** (Tel. 211–8533), at the corner of West and North terraces, near the end of the Port Road. Here's a hotel with genuine creaky
character—it dates back about 130 years.

The centerpiece of the house is its wonderful, freestanding cedar
spiral staircase swirling from the lobby to the upper floor, an architectural feature now protected by the Australian National Trust. It's worth
stopping in to see even if you don't stay there.

An active place throughout the day and night, the Newmarket includes the popular Stockyard restaurant, a cocktail lounge, and a weekend discotheque. The entire establishment is filled with old oil paintings,
Tiffany skylights, crystal chandeliers, marble-mantled fireplaces, and other
Victoriana. The bedchambers, though no longer young, tend to be large,
trim, and cheap. For $45 or so for a double, you'll draw a black-and-
white TV, a phone, a fridge, and an electric jug to boot. (Write the hotel
for reservations at 1 North Terrace, Adelaide 5000.) You may have to lug
your luggage up those historic steps, but at those nonspiraling tariffs, it
could be worth it.

Also justly popular with penny-squeezers is the **Earl of Zetland** (Tel.
223–5500), an ancient entry centrally located at the corner of Gawler
Place and Flinders Street, near Victoria Square: Floral patterns abounding
throughout the edifice; its history posted in the lobby; several bars and a
serviceable dining room; clean, wallpapered bedrooms with tall ceilings;
no views; all rooms with color TV, radio, tea- and coffee-making equipment; larger rooms also boasting air conditioning and refrigerator; singles at about $30; doubles around $40. (Reservations direct from "the
Earl" at the address above, Adelaide 5000.) Very comfy for the price.

The **Ambassadors Hotel** (Tel. 51–4331) at 107 King William St. is
another supposed oldie-but-goodie. There's a lift here, and you'll get

color television and all that, but the rooms are relatively cramped. Most have showers, but few have tubs. A better deal is probably the **Festival Lodge** (Tel. 212–7877) at 140 North Terrace, between the Gateway and the Grosvenor. Doubles are around $40. Sorry, we no longer recommend the **Astor** or the **Plaza.**

Youth hostel? For members only, remember, it's at 290 Gilles St. (Tel. 223–6007), and it has lots of rules. You may check in for about $6.50—a little less if you provide your own bed sheet. Headquarters of the Youth Hostels Association of S.A. (Tel. 51–5583) is at 72 South Terrace.

5. Restaurants and Dining

Adelaide folks like to eat out, and it's an oft-repeated truism that the city has more restaurants per gullet than any other metropolis in Australia.

Observers of Adelaide's restaurant scene say, in fact, that the city has too many restaurants, and that this results in a serious lack of consistency at the top addresses—this, in a city that would otherwise rival Melbourne for elegant dining rooms.

SEAFOOD

Adelaide is famous for ocean specialties, particularly (1) crayfish, (2) prawns, and (3) whiting, whether in restaurants calling themselves seafood houses or in more wide-ranging kitchens. It's not surprising when you consider that there are two large bays, or rather gulfs—Spencer Gulf and Gulf St. Vincent—to harvest.

Look out for dishes labeled "fried or grilled whiting" or "crumbed prawns." More than likely they will be frozen, not fresh. And skip whiting dishes that are smothered with French sauces, as these mask the delicate, distinct flavor of the whiting.

Other favorites, if you can find them, are fresh gemfish (something like barramundi, which is a Northern Territory specialty), tuna, and rock lobster.

And don't forget that some of Australia's best wines—particularly whites—are produced in the nearby Barossa Valley and are just about perfect complements to the seafood specialties.

There are two or three outstanding seafood restaurants. One is **Swain's** (Tel. 79–6449), which now packs 'em in at 249 Glen Osmond Rd. in Frewville, a little southeast on Route 1. Here's a good place to try whiting or crayfish, but it's not cheap. (Closed Sundays.) Some now prefer **Chief Charlie's** (Tel. 574–432), formerly the Adelaide Oyster Bar, 12 Grenfell St., for lunch or dinner. A third choice for high-class ocean fare is **Byron's** (Tel. 294–3844), a 60-seat establishment at 712 Anzac Highway. For fish fanciers with a thinner wallet under their gills, try one of the little ocean-oriented cafes in Gouger Street, an even greater saving when you can bring your own wine. Don't expect the Ritz, but we liked **Gouger's Cafe** (Tel. 51–2320) at No. 98. If you don't mind formica and bright lights, you may come up with an excellent garfish or whiting for about $6.50. It's very popular; reservations are not mandatory, but you may have to wait. Another favorite is **George's**, at No. 108, the only one that is air conditioned and also open Sunday. A Minneapolis reader recommends the "perfectly cooked" barramundi.

OTHER RESTAURANTS

Many of Adelaide's better restaurants will also do very nicely with seafood, of course. This is certainly true at **Henry Ayers** (Tel. 223–2852), in the historic, state-owned Ayers House at 288 North Terrace. This was once the most expensive restaurant in Australia, but prices have become much more realistic. According to Sol Simeon's excellent guide, *Eating Out in Adelaide*, it is Adelaide's most spectacular restaurant, decorated in "Edwardian decadence." The last menu we saw made it difficult to choose between the Supreme de Volaille Roxelane (chicken breast stuffed with pâté, sauteed in butter with tarragon, carrots, leeks, mushrooms, lemon peel, and wine, flamed in whisky, and finished with cream) and the Tournedos Colbert (two panfried filets on medallions of chicken croquette, topped with egg, and served with mushrooms and Madeira sauce). The dining room is under new management, but standards are said to be as high as before.

Another top-drawer choice is the **Chelsea** (Tel. 217–7552), in the Gateway Hotel. You might try the Porc a la Scandinave, with red cabbage, for something different. They're proud of one crayfish dish, too—the Chausson de Langouste Haleakala, named for a Hawaiian volcano. It's baked in pastry with celery, chestnuts, and mushrooms. Another traditional leader is **Possums** (Tel. 267–1503) at 145 O'Connell St. in North Adelaide. It's a BYO that seats about 30 max., but it serves up what might be the best examples of French *nouvelle cuisine* in the country.

The restaurant dubbed "the best value in Australia" by the national magazine the *Bulletin* is **Ellini's** (Tel. 212–6794), a Greek place at 69 Grote St. Some specialties include spanakopita (spinach pie), seafood skewers (octopus, crayfish, scallops, and prawns), and shaved lamb. Mentioned in the same article was the **Arkaba Steak Cellar** (Tel. 51–2221) at Quelltaler House, 22 Gilbert Place. They seat about 400 beef lovers there in an old wine cellar. And while we're passing around accolades from the press, **Reilly's** on King William Road was singled out for singular praise by the American *Gourmet* magazine not long ago. The **Grapevine** (Tel. 267–3766) at 63 Melbourne St. in North Adelaide really is nestled in a genuine grapevine. The cuisine is cosmopolitan, and usually very good.

You'll find good international fare in the **King's Court** (Tel. 223–4355) in the Parkroyal Hotel and the **Riverside Restaurant** (Tel. 51–6430) right next to the main auditorium in the Festival Centre (Adelaide *Advertiser* food writer Stan James said he had his best barramundi there, panfried in butter and topped with Hollandaise sauce). **Rang Mahal** (Tel. 267–3444) in the Oberoi Adelaide Hotel now offers authentic Indian cusine. And **Decca's Place** (Tel. 267–2111), 93 Melbourne St., near the boutiques in North Adelaide, is as well loved for its garden atmosphere as its wiener schnitzel.

There are bargains to be had in little Hindley Street, particularly in the little Greek- or Serbian-run barbecue cafes there. One is **Lubo's** (Tel. 51–2848) at No. 108, and not bad except for some glaring fluorescent lighting. My shashlik was fine. Sara didn't go for the schnitzel, which came with cold veggies. Some say the **Barbecue Inn** (Tel. 51–3033) at No. 196 is much better, especially for Serbian sausages. And the **Hindley Bar-B-Q** (Tel. 51–2090) at No. 179 has always been popular—perhaps a little more so since the waitresses began wearing transparent costumes!

For Italian food, the best bet is **Sorrento** (Tel. 51–6740) at 135 Hindley St. Also popular are the low-priced pasta palaces on Pirie Street, the **Marco Polo Pastificio** (Tel. 223–2159) at No. 131 and the **Fontana di Trevi** at No. 125.

Adelaide now teems with pizza joints, but the best is **Don Giovanni's** (Tel. 223–2125) at 201 Rundle St., just off the mall. Lots of other standard Italian dishes like canneloni and scallopini marinara are also good; servings are large, and prices are reasonably low. The **Adelaide Pizza House** (Tel. 51–6906), 169 Hindley, is also popular.

And Chinese fare? Adelaide has several possibilities, including **Chinatown** (Tel. 212–2501) at 33 Hindley St., usually a good bet; **Dynasty** (Tel. 211–7036) at 26 Gouger St., specializing in dim sum (Chinese snacks); and the **Lantern Inn** (Tel. 297–1629) at 295-B Anzac Highway in Plympton (halfway to Glenelg), where the Peking duck is excellent (but 24 hours' notice is required if you want to order it), and the **Manchurian** (Tel. 295–7839), *all* the way to Glenelg at 16 Jetty Rd.

In Kent Town, a little east of the city, is an English find called **Maggie's Tavern** (Tel. 42–2686). It's at 107 Rundle St. (not to be confused with the Rundle Street downtown), and a fan named John Anderson wrote us that "it has a warm atmosphere, with fireplaces in several of its small rooms, a large wine cellar, and the service is friendly." Thanks, John. The corned beef and cabbage is good, too.

BAROSSA VALLEY

In the famed wine-growing region, one of your best bets for wein-and-wurst Germanic atmosphere might be the **Vintners Restaurant** (Tel. 085 + 64–2488) on Nuriootpa Road at Angaston. We were very disappointed in **Die Galerie** in Tanunda. The weingarten *gemütlichkeit* was delightful, but we felt as if the owner was trying to trick us into ordering more than we really wanted. We did not experience that anywhere else in Australia. Next time we'll try **Die Weinstube** (Tel. 085 + 62–1416) on Lyndoch Road near Nuriootpa, or the reportedly phabulous **Pheasant Farm,** between Nuriootpa and Seppeltsfield.

6. Sightseeing in Adelaide and South Australia

Get all the latest information, maps, folders, tour schedules, etc., from the South Australian Government Travel Centre (Tel. 212–1644) at 18 King William St. It's just about the most on-the-ball state tourist office in Australia.

Ask at the Travel Centre for the pamphlet and map entitled *Your Complete Guide to Adelaide,* which covers the most important sites and sights in the city center.

The **Adelaide Festival Centre** complex, in Elder Park alongside the banks of the Torrens, includes a 2,000-seat multipurpose auditorium, a two-level drama theater, an experimental theater, and an amphitheater. The Adelaide Festival of the Arts takes place in the fall of even-numbered years. The next is March 1986. (Public tours of the Centre are offered from 10 to 3 on the hour Monday through Friday. Recheck hours for Saturday.)

The **Art Gallery of South Australia** (Tel. 223–7200), sometimes called the National Gallery, houses an international collection particularly rich in Australian paintings, ceramics, and sculpture. (Open daily 10 to 5.) Nearby, the Frome Road is very attractive in summer with its copious overhanging trees.

Ayers House (Tel. 223–1196) at 288 North Terrace, headquarters of the South Australian National Trust, is an elegant bluestone home of the middle nineteenth century that is also maintained as a museum. (Two restaurants are on the property—Henry Ayers, expensive, and Paxton's, less formal but still not cheap.) Try to catch a guided tour of the house, Tuesday through Friday at varying hours. (Also open weekends and holidays from 2 to 4 P.M. Closed Mondays. Admission $2.)

In the parklands to the northeast of the center, the collection of water lilies at the **Botanic Gardens** is noted worldwide. The gardens are open daily until sunset. By the way, there's a small riverboat called *Popeye* that sails on the Torrens every 10 minutes between the zoo and the Festival Theatre.

The **Civic Buildings** include the structures just north of Victoria Square—the twin clock towers of the General Post Office and the Town Hall, the Treasury Building, and the Gothic-styled Stow Memorial Church. Of more interest to many is the little pie cart alongside the G.P.O. The specialty is the "floater," an upside-down pie floating in a sea of green pea soup. Adelaideans lap it up with a dollop of tomato sauce. (Another good pie cart is usually outside the railway station.)

At the stalls of the **Central Market,** running between Grote and Gouger, you can buy veggies, fruit, cheeses, meats, flowers, nuts, caviar, smoked salmon, and you name it. It's open Tuesday until 6, Friday until 10, and Saturday until 2 P.M.

The **Constitutional Museum** (Tel. 212–6066), which covers South Australian political history, sounds exceedingly boring. Such is not the case. Set in the 1843 Legislative Assembly Building, next to the railroad station, the light-and-sound, audiovisual techniques seem almost to bring the past to life. We recommend it even to those who know nothing about S.A. (Admission about $3, and worth it.)

In North Adelaide, overlooking the city from Montefiore Hill, stands **Light's Vision.** This memorial and statue of Colonel Light is considered a good place to begin a tour of his city.

The **South Australian Museum** (Tel. 223–8911), sometimes called the Museum of Natural History, has an outstanding mob of stuffed birds and animals. Be sure to stop inside long enough to have a good look at the ground-floor skeleton of the giant Diprotodon, an ancestor of the wombat. (Photograph its portrait head-on, and we'll guarantee you'll have a startling slide to shake up your audience!) Like many sites, the museum is on the elegant North Terrace. It's open 10 to 5 most days.

In the reading room of the **State Library** next door you'll find an excellent collection of current newspapers.

The **University of Adelaide,** also a neighbor to the above, provides a scholarly-looking campus and a route to the little footbridge over the Torrens to the Angas Gardens.

KANGAROO ISLAND

A good, one-day aerial tour is a trip to the island they call "K.I." It features lots of unpenned wildlife—yes, that means kangaroos, plus penguins, goannas, koalas, "flying foxes" (a type of bat), and an occasional platypus. At Seal Bay you can walk among and photograph close up the laziest colony of seals you ever saw. Have a look, too, for squadrons of

pelicans and the rare Cape Barren goose, as well as a group of remark
able rocks, called the Remarkable Rocks.

Kangaroo Island, discovered in 1802 by Mathew Flinders, has a color
ful history all its own, and we could easily do an entire chapter on the
place—and a book on S.A.—if only we had the space.

MOUNT LOFTY TO THE MURRAY

A good day's driving tour from an Adelaide base is to head for the
Adelaide Hills along Route 1 (Princes Highway or Mt. Barker Road)
and thence to **Mount Lofty** via the Summit Road. The outlook is great,
but the real purpose of the journey is to enter the well-designed Native
Fauna Zone of the **Cleland Conservation Park.** There you may walk
among and even pet some of the friendliest koalas, kangaroos, cockatoos, and other animals you ever did see. The park is still being developed,
but it has already begun to rank with the best in the country, and many
say it's better than any. (Open 9:30 A.M. to 5:00 P.M. daily. Feeding time
for koalas, dingoes, and birds is from 2:00 P.M. to 4:00 P.M.)

On the same trip you might drive through—or even stop for lunch
at—the little German-styled town of **Hahndorf,** 18 miles east of Adelaide.
Many Germans immigrated to South Australia because of religious and
economic problems around 1840. The Old Mill Restaurant there is well
known. Tours are available from the blacksmith's shop.

About 30 miles farther along the Princes Highway you eventually come to
Murray Bridge at Australia's famous **River Murray.** It's a total of around 50
miles from Adelaide, so you might want to make it a separate excursion.

BAROSSA VALLEY

This is wine country, and if that doesn't interest you, so be it. But for
those who appreciate the fermented grape, a visit to the best vineyards
of Australia is virtually essential.

Since you will want to stop at one or two established wineries, perhaps
the best way is to take one of the guided tours from the Tourist Centre. But
if you want the freedom of driving, pick up the thorough brochure entitled *Barossa Valley* and head for **Tanunda,** about 45 miles away. This is the
center of the valley and headquarters for many of the German families
who brought their skill to South Australia nearly a century and a half ago.

On odd-numbered years—the opposite to the schedule for the Adelaide
Festival—the Barossa Wine Festival starts on Easter Monday.

Some of the wineries that offer tours, tastings, and "cellar-door" sales
are **Yalumba** (site of our own recent taste test) and **Seppeltsfield.** There
are dozens more. (Tours and tastings are generally free; sales are usually
about 10 or 15 percent less than retail prices in bottle shops in Adelaide.)

NORTHERN SOUTH AUSTRALIA

About 225 miles north of Adelaide begin the rugged mountains called the **Flinders Ranges,** actually an extension of the Adelaide Hills. The Flinders' bright colors, majestic trees, and granite peaks make them a favorite of landscape painters. From September to October the hills are covered with wildflowers. As a base for Flinders explorations, head for the town (and mountain) of Wilpena Pound.

Farther out is the salt lake that is usually *all* salt, called **Lake Eyre.** It may be difficult to get much of a feeling for the salt flats without taking a plane over them.

Near the center of the state are the desolate opal-mining areas of **Andamooka** and **Coober Pedy** (the latter is a somewhat more practical destination for a casual visitor). About $3 million worth of opals is mined each year, much of it by intrepid individuals, many of whom are recent immigrants. The residents live mostly underground in former opal digs where the temperatures are tolerable. Outside, it can easily reach 130 degrees Fahrenheit.

They say Coober Pedy in the local Aboriginal tongue means "white man in a hole." (The town is lucky to have a simple name. A nearby salt lake is called Lake Cadibarrawirracanna.) Sightseeing tours of both communities are available, and they even have a couple of motels. At Coober Pedy you can stay underground inside the Umoona Opal Mine. We'd advise flying in—not driving—because of the hazardous roads in the area.

If you want to "gouge" for some opals yourself, you must buy a Precious Stones Prospective Permit for $20. Otherwise you can "noodle" through a "mullock heap" gratis. If you want to buy opals, we'd advise staying with established dealers. You might get a bargain from a miner, but if you're not an expert you're taking a big chance.

Last, and not really part of South Australia, is the silver-mining town of **Broken Hill,** just over the state line into New South Wales. Check out the Moslem mosque, built by Afghan camel traders, and the 20-pound Silver Tree in the Civic Centre.

7. Guided Tours and Cruises

There are a potentially confusing number of tours offered by several different agencies throughout South Australia, and the picture changes frequently. Better get the latest from the South Australian Government Travel Centre at 18 King William St.

Half-day tours. *City Sights,* 2 afternoons a week, about $15. *Mt. Lofty Ranges and Wildlife Sanctuary,* 2 afternoons a week, about $16. *City Lights,* 2 evenings a week, about $13.

Full-day tours. *Barossa Valley* (including lunch), daily, about $25. *Goolwaa and Murray Mouth* (including a short launch cruise), Tuesdays and Saturdays, about $35. *Victor Harbour and South Coast,* 2 days a week, about $25.

Murray River Cruises. At the moment, long passenger cruises are available on the *Murray River Queen* (5½ days, Goolwa to Swan Reach and back, for around $400) and the newer $1.8-million *Murray Explorer,* which carries 120 passengers on 5½-day cruises from Renmark for about $500. A new vessel, the *Proud Mary,* has been launched on a 5-day cruise from Murray Bridge to Blanchetown for around $500, and on a 2-day cruise to Mannum and back for around $200.

There are a few combination plane/bus one-day tours to *Kangaroo Island,* including a picnic lunch and sometimes a dinner at Kingscote. About $115.

8. Water Sports

Adelaide's principal seaside resort is the town of **Glenelg.** Together with other shoreline sites on the Gulf St. Vincent—like **West Beach** and **Grange**—it offers about 20 miles of good, safe swimming beaches, with no surf. The beaches are virtually shark-free, even though white pointer sharks, measuring 25 and 30 feet, are caught off South Australia. **Maslin's Beach,** about 45 minutes' drive south of Adelaide, was the nation's first official nude beach.

Surfers head for **Victor Harbour, Pondalowie Bay,** and **Cactus Beach** on more exposed waters of the Bight. Skin divers like both gulfs (St. Vincent and Spencer) to view the reefs and wrecks. You can rent skin-diving equipment from **Adelaide Skindiving Centre** (Tel. 51–6144), 7 Compton St., Adelaide.

9. Other Sports

For spectator sports—and in S.A., that means cricket and Aussie Rules football—the main sports grounds are the **Adelaide Oval,** just across the river from the Festival Centre (now devoted to cricket only) and the new **Football Park** at West Lakes. There is horse racing in the parklands southeast of the main grid at **Victoria Park Racecourse.** You can watch free if you walk up to the side of the track, but you have to pay to get a grandstand view. But the premier course is now **Morphettville,** four miles southwest, where the Adelaide Cup is usually run the third Monday in May. Others include **Cheltenham,** five miles northwest, and **Globe Derby Park** in Bolivar for trotting races.

Tennis courts are everywhere. Avid players should call the Department of Environmental Planning (Tel. 216–7862) in order to find an available court.

For golfers, the **North Adelaide Municipal Golf Links** (Tel. 267–2171) are also right in town, in the parklands. Some enjoy the unique character of the **Royal Adelaide** in Seaton (Tel. 356–5511), which has a railway line through the course. But the best and most impeccably groomed course is the **Kooyonga Golf Club** (Tel. 352–5444), at May Terrace, Lockleys, S.A. 5032.

10. Shopping in Adelaide

Shopping activities center around two very compact areas—the **Rundle Mall,** a block south of North Terrace, with several arcades that open onto the mall, and the smart boutiques along **Melbourne Street** in North Adelaide. Most shops are open weekdays from 9:00 to 5:30. Thursday night is late-shopping night in the suburbs. On Fridays, shops in the city operate until 9. Saturday everything goes dead at about noon.

On the Rundle Mall, you'll find the three main department stores. First, there are the two branches of the Melbourne- and Sydney-headquartered outfits, **Myer** and **David Jones.** But there is also one sharp local firm, **John Martin's of South Australia,** often known affectionately as "Johnny's."

For opals, a well-recognized house is **The Opal Mine** (Tel. 223–4023), 30 Gawler Place. Another dependable address is the **Opal Field House** (Tel. 212–5300), just across from the Travel Centre at 29 King William St.

General gifts and souvenirs are pretty good at **The Australian Scene** (Tel. 43–6916) at 235 Henley Beach Rd. in Torrensville, and the **Primitive Arts and Craft Shop** (Tel. 223–8449) at the S.A. Museum on North Terrace.

For antiques, poke around the numerous shops along Unley Road (try **Antique Galleries**), King William Road (near Hyde Park), or, of course, Melbourne Street. You'll probably pay less here for items also sold in Melbourne and Sydney.

Artworks are for sale at **Bonython-Meadmore Gallery** (Tel. 267–4449) at 88 Jervingham St., North Adelaide, and you'll find more jewelry and pottery as well as sculpture at **Greenhill Galleries** (Tel. 267–2887), 140 Barton Terrace in North Adelaide. An excellent new gallery, **La Unique** (Tel. 223–1328), has just opened at Shop 6, Renaissance Arcade. It features a wide selection of ceramics.

An unusual arts-and-crafts operation is at **The Jam Factory** (Tel. 42–5661), 169 Payneham Rd. in St. Peters. No longer turning out jam, of course, it's a project by the South Australian government to boost local crafts, most of them made on the premises.

Bookstores. There are four or five well-stocked bookstores in central Adelaide, Browse through **Mary Martin Bookshop** (Tel. 212–7911), where you might meet Max Harris, *Bulletin* columnist and one of the country's top literary figures. Also, check the **Standard Book Store** (Tel. 223–5380), 136 Rundle Mall, **Liberty Bookshop** (Tel. 223–2386), 32 Hindmarsh Square, or **City Books** (Tel. 223–2773) at 108 Gawler Place. And then there's the well-known **Third World Bookshop** at 103 Hindley St., which never closes!

11. Night Life and Entertainment

The closest thing Adelaide has to Sydney's King's Cross area is Hindley Street, a three-block-long stretch of after-dark activity that, by and large, is pretty tame.

All the standard drinks are available, bolstered by perhaps more kinds of wine than you might find elsewhere in Australia. Neighborhood pubs, of course, are still loyal bastions of beer, and despite the state's reputation for wine it also brews some fair samples of the amber.

Cooper and Sons, the only family brewery in the country, produces the wonderful sparkling Cooper's Ale, which is brewed *in the bottle.* (It's considered one of the best beers in the world, even if it does look like mud!)

A second brewery, the South Australian Brewing Company, produces West End and Southwark, both very bitter beers indeed.

Most beer glasses come in "butcher" sizes—that's 6 ounces. Don't be frightened by the "schooner." Unlike the N.S.W. version, which holds 15 ounces, the S.A. schooner has only 9 ounces.

Out of the pubs, now, and back on Hindley Street, one of the best strip shows Adelaide has seen is at the **Crazy Horse.**

There's discotheque and rock music at **Juliana's** in the Adelaide Hilton, at **Da Vinci's International** at 9 Light Square, at **Regines** in a former church at 69 Light Square, and at the **Old Lion Hotel** on Melbourne Street in North Adelaide. **Jules,** 94 Hindley St., and **The Wellington** at Wellington Square, North Adelaide, also feature some heavy beats. Farther out (that is, farther away), there's the **Arkaba Disco** (Tel. 79–3614), also a restaurant at 150 Glen Osmond Rd. in Fullarton. And the **Green Dragon Hotel** at 239 South Terrace caters somewhat to the gay community.

Something a little cooler, more conservative? You'll find live jazz at the **Flagstaff Hotel** (Tel. 296–6677), South Road, Darlington, and at the **Inglewood Hotel,** Inglewood, but you'd better recheck the days and hours by phone.

In theater-restaurants, that double medium becoming almost as popular as football and pavlova, the choices include the **Bull 'N' Bush** (Tel.

262–3944) at the Hotel Enfield, 184 Hampstead Rd., Enfield, which features Elizabethan trappings. Another dinner/floor-show combination is at the **After Dark Club** (Tel. 212–4580), 63 Light Square.

Live theater is a frequent event in Adelaide, with performances often taking place at the **Festival Centre** (Tel. 51–2291). The 600-seat Playhouse there is the home stage for the South Australian Theatre Company.

Other commercial theaters include the **Sheridan Theatre** (Tel. 267–3751) at 50 MacKinnon Parade, North Adelaide; the **John Edmund Theatre** (Tel. 223–5651) at 89 Halifax St.; the **Opera Theatre** (Tel. 212–6833) at 58 Grote St., the home of the State Opera of South Australia; and the **Troupe Theatre** (Tel. 271–7552), an experimental theater at the corner of Unley Road and Oxford Street, Unley.

For classical music, the South Australian Symphony presents concerts, usually in the 2,000-seat concert theater at the Festival Centre but sometimes in the **Adelaide Town Hall.** Get the latest from the tourist office or the Australian Broadcasting Corporation Concert Department, Gawler Place, in Adelaide.

12. The Adelaide Address List

Ambulance—Tel. 272–8822.

American consulate—Tel. 322–8886.

American Express—13 Grenfell St. (Tel. 212–7099).

Bank—State Bank of S.A., 97 King William St. (Tel. 51–0371).

Bus and tram information—Tel. 210–1000.

Dental emergency service—Tel. 79–7878.

Doctor service after hours—Tel. 223–0230, 45–0222, or 275–9911.

Emergencies in general—Dial 000.

Fire department—Tel. 223–3000.

Hospital—Royal Adelaide Hospital (Tel. 223–0230).

Pharmacy (24-hour chemist)—Burden Chemists, 41 King William St. (Tel. 51–4701).

Police—Tel. 218–1212.

Royal Automobile Association of S.A.—41 Hindmarsh Square (Tel. 223–4555).

Tourist office—S.A. Government Travel Centre, 18 King William St. (Tel. 212–1644).

Train information—Tel. 212–6699.

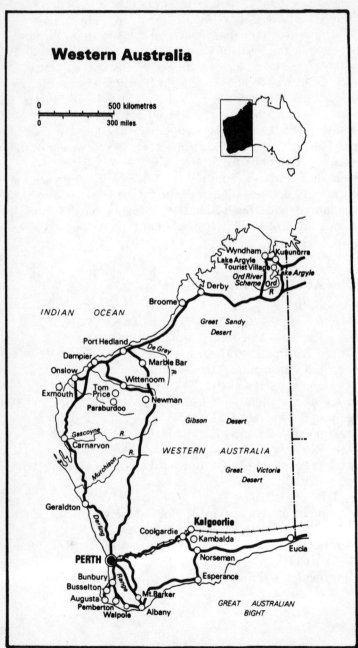

Western Australia

0   500 kilometres
0   300 miles

INDIAN OCEAN

Wyndham   Kununurra
Lake Argyle
Tourist Village
Ord River   Lake Argyle
Scheme   Ord
Derby   R

Broome

Great Sandy
Desert

Port Hedland   De Grey
Dampier
Marble Bar
Onslow   R
Wittenoom
Tom
Exmouth   Price
Paraburdoo   Newman

Gibson   Desert

Gascoyne   R.
Carnarvon   R.

WESTERN   AUSTRALIA

Great   Victoria
Desert

Murchison

Geraldton

Kalgoorlie
Coolgardie
Kambalda

Darling

PERTH   Norseman   Eucla

Bunbury   Esperance
Busselton
Augusta   Range
Pemberton   Mt.Barker
Walpole   Albany

GREAT   AUSTRALIAN
BIGHT

Map courtesy Australian Tourist Commission

10

Perth,
The Star of W.A.

1. The General Picture

Everyone likes Perth. Particularly this year.

You can hold debates at the drop of a beer can about every other city in Australia, but somehow when you come to Perth, the argument stops. Especially right now.

Nitpickers say there are things to criticize about the Western Australians—their provincialism, their overestimation of their importance in the scheme of things. But that's a complaint that could be registered in greater or lesser degree about many other areas in the world. In any case, this year Perth can do no wrong.

You might think the "Tyranny of Distance," a curse supposedly applied to all of Australia, would be visited upon the people of "W.A." (as they like to call the state) more than those living anywhere else in the country. The Westralians are cut off by thousands of miles of desert, not just from the world at large but from the cultural centers of their own nation. People from Perth who travel at all will probably not choose Brisbane, Sydney, or Melbourne for a holiday. More likely they'll fly to Bali, Jakarta, or Singapore.

Still, there have always been some things that are special about Perth. It is the sunniest capital in the country, receiving a yearly average of eight hours of sunshine per day, and it reminds many visitors of the Italian

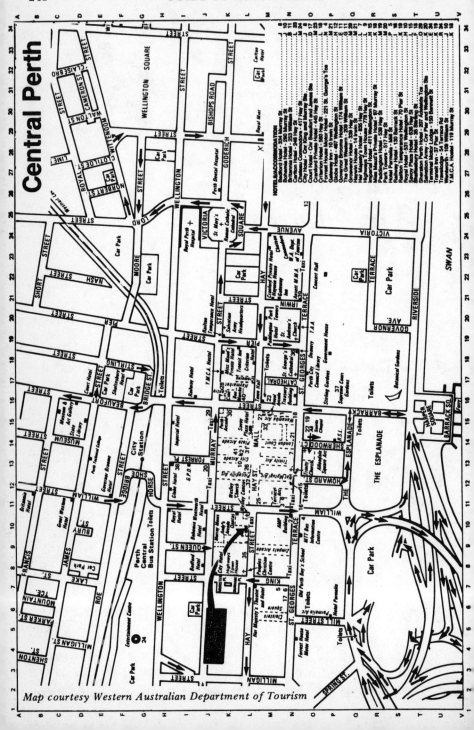

Central Perth

Riviera or of Southern California. It is also unpolluted, with the many heavy mining and manufacturing industries of W.A. installed hundreds of miles away.

There is an attractive river estuary, the Swan, which widens almost into a lake through the city limits. (The river was named in 1696 when Dutch explorers first saw black swans on its waters.) And overlooking the Swan is King's Park, a large piece of flowered bushland atop a hill right within the city. Below it is an architectural pattern of filigreed nineteenth-century buildings set against a few modern skyscrapers. Somehow it's all spread out enough so that, aesthetically, it works.

Every now and then Perth manages to impinge itself on the consciousness of the world, and it's going to do that again in 1986 and 1987.

Back in 1962 the citizens of Perth turned on every electric light they could find as a greeting to pioneer astronaut John Glenn when his orbital path carried him directly over the city. This light of inspiration called Perth to the attention of people around the globe. Perth began calling itself the "City of Light," and investors in New York, London, and Tokyo were soon attracted like moths to the glow. Perth and W.A. grew during the 1960s and 1970s to a degree not previously imagined.

Western Australia is without a doubt the most prosperous state in the country. Iron ore is stripped from the Hamersley Ranges. Elsewhere there is oil, natural gas, bauxite, and uranium. Nickel is mined from the rough-and-tumble towns where Australia's second gold rush occurred in the 1890s, and some marketable gold is even brought up there today. A recent diamond discovery was said to threaten the diamond industry in South Africa. (Much of this underground wealth is being recovered from Aboriginal lands, but due to the intransigence of the mining companies and a tough state premier committed to the industrial interests, Aborigines do not yet collect the royalties they are beginning to receive in other states.)

In 1980 Perth again made world headlines when the American space satellite Skylab fell in pieces over the inland desert to the east. Some thought Perth had quieted down a little going into the current decade, but that was before 1983. That year the Royal Perth Yacht Club went to Newport, Rhode Island, to take part as it had done for years in the America's Cup yachting regatta. Suddenly, to almost everyone's surprise, the Perth crew won the final race and captured the America's Cup for Australia—an event that sparked a national celebration Down Under.

In late 1986 and early 1987, the New York Yacht Club is scheduled to try to win the cup back when the contest is run in the windy waters off nearby Fremantle, at the mouth of the Swan. Again the eyes of the world are turning to Perth. And many foreign yacht crews also hope to win under conditions unfamiliar to the Americans.

It seems that the people of every Australian state like to talk about seceding from the rest of the country, generally acknowledged as an impractical action. They talk about independence, too, in W.A., and if they ever did it there, Perth could conceivably lead the richest country per capita on the globe. Population is a little over 1.3 million in W.A., and more than 70 percent of that number live in the capital.

The people of Perth and W.A. are said to be somehow "more Australian" than the rest of the country—less jaded, more open, and a repository of friendly optimism that seems to some to exist only in the history books. Give a Westralian sympathy for some sort of personal setback, and he's likely to push it aside good-naturedly and exclaim, "No worries!"

Part of Perth's general optimism could also be due to its weather, which is nearly always fine. A little after noon every day, just when it seems the day is building up to be a hopeless scorcher, Perth and its surrounding countryside are suddenly caressed by the "Fremantle Doctor"—a 20-knot sea breeze that bowls over unwary sailors along the coast while it successfully cures a potential fever among those living far inland.

With dozens of 12-meter yachts competing for honors in the America's Cup and other associated races in 1986 and 1987, the "Doctor" may end up doing double duty during these years.

2. Airports and Long-Distance Transportation

If you take Qantas coast-to-coast between Sydney and Perth, and if you're not simply continuing from an international flight, be aware that you have to go through a lot of inconvenient rigmarole. Unlike the flights on Ansett or TAA, the Qantas nonstops leave from Sydney's *international* terminal, and you must be processed through customs and immigration at both ends, standing in lines a domestic passsenger would not normally be subjected to. Be sure to save all the stuff they give you. There's one paper to explain that you're not an international passenger, for example, which must be collected on arrival in Perth. We misplaced ours recently, which caused even more delay. (The flights themselves are fine.)

Perth's airport, 11 miles from town center, currently has a terminal that seems to be one long room. (A new international terminal is under construction on the other side of the runway, and it should relieve the pressure later in 1986.) At this writing, anyway, one end of the older building has the main domestic airlines, including **Ansett Airlines** (Tel. 323–1111), **Ansett W.A.** (Tel. 323–1122), and **Trans-Australia Airlines** (Tel. 323–3333).

At the opposite end of the structure are an amazing number of international carrier counters, including Qantas, Air New Zealand, British Airways, South African Airways, Singapore Airlines, Air India, Cathay Pacific, and more. The terminal offers all the usual facilities, plus a Wines of Australia shop, your last chance to pick up a favorite vintage on the way out, for it's difficult to get W.A. wines anywhere else.

The coach to town, run by **Skybus** (Tel. 328–9777), will cost about $3, and taxi fare about $5 more than that, so two or more together may prefer to split a cab. Better recheck that bus number; the company was having difficulties when we were in town recently.

Ships all dock at Fremantle, the atmospheric port for Perth 12 miles west along the Swan River. You'll tie up at Victoria Quay on the Inner Harbour. Take the train or a bus between the port and the big city if you want at a fare of $1. By taxi, the Fremantle-Perth connection will cost at least $10.

To go to Perth by long-distance train, you can take the famous *Indian Pacific,* the transcontinental express that originates in Sydney. It's three days of travel time from there (a minimum of about $400, unless you have the Austrailpass) or two days from Adelaide. Interstate trains come in somewhat inconveniently at the **East Perth Terminal** on West Parade. (For information, call 326–2811.)

There are air-conditioned buses to Perth over the Eyre Highway from Adelaide, Brisbane, Melbourne, and Sydney. The largest companies are **Ansett Pioneer** (Tel. 325–8855), 26 St. George's Terrace, **Greyhound Coaches** (Tel. 478–1122), now at the Perth Central Bus Station on Wellington Street, and **DeLuxe,** whose address and phone we seem to have left under our seat. It will cost you approximately $120 to make the trip by bus from Adelaide.

Driving to Perth? From Darwin, it's a little better than it used to be, but we would rather not try the 2,800-mile trip without having someone along with Outback driving expertise. There is still about 200 miles of the road that is not paved (between Fitzroy Crossing and Halls Creek), although reportedly a four-wheel-drive vehicle is no longer necessary. From Adelaide you can do it even more easily, but see our remarks in the previous chapter.

3. Local Transportation in Perth

As compared with Sydney and Melbourne, anyway, traffic is light and finding your way around by car is fairly simple. Rentals are also a highly competitive business, so you may be able to get some good rates. The three national firms, as usual, are **Avis** (Tel. 325–7667), 46 Hill St.; **Hertz** (Tel. 321–7777), at 39 Milligan St.; and **Budget** (Tel. 322–1100), 33 Milligan St.

But you might get good bargains for local travel from some others, including **Franchas** (Tel. 277–2384), 20 Wallace St., Belmont; **Houghton** (Tel. 361–1416), 9 Adrian St., Welshpool; **Bayswater** (Tel. 271–7722), corner of Guildford and Garrett roads; **City Centre** (Tel. 322–1887), 789 Wellington St.; or **Barron** (Tel. 271–0300), with offices in the Merlin and Orchard hotels. More may spring up this year. With all these companies note that there are many variations between kilometer and unlimited-distance plans, etc. Some have 150 free kilometers and charges after that.

Local buses, trains, and ferries are run by the city-owned **Metropolitan Transport Trust** (MTT, Tel. 325–8511), 10 Adelaide Terrace, the most efficient public transportation system in the country. By all means pick up their route map and other free folders there. They'll even show you exactly where to wait for a bus in the center of the city.

There are two free buses, the "Blue Clipper" and the "Green Clipper," following short circular routes downtown. Ferryboats span the Swan every half hour between the Barrack Street Jetty and Mends Street, South Perth. The price is around 50 cents. Rent bicycles from **Koala Bike Hire** in King's Park for around $2 an hour. (Open daily.)

4. The Perth Hotel Scene

In 1984 and '85, the number of accommodations in Perth increased by about 2,000 rooms, partly in anticipation of the tourist boom expected in connection with the yacht races during 1986–87. We have just revisited Perth to see some of the new, expanded, and refurbished hotels, guesthouses, and the like. However others are expected to open their doors after these pages come off the press.

Rooms may be tight all through 1986 and certainly in early 1987 during the America's Cup contest. On the other hand, after the 1987 Festival of Perth is over in late February bargains may abound. Whatever the date, if you arrive in Perth without a reservation head immediately for Holiday W.A. Centre, the official state government tourist office at 772 Hay St. or phone them at 322–2999.

EXPENSIVE HOTELS

Perth's acknowledged leader among hotels for nearly two decades has been the 270-room **Parmelia Hilton International** (Tel. 322–3622), taking up the entire frontage on one-block-long Mill Street: Elegant, marble-floored lobby combining modern sculpture with brass pillars and a grandfather clock; an arcade of smart shops to one side; three well-decorated bars; a trio of excellent restaurants including the green-toned Garden

Restaurant, the reasonable Adelphi Steak House, and the Terrace, which offers some interesting international luncheon specials; a quick-service coffee shop also on the premises; Juliana's, a popular disco/nightclub; heated, windless, outdoor swimming pool; sauna and health club facilities.

In the sleeping areas we would insist on one of the bright, blond, balconied rooms on the river side, although most city views are also good. (There are widely varying types of accommodations; stay away from one of the few dark inside units with only half a window like No. 507, which we drew recently. If you don't like your room, call P.R. manager David Weinman and tell him we said to move you.)

All together, some 85 singles, 62 twins, 40 doubles, 28 double suites, 36 twin suites, and 17 VIP suites (those on the 10th—the VIP—floor, running from $200 to $400 a day; normal doubles more like $100 to $125); luxury amenities in virtually every room; colorful wallpapering and good lighting. The Parmelia, built in 1968 to be the best hotel in the country, still keeps up with the times. Hilton International owns it now, and standards seem to have remained high. (Reservations through the Hilton organization, or write to the hotel on Mill Street, Perth 6000.) To those who can afford it, it's worth it.

Occupying a firm second in our book is the pleasant **Sheraton-Perth** (Tel. 325–0501), which overlooks the city scene from 207 Adelaide Terrace: W-i-d-e lobby with patterned carpet, multiple chandeliers, and some weird dented couches; three restaurants—the well-regarded River Room, the Clinker Grill, and the Wandarrah Coffee Shop; Clouds bar and disco; three comfortable drinking bars; good pool and pool deck; a set of computerized elevators that sometimes seem to change their minds; 427 generally comfortable rooms, with good furnishings and excellent floor plans; unsurpassed views over the city and river; rates a little less than the Parmelia, thank heavens—about $95 to $100 for two in regular units, $135 and up, up, up in the suites. (Reservations from any hotel in the Sheraton family.) This house seems like a genuine Sheraton—maybe not "spot on," but certainly a top spot. Firmly recommended.

The brand-new, $25-million **Orchard Hotel** (Tel. 327–7000) we might rank higher if it were a little more conveniently located: Stained-glass entranceway at 707 Wellington St., corner of Milligan; cool, marbled, two-level lobby with glass-bead chandeliers; piano-bar lounge with fountain and black-and-white furnishings; brassy elevators; heated swimming pool; lots of ethnic restaurants in the attractive International Village attached; discotheque; several shops; upstairs hallways in the same salmon pink that seems to be everywhere in Perth hotels this year; 280 bedrooms with state-of-the-art amenities; several king-size beds in king-size rooms; some no-smoking floors; unusual angled windows; most rates in the $110 to $120 range, at least for now. (Reservations from the hotel at

P.O. Box 7244, Perth 6000.) It's too young to flower yet, but if the Orchard succeeds in making its neighborhood bloom, too, it should be fruitful pickings in years to come.

One of Australia's major airlines has one of its dependable trio of establishments in Perth, the **Ansett International** (Tel. 325–0481), formerly the Gateway. (The other two are in Adelaide and Brisbane.) When we went through here again recently, it had just opened a new 15-story tower and temporarily closed its old one, and it was in the midst of a massive refurbishing program: Entrance on busy little Irwin Street; separate check-in for business travelers; enlarged foyer with marble floor and modern glass sculpture; up five steps to a carpeted lounge; delicatessen and wine shop also attached; popular Palm bar; Irwin Restaurant and other new dining areas still on the drawing board during our visit; swimming pool and cabana area up on the roof; well-designed rooms with electronic bedside controls; new units facing noisy Hay Street; air conditioning and double-glazing dulling the traffic sounds, however; some unusual touches like a hidden ironing board in every room; other improvements promised for the revamped Irwin Street tower; twin rates probably nearing $100 by now. (Reservations through Ansett Airlines or the hotel at 10 Irwin St.) If plans are carried out, this should again be classified as a convenient and comfortable landing place.

Some will logically wonder why we have put the flamboyant new $50-million **Merlin Hotel** (Tel. 323–0121) this far down the list. We're not sure of the answer except that if a new hotel is going to look like a World's Fair pavilion, we think it should be more innovative than imitative. Nevertheless, we can't fault its many fine facilities:

Glassy archways and glass roof reminiscent of London's nineteenth-century Crystal Palace; acres of Lego-landish red bricks elsewhere on the façade; cavernous, echoing, nine-story atrium unseen previously in Perth but like so many now on the international hotel scene; tiny lights embedded in reflective granite lobby floor; Atrium piano bar not far away; three restaurants, including the gourmet Langley Room, which is now immensely popular, and a Chinese entry, all below lobby level; Tomorrow disco, as modern as the day after tomorrow; several expensive shops, also open on weekends; sunny, 25-meter rooftop pool; nine squash courts nearby; one tennis court; excellent convention facilities; unintelligible talking elevators announcing the floors.

Four major living wings are marked by four colorful $25,000 kites. ("When you get out of the lift, just look for your kite," explained our guide.) A total of 401 large units; lights turned on with a plastic key, apparently an energy-saving device; room doors using conventional keys; blond wood furnishings and salmon pink fabrics; every luxury facility including hair dryers in the marble loos; good southern views on the park and river side; rates in the $120 to $130 neighborhood for two. (Reservations from the hotel at 99 Adelaide Terrace at Plain Street, Perth 6000.) We judged it about as intimate as a glass garage, but certainly a fashionable parking place this year.

The new, 102-room **Parkroyal** (Tel. 325–3811), near the Merlin, was created from the shell of the old Perth Travelodge, and it now looks very nice: Main entranceway into the skylit bar; reception area to one side; respectable Royal Palm restaurant; wind-sheltered swimming pool; two living areas—a two-story unit of large "cabanas" just a walk up from the lobby and looking toward Langley Park, and a tower block on the opposite side; three floors of nonsmoking rooms; most rooms done up in pink, green, or beige; TVs and all the standard "mod cons"; most units with small balconies; excellent river panoramas on the top "club" (12th) floor; that upper story also with a private butler available in the Club Lounge; fair rates in the $90 range for doubles or twins; good reports from our readers. (Reservations from the hotel at 54 Terrace Rd. or through the Southern Pacific Hotel Corp.) The Parkroyal is a logical choice for the outlay.

More modestly priced is the equally new **Perth Ambassador** (Tel. 325–1455) at 196 Adelaide Terrace, almost opposite the Sheraton: Two entrances on the same street under orange-and-brown awnings; small, high-ceilinged, white-marble lobby with overhead catwalk; lots of brass railings and ashtrays; sounds of shoes squeaking on the polished floor; Chinese restaurant and Australian coffee shop; no pool, but a sauna and hot tub ("spa") available; 171 rooms decorated in beige and salmon pink; TV and all the needed accouterments; rates about $80 for two as 1986 begins. The Ambassador is no embassy, but it's a diplomatically correct address.

Many Australians like the **Chateau Perth** (Tel. 325–0461), formerly the Chateau Regency, which has been around for some time. Somehow it seems overdecorated and hokey with all its heavy medieval froufrou. There are relatively few views, but try for a chamber with a balcony. Rates in the $75 to $85 range for two may make up for a lot. (Reservations from the hotel at Hay Street and Victoria Avenue.) A little odds bodkins, but apparently a comfortable castle.

The **Transit Inn** (Tel. 325–7655), a Flag entry, waves from 37–45 Pier St. Combination foyer/terrace/swimming pool; Boodles Coffee House to one side; Ruby's Restaurant to the other; 120 well-maintained bedrooms; views from the very highest floors; some extras like in-house movies available on the TV, toaster to augment the usual tea-maker, nice long bath towels, etc.; No. 902 a favorite double for about $90; also one single room on each floor for about $80. (Reservations from the hotel.) Not too fancy, but okay.

Another possibility at the lower end of the higher spectrum is the **Town House** (Tel. 321–9141) at 778 Hay St. It has an indoor pool and double rates of around $85. And the **Kings Perth** (Tel. 325–6555) has similar facilities and slightly lower fares at 517 Hay St.

The new **Langley** is under construction at this writing on Adelaide Terrace across from the Sheraton. The 253-room, 11-story hotel will also offer two restaurants, a coffee shop, two bars, two swimming pools, and tennis courts, and will be aimed primarily toward business travelers. Plans call for it to be completed in late 1986.

MEDIUM-PRICE HOTELS

We never used to list a medium price category in this chapter, but since so many hotels have opened there are two or three of note renting in the $40 to $60 range this year.

One is the brand-new **Princes** (Tel. 322–2844), which was unveiled behind an old façade at 334 Murray St., corner of Queen, just on the edge of the principal shopping district: A glass awning welcoming you to a cool, unusually shaped lobby in pinks and purples; two restaurants, the Society and Valentines, nearby; 160 neat rooms upstairs, several on the smallish side; all units with showers; all with direct dialing, in-house movies, and other facilities appealing to businessfolk. Rates at this writing run around $50 for one, $55 for two, but don't hold us to that. Unfortunately this place is flanked by an adult lingerie store and bookshop on one side and something called the Bra Bar on the other. Don't let that put you off. This is a nice, respectable choice for the price.

Once a traditional low-budget favorite, **Miss Maud European** (Tel. 325–3900) has now gone "up-market" (as the Aussies say), relatively speaking. Rooms are not spectacular, but they are usually well serviced. Rates now run about $50 to $60 for two, including breakfast.

The best bet for modest rooms at $55 and below used to be the Salvation Army–run Railton, which was bought and converted into the Inntown Perth and finally into the **Crestwood** (Tel. 325–2133). The phone number has remained the same in all its incarnations, but the facilities haven't, since there is now a licensed restaurant, cocktail bar, and the lot. There are still some nice views on the sixth and seventh floors, and maybe the roof garden is still there. If you go before we do, let us know your verdict.

BUDGET ACCOMMODATIONS

For strict penny-squeezers, by far the best deal in town today has to be the little **Jewell House** (Tel. 325–8488), run by the YMCA at 180 Goderich

St. near Hill. This modern, 11-story high-rise was once the nurses' quarters for a nearby hospital. That means rooms without private bathrooms— not even a private sink: Free "Clipper" bus stop outside the door; walking distance to downtown in any case; small reception area with lots of posters on the walls, etc.; dining room serving breakfast (about $4) and dinner (about $7) or a week's worth of these meals for only $30 (the day we asked, anyway); two TV rooms, one designated no smoking and no alcohol; laundry and ironing rooms; male bedrooms on the odd floors, females on the even; no phones, but wake-up calls and other signals given by a buzzer system; single rooms about $16; doubles about $20; weekly discounts; credit cards accepted. (Reservations are a must from the address above at Perth 6000; send one night's deposit.) The Jewell House is an absolute gem for the price.

After that, things move downhill fast. You might try the **Criterian** (Tel. 325–5155) at 560 Hay St. It's not bad, with such things as room TVs and private showers, but it costs more, too, at tabs of about $40 for two— although perhaps still including breakfast. Another possibility is the **Wentworth** (Tel. 321–6005), not to be confused with Sydney's famous Wentworth. This drinking pub at 109 William and Murray streets sells basic doubles with sinks (and a few with showers) for $25 to $35. A bare-bones establishment is the **Imperial** (Tel. 325–8877) at 413 Wellington St., across from the suburban railroad station, at single and double fares of about $15 and $25 respectively. This place looked on its last legs to us, but somehow it keeps standing.

Australia's busiest youth hostel is the **Perth City Hostel** (Tel. 328–6060) at 196 William St. Members with their own regulation sheets will fork over about $6 for a night's bunk.

5. Restaurants and Dining

There are a large number of ethnic cafes in Perth. Many good dining rooms are in the hotels, of course, but the more exotic establishments you'll find in Northbridge or "North of the Line"—that is, on the other side of the bridge over the railroad tracks from downtown Perth. These are generally along William Street. Many will change owners, managers, prices, and menus more rapidly than some of the long-established central salons.

COSMOPOLITAN AND INTERNATIONAL

One of the best combinations for views and viands is the **Kings Park Garden Restaurant** (Tel. 321–7655), overlooking Perth from the park. Lunch from 12:00 to 2:30; dinner from 6:00 until 11:00. We enjoyed our Dhufish (jewfish), a local specialty, at around $8.

The **Garden Restaurant** (Tel. 322–3622), in the Parmelia Hilton on Mill Street, is formal, expensive, elegant, and delicious. A good place to try W.A. rock lobster, perhaps. **Ruby's** (Tel. 325–7474) in the Transit Inn, 37 Pier St., is similar, but darker. The **Langley Room** (Tel. 323–0121), in the new Merlin, is winning a top local reputation and is often hard to get into. Two good cosmopolitan choices in West Perth are the **Ord Street Cafe** (Tel. 321–6021), a bargain BYO at 27 Ord St., and **Wellington's** at 110 Outram St., whose phone number we apparently left on the table—sorry.

European fare with a Yugoslavian accent is a specialty at **Bohemia** (Tel. 328–7163) at 309 William St. A favorite of owner Mie Andrijcich is Govedina u Vinu (beef in red wine), and you'll also find the usual selections of shish kebabs, goulashes, etc. Some like the seafood, too. Most main courses are in the $8 to $9 range. (Closed Sundays and Mondays.)

Locally respected French choices include **Le Normandy** (Tel. 328–7008) at 73 James St., **Le Chef** (Tel. 381–9858), 292 Hay St., and especially **Luis'** (Tel. 325–2476), 2 Sherwood Court. The **Society** (Tel. 322–2844) in the new Princes Hotel opened to good reviews recently. The **River Room** (Tel. 325–0501) at the Sheraton is rolling right along. Figure $15 to $17 for main courses.

SPECIALIZING IN SEAFOOD

The championship oceanarium is still **Barnacle's** (Tel. 325–7125) in the St. Martin's Arcade. Here you might get some of Perth's blue marlin— or mangrove crabs, which are similar to the mud crabs of Queensland. **Darby's** (Tel. 328–8744), another popular seafood address, has now moved to 124 James St. Just down the street, **The Fishy Affair** (Tel. 328–3939) is a modest but excellent BYO at 132 James. (Some good local white wines to bring include a Swanville Riesling or Chablis or Sandalford's Swan Valley White Burgundy.)

The Oyster Bar (Tel. 328–7888), down the road at No. 88, is less expensive, serves cafeteria style, and closes early. (This is different from the **Oyster Beds** in Fremantle, which is also good and popular.) **Blue Fin** (Tel. 328–5370), at 75 Aberdeen St., doesn't mask the flavor of good seafood with heavy sauces or batter.

ITALIAN RESTAURANTS

The kitchens of Perth are blessed with several seasoned sons of Italy. At 147 Francis St. is the new **Pasta Place** (Tel. 328–8815), which serves up a wide variety of *platos Italianos* for around $10. Lower-priced but also popular are **La Tavernetta** (Tel. 328–3763), next door to Mischa's on James Street (large veal cutlets a specialty), and the **Romany** (Tel. 328–8042), also north of the line at 188 William St.

CHINESE FARE

The **Emperor's Court** (Tel. 328–8860), 66 Lake St., is now the leader in Chinese cooking. Some still swear by the **Golden Eagle** (Tel. 328–5420) at 130 James St. Luncheons of dim sum (Chinese dumplings) are now becoming popular in Perth, according to TV news personality Alison Fan, a Chinese-food fan. Look for these at **Jumbo** (Tel. 325–9987) at 166 Murray St. and at the **Golden Galleon** (Tel. 328–7991) at 40 Francis St. in Northbridge. (Both are open daily for lunch and dinner.)

MEXICAN RESTAURANTS

Verdad! There are some, and *delicioso,* too. The best of the best lately has been **El Gringo's** (Tel. 381–9513), a BYO place at 13 Rokeby Rd. We know a displaced gringo named Duncan MacLaurin in Perth, and join him in his heartfelt *olés.* If the lines are too long there, try the place entitled **Los Gallos Mexicanos** (Tel. 328–4728) at 276 William St. Two others we know less about are **Acapulco Annie's** (Tel. 367–1231) at 15 Labouchere in South Perth and **Pancho's** (Tel. 321–4374) at 903 Hay St.

SPANISH AND PARTLY SPANISH

We must draw a distinction between Spanish restaurants and the Mexican entries above, even if the Westralians might be forgiven for mixing them together. **Franco's** (Tel. 325–4843) is at 323 Hay St., if we remember right. The paella is only available Tuesdays. Other nights the cuisine is more international. Also popular are the **Casa Latina** (Tel. 328–1769) at 245 William St. and the unusual **Casa Pepe** (Tel. 321–8184) on Wellington Place at the Metropolitan Markets. The latter combines *Spanish and Greek* specialties—honest!

INEXPENSIVE DINING

In addition to some of the Mexican, Italian, and Spanish candidates above, look for various bargains near the shopping areas. One possibility is **Miss Maud's Swedish Restaurant** (Tel. 325–3900) at the corner of Pier and Murray. Last we saw it, the all-you-can-eat smorgasbord was selling at $10.95, $13.95, and $14.95, depending on the time of day and the day of the week. (Probably up "something-ti-five" by now.) Sandwiches in the same place come cheaper.

You can still get a full, hot evening meal of the day for around $7 from the dining room at **Jewell House** (Tel. 325–8488), the YMCA at 180 Goderich St. Also, try the **Sun Markets,** the Oriental food stalls behind Boan's Department Store. You may be able to walk along from one food stand to another and fill up your tummy for $5 or less. Similar operations include the **Carillon Food Hall** in the Hay Street Mall and some other barnlike premises in the Northbridge area.

6. Sightseeing in Perth and W.A.

Just as in South Australia, your sightseeing headquarters in Perth ought to be the official T.O. That's the **Holiday W.A. Centre** (Tel. 322–2999), formerly named the Western Australia Government Travel Centre, but still at 772 Hay St. In addition to dispensing free folders, maps, and advice, they will also book you on any sightseeing tours.

Here are some town targets to consider:

The **Art Gallery** (Tel. 328–7233) and the **Western Australia Museum** (Tel. 328–4411) are at Francis and Beaufort streets. The new gallery (enter at 47 James St.) exhibits contemporary and traditional Australian paintings; in the museum you'll find some dramatic blue-whale skeletons and an Aboriginal history and culture section. Also on the grounds of this complex, check out the old jail dating back to 1856. (Open 10 to 5 most days, and 1 to 5 Sundays.)

The **Town Hall,** at the corner of Hay and Barrack streets, was built by convicts from 1867 to 1870 in the style of an English Jacobean market hall. The nearby Colonial-style **Treasury Building,** around the corner on St. George's Terrace, was put up between 1874 and 1897.

London Court, an unusual Elizabethan-style shopping arcade, is a study in "Pseudor Tudor." It looks like it was designed in the 16th century, but was actually built in 1937. It runs between the Hay Street Mall and St. George's Terrace.

Stirling Gardens hosts several government buildings, including the interesting Old Court House (1836). This Georgian building is the oldest one remaining in Perth.

Of all the green spaces, the big one to see is **King's Park** and its bordering **Botanic Gardens.** The 1,000-acre reserve is largely natural forest land that is carpeted with unusual wildflowers from August through November. (There are 7,000 varieties of wildflowers in W.A. Try to find the weird green-and-red fingers of the "kangaroo paw.") Buses 25, 27, and 28 drive right through the park.

On Matilda Bay in Crawley (on Hackett Drive) you'll find the **Royal Perth Yacht Club,** where, at this writing, rests the America's Cup. At the moment, and subject to change, you may be able to view and photograph the famous trophy the Aussies call the "Auld Mug" behind its bullet-proof glass in the observation lounge between 10 A.M. and 5 P.M., Monday through Friday. Ask permission from the club office. (Of course, it may not be there after February 1987!) Better check with the tourist office before going over to see it, just to be sure.

The Old Mill in South Perth, which dates back to pioneer days, has been restored as a folk museum. The small **South Perth Zoo,** which was recently upgraded, also encompasses a superbly designed new botanical garden.

OUT OF TOWN

Fremantle (Pop. 23,000), the port for Perth, was settled 12 miles downstream, at the mouth of the Swan River. It will be the center of action for several 12-meter yacht races and trials in 1986–87, including the America's Cup contest. At Memorial Park you can get a wide panoramic view of the well-preserved nineteenth-century city and its harbors. Other stops include the *two* excellent maritime museums often called by similar names. One, the Fremantle Museum and Arts Centre, was originally built as an asylum at the corner of Finnerty and Ord streets. The other, the W.A. Maritime Museum, is on Cliff Street. *The* place to stay this year, if you can get in, is the old but now expanded and refurbished Esplanade Hotel in the most interesting part of town, opposite the three main yacht harbors. (Doubles about $100.) The Freemason's pub makes and sells its own very bitter Anchor beer right on the premises. Lots of good restaurants and sidewalk cafes, including the popular Papa Luigi's and inexpensive Capri, are on South Terrace.

About 12 miles offshore is the popular resort and wildlife sanctuary at **Rottnest Island.** It was named by a Dutch sea captain who mistook the little quokkas of the island for rats (*rott*, in Dutch). Thousands of these "midget kangaroos" still live there, and almost nowhere else. The diminutive marsupials have proven useful in muscular dystrophy research. No automobiles are allowed on this quiet island, incidentally. Everyone gets around on foot or on bicycles.

The Rottnest Passenger Service run by Boat Torque (Tel. 325–6033) offers a good hydroplane ride between Perth's Barrack Street Jetty and Rottnest Island via Fremantle for a round-trip fare of around $35. A slower service is the regular passenger ferry. It takes about two hours each way, about twice the hydroplane time, and costs about $20.

Tip: The actual race course for the '86–87 yacht races is approximately between Fremantle and Rottnest Island, although more to the north. To watch these contests, take your binoculars and transistor radio and find your way up the coastline to one of several popular beaches. The finish line is almost opposite City Beach, about five miles offshore, but the stretch between City Beach and Swanbourne Beach parallels the entire proposed course. Land-bound spectators will be able to get very good views of the action here. Some of those fortunate enough to book into accommodations up at Scarborough Beach, north of City Beach, or down at Cottesloe Beach, south of Swanbourne, will probably be able to watch the action from their front porch.

In suburban **Armadale,** about 15 miles south, you'll find Pioneer World, a re-creation of a W.A. town of 100 years ago, and Elizabethan Village, another theme park, plus the privately owned Cohunu Wildlife Park, where you can feed the roos yourself. Two other sites promoted in the Perth area include **Yanchep National Park** (with its caves) and the Andalusian stud farm at **El Caballo Blanco** near Wooroloo. We've seen them both, and they're pleasant, I guess, but all of this last group—except maybe the wildlife park—are probably of more interest to Australians for the time spent than to international travelers.

THE REST OF W.A.

If you can easily visit **Kalgoorlie** and **Coolgardie** and the surrounding gold-rush country 375 miles east of Perth, then do so. Due to an inconvenient air schedule—an early-morning arrival from Perth, a late-night departure to Perth—we were at the hands of one of the local tour drivers all day, and had every bloody grade school within a 50-mile radius pointed out to us—when he wasn't cursing the "Abos." We would have enjoyed driving around on our own, going down into the **Hainault Tourist Mine,** seeing the ghost-town buildings at Coolgardie, etc., and then choosing when to leave.

With the rising world price of gold, long-abandoned mines have been revitalized in and around Kalgoorlie. Even weekend tourists with metal detectors have been scouring the landscape ever since some recent successful gold finds by amateurs. One woman discovered gold not long ago while digging her swimming pool! Bars, restaurants, souvenir shops, etc., are being opened and expanded everywhere.

It might be fun to take the train called the *Prospector* one way from Perth to Kalgoorlie (eight hours for about $50), and then stay overnight (the Palace Hotel is an interesting old place). Next day, rent a car for sightseeing and then return to Perth with a taste of Outback driving under your belt. (In Coolgardie, drop in to see Harry Boucher on the main street; he's a most amazing rock merchant. And Ben Prior is as popular as his garage.)

The south is the spring **wildflower country,** blooming in September and October around the towns of Bunbury, Busselton, Augusta, Pemberton, and so forth. At other times of the year the 250-foot-tall karri forests are still impressive. One reader who drove the long South Coast Highway on the way to Perth was ecstatic about wildflowers and beaches she found at Esperance, Albany, and Walpole. Somehow we have not managed to make it to that area yet; we would certainly welcome any more impressions of southern W.A.

North of Perth on Route 1 about 315 miles is **Geraldton,** the center of the crayfish industry and the gateway to the spectacular gorges of Kalbarri National Park. Then 350 miles north of Perth is the strange **Hutt River Province,** where Leonard Casley has declared himself "prince" of an 18,000-acre desert domain that no one else wants for the moment and "seceded" from Australia.

Locals disagree as to exactly how serious Prince Leonard is, and the federal government at Canberra ignores him, perhaps realizing with some sensitivity that some important elements in Western Australia would like to cut off the entire rich state from the rest of the country. Meanwhile, the prince is doing a terrific souvenir business, selling stamps, visas, etc.

The **Hamersley Ranges,** 800 miles north of Perth and including the towns of Wittenoom, Tom Price, and Newman, are the site of massive iron-mining operations, but reported to be ruggedly scenic by survivors of those roads. Marble Bar (hottest town in Australia) is not far away.

Broome, on the northwest coast, is a romantic area once the center of a massive pearl-diving industry, which is still partly carried on there. Further north the town of **Derby,** gateway to the iron-rich Kimberley Ranges, is famous for its baobab or boab trees, whose bottle-shaped trunks actually store water. One particularly fat tree in Derby is hollow and was supposed to have once been used as a jail. **Kununurra** is the site of the Ord River Dam and becoming a recreational center on Lake Argyle. The new diamond mines are near here—also the strange **Bungle Bungle Range,** a recently discovered group of round mountains that look like the ruins of some lost civilization.

7. Guided Tours and Cruises

Some tour operators include **Ansett Pioneer** (Tel. 325–8855), **Feature Tours** (Tel. 271–1131), **Pinnacle Tours** (Tel. 364–2603), and **Parlorcars Tours** (Tel. 325–5488). We'd book all tours from the aforementioned Holiday W.A. Centre (Tel. 322–2999) at 772 Hay St., Perth, W.A. 6000. The following are examples of a few tours available at this writing:

Half-day tours. *City Sights, Beaches, and Landmarks,* about $12. *Swan Scenic Drive* (to Fremantle and back by separate routes), about $11.

Full-day tours. *Perth in a Day,* about $17. *Wildflower Tour* (August through October), about $25.

There are also longer wildflower and other types of "fully accommodated" tours over several days throughout Western Australia. See the tourist office for details.

Cruises. The city-owned MTT (Tel. 325–8511), the same hot-shot outfit that runs the buses, offers afternoon cruises on the river, too. The M.V. *Countess* goes upstream from the Barrack Street Jetty daily for about $8, and the S.S. *Perth* makes a downstream cruise perhaps on Sundays only for around the same price.

The **Rottnest Passenger Service** (Tel. 325–6033), run by Boat Torque at the same jetty, also has several cruises on several vessels, some to Fremantle and back, others to Rottnest Island. Its hydrofoil service via the *Sea Raider* is fastest, making Rottnest Island in an hour each way for around $35 round trip. That trip includes a bus tour of the island.

The *Lady Houghton* and the *Miss Sandalford,* both Boat Torque vessels, go upstream to the Houghton Winery once a day for around $25, including lunch. Reserve through the tourist office.

Multiple-day tours into the Outback by bus and camel are launched by **Bryan Casey Adventure Tours** (Tel. 339–4291) from a base in East Fremantle. Write to Casey for information at 9 Habgood St., East Fremantle. (We have had no personal experience with him, but the itineraries look good.) An excellent free-lance guide we do know is Ralph Hoger (Fremantle Tel. 339–5804). Ralph works out of his home at 16 Essex St., Fremantle 6160, and sets up both urban and Outback tours.

8. Water Sports

There are several popular Indian Ocean beaches along the shoreline north of Fremantle. You can get to **Scarborough** via Bus 260, to **Cottesloe** via Bus 72, and to **City Beach** via Buses 80 and 81. All three are good surfing beaches October to March. The most famous surf beach, however, is **Yallingup,** much further south. **Leighton Beach** (train to Leighton Station) and **North Beach** (Bus No. 250, then transfer to 255) are gentler strands. And **Swanbourne** is the local site for swimming and sunning in your birthday suit. (Look out. No lifeguard on duty there.) Unless you're an expert windsurfer, go to the beach in the morning; the brisk southwesterly called the "Fremantle Doctor" will be in before 1 o'clock, whipping things up too much for other beach activities. (Except for watching the aforementioned yacht races, of course.) Windsurf rentals and lessons are available from the **Maylands Sailboard School** (Tel. 367–2988) at the East Street Jetty next to the Maylands Yacht Club.

You can also swim in the Swan. It's clean, believe it or not—"the cleanest river running through any capital city in the world," says Steve Moir at Holiday W.A. Two river beaches are **Crawley** (Bus 201), near the university, and **Como** (Bus 32), south of South Perth.

Skin diving is supposed to be good on the shallow coastal shelf where you find the occasional wreck of seventeenth- and eighteenth-century Dutch ships. Skin-diving conditions around Rottnest Island, an undersea sanctuary, are also said to be excellent. Contact either of two outfits, the **Australasian Diving Centre** (Tel. 384–3966) at 259 Stirling Highway in Claremont, or the **Perth Diving Academy** (Tel. 344–1562) at 281 Wanneroo Rd., Nollamara.

Boats and water-skiing equipment may be rented from **Bonney Water Skis** (Tel. 361–2038) for skimming over the surface near the Narrows Bridge. You might also like to rent the little "surf cat" boats there or off Mill Point Road in South Perth, or at the Coode Street Jetty.

Deep-sea fishing is available the year around from ports all along the coast, and it has recently been getting more popular. Blue marlin is the big catch. Some charter boats are based at Fremantle. You can also fish on the Swan River. We heard of a chap who got a 76-pound mulloway right on the doorstep of the city!

Yacht racing. The years 1986 and 1987 will be long remembered in Perth and Fremantle for a series of exciting contests between 12-meter boats from all over the world. It all begins in January and February, 1986, with the World 12-Meter Cup Championships. Some of the best racing will be from September to December 1986, with the elimination trials for the America's Cup race. The famous cup match finals themselves are scheduled to begin January 31, 1987, and will carry over into an exciting February. As previously mentioned, the Perth beaches will be crowded with spectators. At this writing some "floating grandstands" —specially designed boats—are also being planned by private companies, with appropriate admission prices.

9. Other Sports

The big spectator sport, of course, is the same as in Melbourne, Tasmania, and Adelaide—Australian Rules football. Matches are at the **Subiaco Oval,** Roberts and Coghlan roads, Subiaco. Cricket is played at the **W.A. Cricket Association Oval** at the end of Hay Street.

Westralians are nuts about racing—horses, dogs, cars, and motorcycles. Flat races are held at two racecourses, **Ascot** in the summer and **Belmont** in the winter. Night trotting races, particularly popular in Perth, are held October through July at the supermodern facilities at **Gloucester Park** on Nelson Avenue in East Perth. Greyhounds run in the new stadium at Cannington. Cars and motorcycles tear up the turf at Claremont.

On the subject of golf courses, Terry Smith, the knowledgeable golfing writer for the Sydney *Sun* and other publications, says that **Lake Karrinyup** (Tel. 447–5777) on North Beach Road is the pride of Perth, although he complains about the need to wear a collar and tie in the clubhouse and the summertime swarms of bush flies out on the links. John Glendon, another golf writer, praises the public courses at Perth, suggesting visitors try **Hamersley** (Tel. 447–7137) on Marmion Avenue at North Beach. There are about two dozen more in the neighborhood, and serious duffers should talk to the W.A. Golf Association (Tel. 384–2513).

Tennis courts are available in the public parks for low fees, but check first with the tourist office or with the W.A. Lawn Tennis Association (Tel. 321–9977), P.O. Box 138, Perth, W.A. 6005.

10. Shopping in Perth

The principal shopping area is the Hay Street Mall running from Barrack Street to William Street, and the little arcades shooting off from it, including the Wanamba Arcade, London Court, Plaza Arcade, Trinity Arcade, City Arcade, National Mutual Arcade, and the Piccadilly Arcade. (Shopping hours are 9:30 to 5:00, Monday to Friday, except on Thursdays until 9:00 and Saturdays until noon.)

The most unique item in the shops of Western Australia is jewelry made of iron ore, something we never knew could be turned into a stone before! It certainly does seem appropriate in a state known for iron ore, but you'll have to decide for yourself whether or not you like the sparkling form of the product. You can buy it as a pendant for $25 or $30. Try the **Gem Centre and Opal Cave** (Tel. 325–5528), at 534 Hay St., for iron ore and other stones.

For a good selection of opals, iron-ore stones, kangaroo-skin products, etc., as well as a wider selection of Australian souvenirs, look into **Swan Souvenirs** (Tel. 321–5551) in the Plaza Arcade, off Hay Street. (Ask for Alex.)

For stones in a rougher state, peek into the **Perth Lapidary Centre** (Tel. 325–2954) at 58 Pier St. It's a rock hound's delight with everything for chip-it-yourselfers.

There are five department stores on Hay Street, including **Ahern's, Woolworths,** and **Cole's. Myer** is on Murray Street. And on the Wellington Street side of **Boan's Department Store** we remember a permanent flashing sign that proclaimed "SALE!" 52 weeks of the year!

11. Night Life and Entertainment

Popular nightclubs include **Romano's** (Tel. 328–4776) at 187 Stirling St. (it's a restaurant, too) and the **Civic Theatre Restaurant** (Tel. 328–1455) at 380 Beaufort.

On William Street, "North of the Line," a lavish illegal casino will occasionally begin spinning until it gets shut down by the law, so you'd better not count on that.

The top discotheque in Perth today is **Hannibal's,** carved out of an old church at 69 Lake St. The deejay is suspended in a glass box above dancers who jump on a lighted glass floor. Other hot spots include **Tomorrow** at the Merlin Hotel, **Eagle One** at 139 James St., with its chrome and black "spaced-out" decor, **Gobbles** at 613 Wellington St., the **Underground** under Newcastle Street, and **Beethoven** at 418 Murray St. The largest disco is **Clouds** in the Sheraton-Perth, and some singles consider it the best for pickups. Perhaps the most expensive, however, is **Juliana's** in the Parmelia Hilton. **Pinocchio's** is a bit teeny-boppish. And the gay crowd, along with some other young "trendies," is said to like the **Red Parrot.** In nearly all top discos membership requirements are waived for holders of overseas passports. (But drinks will not be cheap to any nationality.)

All the beer you'll find in W.A. pubs is made by the Swan Brewery, Besides Swan Draught and Swan Lager, it also produces a brand called Emu in Perth. By the way, a "glass" of beer has 5 ounces and the "middy" is 7. A "pot" can be either 10 or 15 ounces.

For more genteel entertainment, there is usually good live theater in Perth at the **Playhouse** (Tel. 325–3500) at 3 Pier St., the headquarters of the National Theatre, Inc. At the University of Western Australia, at Crawley, downstream a bit, is the **Dolphin Theatre** (Tel. 380–2432).

Special events are usually staged at the modern **Perth Concert Hall** (Tel. 325–3399), 5 St. George's Terrace, also the home of the West Australian Symphony Orchestra, **His Majesty's Theatre** (Tel. 321–6288), or the **Perth Entertainment Centre** (Tel. 322–4766) on Wellington Street.

12. The Perth Address List

Bank—Commercial Bank of Australia, 40 St. George's Terrace (Tel. 325–9877).

Bus information—Bus Information Centre, 125 St. George's Terrace (Tel. 325–8511).

Citizens Advice Bureau—81 St. George's Terrace (Tel. 321–5268).

Dental emergency—Perth Dental Hospital, 196 Goderich St. (Tel. 325–3452).

Emergencies—For fire, police, ambulance, etc., dial 000.

Ferry information—Tel. 325–8511.

Hospital—Royal Perth Hospital, Wellington and Lord streets (Tel. 325–0101).

Immigration department—12 St. George's Terrace (Tel. 325–0521).

Laundromat—Grand Central Wellington Street Launderette, 379 Wellington St.

Library—State Library, 40 James St. (Tel. 328–7466).

Pharmacy—Craven's Pharmacy, Barrack and Hay streets (Tel. 325–4375).

Police station—Hay St. East (dial 000 for all emergencies).

Post office—Forrest Place near Wellington Street (Tel. 326–5211).

Royal Automobile Club—228 Adelaide Terrace (Tel. 325– 0551).

Tourist office—Holiday W.A. Centre, 772 Hay St. (Tel. 322–2999).

Travellers' Aid Society—Westrail Centre, West Parade, East Perth (Tel. 326–2811).

11

The Northern Territory—
Darwin and Alice Springs

1. The General Picture

The Northern Territory is what most of the world imagines when it thinks of Australia.

Here is the Red Centre—the baked desert and stone that has served as the setting for nearly a century and a half of Outback adventures. It's studded by that massive red granite monolith that almost marks the geographic hub of the entire continent, Ayers Rock—what the ancient Aborigines called their sacred Uluru.

The staging area for visiting The Rock and the other sights in Australia's Dead Heart is the strange, often lonely town of Alice Springs, which was sparked by a telegraph relay station and grew up along the banks of a usually dry river. It was made world-famous by Nevil Shute's wartime novel *A Town Like Alice*.

"The Alice," with a population of 21,000, may be the informal capital of the Outback, but the official center of government for the Northern Territory (N.T.) is the coastal city of Darwin, bordering the Timor Sea in the tropical climate near the tip of Australia's "Top End." Some 65,000 people now live there, half the population of the entire territory. (Alice Springs and Darwin are known today as the two fastest-growing cities in Australia.)

Many of Darwin's residents are foreign-born or are descended from a

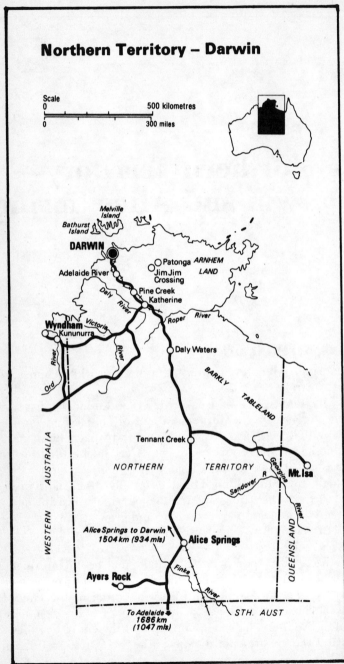

Northern Territory – Darwin

Scale
0   500 kilometres
0   300 miles

Melville Island
Bathurst Island
DARWIN
Patonga
ARNHEM LAND
Jim Jim Crossing
Adelaide River
Daly River
Pine Creek
Katherine
Roper River
Wyndham
Kununurra
Victoria River
Daly Waters
Ord River
BARKLY TABLELAND
Tennant Creek
NORTHERN   TERRITORY
Georgina River
Mt. Isa
Sandover R
WESTERN AUSTRALIA
QUEENSLAND
Alice Springs to Darwin 1504 km (934 mls)
Alice Springs
Finke River
Ayers Rock
To Adelaide 1686 km (1047 mls)
STH. AUST

Map courtesy Australian Tourist Commission

variety of nationalities and races, including the black Aborigines. (More than half of Australia's Aborigines live in the N.T., as a matter of fact. Some of those with homes on reserves outside of Darwin have managed to maintain their dignity, but visitors are sometimes shocked to see results of the cultural lag that causes many Aborigines to live out sad lives drinking in the dry Todd River bed in Alice Springs.) About 300 Vietnamese live in Darwin today—a small percentage of the thousands of "boat people" who arrived in the harbor aboard derelict vessels at the end of the Vietnam War.

Darwin deserves a book of its own. This multiracial town has survived despite repeated ravages of war and weather over the past 110 years. Thousands of Americans were stationed in Darwin during World War II, one reason the settlement suffered no less than 64 Japanese air raids. The town is also smack in the middle of the Indian Ocean cyclone (hurricane) belt, and it has been directly hit by three of these storms to date. The first was in 1897, another was in 1937, and the last was the devastating Cyclone Tracy, which stripped Darwin to the bone during a 5½-hour siege on Christmas Day, 1974. A few of Tracy's scars are still visible.

Darwin and Alice Springs are connected by the thousand-mile Stuart Highway, locally called simply "The Track." This road, paved largely by the U.S. Army during World War II, passes through such history-steeped settlements as Adelaide River, Katherine, and Tennant Creek. It serves as the arterial route from which other tracks lead to poverty-stricken Aboriginal reserves; to huge, battling cattle stations; to teeming wildlife sanctuaries; to current iron mines; and to future uranium mines.

The Northern Territory is full of anomalies, but one that concerns visitors directly is that it has only two seasons. In Alice Springs this is interpreted as summer (very hot days and warm nights) and winter (hot days and cool nights). In Darwin they talk about "The Wet," a monsoon summer season, when it rains nearly nonstop from about November through March, and "The Dry," the cloudless warm days and balmy, pleasant nights occurring from about April to October—the ideal season to experience some of the most varied bird and animal life you'll see in Australia.

This makes the N.T. a practical vacation for Americans and Europeans during their Northern Hemisphere summer—i.e., Australia's winter—when the Alice and Darwin are just right. During the Australian summer we'd probably skip them both, unless we could arrange to stay at least overnight at Ayers Rock. No photograph, no word description does justice to this natural wonder. It's hard to explain, but we firmly believe that a lifetime is hardly complete without having experienced Uluru at first hand.

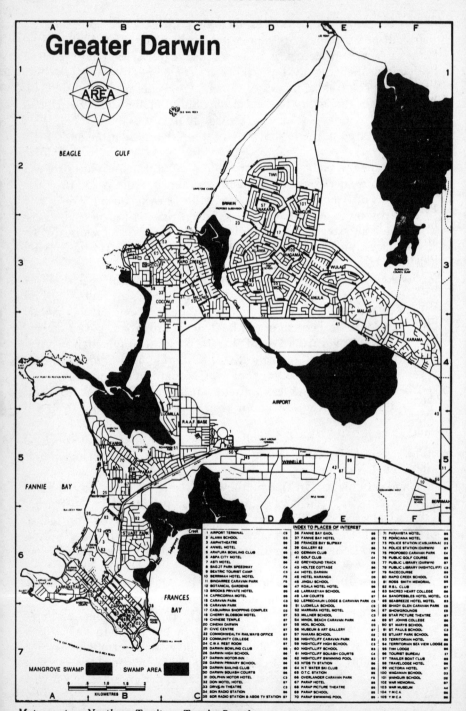

Greater Darwin

Map courtesy Northern Territory Tourist Board

2. Airports and Long-Distance Transportation

Airports at both Darwin and Alice Springs are simple affairs, often crowded with waiting friends and relatives when big flights are due in or out. The new international terminal at Darwin is expected to continue under construction at least through 1987. Try to avoid either airport on weekends. When planes are scheduled, the three main airlines, **Ansett, TAA,** and **Airlines of Northern Australia** (ANA) run buses to and from town. (For phone numbers, see section 12.) Near the baggage-claim areas, look for free telephones to the taxi companies. Pick up a receiver and give your name, and the driver will "sing out" for you when he arrives.

Darwin and Alice Springs are connected over "The Track" by **Ansett Pioneer, Deluxe,** and **Greyhound** coaches. The trip lasts more than 20 hours on the road, and it would be a good idea to break the journey for an overnight stay in Katherine. The bus costs about $100, about half the plane fare.

It's approximately the same fare again to continue on the stretch between Alice Springs, N.T., and Adelaide, S.A.; some of this is still a rough dirt road. Driving Alice-to-Adelaide yourself will become easier as more miles in between become "sealed" (paved). That project is scheduled to be finished in time for South Australia's state sesquicentennial jubilee in 1986—well, at least in time for Australia's national bicentennial celebration in 1988.

You can also take the new, modern version of the historic old train called *The Ghan.* The 1,000-mile trip to Alice Springs from Adelaide (Port Augusta) has its roots in 1877, when the "Afghan Express" was built along an old camel caravan route across what was then believed to be a drought area. But it turned out to be one of the most flood-prone regions of the country.

The old narrow-gauge line has finally been superseded by a new set of tracks about 100 miles to the west, reducing the 60-hour trip to about 24. The latest fares for the new *Ghan* are not out at this writing, but we'll guess it will cost about $200 to ride First Class with your own sleeping facilities this year. (There's a supplementary charge of $25 or so on the Austrailpass if you want First Class accommodations, and we think it's worth it.) The train usually leaves Alice at 3:30 P.M. Friday and Monday and arrives in Adelaide about 3:30 P.M. Saturday and Tuesday. We enjoyed the trip in the opposite direction; in addition to the desert scenery, a real refresher is the idea of taking a shower while traveling at 60 miles per hour through one of the driest areas of the world. And you'll probably make friends in the diner and perhaps around the piano in the bar car.

Stealing some of the thunder from *The Ghan* these days is the new train from Sydney called *The Alice,* which travels over the same tracks after

Darwin—Central Business District

ACCOMMODATION
1   Cherry Blossom Motel
1A Lameroo Lodge
2   Darwin Motor Inn
3   Don Hotel
4   Hotel Darwin
5   Telford Top End Hotel
6   Poinciana Motel
7   Ti Tree Units
8   Tiwi Lodge
9   Travelodge Hotel
10 Windsor Tourist Lodge

BUSINESS
11 A.M.P. Building
12 A.N.Z. Bank
13 Westpac
14 C.B.A. Bank
15 City Mutual Building
16 C.M.L. Building
17 Construction House
18 CBA Building
19 Commercial Union Building
20 Commonwealth Bank
21 Credit Union House
22 Custom Credit Building
23 Darwin Plaza
24 Flinders House
25 Hooker Building
26 Jape Plaza
27 Mallam Chambers
28 Manufacturers Mutual Insurance
    Building
29 M.L.C. Building
30 National Australia Bank
31 National Mutual Building
32 N.T. News
33 N.Z.I. Building
34 Paspalis Centre Point
35 Plaza Building
36 Reserve Bank
37 Tamar House
38 Tem House
39 T & G Building
40 T.I.O. Building
41 Vogliotti Building
42 Woolworths
43 Woolworths

CHURCHES
44 Catholic Cathedral
45 Christchurch Cathedral
46 Greek Orthodox Church
46A Seventh Day Adventist Church
47 Uniting Church

GENERAL
19 Parks and Wildlife Office
22 Dept. of Social Security
29 Auto. Assoc. of the N.T. (A.A.N.T.)
34 Darwin Public Library
48 Immigration Dept.
64 Public Toilets
97 Public Toilets
97 Car Park

GOVERNMENT
48 Arkaba House
49 Beagle House
50 Brennan Building (Block 5)
52 Chan Building (Block 8)
53 Civic Centre
54 Communications Building (Telecom)
55 Customs House
56 Development House
57 Fire Station
58 Fisheries Department
59 Government Information Centre
60 Gregory Building (Block 6)
61 Law Courts
62 Legislative Council Chambers
63 Leichhardt Building (Block 7)
64 Library (Centre Point Building)
65 Mineral House
66 Moonta House
67 Nelson Building (Block 3)
68 Palmerston Building
69 Police Headquarters
70 Port Authority
71 Post Office
72 Royal Globe Building
73 Sasco House
74 Stuart Building (Block 1)
75 Ward Building (Block 4)
76 Wells Building (Block 2)

PLACES OF INTEREST
77 Arnhem Land Aboriginal Art Gallery
78 C.W.A. Rest Room
79 Former Museum
80 Joss House (Chinese Temple)
82 Lyons Cottage
83 Old Naval Headquarters
84 Overland Telegraph Memorial
85 War Memorial

SPORTS AND ENTERTAINMENT
87 Browns Mart
88 Cinema Darwin
89 Police Boys Club

TRAVEL
90 Ansett Office
91 Bus Terminal (Public)
92 Ansett Trailways (Pioneer Coaches)
93 Greyhound Coaches
94 N.T. Government Tourist Bureau
95 TAA House
18 Qantas Travel Centre
    (CBA Building)

Map courtesy Northern Territory Government Tourist Bureau

reaching Port Pirie, anyway. An unusual feature of the train is that it makes "sightseeing stops" en route. Accommodations include "roomettes" for one person or "twinettes" for two. The twinettes have their own showers; occupants of roomettes use showers at the end of the car. *The Alice* leaves Sydney on Sunday, arrives in Alice on Wednesday, leaves the same day, and returns to Sydney on Friday. At the moment of this writing, the 1,775-mile trip costs $357.50 First Class, $229.75 Economy.

Service to and from the railway station or the airport and several Alice Springs hotels is provided by the **Airport & Railway Shuttle Service** (Tel. 52–3843).

We generally don't recommend rental cars for long-distance transportation in this neck of the desert. Therefore you'll find them straight ahead in this chapter, parked under Local Transportation.

One more word: Try not to arrive in either of these or any small Aussie towns on a Sunday. With so many things closed, it's sometimes difficult to get organized.

3. Local Transportation

There are no public buses in Alice Springs. Darwin has a few from 6 A.M. to 11 P.M. Monday through Saturday. They run to the suburbs from the terminal on Harry Chan Avenue (Tel. 81–2150). There is taxi service in both Darwin and Alice Springs, although you may have to pay extra for telephoning and, of course, the weekend supplements. (In Darwin you'll get a cab by calling 81–8777.)

Although you can walk around the central districts of both towns pretty easily, it's a good idea to rent a car for some medium-distance exploring.

Several firms compete in both settlements. For the best bargain, you might consider picking up a popular, jeeplike "Moke," a sort of mobile tin can that will negotiate some rough roads with ease, although admittedly leaving you vulnerable to dust in the open-sided vehicle. (It is not, however, a four-wheel-drive.) You might manage a Moke for $20, plus 16 cents a kilometer (but no promises) from the **Intertourist Centre** at the Hotel Darwin (Tel. 81–8896), or in Alice Springs at a related company, **Moke Rentals, N.T.** (Tel. 52–1405) opposite Ansett on Parsons Street.

The ubiquitous **Avis** (Alice Tel. 52–4366; Darwin Tel. 81–9922) also has Mokes (for more), along with conventional sedans. Other companies represented in Alice Springs are **Budget** (Tel. 52–4133), **Hertz** (Tel. 52–2644), and **Letz** (Tel. 52–7633).

In Darwin look into **Cheapa Rent-A-Car** (Tel. 81–8400), which might have a four-wheel-drive, if you need it. (They also rent mopeds.) Then

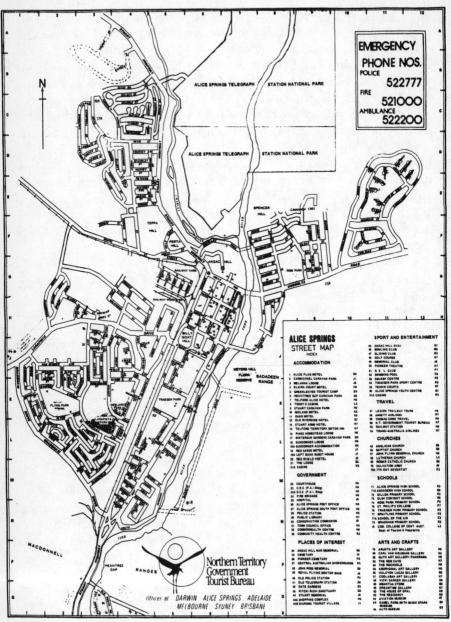

Map courtesy Northern Territory Government Tourist Bureau

Rent A Rocket (Tel. 81–6977) offers used cars. **Hertz** (Tel. 81–6686) is also in Darwin with Datsuns and Holdens on tap. **Letz** (Tel. 81–8400) and **Budget** (Tel. 84–4388) have now opened in town as well.

In both cities **Thrifty Rent-A-Car** (Darwin Tel. 81–8555; Alice Tel. 52–1303) offers campmobiles for rent, and these may be one-way deals between the two locations.

4. The Hotel Scene

Despite what you may have heard, comfortable rooms are available in both Darwin and Alice Springs, if you reserve ahead. If you haven't booked, you might still get a place, but don't expect the Ritz. In the summer, air conditioning is a must. In the winter, it's still highly desirable in the daytime.

HOTELS IN DARWIN

Until the Sheraton opens (see later), the best and most convenient hotel right in Darwin—and a proud, 11-story survivor of Cyclone Tracy—is the 186-room **Travelodge** (Tel. 81–5388) on the Esplanade, somewhat of a hoof from the center of town. (We walk it in ten minutes or so, when the weather's not too hot.) Reserve the inland side for the more interesting views (the ocean side is just that—lots of blank water). There's a good, beef-accented restaurant, swimming pool, and all luxury facilities (including a fridge and bar) in the ample rooms. Since we stayed here the price has been jacked up considerably to about $100 for two—and we can't help wondering if it's improved all that much. (Reservations from the hotel or through the Travelodge chain.) Certainly it's a solid choice.

Just a little out of town is Darwin's proud **Diamond Beach Hotel and Casino** (Tel. 81–7755), which opened in 1983. Known locally as the site of the gambling casino, the 106-room, bright-white resort by the water has been built beside five hectares, as they say, of botanical gardens. (A hectare is 10,000 square meters, or about an acre and a half.) On the other side of the three-story hotel is the beach and the Timor Sea. Besides the roulette tables the hotel boasts a swimming pool, tennis courts, a nine-hole golf course, three restaurants (one Chinese), and six bars, including the Sweetheart Bar, named, believe it or not, after the Northern Territory crocodile (note that some chairs are covered in sweetheart skin!). Guest rooms, at about $110 for two, all have balconies and face toward the ocean and the sunsets. (Reservations from the hotel on Gilruth Avenue, Darwin, N.T. 5790.) When we toured the hotel recently, the new owners were about to embark on a massive $3-million refurbishing project, which should be complete by early 1986. If it all comes together as planned, it could be Darwin's premier landmark.

Another good house, for around $70 per couple, is the low-rise **Telford Top End Hotel** (Tel. 81–6511), just around the corner from the Travelodge at 4 Daly St. This one has a large number of bars and restaurants and is one place to take in the local action.

With loads of tropical character—and almost right downtown—is the 1939-model **Hotel Darwin** (Tel. 81–9211), 10 Herbert St., which was partly rebuilt after the 1974 storm. The dining and bar areas look like something out of an old movie, and the hotel is talking about "improving" them (heaven forbid!). There's an outdoor swimming pool surrounded by some classically kitschy statuary. Upstairs you'll find overhead fans (besides air conditioning, of course) and other tropical accouterments, along with a few rough edges. At double rates of $75 or $80, its value will depend on your individual accommodation. We drew a virtual broom closet when we stayed here last in '85. If you get that one, even as a single, try asking for another.

Right smack in the center of town at 12 Cavenagh St. is the **Don Hotel** (Tel. 81–5311), with 40 not-too-fancy but adequately furnished rooms (even with color tellies) renting for around $70 for two.

Other possibilities include the eight-story **Telford International** (Tel. 81–5333) on Dashwood Crescent, about $80 for twins—but recheck the name. Its precise future is up in the air as we go to press. Then there's the more modest **Lameroo Lodge** (Tel. 81–9733), a two-story, spread-out establishment at 69 Mitchell St. for around $45 for two. The cheapest hotel in Darwin, which we haven't seen, we think is now the **Windsor Tourist Lodge** (Tel. 81–9214), selling doubles for $30 at 30 Cavenagh St.

The youth hostel is in Berrimah, now, about nine miles south of town, back of the navy base on Hidden Valley Road. Beds are about $5 each.

Still under construction at this writing is the 253-room **Sheraton Darwin,** which will provide the first first-class accommodations right downtown in many a year. The 13-story hotel, which will open in about September 1986, will offer views over the water from most rooms yet convenient access to the Smith Street Mall in the city center. Facilities include two restaurants, a swimming pool, bar, and discotheque. Sorry, no phone number was available before our deadline.

Also under construction is the new combination hotel/performing arts center/convention building financed by a Malaysian investment group. It's approximately around the corner from the Travelodge.

HOTELS IN ALICE SPRINGS

Keeping in mind that Alice Springs is synonymous with "roughing it" in most Australians' lexicon, the most dramatic thing to happen to the town in 100 years or so was the opening of the luxurious new **Diamond Springs Hotel Casino** (Tel. 52–5066), not to be confused with its similarly named sister in Darwin. Although given several different names in the past, it is known locally as just "the Casino." The 75-room spread was carved out of a section of desert on the edge of town, near the MacDonnell Range, and it does indeed serve as the venue for Alice's first venture into legalized gambling:

Private courtesy bus from the airport; a guard at the gate to keep out the undesirables; Cinerama-wide reception desk backed by a material mural of appliqué; red-and-green patterned carpet; supermodern lines nearly everywhere; popular Lanai Silver Service restaurant; cabaret show-room in purple and red, seating 200 for dinner and show; open-air amphitheater accommodating 500 for occasional concerts alfresco; small piano bar with a keno display board; spacious casino featuring all the standard stuff, plus the Aussie "two up"; smaller room for V.I.P. sporting; several bars and restaurants including a 24-hour coffee shop; some souvenir shops; a giant, heated swimming pool in the sunny outback; two tennis courts.

Most accommodations in two large separate structures flanking the pool, each surrounding its own central courtyard; lots of greenery; 58 twins, 12 doubles, and 5 suites available, all with wicker accents; gaming instructions available on the "telly"; minibars; push-button phones; walk-in wardrobes; patterned tile bathrooms. Normal tabs should run from about $90 to $110 per night for two this year. (Reservations from the hotel at Alice Springs, N.T. 5750.) It's not Las Vegas, but it's the closest thing to it you can find in these parts.

The 250-room **Sheraton Alice Springs** (Tel. 52–7566) opened in late 1985, too late to be personally inspected for this edition. The 252-room establishment is connected with the Desert Springs Country Club Estate and is a short walk from the Diamond Springs Hotel Casino. It overlooks a new $2.2-million, 18-hole golf course. Facilities include the gourmet Bradshaw Room and the coffee shop called Alice's Bistro (maybe they missed a bet by not naming it Alice's Restaurant), plus several bars and shops. We hope to check in and check it out before our next edition.

Sorry, but we still have not seen the new **Alice Springs Gap Motor Hotel** (Tel. 52–6611), nearby on the Gap Road. It's about $75 for two. And another new and well-regarded entry is the **Ford Resort** (Tel. 53–6699), just across the Todd River from downtown at 34 Stott Terrace. Besides the pool and tennis and volleyball courts, there are 52 units with modern conveniences in the $50 range for two.

We still very much like the modest yet attractive layout at the **Oasis Motel** (Tel. 52–1444) on Gap Road: Tiny, 24-hour reception room where one or two friendly faces try to do everything at once (sign you in, answer the switchboard, sell newspapers, etc.); licensed restaurant; pleasant Afghan Camel Drivers Bar; motel-type courtyards lined with orange and lemon trees, hibiscus bushes, and other desert and tropical flowers; pool in the middle somewhere; a private aviary on the grounds; many different types of accommodations, most with wall-to-wall carpeting and good furniture. Rates of about $50 to $65 for two. (Reservations from the hotel at P.O. Box 549.) We've always wanted to stay here, but never managed to get our booking in early enough.

Some new establishments featuring fridges and full kitchen facilities have now opened in Alice. One of the best is the **Outback Motor Lodge** (Tel. 52–3888) on South Terrace, and we've received letters about its good pool and laundry, helpful owners, etc. A smaller one is **White Gum** (Tel. 52–5144) on the same street. Both have doubles in the $50 range.

Our experience at the **Telford Territory Motel** (Tel. 52–2066) was much less than fun, but that was under the previous management. We still would insist on the refurbished rooms only. Rates are now up in the $65 range. We'd be interested in your reaction to this one. And we no longer recommend the **Melanka Lodge.**

On one trip to Alice we got stuck in the venerable old **Stuart Arms** (Tel. 52–1811), right on noisy Todd Street, which was at that time a dump. Now under new ownership, the place has reportedly improved a lot, although we haven't been back to see it in its new incarnation.

The Alice Springs youth hostel is **Griffiths House** (Tel. 52–1880) at 34 Hartley St. Members pay about $5 per set of Alice springs.

5. Restaurants and Dining

Thanks to its diverse ethnic population, Darwin is lucky enough to have some variety in its restaurants. And this does not mean all fancy "silver-service" dining rooms. Check out the little Thai takeout next to the taco takeout and other takeouts in the arcade under the Darwin Plaza building on the Smith Street Mall, for example. Then Alice Springs is big on beef, although "buffalo steaks" are sometimes available in both cities. That's cut from water buffalo, of course. We've tried it—and it's very good, too. The fish specialty in the area is barramundi.

DARWIN DINING

One top Darwin diner today is **Peppi's** (Tel. 81–3762) at 84 Mitchell St. There's no view, but the food and service more than make up for that. A little farther out, **Holtze** (Tel. 81–6756) in the pleasantly green and growing city Botanic Gardens served us an excellent dinner in the classical mode recently. Another recommendable French entry is **Le Saint Tropez**

(Tel. 81–9726) at 110 Mitchell St. And the smorgasbord offered at **The Top of the Telford** in the Telford International is winning over some local palates. The evening views of town and harbor are also delicious.

The **Capri** (Tel. 81–2931), 37 Knuckey St., is a two-part Italian restaurant that bakes the town's best pizza in the bar out front. We've never been in the back—a fancier spot, apparently. **The French Restaurant** (Tel. 81–6511) in the Telford Top End on Daly Street has some nighttime glamour in its green-and-yellow interior. True to Darwin's beer-drinking reputation, it serves up a Soupe à la Biere for around $4. A good local fish offering with a Gallic accent is Barramundi Grenoboloise for $10 or so. The only Greek place in town is **Christo's** (Tel. 81–8658), at No. 39 on the Smith Street Mall. You might like the Garithes Meskordo (prawns dipped in flour and cooked in garlic, brandy, and cream).

Simply delish for vegetarian specialties is **Simply Foods** (Tel. 81–4765). It's in the Central Mall off Smith Street. On the other side of the cholesterol street is **Jessies** (Tel. 81–2191) in the Parap Hotel on Parap Road. It's the premier steak house in town, and does some amazing things with both buffalo and barramundi, according to Gary and Marion Woodman, our resident Darwin diners. Thanks, chaps; we'll hoe into this local tucker the next time we're in town.

An attractive dining spot, especially for lunch, is the restaurant opened in the refurbished historic old **Vic Hotel** (Tel. 81–4011) at 27 Smith St. There's an excellent carvery for lunch and a downstairs grill for dinner. (We think they may have saved the bullet holes from a Japanese air raid, so have a look.)

A well-respected Chinese establishment is the **Tai Hung Toi** (Tel. 81–6373) at 36 Parap Rd. Takeout ("takeaway") is available, too. Another Chinese address is the **Mandarin Palace** (formerly the Hong Kong, Tel. 81–3498), at 29 Cavenagh St. near the waterfront, catering to all comers—including Darwin's 1,200 resident Chinese, of course.

ALICE'S RESTAURANTS

The best in Alice Springs today is probably still the **Turner House** (Tel. 52–5775), a 50-year-old former private residence at 13 Hartley St., the next street over from Todd. We remember a cozy, homelike atmosphere with several rooms, and we enjoyed a fine piece of veal with an excellent French sauce. Our evening meal was about $18 plus wine for one. We feel you won't be disappointed, either.

We keep getting good reports from readers who try the **Overlander Steakhouse** (Tel. 52–2159) at 72 Hartley St. It's attractive, with rough wooden tables, buffalo horns on the wall, etc. A filet mignon runs around $15, and there's sometimes a good slice of entertainment, too.

An inexpensive Italian address is **Papa Luigi's Bistro** (Tel. 52–2000). We dropped in for a lasagna lunch at two or three dollars. Simple, but good and efficient.

A place for good dining and fun dancing is the **Todd Tavern** at the corner of Todd and Wills streets. The local champion Chinese place is supposed to be **Chopsticks** (Tel. 52–3873) in the Ermond Arcade on Hartley Street, although we had a letter last year from Phillip Lister, a barrister and solicitor from Edmonton, Alberta, who gave that judgment to the **Golden Inn** at the north end of town. And Captain Charles Sweeney from the Aberdeen Proving Ground, Maryland, wrote that breakfasts proved to be very good from 7 A.M. on at **Beauty's Pancakes** in the bowling alley on Gap Road between Strenlow and Kempe streets.

6. Sightseeing in the Northern Territory

You'll get all the latest on what to see and do from the Northern Territory Government Tourist Bureau at 31 Smith St. (on the mall) in Darwin (Tel. 81–6611) and at 51 Todd St. (Tel. 52–1299) in Alice Springs.

One thing you should look for—but certainly not count on—in the N.T. is an Aboriginal corroboree. This singing and dancing extravaganza is unfortunately not often available to visitors, and not well explained on the rare occasions when you can see one. (On our last visit to the N.T. in 1985, they were holding a regular corroboree three times a week at Springvale Homestead near Katherine.)

Much of the rich Aboriginal culture has been erased from the country by repressive religious missions and other unenlightened policies of the past, many of which are still in effect in the present. Hopefully some of their ethnic dignity and colorful ceremonies will be restored in years to come, for the benefit of the Aborigines themselves as well as the appreci ation of international visitors and Australian tourists.

Be sure to dress practically for excursions "out bush." Jeans are worn out of town by both men and women, as are tough, comfortable shoes. Use sandshoes or sneakers for rock climbing, but for other serious hik ing you should have a stronger sole. A sun hat is advisable any time of year. And long sleeves and long trousers help combat sun, brush, and insects.

And while we're on the subject of clothes, we should mention that you'll notice some interesting patterns of apparel in the N.T. Normally, men wear shorts, long socks, and short-sleeve, open-neck shirts during the day. In Darwin, "Darwin Rig" is worn for formal occasions—dark trousers, long-sleeved white shirt, and tie. At Alice Springs, a similar evening uniform is adopted, except that jackets are worn in the winter (it's cool in the desert then). Women wear light dresses during the day and cocktail dresses in the evening.

DARWIN

Pick up the latest copy of *This Week in Darwin* (free at most hotels) and follow the suggested historical walk in the central city, beginning at the old **Hotel Victoria** on the Smith Street Mall. Several buildings described are interesting, but don't miss the significance of **Christ Church Cathedral.** The older gateway in front was left after Cyclone Tracy. The modern structure behind was built after the storm.

Farther from the center, now, we have never attended the fish-feeding operation at **Doctor's Gully,** also called Aquascene, although we will some day. It's only open at high tide, and then, for about $2, you can watch hundreds of fish being fed by hand at the end of the Esplanade. Get exact directions and times from the tourist office.

The 85-acre **Botanic Gardens** (Tel. 81–9155), badly damaged by Cyclone Tracy, are worth seeing for the tropical flora there. Then, about four miles out at **East Point,** wander through the fortifications left from World War II and visit the **N.T. War Museum** (Tel. 81–9702), sometimes called the Artillery Museum.

East Point Road also leads to the **Fannie Bay Gaol Museum** (Tel. 82–4211). This century-old institution was finally closed for good in 1979; the gallows inside were last used in 1952. Also off East Point Road, on Conacher Street behind Darwin High School, is the new **Northern Territory Museum of Arts and Sciences** (Tel. 82–4211). Besides the extensive collection of Aboriginal and other art inside, be sure to notice one of the Vietnamese "boat people" vessels, which arrived in Darwin Harbour and is now permanently mounted outside the museum. (Use Bus No. 4 or Bus No. 6.)

An almost incredible collection of undersea life is on living display at **Indo Pacific Marine** (Tel. 81–5906) at Larrakeyah Lodge on Kahlin Avenue. We hope Helene Pretty will show you through the reef life aquaria herself and explain something about the box jellyfish and some of the other dangerous and beautiful creatures so well exhibited. (Admission is $3 or so, and worth it!) A pleasant water trip is the half-hour cruise across the harbor from Darwin to Mandorah Beach on the **Harbour Ferry** (Tel. 81–6744).

Then, 13 miles down "The Track," you can view **Yarrawonga Park,** a garden of tropical wildlife including crocodiles, buffaloes, brolgas, emus, dingoes, and snakes. And if you visit **Fogg Dam** near Humpty Doo, 36 miles southeast of Darwin, you may see thousands of water birds, parrots, and other winged creatures on the floodplains of the Adelaide

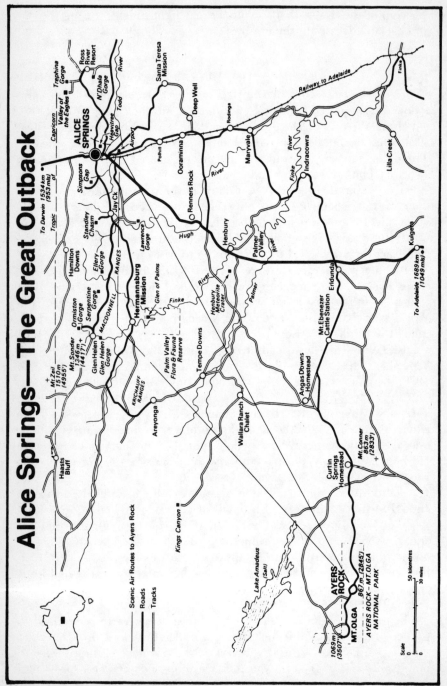

Alice Springs—The Great Outback

Scenic Air Routes to Ayers Rock
Roads
Tracks

Scale

50 kilometres
30 miles

River. On the nearby **Marrakai Plains** are wild wallabies, water buffalo, and the vertical anthills built by different varieties of termites.

There are several areas of interest even farther outside Darwin in the N.T., which are more practically reached on tours from the city than through personal travel arrangements. These include visits to **Melville Island** or **Bathurst Island** and the Aboriginal communities there and the new **Kakadu National Park,** past the Marrakai Plains some 150 miles east of Darwin, now considered one of the wildest and most scenic areas in the entire country. (See section 7.)

ALICE SPRINGS

Alice Springs perhaps qualifies more as a staging area for Outback sightseeing than as host to many points of interest within its city limits. Nevertheless you shsould try not to miss the restored **Old Telegraph Station,** now a national park, about three miles north of town on the billabong that was the real, original Alice Springs. (It was named for the wife of the S.A. superintendent of telegraphs, Sir Charles Todd. His own name stuck on the dry river.) Signs posted around the buildings will explain it all pretty well, and it's a great place for a picnic lunch.

Back in town, the **Royal Flying Doctor Service** is headquartered on Stuart Terrace, between Todd and Simpson streets. Contrary to most people's impressions, the doctors seldom fly to the distant cattle and sheep stations any more, but mostly diagnose patients and dispense medical advice by radio. You can watch and listen weekdays from 9 to 11 and 1 to 4, and Saturdays from 9 to 10 A.M. (admission 50 cents). Also in town is the **School of the Air,** on Head Street, where you can sometimes listen to children in Outback homesteads taking part in their radio lessons. Classes begin at 8:30 each weekday. Check at the tourist office to make arrangements to audit the classes.

The **Pitchi Richi Sanctuary,** just three miles south of town, features sculptures by William Ricketts. (Open daily from 9 to 5; admission $2.) And just north of the main part of town, **Anzac Hill** provides an elevated viewpoint over the area. (Drive or walk via "Lions Walk" opposite the Catholic Church on Wills Terrace.)

We haven't been there yet, but the **Emily Gap Camel Farm** is just off the airport road, and there you can ride a camel for around $3. There may be 30,000 wild camels roaming the Red Centre. They were introduced in the 1840s for transportation. (The Camel Cup races, organized by the Lions Club, are run on a Saturday in mid-May in Alice Springs.)

Be sure to stop by that strangely shaped building at 65 Hartley St. to see the **Panorama Guth** (Tel. 52–2013), the unusual 360-degree, 200-foot painting by Henk Guth, who might well be the gent selling you your ticket. Entrance is about $3, as we recall. It's worth it, in any case, and don't miss the minimuseum he has set up outside the principal panorama.

AYERS ROCK

Nothing seems more of a shame than for a Northern Hemisphere visitor to fly all the way to Australia and not go to Ayers Rock. To any but the most jaded or the most superficial traveler, it is not "just a big pebble." Ayers Rock, 210 air miles southwest of Alice Springs, is, of course, the largest monolith in the world. It is two miles long, 1½ miles wide, and 1,143 feet high.

But beyond that, the rock—a type of feldspar-rich sandstone called arkose—was the sacred Uluru to the Aborigines, and their paintings and the remains of ancient rites and ceremonies are in evidence in the rock's folds and caverns. If you're in good physical condition and wearing appropriate shoes, you can climb the rock in about 45 minutes, something many Aussies feel they must be able to boast they have done.

The rock is interesting from dawn until dusk; it changes colors throughout the day, ending usually with a brilliant orange blast exactly at sunset. No photograph we've seen does it justice, and yes, it's worth a special trip from Sydney if you can swing it. (You may have to change airlines in Alice Springs.) It's also worth braving all the annoying flies you'll find in hot-weather months. (Take some kind of repellent.)

Ayers Rock is only one of the big lumps in the area. Also in the same national park is **Mount Olga,** or, as it is better known, "The Olgas." It consists of about 30 dome-shaped protuberances down a dusty orange road 20 miles from Ayers Rock. Some think they're more dramatic than Ayers. The Olgas are not related to Ayers Rock, incidentally. Look closely and you'll see the stone is a conglomerate of many other rocks—a sort of pre-Cambrian concrete.

In the recent past Ayers Rock was ringed with rather rickety motels, but the picture has changed with the opening of the snazzy new government-sponsored **Yulara Tourist Resort.** It's almost a small town, running partly on solar energy, just outside the park boundary but still within sight of Ayers Rock and The Olgas. The 100-room Four Seasons has double rooms at around $100; the 230-room "international-standard" Sheraton packs 'em in at $120 for two. The resort also includes landscaped campgrounds and "holiday cabins" for perhaps $35 per couple per night. Also, the 54-room Erldunda Motel has opened midway between Alice and Ayers.

MACDONNELL RANGES

The mountain ranges to the west and east of Alice Springs contain several worthwhile tourist targets. **Simpson's Gap,** 14 miles west, is a colorful park. Farther on, 30 miles from Alice, is the well-known **Standley Chasm,** which you're supposed to see at exactly noon to appreciate the 200-foot cliffs that are just 12 feet apart. **Ormiston Gorge** (80 miles west of town) features red and purple rock walls rising above the creek, and 5 miles south of that **Glen Helen Gorge** displays remarkable vertical rock formations known as the Organ Pipes. **Hermannsburgh Mission** (83 miles west) contains the school where the late Aboriginal artist Albert Namatjira learned to paint. (The school might not be open to the public, but check at the little museum there.)

East of Alice Springs about 50 miles, **Trephina Gorge** displays magnificent "ghost gum" trees. The nearby **Corroboree Rock** and the **Valley of the Eagles** had considerable significance to the ancient Aborigines. And 50 miles east of town is the **Ross River Resort** (Radio Tel. 135), Australia's equivalent of the dude ranch.

KATHERINE

The small town of Katherine, about 200 miles down "The Track" from Darwin, is famous mainly for **Katherine Gorge National Park,** 20 miles east of town. You can arrange cruises on the river and safaris through the park through the Katherine Gorge Tourist Agency (Tel. 72–1810) on Katherine Terrace. (The Paraway Motel, overlooking the river, opened in 1983 and is the newest in a series of hotels there.) The gorge, incidentally, is the home of the fish-eating Johnstone River crocodile, apparently the most benign crocodile in the world, taking no interest in man whatsoever. (But we'd take no chances whatsoever, either. There are two types of crocodiles living in the N.T., and the other, considered a saltwater species, is highly dangerous.)

TENNANT CREEK

Farther down the same Stuart Highway, Tennant Creek is closer to Alice Springs, but still more than 300 miles from it. The town is the commercial center for a few mineral mines. South of the settlement about 80 miles are the **Devil's Marbles,** a group of gargantuan granite gibbers. Some measure about 20 feet in diameter.

7. Guided Tours and Cruises

Up here there's a chance to enjoy the genuine wilderness of Australia—not only strange land forms, but also flocks of bright-colored parrots and other strange birds, plus beasties like wallabies, buffaloes, dingoes, goannas, crocodiles, etc.—without the formality of a zoo or fenced-in sanctuary.

The Outback is ideal guided-tour country. Many of the trips are called "safaris," and with good reason. These sights and sites take expert drivers and lecturers, usually a combination of the two. On your own, you not only might get stuck in a bog, you won't know what you're looking at either.

(Some of the safaris are multiple-day or -week arrangements up from Sydney or Melbourne. We hope to be able to report on these in a future edition of this book. Meanwhile, here are a few of the locally conducted tours.)

DARWIN

In Darwin there were two dozen tour outfits around last season. There will probably be as many this year, but only some of them will be the same companies. In fact the tour business is so volatile that the best procedure we can recommend is to check on available tours at the government tourist bureau, which is probably where you'll make your bookings anyway.

At this writing the shorter, afternoon tours around the city are mostly operated by **Ansett Trailways** (Tel. 81–6433) and **Greyhound Coaches** (Tel. 81–8510). Current price is around $25 for a quick trip that includes Darwin, the harbor, East Point with its wartime relics, the Northern Suburbs, and Yarrawonga Wildlife Park.

Several agencies may offer a sunrise wildlife tour in the bush country just south of Darwin around Fogg Dam and Humpty Doo. This is the best time to see kangaroos, wallabies, goannas, water buffalo, and lots of birds. Our guess is that a five-hour morning tour will cost about $50 this year. (Check at the tourist office for the latest information.)

Lots of people will be promoting their tours lasting from one to several days at Kakadu National Park. Of these, one of the biggest and best-organized is **Australian Kakadu Tours** (Tel. 81–5391), which lists 12-hour tours from around $100, plus several two- and three-day tours and safaris to the area. This is one of the few outfits that may also be running tours in The Wet (summertime), too.

Other tours to Kakadu, some of them in combination with short air flights, may be offered by **Air North** (Tel. 81–6611), **Ansett Trailways** (Tel. 81–6433), **Dial a Safari** (Tel. 81–1155), the **South Alligator Motor Inn** (Tel. 79–0166), **Terra Safari Tours** (Tel. 81–1006), and **Wimray Safaris** (Tel. 84–3314).

One-day tours to Katherine are usually launched by **Dial A Safari** and **Greyhound** (Tel. 81–8510). Several agencies also have extended tours to Katherine and surrounding areas.

Half-day flying tours to Aboriginal communities on Bathurst Island (about $125) and full-day trips to both Bathurst and Melville islands (about $200) are the specialties of **Tiwi Tours** (Tel. 81–5115).

ALICE SPRINGS

A bewildering number of tours also leave from Alice Springs, the traditional jumping-off place for nearly everything of interest in the Outback. Here are just a few of the operations, nearly all of which offer day tours or overnight arrangements to Ayers Rock:

CATA (Central Australia Tours Association, Tel. 52–1700), in the TAA Building on Todd Mall, operates bus/air packages with TAA and offers about two dozen tours ranging from an *Alice Town Tour* to air tours of several days. Its 6-hour *Standley Chasm* tour costs around $35, including lunch.

Ansett Trailways (Tel. 52–2422) at the corner of Todd and Parsons streets, the local branch of the national outfit, has at least a half-dozen offerings. Sara took the 10-hour *Valley of the Eagles* tour (about $50), which was enjoyable if sometimes frightening because of road conditions. Another large company listing several tours out of Alice Springs today is **Arura Safari Tours** (Tel. 52–3843).

A more personal approach may be available through Rod Steinert's **Dreamtime & Namatjira Tours.** Steinert's unusual Aboriginal-heritage and cattle-station tours may be booked through CATA (see above) or through any Northern Territory tourist office. Prices range from around $50 for some half-day trips up to around $80 for day-long experiences. A similar one-man operation, also with a good reputation, is Jim Lane's **Landscanner Tourist Services** (Tel. 52–4767). Unlike most companies, Lane has a two-day tour that includes both Ayers Rock and King's Canyon. And another family operation, specializing in two-day tours to Ayers Rock, is **Worana Tours** (Tel. 52–5710). Last year, at least, Worana had some especially good rates during the summer. It also offers tours to the opal fields at Mintabie.

Airlines of Northern Australia (Tel. 52–4455) has inherited the all-inclusive one-day air tour to Ayers Rock this year. The tour leaves at 8 A.M. and returns to Alice Springs at dusk daily for a per-person tab of around $300.

Chartair (Tel. 52–6666) launches scenic flights over the rugged desert country, starting at about $100 for five hours. Some flights include a visit to an Outback cattle station.

8. Water Sports

Do not swim in the ocean near Darwin in the summertime! That's a warning we'll get in right off the bat because of an often-deadly jellyfish that lives there November to May called the sea wasp. Other times of the year swimming is pleasant and safe. Popular beaches include **Mandorah Beach**—take the ten-minute *Darwin Duchess* (Tel. 81–3894) across the harbor from Stokes Hill Wharf; **Mindil Beach,** on East Point Road, site of the world-famous Beer Can Regatta in June (all kinds of boats made from empty beer cans compete in various classes); and **Casuarina Beach,** at the end of Trower Road. For freshwater swimming, drive 20 miles down "The Track" to **Howard Springs,** a cool and green swimming hole near a popular picnic area. (Notice the bower birds and the ibis, too.) And boaters can rent a catamaran or a windsurfer at Mindil Beach during the dry season.

Deep-sea fishing is catching on in Darwin, with most anglers casting about for queenfish, Spanish mackerel, and—from January to May—barramundi and barracuda. Check at the tourist office for information on chartering a boat.

9. Other Sports

You'll find the Territorians interested in football (rugby, "Rules," and soccer), cricket, and horse racing, of course. In Alice Springs there's quite brisk competition in basketball, baseball, and softball, partly brought on by the number of American military men and dependents living in or near the community. (A supersecret American communication base is at Pine Gap, outside of Alice Springs.) There's also a big baseball- and softball-playing community in Darwin, where local boosters say the popularity of the game has little or nothing to do with any American forces that may have been stationed in the Territory.

The big spectator sport of the year, however, is the Henley-on-Todd Regatta, held in late August or early September. It's run on the dry Todd River bed, and contestants fashion boatlike contraptions with sails but no bottoms so that the eight-man "crews" can pick them up and run with them. In May the Camel Cup races draw thousands to Blatherskite Park.

Golfers visiting Darwin should make contact with the **Darwin Golf Club** (Tel. 27–1322) at McMillan's Road. In Alice Springs, visitors are welcome at the 18-hole **Alice Springs Golf Club.**

Tennis courts are installed at some hotels. Otherwise, call the **N.T. Tennis Association** (Tel. 81–2181) on Gilruth Avenue in Darwin. And in Alice Springs you can rent public courts at **Traeger Park** (make the arrangements at the Council Offices in Todd Street.)

10. Shopping

In either Darwin or Alice Springs some of the widest choices are in

Aboriginal products, and you'll find some local shopkeepers able to discuss the differences in patterns and styles made by various Aboriginal tribes. Be aware that much Aboriginal material is turned out almost in mass production by artisans under central direction at various mission stations.

In Darwin, the best of the type is the **Aboriginal Heritage Gallery** (Tel. 81–1394) at 41 Smith Street Mall, across from the tourist office. Be sure to see the fabric designs as well as the better-known wood carvings and paintings. (By the way, a more representative boomerang is not the common returning type, but the hook-style hunting boomerang.) Also on the same mall, you might check the **Saddle Shed and Craft Centre** and the nearby **Studio Arts** in the Vic Complex, just off the mall.

In Alice Springs, have a look at products at two addresses. For N.T. Aboriginal work only, try the **Center for Aboriginal Artists and Craftsmen** (Tel. 52–3408) at 86–88 Todd St., also open Sunday afternoons from 2 to 5. There's a wider selection from all over the country at the little store called the **All-Aboriginal Art Gallery** (Tel. 52–3662) at Todd and Gregory streets.

Rock hounds in Alice Springs will dig **The Gem Cape** (Tel. 52–1079), 99 Todd St., which sparkles with an excellent collection of semiprecious stones—opalite, mica, amethyst, even rock salt—destined to whet the appetite of a minerals gourmet. **The Rockhole** (Tel. 52–1480), at 50 Hartley St., has similar specimens presented more informally. We wished later we'd picked up the souvenir card of 20 gemstones we saw there for $5.50.

For books, magazines, postcards, and the like, see the **Darwin Newsagency** (Tel. 81–8222) at 28 Smith St., Darwin; in Alice Springs try **Marron's Newsagency** (Tel. 52–1024) on Todd Street, opposite the Flynn Church, or the **Connoisseur Book Shop** (Tel. 52–4057) in the Fan Arcade.

11. Night Life and Entertainment

As elsewhere in Australia—probably *more* than anywhere else in Australia—the principal nighttime entertainment throughout the N.T. is drinking, mainly beer. There's a brewery in Darwin, jointly owned by C.U.B. and Swan, turning out local beers, notably the brand called N.T.

In a vain attempt to beat the heat, draft beer is often sold too cold in these climes—as low as 35 degrees F., whereas the most flavor is released at temperatures closer to 42 degrees. Before buying a *bottle,* be sure you want what you'll get. The famous "Darwin Stubbie" contains 75 ounces of beer! (The bottles are becoming a collector's item, by the way—even empty.) This year you might find full bottles at Woolworths for about $10.

Some of the pubs in Darwin can be a little rough. We looked at each of a group of better-run bars in the Koala Welcome Inn: **The Beachcomber,** serving tropical drinks, probably will have live entertainment. **The Board Room** is the "gentlemen's club bar." Then there's **The Verandah,** a "saloon" bar, for eating in, too, and **The Sportsman,** a "public bar," which means there are minimum dress standards (footwear and a shirt)—and no ladies.

The Vic is becoming a popular wateringhole on the Central Mall. And somewhat run-down, but fiercely defended by loyal clientele, is the old-world-style **Hotel Darwin.** The air conditioning is almost as cold as the beer, and it's a great place to watch the sun set, too.

You'll find nightclub and disco entertainment in Darwin at **Fannie's Disco,** 3 Edmund St., the **Aspa Cabaret Room,** Dashwood Crescent, the **Don Hotel,** 12 Cavenagh St., and at the casino, cabaret, and environs at the **Diamond Beach Hotel** out at Mindil Beach. Jazz is often on tap at the **Beachfront Bar** behind the Vic Hotel. (The Beachfront is also the location for crab-tying contests(!) from time to time.) The often-rough bar at the **Berrimah Hotel** is now off our list.

Occasional outdoor performances by local thespians and other groups take place at the amphitheater in the Botanic Gardens and also, believe it or not, under the shelter of a large abandoned gun turret near the military museum at East Point. In the latter, the Northern Territory Folk (Music) Club gives a concert at 8 P.M. every Sunday. Admission is probably still $1. Darwin's new **Performing Arts Centre** is scheduled to open soon near the Travelodge.

At Alice Springs there's usually some kind of a country and western show at the **Stuart Arms Hotel** on Todd Street and often out at the new **Diamond Springs Hotel.** Keep an eye out in either Darwin or Alice for Slim Dusty, an Outback C&W entertainer. Ted Egan, another locally popular entertainer, may still have a venue at the **Melanka Lodge** on Todd Street. There's a disco nearly every night in the **Todd Tavern** (Tel. 52–1255) on Wills Terrace—sometimes a live act plays there, too. Alice likes to drink all right, but generally speaking she turns in early.

12-A. The Darwin Address Book

Airlines—Ansett, Smith Street Mall (Tel. 80–3333). TAA, 8 Bennett St. (Tel. 80–1222). Airlines of Northern Australia, 51 Todd St. (Tel. 52–2644).

Ambulance—Tel. 27–9000 (or dial 000 for all emergencies).

Beauty salon—Shirley Ann, Cavenagh Street (Tel. 81–9711).

Bridge players—Darwin Bridge Club (Tel. 85–4568).

Dental clinic—48 Mitchell St. (Tel. 81–9688).

Fire brigade—Tel. 81–2222. (Dial 000 for all emergencies.)

Florist—Gardener's World, 63 Smith St. (Tel. 81–4607).

Hospital—Darwin Hospital, Mitchell Street West (Tel. 89–2211).

Laundry—City Laundromat, Smith Street West (Tel. 81–3561).

Lions Club—Bill Binns, 913 Chrisp St.; Rapid Creek (Tel. 85–3267).

Pharmacy—Jim Berry, 7 Westralia St. (Tel. 81–8075).

Police station—Mitchell Street (Tel. 81–5555, 85–2444).

Post office—Knuckey Street.

Supermarket—Alawa Supermarket, 53 Alawa Crescent, Casuarina.

Swimming pool—Casuarina Pool, opposite the shopping center.

Taxis—Darwin Co-op (Tel. 81–8777) or Keetley's (Tel. 81–2933).

Tourist office—Northern Territory Government Tourist Bureau, 31 Smith St. (Tel. 81–6611).

Youth Hostel Association of N.T.—Hidden Valley Road (Tel. 84–3107).

12-B. The Alice Springs Address List

Airlines—Ansett, Todd St. (Tel. 52–4455). TAA, Parsons and Todd streets (Tel. 50–5222).

Ambulance—Tel. 52–2200.

Bank—Westpac on Todd Street, opposite Woolworths (Tel. 52–1066).

Camping equipment rental—Outdoor Territorian, Milner Road and Elder Street (Tel. 52–2848).

Fire brigade—Tel. 52–1000.

Hospital—Alice Springs Hospital (Tel. 50–2211).

Laundry—Whistlestop Laundromat, Todd Street, opposite Melanka Lodge (Tel. 52–4461).

Pharmacy—Alice Springs Pharmacy, Todd Street (Tel. 52–4274).

Police—Tel. 52–2777.

Post office—Hartley Street, between Parsons and Gregory.

Supermarket—Egars, Todd Street (Tel. 52–4000).

Tourist office—Northern Territory Government Tourist Bureau, 51 Todd St. (Tel. 52–1299).

Youth Hostel Association of N.T.—Todd Street (Tel. 52–5016).

Queensland

Cape York

GULF OF
CARPENTARIA

SOUTH

PACIFIC

OCEAN

Cooktown

Lakeland
Downs

GREAT

Normanton

Cairns

BARRIER

To Tennant Creek

Agate
Creek

GREAT

377 km
(234 mls)

REEF

Townsville

414 km
(257 mls)

Cloncurry

DIVIDING

Mt Isa

Mackay

396 km (246 mls)

Colston
Sheep Station

Longreach

Anakie

QUEENSLAND

Rockhampton

Jundah

Carnarvon
National Park

Fraser
Island

Hervey Bay

Charleville

420 km (247 mls)

Maryborough

RANGE

Maroochydore

Sunshine
Coast

Rosevale
Sheep
Station

Caloundra

SOUTH

Glass House Mtns.

AUST

Toowoomba

BRISBANE

Cunnamulla

Warwick

N.S.W

To Sydney
1043 km (648 mls)

To Sydney
1021 km
(634 mls)

Scale
0   300 kilometres
0   200 miles

Map courtesy Australian Tourist Commission

12

Brisbane and Queensland

1. The General Picture

Queensland might hit you in three stages.

At first, the state seems to be like Hawaii—coastlines of yellow sand, solid blue waters, bright green islands, then fertile plains of sugar, pineapple, rustling palms, and hills of flowering trees and plants—all backgrounded by the mountains of the Great Dividing Range.

But just beyond that first impression, the state begins to feel more like Florida. Its capital, Brisbane, bears the remnants of a traditional "wowserism" that is not unlike the "cracker" influence still at work in America's southern resort state.

Still later, Brisbane and Queensland take on their own personalities, as complex and as interesting as that of any other location in Australia.

Queensland's conservative tradition is an outgrowth of a long agrarian history. In the past, the great labor-intensive industries were operated by those who shanghaied and shipped in thousands of "kanakas"—Pacific islanders—to provide the brawn needed to harvest the sugar, pineapple, and banana plantations. There was little but scorn for the Aborigines who understandably enough did not see the percentage in this kind of backbreaking work.

And the racist attitudes of the past have still not entirely disappeared in Queensland. This, together with its otherwise hospitable personality,

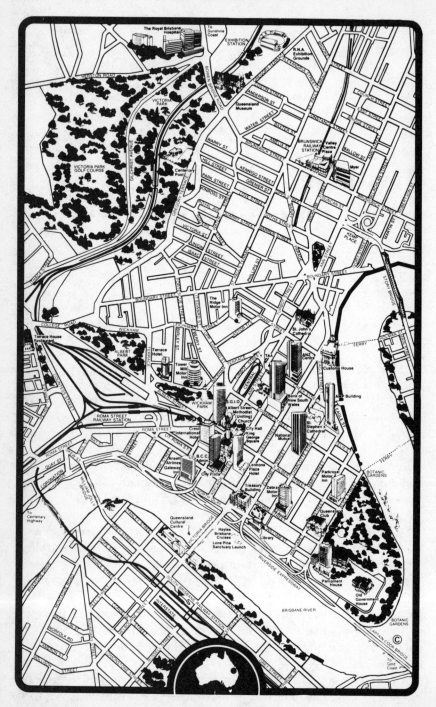

Map courtesy Stuart Powell and Associates, Brisbane

makes it a paradox comparable to the anomalies still found in the American South.

Physically, Queensland varies from the treeless, fly-ridden mining country and desert Outback around Mount Isa and elsewhere in the west through junglelike Aboriginal reserves and other little-explored and hardly civilized territory to the north, especially in the York Peninsula. One feature of its sun-bathed northwest coast is world-famous—the 1,250-mile-long Great Barrier Reef, once hazardous to navigation and today a repository of some of the most varied and beautiful marine life on earth. This massive ridge of regenerating coral polyps is now considered to be the world's largest living thing.

To the southern Australian, Queensland is a winter playground—the tropical home of the Sunshine Coast, a string of beaches and resorts from Brisbane north to Noosa, and most especially the Gold Coast, a long, narrow equivalent to Miami Beach extending along the southern shore for the last 20 miles before reaching the border of New South Wales.

Queensland's premier for the past several years has been an authoritarian figure who some say sets an anti-intellectual, ultraconservative tone for the state, Sir Joh Bjelke-Petersen. He has the power, which he exercises, to ban public demonstrations and to arrest those who challenge this authority, which they do.

When rich bauxite was found on ancestral land at a Queensland Aboriginal reserve not long ago, the premier's decision was merely to move the tribe off the property and start mining. When church missions came to the aid of the Aborigines, Bjelke-Petersen closed down the churches, too! (With the help of the federal government in Canberra, some compromise has been reached, although the controversy seems destined to continue.) Sir Joh's knock-down, drag-out battles with labor unions are also legendary in Queensland, and will probably continue as long as the 75-year-old premier is in power.

Outside of the wildest areas, the Queensland countryside is still very agricultural; in addition to the giant sugar plantations there are vast acres of vegetables and fruits plus huge cattle stations raising some of Australia's best beef. An occasional impediment to this activity are numbers of wild animals who compete for the forage of the plains. Most of these are shot on sight—creatures like kangaroos, dingoes, and "brumbies" (wild horses that cannot be captured).

Brisbane (they pronounce it "*Briz*-b'n") grew from a crude convict settlement in 1824 to a very large country town, which it remained until recently. But thousands of American GIs who were stationed in Brisbane during World War II would hardly recognize it today; it has now grown to a population of nearly a million.

With a few exceptions, Brisbane is not known for holding onto evidence of its past. Many of the city's landmarks, including the famous hotel where General Douglas MacArthur issued orders during the darkest days of the war, have been razed to make way for other, more modern, more lucrative structures. Every year it seems like one more historical building has disappeared.

Happily the city's tropical gardens and parks remain, as well as a few of its more revered sandstone, Victorian-style public buildings. Most of these have recently been cleaned and sandblasted, partially in preparation for 1988. Then the city will celebrate the nation's 200th birthday by holding a compactly designed world's fair just across the river from the downtown area. (We will devote considerable attention to this exhibition in the 1988–89 edition of this volume.)

Meanwhile, with her face freshly scrubbed, Brisbane has become a very bright-looking place to visit indeed.

2. Airports and Long-Distance Transportation

The Brisbane *Sunday Sun* not long ago dubbed the city's aging airport terminal at Eagle Farm the "Jet Shed," and it is certainly true that the hodgepodge left over from the former U.S. World War II base has about outlived its usefulness. From time to time both the international and domestic sections have been spruced up, but these have always been temporary measures. An entirely new airport terminal is expected to be completed in 1988, considerably delayed from the originally announced 1986 opening.

(Note: The new Gateway Bridge in the airport complex may already be finished. The span crosses the nearby river to give passengers direct access to the Pacific Highway, bypassing Brisbane on the way to the Gold Coast, and cutting the 90 minutes' driving time between the Gold Coast and the airport by more than half.)

Unless you come in on one of the international flights from Hawaii, Papua New Guinea, New Zealand, and a few other foreign gateways, you'll most likely arrive either on **Ansett Airlines** (Tel. 226–1111) or **Trans-Australia Airlines** (Tel. 260–3311). Some flights from Sydney are also shuttled by **East-West Airlines** (Tel. 229–0455) or **Air New South Wales** (same phone number as Ansett, above), and flights arrive from the north on **Air Queensland** (formerly Bush Pilots Airways, Tel. 229–1311), which still flies a few World War II–vintage DC-3 "Gooney Birds," among other things.

Arriving on a domestic flight, you stand a good chance of getting rained on between the plane and the shelter. Once through the crowded terminal, you may have to wait until next Tuesday for a cab, so if it's a toss-up anyway, better take the airport bus for the four-mile, 15- or 20-minute trip into town. **Skennars Transport Industry** (Tel. 832–1148) charges about $3, and drops off and picks up at some Brisbane hotels. If you do get a taxi, the fare will run about $7—probably a good deal for three traveling together.

You step off the air-conditioned *Brisbane Limited Express* train from Sydney, after a 16-hour trip, at the **Interstate Station** in South Brisbane. Fares run about $90 Economy and $70 First Class. Now that Qantas is landing in Cairns, another popular train for Americans and Canadians is the *Sunlander* between Brisbane and Cairns. The two-day trip costs about $85 Economy and $100 First Class, plus $10 or $20 respectively if you choose a berth.

Four long-distance bus ("coach") lines link Brisbane with other cities: **Ansett Pioneer** (Tel. 226–1184), 16 Ann St., **Greyhound Coaches** (Tel. 240–9333), 79 Melbourne St., **McCafferty's Coaches** (Tel. 44–4015) on Gray Street, and **Skennars Transport** (Tel. 832–1148) in Fortitude Valley. If you don't have a special pass, the fare between Sydney and Brisbane runs about $70 each way for a 17-hour overnight trip. There is an inland and a coastal route (choose the latter). From Cairns, the bus ride will run a little more.

Travel by car along the east coast of Queensland can be delightful at any time of the year. You'll find several competing rental agencies in Brisbane. The three biggies are **Avis** (Tel. 52–9111), 275 Wickham St., **Hertz** (Tel. 229–0990), 55 Charlotte St., and **Budget** (Tel. 52–0151), corner of St. Paul's Terrace and Baxter Street. This trio also meets the planes at Eagle Farm. Rates start at about $25 a day plus 25 cents a kilometer.

Manx (Tel. 52–7288), a well-known local outfit at 325 Wickham St., is considerably cheaper. Also, you might check out **Scotty** (Tel. 52–7400), 100 Abbotsford Rd., Mayne, **Crown Cars** (Tel. 832–4544) at 59 Barry Parade in "the Valley," and **Thrifty** (Tel. 52–5994), at the corner of Ann and Brooke streets.

3. Local Transportation

The urban bus service (Tel. 225–4444) run by the City Council isn't bad. You can buy a Day Rover ticket and go anywhere all day for a dollar, if you want. There's also good train service to several suburbs; most of these trains depart from the Central Station.

Despite the ubiquitous bridges across the meandering Brisbane River, there are still a few ferryboats bouncing back and forth, notably the **Edward Street Ferry,** which crosses between the Botanic Gardens and Kangaroo Point, and the **Customs House Ferry,** a few hundred yards downstream.

We recently found one conveniently located place where you can rent a bicycle for about $3 an hour: **Brisbane Bicycle Hire** (Tel. 229–2592), open seven days, is at 214 Margaret St., next to the Botanic Gardens.

Taxi services include **Ascot** (Tel. 831–3000), **Black & White** (Tel. 229–1000), and **Yellow** (Tel. 391–0191).

4. The Brisbane Hotel Scene

Brisbane still doesn't have enough hotels for the demand, so make sure your bookings are nailed down tight or you may find yourself camping at the airport during busy periods.

EXPENSIVE HOTELS

Occupying undisputed center stage on the Brisbane hotel scene today is the new 441-room **Sheraton-Brisbane** (Tel. 835–3535). It was built by the State Government Insurance Office (S.G.I.O.) on an unusual and dramatic site on the side of a hill and at the same time directly above Brisbane's historic Central Station: Bus and car entrance conveniently off busy Turbot Street; pedestrian entrance from Anzac Square via a series of underpasses and escalators through the station complex; large marble lobby, often echoing with live piano music; three restaurants, including the viewful Denisons up on the roof, the colorful Carriages Grill off the lobby, and the Sidewalk Cafe, which is actually a long way from the sidewalk at face level with the station clock tower; several bars, including one next to the outdoor swimming pool; a Clark Hatch Fitness Center adjoining.

Two different sets of rooms—the normal hotel rooms (standards and suites) up through the 26th floor and the new Tower Floors, a "hotel within a hotel" concept, relatively new in Australia, from the 27th through the 29th; all rooms with modern amenities, good furnishings (even the standards with choice of double-double beds or one king-size, plus writing desks—or "work stations," as they're beginning to call them) and excellent views over the cityscape; Tower Floor clients enjoying several extras in their suites (hair dryers, remote-control TVs, etc.) plus froufrous like a floor butler; standard room rates hovering in the $100 range as 1986 begins; Tower Floor units beginning at about $150; the basic presidential suite "a steal," someone told us, at around $350 a day. We were comfortable enough in our own standard room. (Reservations through the Sheraton organization or the hotel itself at G.P.O. Box 1211, Brisbane 4001.) From its lofty location, the Sheraton almost seems to command the center of town, a position it well deserves.

The 1972-model **Lennons Brisbane** (Tel. 32–0131) is at 66–76 Queens

St., over three blocks from the site of the original historic Lennons, where General MacArthur publicly vowed to return to the Philippines: Convenient location in the center; large, plush, high-ceilinged lobby in modern "grand hotel" style; several thick-carpeted, very decorated bars; three different dining areas, including the elegant Colosseum Restaurant, the tropical-toned Hibiscus Room on the top floor, and a coffee shop on street level; several function rooms; 150 well-designed accommodations, all with luxury fittings; higher floors featuring the views. Doubles in pleasant colors like yellow, dark green, and maroon run from about $90 to $100. Spacious suites are about $150. (Reserve from the hotel or through the Zebra chain.) This was our own address once, and we found it a solidly professional operation.

Perhaps with a little more distinguishable personality, though, is the **Brisbane Parkroyal** (Tel. 221–3411), which is labeled a "motor inn." (For some reason Australians insist on drawing a definite distinction between "hotels" and "motels," although the latter term is going out of favor.) Lovely green site next to the Botanic Gardens and within walking distance of the river ferry; long, carpeted lobby (with courtesy coffee) leading eventually to a refreshing outdoor pool; wood-lined sauna available; spotless and spacious cocktail bar; dark-paneled Walnut Room Restaurant; ample, warm-toned rooms, all with unusable balconies; front units overlooking the gardens and the river beyond; all top-class amenities installed; a small amount extra for some units with water beds. Doubles begin at $100 or more, but the best views are higher than that; 7th floor for nonsmokers; 9th and 10th floors equipped with king-size mattresses; some swellegant VIP suites at around $200. A massive, million-dollar face-lift has just been completed; sorry, we haven't seen it since. (Reservations through the Travelodge organization or the hotel, corner of Alice and Albert streets.) We're going to try to get in here another time.

We've also had a brief stay at the **Gateway Hotel** (Tel. 221–0211), a successful and well-concocted formula run by the Ansett organization above their bus terminal at 85 North Quay, off Ann Street. Its efficiently designed rooms are virtual duplicates of the Gateway in Perth, except that if you draw a front room here you get a nice view of the spiffy new Cultural Centre, Victoria Bridge, and the mid-channel Elizabeth II Jubilee Fountain that springs to life from time to time in the Brisbane River. There's a pool, restaurant, and bar, too, of course. Even though we might prefer the more open feeling of the Parkroyal, we have no complaints about the Gateway, which you may find more convenient, anyway. Rates about $85 and up. (Book through Ansett or the hotel at Brisbane 4000.) Firmly recommended.

The centrally located, 16-story **Crest International** (Tel. 229–9111), right opposite a corner of King George Square, was our Brisbane headquarters on one occasion. This recently expanded businessmen's bulwark has traditionally boasted more single than double rooms and sometimes offers discounts on the weekends: New lobby in the new Roma Wing; lots of wining and dining facilities—some of these with Yankee accents, including George & Martha's Washington Bar, Sachmo's Bar, the Presidential Ballroom (which can be divided into Lincoln, Roosevelt, and Kennedy rooms), the General Jackson Room, and the Early American Inn; rooftop pool on top of the older wing; gymnasium and sauna adjoining; second pool and jogging track designed for the new wing; total of 436 rooms, all with luxury appointments; generally larger accommodations in the new wing; better views over the square in the original structure. Double rates are expected to be in the $90 to $110 range in 1986 and 1987, but you should ask about those weekend discounts. Solid and dependable.

The **Bellevue Hotel** (Tel. 221–6044), formerly the Zebra, is also near the center of things at 103 George St. (the new name honors an old hotel which was recently demolished nearby): Modern entrance decorated by stickers proudly displaying the scores of credit cards and traveler's checks it accepts; outdoor advertising pushing for more restaurant business; dining and dancing in the Raindrop Room; swimming pool; bedchambers all neat and clean; mostly showers, not tubs; some TVs in color; furniture running toward raffia; some with kitchenettes; not as much view as the previous two; rates a little less than for the Lennons, its partner in the profession. (Reservations through the Zebra chain or the hotel at the above address.) A businessmen's favorite, and a decent deal.

The new 340-room **Brisbane Hilton** is under construction as part of a shopping complex at 197 Queen St. (where Her Majesty's Theatre was razed three years before her 100th birthday) and extending to frontage on Elizabeth and Edward streets. Like the Hilton in Sydney, the hotel will begin considerably up off the street. Reached by escalators, its lobby will be four levels above the ground. An interior atrium is scheduled to climb 25 stories up and to drip with plants and flowers of the region. The hotel should open in early 1987.

BRISBANE BEDS ON A BUDGET

You might draw a very nice double for $50 at the **Parkview Motel** (Tel. 31–2695) at 128 Alice St., near the more prestigious Parkroyal. A member of the Flag chain, it runs up an outdoor pool but no restaurant. Almost next door, at 132 Alice St., is the **Motel Regal** (Tel. 31–1541), which does have a restaurant as well as a pool. It's also a Flag, waving rooms at around the same price. You'll find TVs, complimentary newspapers, and several touches associated with the big boys.

The well-advertised **Canberra Hotel** (Tel. 32–0231) up the hill at Ann and Edward streets has a plaque outside declaring that it has been a temperance hotel since opening day, July 20, 1929. We've nothing against their not selling liquor, but we wonder what they've got against having pictures on the walls. The rooms in the new wing would look nice if it weren't for those acres of blank space above the furniture. Doubles were running a fair $50 to $60 when we looked in, most with TV, tea- and coffee-makers, etc. Not a bad choice—especially if you want some place to project your slides.

If you can take the hilly hike, or if you have your own transportation, a good low-budget choice is the ambitious little **Yale Budget Inn** (Tel. 832–1663) at 413 *Upper* Edward St. Public areas include just the tiny lobby, a breakfast room, a laundry area, and a common TV room. Most of the 70 or so rooms have washbasins, at least, but other facilities "down the hall." After a new refurbishment, however, there may be a couple of doubles with all their own plumbing. No air conditioning; fans will do the job except on the hottest days of summer. Predicted 1986 rates of about $30 for two, $20 for one, include breakfast. The owner of this hotel lives in San Diego, California, interestingly enough, but you can write or see the enthusiastic manager, Jack Castle, or his wife Shirley.

At the **Embassy Hotel** (Tel. 221–7616), the "XXXX" sign outside the old brick building does not a four-star hotel make. That's just the brand of beer featured in the pub. It's a convenient location (the No. 37 bus stops right outside), and the renovations attempt to take the edge off some of that 1924 mustiness. Believe it or not, there are just 29 sleeping nests and 7 bars. One reader undiplomatically reported to us his own unhappiness at the Embassy recently. It's no palace, that's for sure.

Last, Brisbane's youth hostel is about five miles out at 15 Mitchell St. in Kedron. (Book through the YHA in town, Tel. 57–1245.) Beds run about $6 for members here.

5. Restaurants and Dining

An unsubtle delicacy, the Queensland mud crab is famous, gigantic, and delicious. Also the Moreton Bay bug, a lobster, is brought in from the bay outside Brisbane.

The restaurant for seafood is **Gambaro's** (Tel. 369–9500) at 34 Caxton St. in Petrie Terrace. Dominic Gambaro is famous for his Cold Seafood Platter, which includes the bug and the crab, along with oysters and other seasoned goodies. This is not a fancy-looking place. In fact, it started out as a fish-and-chips shop, although it's now been built up into one of the best of its type in the country.

Just across the street from Gambaro's, **Rag's** (Tel. 36–6794) at No. 25

Caxton has a name that belies its serious French intent. Try the Boeuf Grand Veneur (beef marinated in red wine). Some now rate this the best Gallic kitchen in town. Vigorous competition comes from **Allegro** (Tel. 229–5550). Despite the Italian name, the cuisine is *très français* and *très bon*. The new **Matilda's** (Tel. 32–0131) in the Lennons hotel is making a good initial impression. Ditto **Agatha Christie's** (Tel. 229–6744) in an old Orient Express car permanently parked at the corner of Adelaide and George streets.

On the Italian front, we liked our excursion into Scallopine Picante at **Milano's** (Tel. 229–3917), 78 Queen St., a short lob from Lennons. Hmm . . . or was that Veal Stuffato di Manzo al Barolo? Our notes are not clear on the subject, but our memory is of a vividly excellent meal, well prepared and served faultlessly. The elegant upstairs setting featured white tablecloths, rosebuds in stainless-steel vases, pivoting, hip-hugging chairs, and someone playing Gershwin on the goanna in the background. There are many French specialties on the menu, and we understand they're good, too. Figure about $55 for two, with an obscure (but quite acceptable) house wine. However, Milano's can boast one of the best cellars in Australia.

A much more modest Italian entry, but still fun for lunch or perhaps unpretentious evening dining, is **Gino's East of Chicago** (Tel. 221–0966) in the Brisbane Arcade, down the stairs from the Queen Street Mall. The spicy fare was reminiscent of Southern Italian cooking we've had north and west of Chicago. "Four-Ex" is on tap. Pleasant and inexpensive, and you can even take out a pizza if you want.

Crowning culinary achievements are the rule at the **Coronation** (Tel. 369–9955) in Milton. It's expensive, though—about $70 for two, with wine. Ditto the prices at the **Fountain Room** overlooking the river in the new Cultural Centre. The setting is magnificent. **The Courtyard** (Tel. 52–5431), 67 O'Connell Terrace near Brisbane Hospital, has indoor tables as well as seating *alfresco*. The atmosphere amongst the greenery is delightful, and the specialty is dependable Queensland beef.

Arts & Battledress (Tel. 369–2406), a BYO at 216 Petrie Terrace, displays gourmet skills in a tiny, midtown setting. The Steak Bermuda combines beef, bacon, banana, and brandy! The nearby **Terrace House** (Tel. 36–6374), at No. 230, is recommended for food and atmosphere by Peter Newland, a knowledgeable local lad.

For lunch, look for the outdoor beer gardens. Excellent of the type is the **Victory Hotel** at 127 Edward St. A more modest one is the **Port Office** (opposite the old post office), which offers 70-cent hamburgers, etc. They go down well with a glass of Brisbane Bitter or Castlemaine XXXX. The garden of the **Breakfast Creek Hotel** (Tel. 262–5988), at 2 Kingsford Smith Drive, is also fun. It has a national reputation as a no-nonsense steak house, day and night. And across the creek from the BCH, at 194 Breakfast Creek Rd., try the **Coral Trout** (Tel. 52–1741) for seafood.

Back downtown again, there are budget-conscious meals in the **Wool Press Restaurant** (Tel. 229–5064) in the S.G.I.O. Building on Albert Street. Another inexpensive choice for day or night dining is **Mama Luigi's** (Tel. 52–2320), a pasta palace at 240 St. Paul's Terrace that dates back half a century. Bring your own wine and enjoy the simple spaghetti and/or chicken served on rough-hewn wooden furniture. *Molte bene,* and you may get away for around eight bickies!

6. Sightseeing in Queensland

Long a vacationland for Australians, Queensland lays out an incredible number of attractions, only relatively few of which we can touch on in a guidebook for international visitors to Australia. We've divided this section into four areas—Brisbane, the Gold Coast, the Great Barrier Reef, and North Queensland (Townsville, Cairns, etc.).

BRISBANE

First pay a visit to the **Queensland Government Travel Centre** (Tel. 31–2211) at the corner of Adelaide and Edward streets. This is the place to ask for maps and folders, not only for Brisbane but for attractions throughout the state. They'll book you on tours, too, if you want, or for trips north, south, or west of the city.

If you see nothing else in Brisbane, don't miss a visit to the privately owned **Lone Pine Koala Sanctuary** (Tel. 378–1054), about seven miles up the river. (In fact, a delightful way to arrive is by launch; see section 7.) The sanctuary was established in 1927 specifically to protect the koala (the Australian "Teddy Bear") then being slaughtered in huge numbers. At Lone Pine the Queensland koalas prove their penchant for gentleness, and the curators will even photograph you with a Polaroid holding a koala in your arms.

Other animals at Lone Pine include kangaroos and emus (you can walk among them, scratch their ears, and feed them all you want—but *they'll* want only a little, being so well fed), plus a platypus, wombats, echidnas (spiny anteaters), Tasmanian devils, dingoes, and various kinds of weird reptiles and native birds including kookaburras, cockatoos, galahs, etc. (Get there early to see all the animals at their friskiest.) We thought the whole experience was wonderful. (Open 9:30 A.M. to 5:00 P.M. daily; admission about $5.)

On the way to or from Lone Pine, many newcomers drive up to **Mount Coot-tha Forest Park,** a piece of natural bush that also provides a view over Brisbane, the meandering river, Moreton Bay, and the surrounding area sometimes as far as the rock pillars called the Glasshouse Mountains, 50 miles away. The park features many kinds of aromatic gum (eucalyptus) trees, and lots of tropical flowers like fragrant frangipani (plumeria), poinciana, etc. Maureen Millar, a knowledgeable local lady, advises us to take the "scented shrubbery walk" through the gardens. Also the new **Mount Coot-tha Botanic Gardens** were opened recently on Sir Samuel Griffith Drive. (The tearoom overlooks the lake there. And ask about the Rolls Royce tour.)

Other gardens worth looking into are at **New Farm Park,** a "must" during early summer. Some 12,000 rosebushes bloom from September to November, but—even more dramatic and unusual—millions of lavender jacaranda blossoms come out during October and November, and the brilliant red poinciana trees bloom in November and December. Also, right in town, the **Brisbane Botanic Gardens** surrounding Parliament House and other public buildings provide Queenslanders with some serendipitous Sunday walks.

In the center of the city, a stop at the symbol of Brizzie, the 1930 Queensland stone **City Hall,** is considered a must by some. They say it's still worth the 20 cents or so they charge to take the elevator up into the tall clock tower, but we've never gotten around to that ourselves. **King George Square,** in front of the building, gives a pleasant open look to this area of town. A couple blocks up either Ann Street or Adelaide Street is **Anzac Square,** with a memorial made from that same handsome sandstone. The park also sports one water-swollen boab (baobab) tree, and stairs to walk up the steep hill from Adelaide to Ann Street in front of the Central Station. The new **Post Office Square,** with its underground shopping arcade, is between Anzac Square and the post office.

Further up the hill, next to Wickham Park, is the **Tower Mill,** also called the Old Observatory. It was built by convicts to be a windmill, but somehow it didn't work. The sails were then removed, and it was converted to a treadmill, run by convict foot power and used to grind corn. (We wonder if the same convicts turned it after failing to build it correctly.)

There are a few museums in the city, ready for rainy-day visitors. The **Queensland Museum** (Tel. 52–2716) is temporarily housed at the corner of Gregory Terrace and Bowen Bridge Road, but will move in 1986 to the new **Queensland Cultural Centre,** just across Victoria Bridge on the south bank of the river. Also worthwhile is the **Queensland Art Gallery** (Tel. 229–2138), which has now opened in fine new quarters in that Cultural Centre. (The Performing Arts Centre and the Lyric Theatre are just across the street in the same complex.) Queenslanders are also proud of **Newstead House** (Tel. 52–7373), at Newstead Park, the city's oldest surviving home. Its memorial to the Battle of the Coral Sea will be of interest to World War II vets.

Also in downtown Brisbane, don't miss the intricate facade of the 1888 **Treasury Building.** The collection of columns and archways carved from local sandstone is now dubbed "one of the finest Italianate buildings in (you guessed it) the Southern Hemisphere." Like many of the city's public buildings, it has recently been sandblasted back into the elegance it possessed a century ago.

We still haven't managed to get to the **Australian Woolshed,** a little out of town at 148 Samford Rd. in Ferny Hills. Shearing and spinning demonstrations are augmented by a "ram parade." Also, there is now the **Earlystreet Historical Village,** a restored pioneer settlement off McIlwraith Avenue in Norman Park.

We shouldn't leave Brisbane without mentioning two islands in Moreton Bay: **Moreton Island** (and its Tangalooma resort) and **North Stradbroke Island** ("Straddie"). They feature some fine, uncrowded beaches, and there are day trips to both.

THE GOLD COAST

Believe it or not, the Gold Coast is officially one long city, stretched out for 20 miles (and about a half-mile wide). It begins at a place called **Southport,** about 50 miles down the Pacific Highway from Brisbane, then continues through a dozen and a half other communities along the shoreline, notably **Surfers Paradise, Burleigh Heads,** and **Coolangatta.** Some call it a "concrete jungle," and say that development is more sensitive to the environment on the Sunshine Coast north of Brisbane.

There are lots of ockerous things to see and do on the Gold Coast— fake medieval castles, wax museums, zillions of lion parks, miniature golf courses, and the like. Without going into detail, however, two locations we rather liked were **Sea World** (Tel. 32–1055) in Surfers, whose dolphin and seal performances are terrific for the nippers ($6.50 for grown-ups, $3.50 for nippers), and the nearby **Fisherman's Wharf,** on the spit at Southport, which is home to many of the local fishing trawlers. There are good seafood restaurants, a nice pub, and shops there, now.

Many fanciers of fancy birds have written to recommend the **Currumbin Sanctuary** at Currumbin Beach. You may be able to feed those garish wild lorakeets there yourself. We haven't seen **Dreamworld,** the Down Under Dizzyland, or **Lamington Park,** the national park farther inland from the Gold Coast. (Locals sometimes call this region "the green behind the gold.") Look for O'Reilly's Hotel or Binnabura Lodge in that area.

The English novelist and playwright J. B. Priestley dismissed the Gold Coast and Surfers Paradise as "a cardboard Miami," but that's perhaps a little unfair today. Although it has suffered from years of unplanned growth, and although commercialism is rampant, it serves as an attractive playground for a young segment of Australia's population, and its higgledy-pigglediness at least gives an interesting insight into the directions taken by an unbridled antipodean pop culture.

It's also worth noting that because of the fierce competition between facilities here, prices for such attractions as hotels and restaurants are some of Australia's lowest for quality among the highest. The River Inn is a very nice restaurant at 32 Ferny Ave. in Surfers Paradise, just across from the luxurious Chevron Paradise Hotel. The several Quality Inns are also good places to stay. Most are on the Esplanade. If you can't find a reasonable room in Surfers, look at Mermaid Beach, just to the south, for better bargains.

We can't say good-bye to the Gold Coast without mentioning its best-known assets—the meter maids. As the brief bathing suit is the unofficial uniform of the place, these maids are bobby-dazzlers dressed in gold lamé bikinis. Their job is not to ticket overparked cars but to put coins *into* the meters for forgetful motorists as a public-relations service of the Merchants Progress Association. Good-on yer, Gold Coast. Yer cahn't be all bad, at that!

THE GREAT BARRIER REEF

The massive coral growth that extends along 1,250 miles of the East Coast from Gladstone to Cape York is, of course, one of the genuine wonders of the world. Who hasn't seen the magnificent, colorful creatures spread across the pages of *National Geographic* and other magazines? It's the site of some of the best underwater photographs ever taken. As the travel posters say, at the reef you can see more kinds of fish in the sea than anywhere else on earth.

But here's the rub. To fully appreciate the Great Barrier Reef, you should be a qualified scuba diver. At least, you must find a good, shallow location to put on a face mask and snorkel and paddle around on the surface to see things as clearly and as close up as they should be. If you can't do that, you could still be lucky, of course. If conditions are perfect on the day you go out, you *might* be able to get some idea about coral patterns and a few small fish that float by from a glass-bottom boat or the new "semisubmersibles," in which you ride about six feet under the surface. And again, when conditions are just right, you can put on a pair of boots or old tennis shoes to protect your feet and walk on the reef at low tide, getting one on one with the sea in that manner.

Most Australians who go to the reef do very little of this. To the "oldies," the G.B.R. means a holiday on a tropic isle, with plastic leis and old-fashioned, syrupy Hawaiian guitar music, community sings, and 1940s dance steps. If you want to learn how to do the "sugar shake," try Brampton Island, for one. To the "youngies," it's sex, rock music, and beer; you'll find sociological specimens of this species at Great Keppel Island.

A couple more general observations: There are two types of islands in the G.B.R. One is an island like any other, the tip of an undersea range of hills. The other is a genuine reef island, or "coral cay," which has been gradually built up to the surface on the coral itself by layers of sand and dirt. These islands are never hilly, and they are also sometimes called "low islands." In general, we believe the latter is more likely to be able to provide the true flavor of the reef, despite what some would consider the monotonous flatness of the territory. The very best months to see the reef are August, September, and October, when you'll find fewer storms, clearer weather, and fewer tourists.

Here is our island-by-island description of the ones easily reached, beginning in the south and continuing north. Nearly all are accessible by boat and/or plane from ports on the nearby mainland. Unless indicated, all offer accommodations for overnight or longer. (If you're going to stay, we would choose either Heron, Hayman, Dunk, Green, or Lizard islands as the best bets.)

Lady Elliot Island, considered the southernmost island on the Reef, is a coral cay that is close enough to Brisbane to visit in a one-day aerial tour. There are a few cabins on it, too, but you'll have to share the shower and the loo.

Heron Island is a small coral cay with a good resort catering to scuba divers and snorkelers and perhaps outfitted for them better than anyone else. There are some wonderful big "bommeys"—coral heads—where you can hand-feed the fish who live there. It's also a nesting site for the sea turtle and hundreds of seabirds. The 68-unit resort also has communal plumbing, but no one seems to mind. In fact, we've never had a single letter of complaint from any reader who has visited or stayed on Heron Island.

Great Keppel Island has been "upgraded" into a big, go-go entertainment center—something going on every minute from water-skiing to rock bands, and appealing largely to the under-25s. One slogan used by the promoters of this southern reef island: "Get wrecked on Great Keppel."

Brampton Island is the top of an undersea mountain, not a true coral island. We enjoyed walking entirely around it one afternoon, accompanied at times by a tame, high-stepping emu named George. However, without going into depressing detail, the resort itself was the pits, and we weren't surprised when we heard that Brampton had gone broke. But

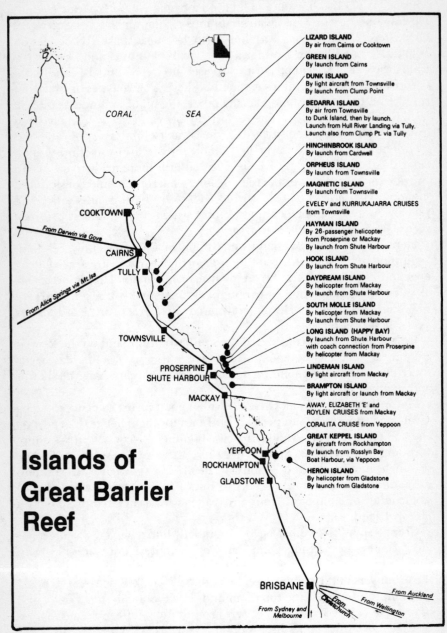

LIZARD ISLAND
By air from Cairns or Cooktown

GREEN ISLAND
By launch from Cairns

DUNK ISLAND
By light aircraft from Townsville
By launch from Clump Point

BEDARRA ISLAND
By air from Townsville
to Dunk Island, then by launch.
Launch from Hull River Landing via Tully.
Launch also from Clump Pt. via Tully.

HINCHINBROOK ISLAND
By launch from Cardwell

ORPHEUS ISLAND
By launch from Townsville

MAGNETIC ISLAND
By launch from Townsville

EVELEY and KURRUKAJARRA CRUISES
from Townsville

HAYMAN ISLAND
By 26-passenger helicopter
from Proserpine or Mackay
By launch from Shute Harbour

HOOK ISLAND
By launch from Shute Harbour

DAYDREAM ISLAND
By helicopter from Mackay
By launch from Shute Harbour

SOUTH MOLLE ISLAND
By helicopter from Mackay
By launch from Shute Harbour

LONG ISLAND (HAPPY BAY)
By launch from Shute Harbour
with coach connection from Proserpine
By helicopter from Mackay

LINDEMAN ISLAND
By light aircraft from Mackay

BRAMPTON ISLAND
By light aircraft or launch from Mackay

AWAY, ELIZABETH 'E' and
ROYLEN CRUISES from Mackay

CORALITA CRUISE from Yeppoon

GREAT KEPPEL ISLAND
By aircraft from Rockhampton
By launch from Rosslyn Bay
Boat Harbour, via Yeppoon

HERON ISLAND
By helicopter from Gladstone
By launch from Gladstone

CORAL   SEA

COOKTOWN
From Darwin via Gove
CAIRNS
TULLY
From Alice Springs via Mt. Isa

TOWNSVILLE

PROSERPINE
SHUTE HARBOUR
MACKAY

Islands of Great Barrier Reef

YEPPOON
ROCKHAMPTON
GLADSTONE

BRISBANE
From Sydney and Melbourne
From Christchurch
From Wellington
From Auckland

Map courtesy Australian Tourist Commission

now, just at press time, we have learned that it has just been taken over by TAA and is being managed by Roger Irving, a pro we saw in operation at Dunk Island. This rescue operation may eventually succeed in light of TAA's high-flying successes at Dunk and other islands.

Lindeman Island, owned by P & O Lines, is very much a family resort on a hilly island. There's lots of organized entertainment. It wouldn't be our first choice, but some reef activities are also featured.

Hamilton Island, one of the Whitsundays, was practically unknown a few years ago, but is now being developed into the reef's largest resort with something for almost everyone. Spectacular hotels, condominiums, restaurants, yacht harbors, and other facilities are being built from shore to shining shore by Keith Williams, the well-known Queensland resort entrepreneur who developed Sea World. Williams wants to make Hamilton a world-class resort, and perhaps he will succeed. At the moment it is the only island on the G.B.R. with an airport capable of landing large jets, and Ansett is scheduled to begin regular service from Sydney and Brisbane—and perhaps Melbourne—by the time the ink is dry on these pages.

Long Island, the Whitsunday 100 resort, is a former community-sing and Bingo retreat now becoming known as "the rock-and-roll resort" for young adults. It's locked in fierce competition with Great Keppel for the same fuzzy-cheeked clientele.

South Molle Island is a mountain island that seems to offer a fairly good compromise between isolation and sociability. We'd like to have some reader reports on this one.

The very tiny **Daydream Island** has chosen a Hawaiian/Mexican motif for its resort. There's an unusually large swimming pool—nay, a sort of swimming lagoon. It may depend a lot on the crowd. You don't have to scuba dive or snorkel at **Hook Island,** because you can go down under the water in a special observatory. (The fish float by thinking that you are the one in the aquarium!) There are no hotel rooms on the island; a daily launch comes over from Shute Harbour.

Hayman Island, once the most sophisticated resort among the G.B.R. islands, is still an active Ansett operation that has a wide choice of everything, both in day and night life. In general it appeals to a young crowd equally at home with rock music and oxygen tanks and flippers. The Air Whitsunday *Reef Adventure* aerial tours, which leave from Hayman, are recommendable.

Much farther north, now, there is **Magnetic Island.** It attracts hundreds of day trippers every weekend due to its closeness to Townsville, and it's big enough to be a national park and host several resorts. You might pick this one for bush walking and animal appreciation, but hardly for coral and fish viewing. **Orpheus Island,** a seven-mile-long island in the Palm group, is fringed with reef. Some say they consider it the ultimate away-from-it-all location. **Hinchinbrook Island** is a national park with dense rain forest, waterfalls, and wildlife. **Bedarra Island** is small, tropical, and isolated; its quiet and well-run Hideaway resort sleeps only 10 souls.

Dunk Island now appeals to the sophisticated over-30s vacationer. Capped by 800-foot-high Mount Koo-tal-oo, it's a tropical rain forest and a biologist's paradise. There is an amazing variety of birds, bats, lizards, echidnas, and insects, including the iridescent blue Ulysses butterfly and the fierce-looking (but harmless) rhinoceros beetle. TVs, radios, telephones, and video games are forbidden at the well-run TAA-owned resort, and we enjoyed our own brief stay here not long ago.

Green Island is a genuine coral cay 16 miles offshore from Cairns and officially a Marine National Park. Snorkeling and coral viewing are good, and the underwater observatory now installed is sometimes effective. You can walk around Green in about 30 minutes. There's a small hotel here, but on the weekend, at least, the island suffers from TMT—too many tourists, most of them day-trippers over from Cairns. We liked the beach, though. **Lizard Island,** closer to Cooktown and with a magnificent coral reef, has a recently expanded, somewhat exclusive facility sleeping about 60 people, about half in the lodge and half in the new beachfront units. We hit this one once on a very brief tour. Perhaps a good choice for splendid isolationists.

NORTH QUEENSLAND

Suddenly everyone in Australia seems to have discovered the touristic charms of North Queensland, the mainland coastline paralleling the Great Barrier Reef. Beware of swimming in the summer months, however, unless you receive assurances from a local lifeguard. The box jellyfish sometimes floating near the shoreline are members of one of the world's most deadly species, similar to the sea wasp found at Darwin. (Treat any stings with vinegar and call a doctor.)

The unofficial capital of North Queensland is **Townsville.** North of Brisbane by about 1,000 miles, the attractive and sophisticated city of 100,000 is dominated by 900-foot-high Castle Hill and is the jumping-off place for Magnetic Island and some other islands of the Great Barrier Reef (see previous pages).

Townsville's traditional top hotel is the International (Tel. 72–2477), which dominates the city center. The new Sheraton Breakwater Hotel & Casino will open late in 1986. Lowths and Travelodge are also good. Gourmet restaurants include Rudy's and L'Escargotiere, but the Seabreeze Inn, a BYO at 57 Mitchell St., is also an excellent choice, according to

Stephen Barton, a resident Yank, and Katie Marthick, his dinkum Aussie bride. One new attraction is the *Reef Link,* a fast catamaran out to the Great Barrier Reef. Check in with the tourist office in the century-old bank building on the Flinders Mall.

Cairns (Pop. 40,000), another 200 miles up the coast, has a very different atmosphere. The town pretty much sleeps in the sun during the hottest months, but it sizzles with activity from September to December when it is the base for the world's sport fishermen searching for record-size marlin. It's also the launching point for trips to some G.B.R. islands, including Green and Fitzroy islands and Michaelmas Cay, seemingly the island of a thousand screaming terns. Qantas has now begun nonstop flights from Honolulu to the new Cairns airport, opening another gate through which Americans can enter North Queensland.

The top hotel is the Pacific International, and we have found it comfortable ourselves on two occasions. The Lions Four Seasons is one of several other choices. The historic Hides Hotel, recently tanned and cured, is a less pricy place positioned right on the new City Mall. Young folks like the Cairns Hostel, smack on the Esplanade. Look for good tucker in the Outrigger Restaurant, Barnacle Bill's, Riccardo's, and perhaps at the Trade Winds Motel (although some readers didn't like staying there). We've also had reports of excellent atmosphere, food, and prices at the Avocado Restaurant on Sheridan Street.

You can board the famous narrow-gauge railroad for a dramatic 21-mile journey from Cairns through the rain forest and into the mountains. The train first cuts through sugarcane fields and lush jungle, then chugs past the Great Barron Falls (stopping so you can take pictures) and hugs the precipitous Barron River Gorge while climbing to cool **Kuranda**—a village on the edge of the 2,000-foot-high Atherton Tableland—and its quaint, fern-covered railroad station. We paid about $5 each way for the trip in the atmospheric old carriages and enjoyed every mile of it. (There are also some bus excursions that meet the train at Kuranda.)

A charming village at the end of the paved road a few miles north of Cairns is **Port Douglas,** identified in some people's minds principally as the home of actress Diane Cilento. But this former gold-rush and fishing town has a rustic charm of its own. We enjoyed our trip aboard the *Quicksilver* on the Outer Barrier Reef Cruises out of Port Douglas not long ago. Fare is around $60 for the all-day trip. (Say "hi" to Captain Jim Wallace for us.) Ms. Cilento's own restaurant, the Nautilus, is atmospheric and popular, and we had an excellent Queensland steak outdoors at Danny's. Two good places to stay are the Rusty Pelican and the Vacation Village.

About 200 miles north of Cairns, **Cooktown** stands on the Endeavour River, where Captain James Cook beached and repaired his ship *Endeavour* during his historic 1770 voyage. Early relics are preserved in the Cook Museum. This includes one of Cook's own cannons, recently recovered from the reef where it was dumped two centuries ago to lighten ballast.

7. Guided Tours and Cruises

The following are only a few representative samples of the tours available in Brisbane and other North Queensland communities. As always, get the latest from the government tourist office. The helpful people there can also book you on all these tours and many others.

In Brisbane, **Boomerang Tours** (Tel. 221–9922) operates morning and afternoon excursions to different parts of the city, either for around $9 or $10 per ticket. Several full-day tours are also offered. Boomerang runs one to the *Gold Coast* and another to the *Sunshine Coast* (the less intensely developed shoreline north of Brisbane), either for around $20. **Scenic Tours** (Tel. 48–0060) has a full-day excursion called the *Jungle Day Tour* to Lamington National Park for around $25.

A newer competing operation is **Aladdin's** (Tel. 345–8300). Last we checked they listed abut 10 different tours. Morning and afternoon tours of Brizzie will run around $10 each. Their full-day tours include *Noosa and the Sunshine Coast,* the *Great Dividing Range, Gold Coast Hinterland,* and others, all for around $25.

Cruises in Brisbane include the trip up the Brisbane River past the University of Queensland to *Lone Pine Sanctuary.* It's run by **Hayles Brisbane Cruises** (Tel. 229–7055) from the quay off Queens Wharf Road under the expressway near Victoria Bridge. The 3½-hour afternoon trip costs around $10 (half price for children). Hayles's new, 200-passenger vessel *Captain Cook* also offers lunch and dinner cruises along the river.

A popular multiple-day trip is the *Daylight Rail Tour,* a six-day excursion from Brisbane to Rockhampton, Townsville, and Cairns, including overnights in motels, for a fare of around $500. There are several similar tours to other areas, all of which do their traveling during the daylight hours only.

OUT OF BRISBANE

Several cruises wend through the islands along the Great Barrier Reef, and this could be one of the best ways to see the area, depending on a number of variables—like the condition of the vessel, the quality of the food, and the compatibility of your fellow passengers. From Mackay, the 112-foot cruiser **Elizabeth E** carries 24 passengers on a four-day cruise in the Whitsunday group for about $500. **Roylen Cruises** also operates several cruises from Mackay. The newest and brightest is aboard the

315-foot, air-conditioned *Roylen Endeavour.* It makes a five-day cruise of the Whitsunday Passage, including a visit to the outer reef, for around $500, depending on your accommodations.

Several day cruises are run by different companies from Shute Harbour near Mackay. Look over their itineraries carefully. The latest information is on tap at the tourist office on River Street in Mackay.

From Townsville, five-day cruises are operated on the 85-foot *Evely Beaver* by **Evely Cruises,** perhaps still for under $300. **Air Whitsunday** offers several seaplane tours out to the Whitsunday group of islands on the G.B.R. from the traditional reef-cruise launching communities of Airlie Beach (near Proserpine) and Shute Harbour.

From Cairns, the all-day diving and snorkeling trips launched by Graham Johnson aboard the 53-foot **Malawondi** (Tel. 53–3463) are pretty good. The fare (about $40) includes mask, snorkel, etc. We recently took the interesting cruise aboard the **M.V. Coral Seatel** to Green Island and Michaelmas Cay. (But we paid extra to have our picture taken during a scuba lesson on the cruise, and never received it.)

A reader also wrote us enthusiastically of an excellent cruise to the Low Islands out of Port Douglas aboard the **Martin Cash** for not too much cash, although another believed the same boat needed some stabilizers in rough weather. And another Maverick traveler was especially enthusiastic about her **Air Queensland** tour from Cairns to Cooktown, Lizard Island, and back. "It cost $150 for the day but was worth every cent of it!" said Mary Ann Fennie of Laguna Hills, California. We have since taken this same trip ourselves and heartily agree.

8. Water Sports

As already indicated, **surfing** and **swimming** on the Gold Coast are some of the best in the world. Go in the water only at designated beaches, however. These are protected with effective shark nets. Almost the entire coastline is lined offshore by these Nylon meshes, at least as far up as Noosa at the top of the Sunshine Coast.

You can go **water-skiing** at Sea World, at Lake Terranora, and on the Tweed River. You can rent boats from most resorts, too. **Windsurfing** is now available at vacation areas all the way up and down the coast.

Skin diving is best, of course, on the islands of the Great Barrier Reef, mostly done with masks and snorkels. However scuba equipment can be rented at Heron Island, Daydream Island, Hayman Island, and Dunk Island. That's the best way to appreciate the reef and the marine life associated with it. The waters between the reef and the mainland are home to 870 kinds of fish, some of which are found nowhere else in the world.

Big-game fishing at Cairns is world-famous, with many anglers trying for the elusive 2,000-pound black marlin. There's a $100,000 prize waiting for the first to get one. (You might catch Marlon Brando, Lee Marvin, Ernest Borgnine, and other famous fisherfolk at Cairns during the October-to-December marlin season.) Some other fish regularly brought in include barracuda, sailfish, wahoo, several kinds of tuna, and Spanish mackerel. Dozens of boats are available for charter at Cairns at around $300 to $500 for a day's outing, depending on the size of the boat and the season.

You can book all boats through the **Great Barrier Reef Travel Agency** (Tel. 51–3877) on Shields Street in Cairns 4870. The Queensland Government Travel Centre, at 81 Abbott St., Cairns 4870, is also ready to hand out good oil on the fishing scene.

9. Other Sports

Being a northern state, Queensland is nuts about rugby, of course, both the professional League and the amateur Union, with New South Wales the principal rival. The big matches are played at **Lang Park.** Cricket is also big, again with the custody of the Sheffield Shield at stake, usually in competition with N.S.W. Cricket matches are played at **Woolloongabba,** more commonly called just "Gabba" or "the Gabba."

Racing, both with dogs and horses, is popular. The principal tracks are at **Eagle Farm,** a fast grass track and the home of the Queensland Turf Club, and at **Albion Park,** a sand track. Also you can "go to the trots"—trotting races—at Albion Park. Greyhound racing takes place at "Gabba," and it's considered most fun while eating dinner at the picture-window restaurant, just a nostril or two away from the dogs.

You can play tennis by hiring a court at **Milton** (Tel. 36–5798), Milton Road, the home of the Davis Cup.

If you like golf, the **Royal Queensland** (Tel. 268–1127) in Hamilton and the **Brisbane Golf Club** (Tel. 48–1008) in Yeerongpilly are private clubs known to be hospitable to visitors, although they apparently hate each other with an intense rivalry that goes back to 1921. (At either club you may get one version of the story, anyway.) Public golf courses, more convenient for visitors, include the one in **Victoria Park** (Tel. 52–4244).

10. Shopping in Brisbane

As in most of Australia, stores are open until 5:00 P.M. most weekdays and until 11:30 A.M. Saturdays. Late-night shopping is available in Brisbane on Friday until 9:00 P.M. There are two main shopping areas. The downtown area is centered vaguely around the Queen Street Mall (between Edward and Albert streets) and includes such popular complexes as City Plaza and Post Office Square. The second area is out in "The Valley"—Fortitude Valley, to be specific. Another and perhaps more atmospheric shopping area is known as Paddington Circle. It is in several old buildings generally along Latrobe and Given terraces and Caxton Street, somewhat east of the center. Antique hounds should find their way to the area around Sandgate and Junction roads in Clayfield. Saturday-morning browsing and buying is fun at the Caxton Street Market at 17 Caxton St., Petrie Terrace.

By the way, if you see a little stand in the mall labeled something like: "LUCKY LARRY, THE CASKET KING," be assured that Larry doesn't sell coffins. Casket is the name of the local lottery.

The official Aboriginal art outlet is **Queensland Aboriginal Creations,** 135–47 George St. (If you buy a boomerang, see if they still have the little pamphlet explaining how to throw it.) **Arunga Gifts** (Tel. 221–0892) at 197 Adelaide St., corner of Edward, has a fairly wide selection—some good, some junk. At the **Artifacts and Souvenir Centre** (Tel. 229–6242), 183 Edward St., Mr. and Mrs. Beard also feature a lot of things from New Guinea and the Pacific islands.

Currans Corner (Tel. 229–3690), 174 Adelaide St., corner of Edwards and across from the tourist office, also displays a bewildering variety of things, plus a book, magazine, and foreign-newspaper section. **The Rock Shop** (Tel. 229–6009) at 193 Adelaide St. has souvenirs but especially Australian rocks and gemstones. And you might find some good opals at **Darryl James,** 260 Adelaide St.

Major department stores, all on Queen Street, include **David Jones** at No. 194, **Myer Queensland Stores** at No. 94, and **G. J. Coles** at No. 210.

11. Night Life and Entertainment

It may be a while yet before conservative Brisbane develops much of a reputation for after-dark shenanigans. It's a commuting city, and the central area says good night to most of its citizens while the sun is still high in the sky.

If you're going on a pub crawl, remember that Brizzie's most popular beer is Castlemaine XXXX Bitter Ale (just ask for "Four-Ex"), a good, strong brew.

A few pubs—they call them "hotels," by the way, but many are better known for their libations than accommodations—stand out. The **Crest International Hotel** on King George Square houses several good bars, at least one of which sometimes has live music. The **Lennons Plaza** is another good bet. Popular pubs also include the **New York Hotel,** 69 Queen St., where the daytime smorgasbord turns into a nighttime discoboard, the **Belfast** at 388 Queen St., and the **Treasury Hotel** on George Street. You'll usually hear some good jazz at the **Cellar Club,** 264 Adelaide St.

The premier discotheque is the **Brisbane Underground** at Caxton and Hale streets. Newcomers challenging that position include **Sybil's** on two or three floors at 383 Adelaide St.; **Pipps,** 74 Elizabeth St. (which sometimes features live rock); **Knights,** 81 Elizabeth St.; **Images,** on the 24th floor of the S.G.I.O. Building on Turbot Street; **Reflections,** in the Sheraton; and especially **Whispers,** 195 Brunswick St. in "the Valley."

You'll find six or seven legitimate theaters. Among them, the 600-seat **S.G.I.O. Theatre** (Tel. 221–3861), in the S.G.I.O. Building on Turbot Street, is the home of the Queensland Theatre Company. **LaBoite** (Tel. 369–1622), 57 Hale St. in Milton, is the headquarters for the Brisbane Repertory Company, which often stages contemporary and experimental productions. The **Schonell Downstairs Theatre** is part of Queensland University in St. Lucia but is open to the public, too. The **Brisbane Arts Theatre** (Tel. 369–2344) is now at 210 Petrie Terrace. And the **Edward Street Theatre** (Tel. 221–1527) at 109 Edward St. is the home of the Brisbane Community Arts Centre.

If you're heavily into films, you might want to skip them in wowserist Queensland, where they are subject to itchy-scissored censors. And we'd avoid any opera, concert, or ballet at the **Festival Hall** on Charlotte Street. The acoustics are awful, the air conditioning is often faulty, and the seats are rock-hard. The new **Lyric Theatre** has now opened in the Queensland Cultural Centre.

If you're in Brisbane in late September, don't miss **Warana,** the annual Mardi Gras–type "Blue Skies" festival. Starting on the last Saturday in the month, it's a week-long wingding with an assortment of activities like art shows, concerts, beer festivals, an air race, a rodeo—you name it. A dinkum shivoo!

12. The Brisbane Address List

American Chamber of Commerce in Australia—10 Market St. (Tel. 221–8542).

American Express—229 Queen St. (Tel. 229–2022).

Bank—Westpac Banking Corp., 260 Queen St. (Tel. 277–2222).

Barber—John Le Count, City Plaza, Adelaide Street (Tel. 229–6113).

Beauty shop—Webster & Wood, Adelaide and George streets (Tel. 31–2432).

Brisbane Chamber of Commerce—243 Edward St. (Tel. 221–1766).

British consulate—193 North Quay (Tel. 221–4933).

Bus information—Tel. 225–4444.

Citizens Advice Bureau—69 Ann St. (Tel. 221–4343).

Emergencies (fire, police, ambulance)—Dial 000.

Hospital—Royal Brisbane Hospital, Herston Road, Herston (Tel. 253–8111).

New Zealand consulate—288 Edward St. (Tel. 221–3722).

Police headquarters—30 Makerston St. (Tel. 226–6001).

Royal Automobile Club of Queensland—190 Edward St. (Tel. 221–1511).

Tourist office—Queensland Government Travel Centre, Adelaide and Edward streets (Tel. 31–2211).

Index

Gold Coast, 202, 297, 305, 307-8, 315
Gold digging license fees, 72
"Golden Mile" (Melbourne), 194-99, 209
Gold Pass plans, 27, 29
Gold rushes, 53, 71-72, 75, 249, 262
Golf clubs: Adelaide, 243; Alice Springs, 290; Brisbane, 316; Canberra, 172-73; Darwin, 290; Melbourne, 204; Perth, 266; Sydney, 144; Tasmania, 223
Goolagong, Evonne. *See* Cawley, Evonne
Goolwa, 242
Gordon, Adam Lindsay, 75, 195
Gosford (N.S.W.), 107, 137
Goulburn, 161
Government, 76-77, 81, 82, 83-84, 85-86
Government House: Melbourne, 198; Sydney, 132
Governor La Trobe's Cottage (Melbourne), 198
Grainger, Percy, Museum (Melbourne), 199
Grampian Range, 200
Grange (S.A.), 242
Grasshoppers, 61
Grass tree ("black boy"), 55-56
Great Australian Bight, 228
Great Barrier Reef, 17, 25, 36, 63, 66, 297, 305, 308-312, 313, 314, 315
Great Britain. *See* England
Great Depression, 76, 80, 131, 157
Great Dividing Range, 69, 70, 295
Great Keppel Island, 309
Great Ocean Road, 200
Greek restaurants: Adelaide, 236; Canberra, 166; Sydney, 128
Green Island, 309, 312, 313
Greenway, Francis, 45, 69, 136
Greer, Germaine, 88
Greyhound Australia, 26-27, 107, 161, 182, 230, 251, 273, 299
Greyhounds. *See* Racing
Griffin, Walter Burley, 76, 157, 167
Gulf of Carpentaria, 70, 74, 199
Gulf St. Vincent, 235, 242
"Gum trees." *See* Eucalyptus
Gunther, John, 91

Hahndorf (S.A.), 240
Hainault Tourist Mine (W.A.), 262
Hamersley Ranges, 249, 263
Hamilton Island, 311
Hancock, Lang, 88
Harbord (N.S.W.), 140
Hardware stores, 146
Hardy, Frank, 88
Hargrave, Lawrence, 45
Hargraves, Edward H., 71
Harris, Max, 80

Harris, Rolf, 88
Hastings Caves (Tasmania), 222
Hawaii, 6, 16, 18, 19, 23, 41
Hawke, Robert, 85-86, 88
Hawkesbury River (N.S.W.), 139
Hayden, William, 88
Hayman Island, 309, 311, 315
Healesville (Victoria), 58, 183, 200, 201. *See also* Mackenzie, Sir Colin, Wildlife Sanctuary
Health card, 47
Hectares, 42-43
Heidelberg School, the, 75
Helicopter tours (Sydney), 139
Helpmann, Sir Robert, 88
Henley-on-Todd Regatta (Alice Springs), 290
Herald, Sydney Morning, 153
Hermannsburg Mission (N.T.), 287
Heron Island, 309, 315
Hibberd, Jack, 88
Highway One, 103, 161, 182, 230
Hiking and backpacking, 173, 225
Hilton Hotels: Adelaide, 232-33; Melbourne, 184-85; Perth, 252-53; Sydney, 114-15, 117
Hinchinbrook Island, 312
History, Australian, 64-86
Hitchhiking, 31-32
Hobart (Tasmania), 11, 24, 34, 39, 54, 82, 211-25
Hogan, Paul, 88
Holden car, 81
Holiday W.A. Centre, 252, 260, 263
Holidays: public, 39; school, 23
Holt, Harold, 82
Honolulu, 10, 11, 16, 17, 18, 19, 21, 22, 23, 47, 79, 313
Hook Island, 311
Hope, Alec Derwent, 143
Horne, Donald, 83, 88
Horses. *See* Racing
Hospitals, 133, 155, 176, 210, 225, 245, 268, 293, 319
Hotels, 92, 95: Adelaide, 232-35; Alice Springs, 278-80; Brisbane, 300-303; Canberra, 161, 163-65; Darwin, 277-78; Melbourne, 183-89; Perth, 252-57; Sydney, 111-21; Tasmania, 215-18
Howard Springs (N.T.), 290
Hughes, Robert, 88
Hume Highway, 182
Humphries, Barry, 88
Humpty Doo (N.T.), 283, 288
Hunter's Hill (Sydney), 135
Hunter Valley (N.S.W.), 103, 137, 139
Hutt River Province, 263

Please tell us about your trip to Australia below.

(You may use this page as an envelope. See over.)

Cut along this line.

Cut along this line.

Place
first class
postage
here

re: 1986-87 edition Aust.

Bob and Sara Bone
The Maverick Guides
Pelican Publishing Company
P.O. Box 189
Gretna, Louisiana 70054

TRAVEL NOTES

TRAVEL NOTES

TRAVEL NOTES

TRAVEL NOTES

REVIEWER COMMENTS

"An amazingly compact and complete compendium written for thinking tourists who want to know all about this three-million square mile country—and who want help in budgeting time and money for maximum enjoyment.... Covers every type of question the traveler may have."

TRAVEL MARKETING MAGAZINE

"This 320-page paperback advises on a host of essentials...Even without plans for a sojourn in Australia, The Maverick Guide makes good reading simply because, physically and historically, Australia—the world's largest island and smallest continent—is a fascinating place.... Bone makes it difficult to leave Australia out of vacation plans."

CHRIS HEATH
Signature

"For travelers heading down under...almost required reading. Informal but not too casual, comprehensive but not verbose."

ALA BOOKLIST

"All aboard for down under! This new edition of Pelican's Maverick Guide Series is first rate. It provides just about everything one needs to know for visiting the continent of Australia, well arranged and amusingly, but authoritatively written."

THE (New Orleans) TIMES-PICAYUNE

"...complete, authentic and entertaining. There are maps galore, historical background, a slang dictionary and plenty of rich detail...And [Bone] has a sense of humor..."

GORDON A. MOON, II
Editor, *Commerce*

"...the type of book you read before you depart, and carry with you every day while 'Down Under.'"

ALLISON CRAWFORD
International Travel News

"When Robert Bone did The Maverick Guide to Hawaii...we knew that here was a writer who by some magic makes even the dull-though-necessary facts of a basic guidebook palatable (we suspect he might even make a telephone directory more interesting) while also reporting with a refreshing honesty and an eye on value received. The new Maverick Guide to Australia is more of the same. Everything the prospective traveler needs to know is there."

PACIFIC TRAVEL NEWS

"...comprehensive coverage of the tourist attractions of Australia...filled with first-hand descriptions, up-to-date prices and specific recommendations of what to see and do ..."

JEAN SIMMONS
Travel Editor, *The Dallas Morning News*

"I've been a Maverick fan ever since I took Bone's Guide to Hawaii on a tour of the Islands...His information is usually right on the money, and he doesn't mind telling you straight out when he thinks the food is overpriced, the service ho-hum, or the hotel rooms like cubicles. Bone's 'Mavericks' are guidebooks you can trust."

JACKIE PETERSON
The Sacramento Union

"...a refreshingly independent view of the island continent...jammed with information...It is an effective guide and contains the kind of detail travelers want, plus a good smattering of entertainment."

RUSS LYNCH
Honolulu Star-Bulletin

"Once again, Bone tells it like it is...Plenty of maps, facts. One of the best guides on Australia to hit the bookstores in a long time."

JERRY HULSE
Travel Editor, *Los Angeles Times*

mav·er·ick (mav'er-ik), *n* 1. an unbranded steer. Hence [colloq.] 2. a person not labeled as belonging to any one faction, group, etc., who acts independently. 3. one who moves in a different direction than the rest of the herd—often a nonconformist. 4. a person using individual judgment, even when it runs against majority opinion.

The Maverick Guides
The Maverick Guide to Hawaii
The Maverick Guide to New Zealand
The Maverick Guide to Australia